Daily Preschool Experiences

For Learners at Every Level

Kay Hastings, Cathy Clemons, April Montgomery

Dedicated to Jim and Madison—My Joy & My Inspiration

Dedicated to my husband, Kelly—Thank you for your unconditional love and support and to my son Brandon. You are the true happiness in my life and I love you more than words can say.

Dedicated to John, Albert, Russell, Kenneth & John Stephen—all my boys tall and small.

And, to all our friends and our families who "stood in the gap" and made it possible for us to accomplish this educational endeavor.

Daily Preschool Experiences

For Learners at Every Level

Complete Developmental Plans for 100 Days

Kay Hastings
Cathy Clemons
April Montgomery
Illustrations by Mary Rojas

© 2008 Kay Hastings, Cathy Clemons, April Montgomery
Printed in the United States of America.

Published by Gryphon House, Inc.
10726 Tucker Street, Beltsville, MD 20705
301.595.9500; 301.595.0051 (fax); 800.638.0928 (toll-free)

Visit us on the web at www.gryphonhouse.com

Kay Hastings, Cathy Clemons, April Montgomery
Illustrations: Mary Rojas

LIBRARY OF CONGRESS CATALOGING-IN-PUBLICATION DATA

Hastings, Kay, 1960-
 Daily preschool experiences for learners at every level / Kay Hastings,
Cathy Clemons, April Montgomery ; illustrations, Mary Rojas.
   p. cm.
 ISBN 978-0-87659-010-2
1. Education, Preschool--Activity programs. I. Clemons, Cathy. II.
Montgomery, April, 1955- III. Title.
 LB1140.35.C74H37 2008
 372.21--dc22

                        2008006560

BULK PURCHASE

Gryphon House books are available for special premiums and sales promotions as well as for fund-raising use. Special editions or book excerpts also can be created to specification. For details, contact the Director of Marketing at Gryphon House.

DISCLAIMER

Gryphon House, Inc. and the author cannot be held responsible for damage, mishap, or injury incurred during the use of or because of activities in this book. Appropriate and reasonable caution and adult supervision of children involved in activities and corresponding to the age and capability of each child involved, is recommended at all times. Do not leave children unattended at any time. Observe safety and caution at all times.

Every effort has been made to locate copyright and permission information.

Gryphon House is a member of the Green Press Initiative, a nonprofit program dedicated to supporting publishers in their efforts to reduce their use of fiber-sourced forests. This book is printed on paper using 30% post-consumer waste. For further information, visit www.greenpressinitiative.org.

Table of Contents

Introduction

We are so excited to share this book with you. The idea for this book came as a result of our search for a curriculum resource book that would meet the daily needs of all the preschoolers at our school. Our classrooms are like most. We have a wide range of learners—from beginning to developing to advanced. Within these levels, our children learn in a variety of ways and have a variety of interests. These are constantly changing. Some children might be beginning learners in math but advanced learners in art. They might be developing learners this week and advanced learners next week. We wanted a curriculum that would meet the needs of every child every day.

In addition to having activities that were differentiated, the curriculum also needed to be engaging for the children and serve as a necessary foundation for kindergarten. Most of the curriculum materials we found focused on traditional themes that are common in early childhood programs (self-concept, family, community helpers, and so on). But we noticed that they did not create a relationship or logical connection between these themes.

We also noticed that many activities did not incorporate the everyday experiences of the young child. Current brain research indicates that children learn best when they are encountering things that are meaningful to them, things that they can relate to their own "real-world experiences." The research also states that it is extremely important for children to be able to see how the information they are learning is related to and different from what they already know.

We love children and are dedicated to providing the very best educational experiences and opportunities for them. Having taught preschool for over 24 years, our goal in writing this book is to share some of our own ideas with you. With this curriculum, you can meet the daily needs of each and every student in your class, and you can help build a strong foundation for future educational experiences. Your children will learn to see relationships and build connections between their own experiences and the skills, ideas and concepts that they encounter on a daily basis.

If you, too, are dedicated to providing the best educational experiences for every learner, and you are excited about learning alongside young children, then this is the perfect curriculum resource book for you. Your children will catch your enthusiasm and they will love learning every single day.

Kay Hastings, Cathy Clemons, April Montgomery

About This Book

DAILY PRESCHOOL EXPERIENCES FOR LEARNERS AT EVERY LEVEL

One major component of this curriculum is building connections between what children already know and the new information that they are learning each day. We also have connected the various academic content areas of Math, Science, Art, Language and Dramatic Play so that the children can begin to see the relationships between one concept, skill and idea and others related to it. To help the children make further connections, we have connected one day to another so that the topics of study are related and naturally build on one another.

CURRICULUM ORGANIZATION

Early-childhood educators have the unique opportunity in many cases to be the first ones to expose children to different topics of study, ideas, and concepts that may be unfamiliar to them. In essence, the job of early childhood educators is to build "file folders" of information in the brains of the young child. As children encounter new information, they will learn to sort and re-organize what they are learning based on how it is alike and different from what they already know.

Traditional early-childhood and elementary education tends to present disconnected pieces of information to children in the subjects of Math, Science, Language, Art, and Dramatic Play without showing relationships or connections between these areas. This curriculum ties information together across academic areas and seeks to teach children a way of thinking that will encourage them to learn to see the relationships. This type of critical thinking and analysis will enhance their creativity and their problem-solving skills in all areas and benefit them throughout their lives.

This curriculum book is unique in that it is organized in such a way that the topics of study flow naturally into one another. It is easy to see that relationships are evident between topics of study and the academic areas. Attention has been given to seasons and times of year so that the topics flow logically in relation to time.

UNIT THEMES AND DAILY TOPICS OF STUDY

This curriculum has 20 thematic units of study and is built around 140 daily topics of study. To arrive at the daily topics of study that we incorporated in this curriculum, we did some research of our own to determine things that are naturally of interest to young children. We built this curriculum around those topics. Our thinking is that if children are already interested and excited about a topic, their attention will automatically be captured and the children will be engaged in the learning process.

The curriculum has been written in a child-friendly way based on the natural characteristics of young children. It capitalizes on their curiosity, playfulness, and interactive nature.

MORNING CIRCLE

Current research on the brain development of young children suggests that children must be actively engaged in the learning process in order for learning to be meaningful for them. Based on this research, we have included a daily motivational activity to be done with the children at the beginning of each day. We have planned these activities to draw children in and excite them about the daily topic of study. These activities capitalize on the fun and playful nature of young children.

STORYTIME

Quality children's literature has been used for the daily story presentations. The focal story selections that we have selected will capture and hold the children's attention and encourage them to develop a life-long love of literature. A wide variety of literature has been selected to enhance children's listening abilities. The story selections provide a starting point by introducing the topic of study for the day. In some instances, the story is just a "spoke in the wheel" of learning for the day, and on some days the daily activities draw lots of inspiration from the story selection.

DAILY CENTER ACTIVITY IDEAS

Current brain research says that in order for children to be able to use knowledge, they must be able to organize it. The teaching methodology of this curriculum involves daily experiences in learning centers where the children are involved in active exploration, repetition, and sensory stimulation, all of which takes place in a fun-filled learning environment. The daily activities are all multi-sensory and experiential in nature.

This curriculum will offer children many opportunities to ask questions, seek information, test their assumptions and evaluate their findings. These are the higher-level thinking skills that the gifted scientists, mathematicians, technology professionals, artists and musicians, and corporate executives exhibit in our world today. These are the skills that children will need to have in order to be successful in the future. Therefore, these are the skills that children need to begin developing at early ages.

By participating in the daily activities of this curriculum, the children will not only develop knowledge and skills related to specific topics, but they will also develop their abilities to organize and represent that knowledge. The children will develop the very important skill of being about to transfer that knowledge to other areas. This curriculum will engender a new way of thinking and help the children develop a keen awareness of their environment with attention to details.

LEVELS OF LEARNING: BEGINNING LEARNER, DEVELOPING LEARNER, EXPERIENCED LEARNER

This curriculum was developed with a wide range of interest levels in mind so that there is something for everyone. Developmental levels have been incorporated for each activity. We have assigned these labels: Beginning Learner, Developing Learner, and Experienced Learner, and we have purposely not assigned ages to these levels. We are aware that you know your children and their skill levels best. And, we know that children do not develop at the same time in all four areas of development: socially, emotionally, cognitively, and physically. In this curriculum, we have provided three levels of each activity so that you can select the level that most appropriately fits the developmental level of each child. The levels of the activities presented progress from simple to more difficult.

ART CENTER

The art activities have been designed to be process oriented and not product based. We believe that children learn art skills best by exploring and experimenting with art materials and by using them to creatively express themselves. The emphasis is not placed on what the children "make" or "create" in terms of a product, but the process by which they arrive at their creation. We believe that a child's "art" is a unique creative and expressive act.

MATH CENTER

The math activities presented in this curriculum are designed to help prepare the foundation for mathematics in kindergarten. The activities presented promote knowledge of the number system by providing activities for recognizing numbers, understanding numbers, representing numbers, understanding the relationship among numbers, recognizing patterns, recognizing shapes, organizing and displaying data, and problem solving. The units also incorporate the use of language that encourages the child to express numbers and the relationships of numbers. Again, the underlying intention is to help children to determine similarities and differences in the world of mathematics. The goal of the math activities in this curriculum is to help children understand and be able to use numbers in their everyday world.

SCIENCE CENTER

The goal for the science activities included in this curriculum is to encourage exploration and inquiry. The activities have been designed to provide opportunities in experimentation as a means of exploration. There are activities that incorporate physical science, life science, and earth science. Fortunately, children by nature are eager explorers and simply providing meaningful opportunities yields rewarding results. The concepts in mathematics and science are intricately related. The foundation on which children develop their scientific knowledge is based on their ability to gather, organize, classify, group, and sort information. Once again, the children's abilities to determine the similarities and differences between objects and ideas is one of the key elements in scientific investigation.

LANGUAGE / DRAMATIC PLAY CENTER

The activities that we include in this category serve many purposes. We want to encourage children to interact with each other and develop their oral language and communication skills as they share their thoughts and ideas with each other as they play. We also want children to be exposed to quality literature and listen to and respond to stories, poems, and nursery rhymes. It is our hope that through participating in these activities the children will develop an appreciation for stories and literature and, in turn, develop a life-long love of reading.

In this curriculum, we have planned many activities to enhance the children's letter recognition and letter-sound skills, as well as activities that focus on rhyming words and beginning sounds. We have incorporated activities that cover all of the necessary pre-reading skills that young children will need to master in their preschool years. There is repetition, and skills are revisited in hopes that the children will build new skills while strengthening their existing ones.

LANGUAGE DEVELOPMENT / VOCABULARY

Vocabulary and language development are a major aspect of any early-childhood curriculum.

One exciting aspect of this curriculum is the inclusion of a section entitled vocabulary development and new words. These words are provided for you to include in your conversations as you explore the various topics of study with the children each day. The words are uniquely related to the daily topic of study. Research in the field of early childhood education indicates that children's vocabulary skills can be enriched and enhanced by teachers as they introduce new words each day and use them in context with regards to the topics that the children are studying. Brain research suggests that children are capable of developing much larger vocabularies than they currently have if the adults in their world will use new words with them, in context, on a regular basis. It is our hope that you will use the words as part of your daily routine and interactions with the children.

REFLECT

This section provides closure to each day's activities by reminding children what the topic of study was yesterday, the topic for today's activities, and an introduction to the topic of study for tomorrow. As you make these connections each day, the children will begin to develop an organized way of thinking about what they are learning. The children will in turn begin to make connections and see relationships between objects, ideas, and topics as they learn about them.

EXTEND AND ENRICH

In this section we have listed additional activity ideas and suggestions for you to use to supplement and enrich your daily lesson plan.

You will find suggestions throughout the curriculum for ideas on how you can include family members in special events or celebration days. Family participation in the preschool program further enhances the connection between home and school, which is very important in the learning process.

FINAL THOUGHTS FROM THE AUTHORS

As young children grow and develop, they are constantly encountering new learning challenges and opportunities. By nature, children's curiosity leads them to become problem-solvers. In the early years of development, children need many, many opportunities to test and refine their problem-solving abilities. This curriculum was written with that goal in mind.

An important goal of any early-childhood program or curriculum should be to make use of the knowledge and experience that children bring to each new learning situation. This curriculum seeks to make use of the existing body of knowledge that the children arrive at preschool with and to help them begin to see relationships between that information and new concepts and ideas.

The outward development that the children are experiencing as they see "connections" and "relationships" in their world is not unlike the "inward connections" that are taking place in their brains as the synapses are being connected.

It is such an exciting thing to be a part of the lives of young children and to watch them grow and learn and develop each day. The joy of being an early childhood teacher comes from joining young children on the journey as they discover all that life has to offer and all of the exciting things there are to explore in their world.

We have written this curriculum based on our perceptions of how the world looks "through the eyes of a child." It is our hope that you will enjoy using this curriculum each day to brighten the lives of the young children that you teach.

We hope that you will use this curriculum to inspire and ignite within each child a "life long-love of learning".

Kay Hastings, Cathy Clemons, April Montgomery

Things that Are Unique About Me

My Face

Morning Circle

Show the children pictures of faces from magazines. (Be sure to include faces that represent different ethnic groups, different ages, and both genders.) Hand out mirrors for the children to look at their faces and discuss their facial features. Have them pay special attention to features such as eyes, noses, and mouths. This is a good time to discuss how they use their faces to express different emotions and feelings. The children will enjoy making silly faces and expressions to exhibit different emotions, such as happy, sad, angry, and afraid.

Storytime

The Little Scarecrow Boy by Margaret Wise Brown

Daily Center Activity Ideas

ART CENTER

For developing and experienced levels, place an overhead projector or other light source on a table or on the floor and place a chair in front of the wall. Tape a large piece of black paper on the wall.

Beginning Learner: Face of Someone Special
Provide white drawing paper and crayons and encourage the children to draw the face of someone who is very special to them. Discuss with each child the emotion their special person is showing.

Developing Learner: Silhouette Profile
Invite the child to sit in a chair. Use white chalk to trace the child's side-view silhouette on the black paper taped to the wall. Explain that what he sees on the paper is his *profile*. It's what his face looks like from the side.

Experienced Learner: Silhouette Art
Follow the steps described for the developing learner to trace the children's silhouettes. Encourage the children to cut out their own silhouettes and then glue them to construction paper in their choice of color.

MATH CENTER

Discuss facial symmetry with the children by showing them a paper plate divided in half. Draw one eye on each half of the plate, a nose in the middle, and a half of a mouth on each side of the paper plate. Discuss how they have *one* nose and *one* mouth, and *two* eyes, *two* eyebrows, and *two* lips. You may also discuss shapes such as circle eyes, triangle noses and oval faces.

■ Beginning Learner: Face Collage

Cut out a variety of pictures of faces from magazines. Be sure to include different ethnicities, different age groups, and both genders. Encourage the children to glue the faces on pieces of construction paper to make face collages.

■ ■ Developing Learner: Face Puppets

Provide pictures of eyes, noses, and mouths cut from magazines. Invite the children to choose facial features to use to create a face. The children glue the facial features on a paper plate. Staple a craft stick to the backs of the paper plates and encourage the children to use the paper plate faces as puppets.

■ ■ ■ Experienced Learner: Face Puppets/Finding Facial Features

Invite the children to cut out pictures of eyes, ears, noses, and mouths from magazines. Continue with the directions for the developing learner activity.

SCIENCE CENTER

■ Beginning Learner: Describing Me

Give each child a small hand mirror. Invite the children to look in the mirror and describe the color of their hair, the color of their eyes, and other distinctive features unique to their faces. Discuss with the children how each of their faces is unique to them and different from the faces of their family and friends.

■ ■ Developing Learner: Symmetry

Cover half of each hand mirror vertically with black construction paper so that children can see only one half of their face when looking in the mirror. Ask the children to look in their mirrors and tell what is missing. Discuss the concept of *symmetry* and how their faces are symmetrical, with one eye and one ear on each half of their face. Show the children how they can hold a small piece of yarn across their faces to divide them in half horizontally and vertically.

Experienced Learner: Symmetry Art

Use the small hand mirrors from the developing learner level of this activity, but make an additional set by covering half of each mirror horizontally. Invite the children to look in the two sets of mirrors and discuss what is missing from their faces. Discuss the fact that their faces are symmetrical when divided vertically, but not when divided horizontally. Provide paper and black paint. Show each child how to fold the piece of paper vertically, unfold the paper, and then use black paint to paint one eye, half of a nose, and half of a mouth. Encourage the children to fold their papers in half again and rub them gently with their fingers. When the children open their papers, they will see a complete face.

LANGUAGE/DRAMATIC PLAY CENTER

Beginning Learner: Funny Faces

Show the children pictures of people wearing clown makeup. Discuss with the children all of the different emotions depicted on the clowns' faces. Provide a variety of masks and invite children to try them on and look in a mirror.

Developing Learner: Face Painting

Show the children clown pictures as described above, and then provide face paint and small brushes to paint the children's faces. Provide a poster with designs or pictures to give the children ideas. Let the children decide if they want to be a clown or animal or if they want a design such as a rainbow, sun, or balloons on their faces. If a camera is available, take photos of the children and put them in a class book.

Experienced Learner: Designing Faces

Have the children use paper, pencils, markers, and crayons to make designs and patterns that they would like to have painted on their faces. When each child has drawn his design, paint that design on the child's face. Provide mirrors so that the children can see themselves.

VOCABULARY

circle, emotions, expressions, eyebrows, eyelashes, eyes, face, facial features, frown, mouth, nose, oval, profile, reflection, silhouette, smile, symmetry, unique

Reflect

Say to the children, "Today we learned about our faces and how some things on our faces are alike and some things are different and unique. Tomorrow we will learn about our bodies, how they work, and how they help us work and play every day."

Extend and Enrich

Use the following ideas to extend and enrich what children know about their faces.

◆ Make a class face collage on poster board using glue and pictures of faces cut from magazines.

◆ Show children real masks or pictures of masks and provide collage materials so that they can create their own masks. (**Note:** Plain white face masks are inexpensive and can be purchased at craft stores.)

◆ Discuss emotions, such as happy, sad, angry, scared, and mad.

◆ Discuss the importance of washing one's face and go over the steps involved.

◆ Encourage the children to experiment with textures by taking skin-colored construction paper and crayons outside and making rubbings on tree bark, concrete sidewalks, corrugated cardboard, and other rough or bumpy surfaces. Help them cut their rubbings into face shapes (oval or circle) and ask them to add facial features. The rubbings will look like lines and wrinkles.

◆ Discuss similarities and differences between human faces and animal faces.

My Body

Morning Circle

Explain to the children that they are going to learn about how their bodies are unique. Specify that most bodies are alike in some ways and different in others. Most people have one head, two arms, and two legs. Bodies come in many different sizes. There are babies with small bodies, children with a little bit bigger bodies, and teenagers and adults with much larger bodies. Show the children actual pieces of clothing, such as a baby jumpsuit, a pair of children's overalls, a pair of women's blue jeans, and a man's suit coat. Also, provide examples of shoes, including a baby's shoe, a child's shoe, and an adult's shoe. Discuss which person would wear each item of clothing and pair of shoes. Also discuss how some people are very tall, and some people are very short; some people are big, and some people are small.

Note: This is a good time to discuss individuals with disabilities.

Storytime

Here Are My Hands by Bill Martin and John Archambault

Daily Center Activity Ideas

ART CENTER

For all levels, invite each child to lay down on a large piece of white paper, and then trace around the child's body with crayons.

Beginning Learner: Coloring My Body Buddy

Cut out the body shapes and provide crayons for the children to add facial features and clothing.

Developing Learner: Painting My Body Buddy

Provide mirrors for the children to look into and explore their facial features. Ask them to look at the color of their hair, their eyes and their clothing. Provide paints for the children to use to add details to their faces and clothing on the cutout body shape.

Experienced Learner: Body Buddy Collage

Encourage the children to choose a friend and trace each other's body outline on paper. The children take turns tracing their friends and being traced on the paper. Next, have the children cut out their body shapes. Provide collage materials such as fabric and wallpaper for the children to use to make clothes for their body shapes, and provide yarn for their hair. Also, provide markers and crayons to add facial features and clothing details. When the children have completed their body shapes, take photographs of the children standing beside their "body buddy."

MATH CENTER

To do this activity on all three levels, weigh children on a bathroom scale and record their weights on small construction-paper person cutouts. Use a yard stick or other measuring device to measure each child's height and record that measurement on a cutout figure.

Beginning Learner: Exploring Weight

After weighing the children and measuring their heights as described above, provide a variety of different types of scales for the children to use to experiment with weighing objects. Collect objects in the classroom for the children to explore and weigh.

Developing Learner: Comparing Weight

Provide several 1-gallon milk jugs filled with water (put the lids on the jugs to prevent water from spilling), blocks, or some other heavy objects so the children can experiment with making comparisons between their own body weight and the weight of other objects.

Experienced Learner: Comparing Height and Weight

Encourage more than one child at a time to stand on the scale to see what numbers they can reach. Use colored tape or masking tape to mark each child's height on a wall or doorway and encourage the children to use blocks and other building materials to build towers to equal their heights.

SCIENCE CENTER

Beginning Learner: People Picture Sort

Provide pictures of people of all ages and sizes, including babies, children, teenagers, mothers, fathers, and grandparents. Encourage the children to sort the pictures into categories based on the person's age, size, and any other characteristics that they wish. (Keep in mind that the beginning learner will only be able to sort pictures based on one characteristic at a time, such as age or size.)

Developing Learner: Outer Coverings or "Skins"

Talk about how our skin acts as a protective covering that helps to protect us. Point out that animals and fish have protective "skins" and "coverings" too. Place items that provide protective covering on the science table, including a piece of tree bark, examples of animal fur (fabric that represents animal fur), and fruits and vegetables with skins or peels (have children focus on the outside of the fruit or vegetable). Ask the children to examine and explore the items, and then discuss the ways each item helps to protect the object from which it came.

■ ■ **Experienced Learner:** Protective "Skins"

Give the children small pieces of each item on the science table (See developing learning activity above. For the fruits and vegetables, use a vegetable peeler or knife to give each child a small piece of each.). Encourage the children to glue their samples on paper. Provide word cards, including *tree bark, fur,* and *skin* for the children to copy and write under their examples of protective coverings. As the children are working, ask them how they think each example protects the animal, tree, vegetable or fruit.

Ideas

♦ Introduce the idea of *camouflage,* which has to do with the color, shape, and pattern of the skin. Some animals, including some birds, fish, and butterflies, camouflage themselves for protection from predators.

♦ Introduce the concept of *metamorphosis.* Some animals, such as caterpillars, can change their bodies through the process of metamorphosis. People also experience changes in their bodies as they grow older. To demonstrate this, compare a baby to an elderly adult.

LANGUAGE/DRAMATIC PLAY CENTER

■ **Beginning Learner:** Twister

To help children think about the many ways that their bodies move, bend, and twist, play Twister. If you do not have the commercially available game, make a similar version by cutting out circles from four different colors of construction paper and taping them on a plastic shower-curtain liner. Make a die from a small cardboard box and attach hand and foot shapes onto each side of the box with tape or glue. In place of a color spinner, you can draw colored pieces of construction paper from a paper bag to determine your moves.

■ ■ Developing Learner: Body Moves

Hang a white sheet from the ceiling and provide a light source behind the sheet. Turn out the classroom lights. Invite the children to go behind the sheet, one at a time, and make action movements, such as swimming, jumping, or moving like animals (for example, hopping like a rabbit or galloping like a horse). While one child is moving behind the sheet, the other children try to guess what action the child is performing.

■

■ ■ Experienced Learner: Body Moves and Shadow Puppets

Do the developing learner activity above. After every child has had a turn to pantomime an action behind the sheet, turn on the classroom lights and provide black construction paper for the children to create their own shadow puppets. Talk about different body shapes they could use for people and animals. Tape the puppets to straws or tongue depressors. Then, turn out the lights and invite the children to go behind the sheet and use their puppets to make shadows. Encourage the children to take turns so that every child has an audience. After the children demonstrate their puppets, they might want to combine their puppets and create a play or act out a story. (**Note:** This could be a week-long activity in which children create puppets and use them to act out their favorite stories.)

VOCABULARY

arms, big, bodies, body, camouflage, change, develop, face, feet, grow, hands, head, height, legs, metamorphosis, protective coverings, short, shoulders, small, spine, stomach, tall, torso, weight

Reflect

Say to the children, "Yesterday we talked about our faces and how faces are alike in some ways and different in some ways. Today we learned about our bodies and how they help us in many ways. Tomorrow we will learn about our voices and how each of our voices has a unique sound."

Extend and Enrich

Use the following ideas to extend and enrich what children know about their bodies.

◆ On a sunny day, go outside and trace the children's shadows on the sidewalk with chalk. Children can choose to stand or lie down while they are being traced.

◆ Explore the many ways that bodies move by jumping, skipping, hopping, running, twisting, and bending.

◆ Play music and invite the children to dance and move. Stop the music and have them freeze their bodies in funny poses.

◆ Sing children's songs that focus on body parts, such as "The Hokey Pokey" and "Head, Shoulders, Knees and Toes."

My Voice

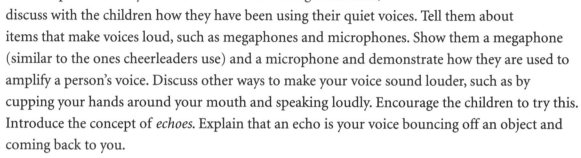

Morning Circle

Greet the children at the door and whisper, "Good morning." Ask the children to go to circle time quietly and whisper when they talk to their friends. During circle time, discuss with the children how they have been using their quiet voices. Tell them about items that make voices loud, such as megaphones and microphones. Show them a megaphone (similar to the ones cheerleaders use) and a microphone and demonstrate how they are used to amplify a person's voice. Discuss other ways to make your voice sound louder, such as by cupping your hands around your mouth and speaking loudly. Encourage the children to try this. Introduce the concept of *echoes*. Explain that an echo is your voice bouncing off an object and coming back to you.

Storytime

Little Beaver and the Echo by Amy MacDonald

Daily Center Activity Ideas

ART CENTER

Beginning Learner: Cup Megaphones
Make a megaphone for each child by cutting out or punching out the bottom of a paper cup. Encourage the children to decorate their cups with stickers. Invite the children to use their megaphones to amplify their voices.

Developing Learner: Paper Tube Megaphones
Provide paper towel tubes and colored construction paper cut to fit the tubes. Invite the children to tape the construction paper around their tubes and then use markers, crayons, and stickers to decorate their megaphones.

Experienced Learner: Paper Cone Megaphones
To prepare for this activity, fold an 11" x 13" sheet of construction paper into a cone shape. Cut off any excess not needed for the cone. Open the cone shape and make a cardboard pattern for the children to trace. Provide cardboard patterns, pencils, and construction paper. Have the children trace their shapes and then cut them out. Provide stickers and markers for the children to decorate their megaphones. When the megaphones are decorated, assist the children with stapling or taping their megaphones into a cone shape.

MATH CENTER

■ **Beginning Learner:** Making Animal Sounds

Make a set of cards using dot stickers and numerals. Place one dot and the numeral 1 on the first card, two dots and the numeral 2 on the second card, and so on to make a set of five cards. Provide a set of small toy animals in a cardboard box. Place the set of cards face down on the table. Invite the children to take turns reaching into the box and pulling out an animal. Each child then draws a card from the pile and makes the sound of that animal the number of times indicated on the card.

■■ **Developing Learner:** Counting Animal Sounds

Talk to the children about the sounds that different animals make and how their "voices" sound different. Include in your discussion animals that are familiar to the children, such as dogs, cats, pigs, snakes, bears, and tigers. Invite the children to practice making their own animal sounds. Provide a tape recorder and microphone and invite the first child to choose an animal and make its sound one time. Invite the next child to choose an animal and make its sound two times. Repeat until each child has had a turn making animal sounds up to five. Replay the tape so the children can count the number of animal sounds that they hear.

■
■■ **Experienced Learner:** Counting Animal Sounds II

Play the game described for the developing learner and provide teddy bear counters for the children to use to indicate how many animal sounds they hear on the tape. Play the tape again and provide numerals written on index cards for the children to use to indicate the number of animal sounds they hear. Encourage the children to practice writing their own numerals on index cards.

SCIENCE CENTER

To prepare for this activity, ask the children to place the fingertips of one hand on their throats and make sounds. Ask, "Do you feel the movement and vibrations inside your throat?" Explain that the vibration they feel is actually the movement of their vocal chords. Set up a vibration experiment by placing plastic wrap tightly over the top of a large bowl. Secure the plastic wrap with a rubber band. Provide small bowls of sugar, salt, and sand for the experiment.

■ **Beginning Learner:** Sound Vibrations

Invite the children to take turns placing small granules of sugar, salt, or sand on top of the plastic wrap. Show them how to bend down close to the bowl and shout or make loud sounds. Watch the bowl to see if the sound vibrations cause the small granules bounce and move across the top of the plastic wrap.

Developing Learner: Comparing Vibrations

Instead of one large bowl for everyone to share, provide several small bowls and encourage the children to choose different materials, such as sugar, salt, sand, and pepper, to place on top of the plastic wrap. The children bend close to their bowls and use their voices to make vibrations so the materials will move. Have them experiment to see which granules are the easiest to move and which are the hardest to move. Encourage the children to find out how loud their voices have to be to move the materials.

Experienced Learner: Comparing Noisemakers

Set up the experiment as described in the beginning learner level and provide a variety of noisemaking objects for the children to experiment with to make vibrations, such as musical instruments, pot and pan lids with wooden spoons, and a megaphone. Encourage the children to experiment to see which objects do the best job of creating the vibrations necessary to move the granules on the plastic wrap.

LANGUAGE/DRAMATIC PLAY CENTER

For every level, make several sets of aluminum can "telephones." Cut out the bottoms of two cans and use an ice pick (teacher only) to poke one hole in the other end of each can. (**Safety note:** Cover the rough edges of the

cans with masking tape before letting the children use them.) Thread a string, about 3 feet long, through the hole in one can and tie a knot on the inside. Pull the other end of the string through the hole in the other can and tie a knot. Pull the cans apart so the string is taut.

Beginning Learner: Aluminum-Can Telephones

Provide the "telephones" as described above and encourage the children to experiment with them. Also provide a variety of other play telephones and old cell phones for the children to use to role play having a conversation with their friends.

Developing Learner: Recording Conversations

Provide a tape recorder and microphone for the children to use to record their own voices. The children may want to talk, sing a song, tell a story, or make funny noises. Invite the children to use the aluminum-can telephones to speak and listen to each other's voices. Encourage the children to practice talking loudly and whispering to see how their voices are amplified by the "telephones."

■
■ ■ **Experienced Learner:** Telephone Game

Implement the activity as described for the developing learner and then play all of the recordings back and encourage the children to make a game of trying to match the voices they hear to their classmates. Be sure to include your own voice for comparison.

VOCABULARY

amplify, echo, laughter, loud, megaphone, microphone, recording, soft, sounds, speech, talking, vibrations, vocal chords, voice box, voices, whisper

Reflect

Say to the children, "Yesterday we learned about our bodies and how they are alike in some ways and different and unique to us in other ways. We also learned how our bodies help us work and play. Today we learned about our voices and vibrations. We learned how all voices sound different. We talked about echoes and how to make our voices loud and quiet. We also talked about some different animals and how their voices sound. Tomorrow we will learn about our hands and fingers and ways that they are unique to each of us and how they help us work and play."

Extend and Enrich

Use the following ideas to extend and enrich what children know about their voices.

◆ Play the game "Telephone." Invite the children to sit in a circle. Choose one child to start the game by whispering something to the child sitting next to him. The "secret" travels around the circle until everyone has heard it. The last child to hear the secret announces what he heard. The child who first shared the message tells the group what he originally said.

◆ Discuss with the children how different people's voices sound, including men's and women's voices, children's voices, and babies' voices.

◆ Provide a board with nails and rubber bands stretched across it at various widths. Children strum the rubber bands to hear their sounds and watch the vibrations.

◆ Show the children a guitar, autoharp, or other stringed instrument. Pluck the strings and listen to the sounds and watch the vibrations. If possible, invite the children to pluck the strings on the guitar and feel the vibrations with their hands.

◆ Encourage the children to listen to the voices of their family members at home and to make comparisons.

◆ Discuss with the children where they might hear loud voices, such as sporting events, musical concerts, and the playground. Discuss places where they would hear quiet voices, such as the library, a church, places where babies are sleeping, and a classroom where children are working.

My Fingers and Hands

Morning Circle

Discuss with the children all of the things that their hands can do, such as wave, clap, snap, tie shoes, blow a kiss, write, draw, and so on. Make a list of the children's ideas. Read the story *Hands Can* and discuss how many of the children's ideas were in the story and how many new ideas the author shared.

Storytime

Hands Can by Cheryl Willis Hudson

Resources for the day's art center activities:
Ed Emberley's Complete Fun Print Drawing Book by Ed Emberley
Ed Emberley's Great Thumbprint Drawing Book by Ed Emberley

Daily Center Activity Ideas

ART CENTER

Beginning Learner: Fingerprints
Provide washable stamp pads and white paper, and invite the children to make fingerprints all over their papers. Provide magnifying glasses so the children can examine their fingerprints and see how they appear when magnified.

Developing Learner: Fingerprint Animals
Show the children Ed Emberley's fingerprint books. Encourage the children to use washable stamp pads and paper to recreate some of the animals shown in Emberley's book. Provide colored pencils and markers for the children to use to add eyes, facial features and bodies.

Experienced Learner: New Fingerprint Creatures

The children use stamp pads to make animals as described above. Next, encourage the children to experiment by connecting their fingerprints on paper in interesting ways to create all new creatures of their own design. Provide magnifying glasses for the children to use to examine their fingerprint creations. Encourage the children to compare their creations with those of their friends.

MATH CENTER

Beginning Learner: Hand Tracing

Trace each child's hand on white paper or construction paper and count the five fingers on each of the child's hands both in the drawing and on his hand. Encourage the children to practice counting their own fingers from 1–5, first from pinky to thumb and then in the reverse direction.

Developing Learner: 5 Fingers

Do the beginning-learner activity. Write the numeral 5 on the palm of the paper hand, and write the numerals 1–5 on each finger. Provide small stickers for children to place on each finger (one sticker on the thumb, one on the forefinger, and so on). When each finger has a sticker, demonstrate how to count each sticker from 1–5.

Experienced Learner: 10 Fingers

Do the beginning-learner activity, but trace both of the child's hands on construction paper. On the paper, write the numeral 5 on the left hand and the numeral 10 on the right hand. Help the children write the numerals 1–5 on each finger of the left hand and the numerals 6–10 on each finger of the right hand (one numeral on each finger). Use crayons to draw dots on the fingers to match the numerals that they have written.

SCIENCE CENTER

Beginning Learner: Feely Box

Talk about the sense of touch and how our hands help us to explore the world. Explain that our fingers give information to our brains. Provide a variety of items, such as a soft blanket, a comb, a hairbrush with bristles, and sandpaper for the children to touch. Put these items in a feely box, and invite the children to reach inside the box, describe the items, and guess what they are without looking at them.

Developing Learner: Things Hands Do

Invite the children to experiment using their hands by making sock balls to throw, sewing with plastic needles and yarn, typing on a keyboard, and playing musical instruments.

Experienced Learner: Sense of Touch

Provide a bowl of ice water and a bowl of cool water. Invite the children to place their hands in ice water for a few seconds and remove them. Then have the children place their hands in cool water. The children will discover that the cool water will feel warm compared to the ice water. Discuss with the children how their fingers are very sensitive to hot and cold temperatures.

LANGUAGE/DRAMATIC PLAY CENTER

Beginning Learner: Play with Puppets

Provide a variety of hand puppets, finger puppets, or homemade sock puppets and encourage the children to use the puppets in pretend play.

Developing Learner: Puppet Theaters

Implement the beginning-learner activity and provide several large appliance boxes (such as a refrigerator box) for the children to use as puppet theaters. Cut out a large square from the top half of one side. Provide markers and collage materials for the children to decorate the boxes to look like stages. When the stages are complete, encourage the children to use the puppets and stages to tell stories.

Experienced Learner: Making Puppets

Give the children garden gloves or rubber dish gloves (**Safety note:** Some children may be allergic to latex rubber, so you may consider synthetic alternatives available at most drug stores.). Provide markers, sequins, collage materials, and glue. Invite the children to make their own puppets and use them to tell stories to their friends.

VOCABULARY

applause, clap, clutch, feel, fingers, fingernails, fingerprints, fingertips, fist, forefinger, gloves, grasp, handprints, hands, lift, middle finger, palm, pinky, ridges, ring finger, snap, texture, thumb, touch, wave

Reflect

Say to the children, "Yesterday we learned about our voices and how each person's voice sounds different. We also learned about vibrations and sound. Today we learned about how important our fingers and our hands are in helping us to work and play and to learn about and explore our world. We also learned how our fingerprints are unique to each of us. Tomorrow we will learn about our names and how they represent and identify each of us and how they are unique to us."

Extend and Enrich

Use the following ideas to extend and enrich what children know about their fingers and hands.

◆ Provide a hand-washing poster and demonstrate the steps of proper hand washing. Talk about the importance of washing our hands.

◆ Fill resealable bags with shaving cream and zip the bags closed. Invite the children to use the bags to draw designs with their fingers, practice drawing numerals, or write the letters in their names.

◆ Talk about various animals and the distinct differences in their "hands" and "fingers" when compared with humans.

◆ Show the children an American Sign Language poster and have them practice using their hands to make some of the signs.

◆ Show the children some examples of Braille and discuss how Braille was invented to help blind people read by using their sense of touch.

◆ Use plaster of Paris to make handprints.

◆ Invite the children to dip their hands in paint and to make colorful handprints.

◆ Add different textures such as salt, sand, rock salt, or cornmeal to fingerpaint or tempera paint, and encourage the children to explore with their hands.

My Name

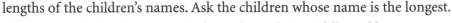

Morning Circle

When all of the children arrive at circle time, discuss their names and the first letter of each child's name. Write all of the children's names on a poster and discuss the letters in each of their names. Compare the lengths of the children's names. Ask the children whose name is the longest. Whose name is the shortest? Ask them about their middle and last names.

STORYTIME

A, My Name Is Alice by Jane E. Bayer

Daily Center Activity Ideas

ART CENTER

■ **Beginning Learner:** Doodle Names

Write the first letter of each child's first name on a poster board square in large uppercase letters. Invite the children to glue collage materials on their letter.

■ ■ **Developing Learner:** Name Collage

Write each child's first name in large uppercase letters on poster board and invite the children to use markers and crayons to decorate the letters in their name.

■
■ ■ **Experienced Learner:** Painted Names

Provide uppercase and lowercase letter stamps and colorful washable stamp pads. Invite the children to stamp the first letter of their name with an uppercase letter stamp and the remaining letters in their name with lowercase stamps. Encourage the children to stamp their name as many times as they wish.

MATH CENTER

■ **Beginning Learner:** Counting Letters

Write the letters of each child's first name in uppercase letters. Help each child count the number of letters in his name and write that numeral below the child's name. Encourage the child to find the same number of small objects in the classroom as the number of letters in his name. The child places one object on each letter in his name. Help the children count their objects.

Developing Learner: Ordering Names

Write each letter of a child's first name in uppercase letters on small pieces of construction paper. Encourage the child to place the letters of his name in order on the table. Invite the children to count the letters in their names as they touch them. Provide paper and crayons for the children to write the numeral that corresponds with the number of letters in their name. Just for fun, the children can mix up the letters in their name and then put them back in order.

Experienced Learner: Comparing Names

Provide squares of construction paper that are uniform in size. Each child writes his first name on the small squares, one letter on each square. After writing their names, the children tape their letter squares, forming their names, on a wall or on large mural paper. When all of the names have been taped to the wall, discuss who has the most letters in his name, who has the same number of letters, and who has the least number of letters in his name.

SCIENCE CENTER

Discuss with the children that all people, animals, and objects have names. Talk about the names of famous people, animals, storybook characters, and common household objects.

Beginning Learner: Common Names

Play a hide-and-seek name game with the children by hiding objects such as an apple, a key, a book, a shoe, or a stuffed animal in the classroom.

Developing Learner: Hide and Seek

Write each child's name on a card and hide it somewhere in the room. Say a child's name, and encourage that child to find the card with his name on it.

Experienced Learner: Name Race

Write each child's name on a piece of paper (or the child can write his own name if he can). Provide magnetic letters and ask the children to find the letters that spell their name and place them over the letters on the paper. Add a small sand timer for fun, and see if the children can find their letters and spell their names before the time runs out.

LANGUAGE/DRAMATIC PLAY CENTER

For every level, photocopy the pages of a telephone book that contain the last names of the children in the class.

Beginning Learner: Finding Names

Show the children a local white pages telephone book and help them find their last names in it. Photocopy the page with each child's last name on it. Give the children their photocopied page and a highlighter marker. Encourage them to find their name on the page and highlight it.

Developing Learner: Copying Names

Help the children find their last name in the telephone book as described above. Provide paper and markers for each child to copy his last name and practice writing it.

Experienced Learner: Paper Chain Names

Write each child's last name on an index card. Give the children their photocopied page from the phone book, their index card, and a highlighter pen. Encourage each child to find his last name on the photocopied page and then highlight it. Provide construction paper strips and markers, and have the children write their names on the strips, one letter on each strip. Connect each child's letter strips together by stapling them (adult only) in order to make a paper chain.

VOCABULARY

alphabet letters, first name, last name, middle name, names, nicknames

Reflect

Say to the children, "Yesterday we learned about our fingers and hands and how they help us work, play, and learn about our world. We also learned how our fingerprints are unique to each of us. Today we learned about our names and how they help identify us and help people recognize us. Next, we will learn about things that are special to each of us. We will begin by learning about our families."

Extend and Enrich

Use the following ideas to extend and enrich what children know about their names.
- Invite the children to make their own name tags or name badges.
- Use commercially available alphabet beads to make name bracelets.

Things that Are Special to Me

My Family

Morning Circle

Prior to this day's activities, send a note home to families asking them to send a family picture to school with their children. When the children arrive, ask them to bring their family pictures to group time. Invite them to share their family pictures with the class. With the children, make a list of all kinds of family members. Discuss with the children different family configurations and the concept of what makes up a family. Also talk about the word "family" and how it can be used to describe different things, including people, animals, and groups of objects.

Storytime

What Daddies Do Best and *What Mommies Do Best* by Laura Numeroff

Daily Center Activity Ideas

ART CENTER

Beginning Learner: Circle Families

Provide construction paper circles of different sizes. Encourage the children to choose one circle to represent each member of their family and glue the circles on paper. The children use crayons to draw eyes, ears, a nose, and a mouth on their circles to represent each member of their family. Help each child write the name of the family member that each circle represents.

Developing Learner: Tracing Circle Families

Provide different sizes of cardboard circles as patterns for the children to trace. The children choose bigger circles to represent the adults in their family and smaller circles for themselves and their siblings. The children trace the circles on paper and then use markers to add hair, eyes, noses, mouths, and bodies for each member of their family. Help the children to label each drawing.

Experienced Learner: Painting Circle Families

Provide cups of different sizes. Invite the children to dip the cups into skin-colored paint and paint a circle on their paper to represent each member of their family. When the circles dry, the children use small paintbrushes to add facial features and bodies to make their family-member pictures complete. Invite the children to label their paintings, helping them as necessary.

MATH CENTER

Beginning Learner: Groups of Objects

Discuss with the children that a family can be a unit of people or a group of objects that belong together or are alike in some way. Provide a variety of objects that are related in different ways, such as an apple, an orange, and a banana; a sock, a shoe, and a hat; a toothbrush and toothpaste; and a fork, a knife, and a spoon. Mix all of the items together and ask the children to sort the objects. Discuss the many ways they can group the objects.

Developing Learner: Things That Go Together

Provide sets of small play figures from the classroom (farm animals, jungle animals, action heroes, cars, trucks, dinosaurs, and so on). Mix the play figures together and ask the children to sort them into groups or units. Discuss how the children decided on each grouping.

Experienced Learner: Family Members

Provide several sets of dollhouse people to represent family members. Encourage the children to sort the dollhouse figures into groups based on different characteristics. After the children have sorted the figures, discuss with them the different groupings.

SCIENCE CENTER

Beginning Learner: Animal Families

Provide magazines with photographs of animals. Invite the children to tear out the pictures and glue them on paper. Discuss the names of the animals and where they live. Talk to the children about animal families.

Developing Learner: Animal Grouping

Provide magazines and old calendars with a variety of animal pictures (farm animals, fish, jungle animals, zoo animals). Ask the children to choose pictures they like, cut them out, and glue them onto construction paper in family groups.

Experienced Learner: Animal Habitats

Provide magazines with pictures of many different types of animals (fish, farm animals, jungle animals, and pets). Encourage the children to cut out pictures of animals they like. Have them create a habitat page

for their animal families by drawing, painting, or cutting construction paper to create water, grass, trees, houses, or any other habitat where the animals can be found. When the habitats are complete, the children glue the pictures of animals to the page.

LANGUAGE/DRAMATIC PLAY CENTER

Before doing this activity, send a note home to families asking them to send in a photo of each family member. Let families know that the pictures will be used for an activity and that the children may cut the photos and glue them to paper.

Beginning Learner: Family Photo Albums

Prepare for this activity by folding 8 ½" x 11" sheets of white paper in half and stapling several sheets together to make a book. On the outside cover, write the words "My Family." Ask each child, "Who is in this photo?" "How is he or she related to you?" Invite the child to glue a photo on each page. Write *my dad, my mom, my sister, my brother*, and so on under each photo. The children can use crayons and markers to decorate the front covers of their photo albums.

Developing Learner: Family Photo Albums/Writing Names

Invite the children to glue a photo on each page of their photo albums. Write the words *my mom, my dad, my sister, my brother*, and other represented family members on sentence strips or index cards for the children to copy. Help the children write the words on the bottom of each page, under each photograph in their books.

Experienced Learner: Family Photo Collage

Invite the children to make a family photo collage by cutting out the pictures of their family members and gluing them on an 8 ½" x 11" sheet of white or colored poster board to make a collage. Provide a sentence strip or index card with the words "My Family" so the children can write the words on the top or bottom of their collages. Also, provide word cards with the words *my sister, my brother, my mom, my dad*, and others as appropriate so the children can copy these words under their photographs.

VOCABULARY

aunt, brother, cousin, daughter, family, father, grandfather, grandmother, grandparents, groups, mother, parents, relatives, siblings, sister, son, uncle

Reflect

Say to the children, "We have learned about ourselves, and we learned about our faces, our bodies, our voices, our hands and fingers, and our names. Today we learned about things that are special to us, starting with our families. Tomorrow we will learn about our friends and how they are special to us."

Extend and Enrich

Use the following ideas to extend and enrich what children know about their families.

◆ Encourage the children to make family trees by drawing a tree and then drawing pictures of their family members on the tree branches.

◆ Provide laundry baskets and an assortment of clothes for the children to practice sorting and folding.

◆ Research different names used for grandparents such as *mimi* and *papa*. Discuss names for grandparents used in other countries. Invite the children to share the names that they call their grandparents.

◆ Encourage the children to talk to their grandparents about things they enjoyed doing when they were children. Encourage the children to ask their grandparents about their favorite places to visit, their favorite foods, or favorite games they enjoyed playing when they were young.

My Friends

Morning Circle

To prepare for this activity, cut out a heart shape from construction paper for each child. Use a marker to write, "I like_____" on each heart. When the children arrive, greet each child at the door and give

her a heart and a crayon. During circle time, encourage the children to use their crayons to draw a picture of something they like. Ask each child to tell you what her picture is about and help her write the words to finish the sentence, "I like_____." When everyone has finished their pictures and written their words, discuss the concept of friendship. Let each child share her picture and tell the other children about something she likes. Point out that no two people are exactly alike, but they can be friends anyway. Brainstorm a list of things that friends share and things they enjoy doing together.

Storytime

Being Friends by Karen Beaumont

Daily Center Activity Ideas

ART CENTER

Beginning Learner: Friendship Pictures

Provide white drawing paper and crayons and encourage the children to draw a picture of themselves with a special friend. Invite children to share the picture with the special friend.

Developing Learner: Friendship Bracelets

Provide chenille sticks and colorful beads for children to make friendship bracelets. Invite the children to make bracelets for themselves and exchange bracelets with their friends.

Experienced Learner: Friendship Necklaces

Provide a salt dough recipe for the children to use to make their own beads. Encourage the children to roll and form the dough or clay into bead shapes and then use a pencil to make a hole inside the bead shape for stringing. When the clay or dough has dried, encourage the children to paint their beads and then string them on a necklace. Invite them to exchange necklaces with their friends.

MATH CENTER

■ **Beginning Learner:** Paper Friendship Chains

Provide strips of colored construction paper for the children to use to make colorful paper chains. Have the children partner with a friend to make a paper chain. Help the children roll the paper strip to form a circle, and tape or staple the paper to hold it in place. Show them how to thread another construction paper strip through the middle of the first circle, form it into a circle, and tape or staple in place. Encourage the children to continue this process until they have a long paper chain, then count the links when they are done.

■ ■ **Developing Learner:** Paper Friendship Chains/Color Patterns

Implement the activity as described for the beginning learner. Encourage the children to choose a color pattern for their chains (for example, red/red/green or yellow/blue/yellow). Encourage the children to repeat their patterns several times. Children may choose to keep their paper chains or exchange them with friends.

■
■ ■ **Experienced Learner:** Paper Friendship Chains/Following Pattern Cards

Provide index cards and markers for the children. Encourage them to look at the colored construction paper and decide what pattern they would like to reproduce as they make their paper chains. When they each have chosen a pattern, encourage them to use colored markers to draw dots on the index cards to represent the pattern they intend to make. Provide scissors and encourage the children to cut construction paper into strips and begin to staple their strips together to make a paper chain that follows the pattern on their index cards. When they are finished making their paper chains according to their pattern cards, they might enjoy switching pattern cards with a friend and making another paper chain according to their friend's pattern card.

SCIENCE CENTER

■ **Beginning Learner:** Autograph Book/Color Mixing

Provide eyedroppers and liquid watercolors in primary shades for the children to drop onto white paper to make splatter paintings. Encourage the children to notice which primary colors mix to make new colors. When the designs are complete, show the children how to place a piece of paper on top of a painting to make a print. When the prints have dried, cut the paper into smaller pieces and staple enough pages together to make an autograph book for each child.

■ ■ **Developing Learner:** Autograph Book/Homemade Paper

Help the children make their own paper by tearing up old construction paper, wrapping paper, and other paper that is not glossy. Be sure they tear it into very small pieces. Place the torn paper in a blender and add warm water (add equal parts water to paper). Let the paper soak in the warm water until it is completely saturated, and then turn on the blender. Blend the paper mixture until it turns into pulp. Add more water, if necessary. Attach a piece of screen to an empty wooden picture frame (just the frame, no glass or backing). Place the screen and frame in a dish pan and pour the mixture through it. Have the children use their hands to press the remaining water out of the paper mixture. Place the paper on a grocery sack to dry. When the paper is completely dry, let the children use it to make autograph books.

Experienced Learner: Autograph Book/Cover Collage
Invite the children to make covers for an autograph book. Provide a piece of cardboard or poster board, markers and paints, and a variety of collage materials such as ribbon, and beads. When they are finished, staple white paper together (adult only) with the covers on top to finish each book. **Note:** If the book covers are too thick to staple through, use a hole puncher and ribbon or yarn to bind the pages instead of staples. Invite the children to share their books in the language center. Friends can sign their names and draw pictures in the books.

LANGUAGE/DRAMATIC PLAY CENTER

Beginning Learner: Autograph Books/Drawings
Encourage the children to share their autograph books with their friends by drawing pictures in each other's books. As each child draws a picture, write that child's name on the page. At the end of the day, the children will have many pages of pictures drawn for them by their friends.

Developing Learner: Autograph Books/Fancy Pens
Provide feathers, ballpoint pens, and florist tape for the children to use to make fancy pens. Invite the children to share their autograph books with their friends, who sign their names or draw a picture using the fancy pens they made.

■
■ ■ **Experienced Learner:** Autograph Books/Photos

Use a digital camera to take a photograph of each child. Make multiple copies so that every child has a picture of each of her classmates. The children cut out the pictures of their friends and glue one on each page of their autograph books. Invite them to give their books to their friends to sign their names or draw a picture on the page that has their picture on it.

VOCABULARY

companions, friends, friendships, giving, neighbors, pals, relationships, sharing, together

Reflect

Say to the children, "Yesterday we learned about families and how there are many different kinds of families. We also learned that families can be made up of people, animals, or groups of objects that are related in some way. Today we learned about friends and how important they are, and how much fun friends can have growing and sharing together. Tomorrow we will learn about pets and how special they are to people."

Extend and Enrich

Use the following ideas to extend and enrich what children know about their friends.

◆ Encourage the children to use crayons and markers to write a letter or draw a picture for a classmate or a special friend.

◆ Provide a postcard so each child can draw a picture or write a letter to a classmate or a family member. Address the postcard and give it to the child to add a stamp. Put the cards in the school mailbox for the school mail carrier to pick up. (The children love giving the letters to the mail carrier directly). This is a fun activity to do around Valentine's Day.

◆ Teach the children ways to say "friend" in different languages.

My Pets

Morning Circle

Prior to this day's activities, send a note home to family members asking them to let their child bring a stuffed animal (preferably a dog, cat, or other typical family pet) to school. Cut out small "Blue Ribbon" shapes from construction paper. Write simple messages on the ribbons, such as "Most Cuddly Kitten," "Most Precious Puppy," and "Silliest Snake." As the children arrive, give them ribbons for their "pets." At morning circle, ask the children to name animals that make good pets. List the children's ideas on poster board or on a dry-erase board. Next, ask the children to name animals they would love to have as pets. This list may have more interesting animals on it. Discuss the two lists and how they are alike and how they are different. Which animals are on both lists? Which animals are missing from each list? Encourage the children to discuss why some animals do not make good pets.

Storytime

Pet Show by Ezra Jack Keats

Daily Center Activity Ideas

ART CENTER

Beginning Learner: Paper Snakes

Cut large white paper into snake shapes and give one to each child. Encourage the children to use the watercolor paint to make designs on their snakes.

Developing Learner: Stocking Snakes

Provide one knee-high stocking for each child and cotton batting. Invite the children to stuff their stockings with the batting to make "snakes." Help the children tie a knot in the end of their stockings. Provide tempera paint for the children to use to decorate their snakes.

Experienced Learner: Stocking Snakes II

Encourage the children to follow the steps described for the developing learner to make a stocking snake. Provide pieces of colored felt and encourage the children to cut stripes, spots, and designs to decorate their snakes. Show them how to use red felt to make a tongue. Attach all the pieces using glue. Provide wiggle eyes for the children to add to their snakes.

MATH CENTER

▪ Beginning Learner: Sorting Animals

Invite the children to place their stuffed animals on the floor and discuss how they are alike and different. Encourage the children to sort their animals into categories by color, size, or type of animal.

▪ ▪ Developing Learner: Sorting and Counting Animals

Place large hula hoops on the floor for the children to use to sort their stuffed animals. The children place the animals into the hula hoops based on the categories they choose, such as color, shape, size, or other category. When they are finished sorting the animals, ask them to count how many animals are in each hoop and encourage them to write those numbers on pieces of paper. Ask them which circle has the most animals and which has the least animals.

▪ ▪ Experienced Learner: Ordering Stuffed Animals

Invite the children to place the stuffed animals in order from largest to smallest or from smallest to largest. Encourage them to count the animals when they are all in a row. Ask the children, "Which animal is the biggest?" "Which animal is the smallest?"

SCIENCE CENTER

▪ Beginning Learner: Pet Care/Dogs

Provide items used to care for a dog, such as dog bowls (large, medium, small), dog food (canned and dry), dog treats (large, medium, small) leashes and collars (large, medium, small), dog beds (large, medium, small), dog toys, and books on the care of dogs. Provide three sizes of stuffed dogs. Encourage the children to look at the items and discuss them. Invite the children to sort the items based on which ones they think would be used by the big dog, the medium dog, and the small dog. Which items would be used for dogs of all sizes?

Developing Learner: Pet Care/Dogs and Cats

Provide the items from the beginning-learner activty for three sizes of dogs, and add items for cats as well (cat food, cat treats, cat bed, cat toys, cat collars, and books on the care of cats). Provide stuffed dogs and cats in a variety of sizes. The children discuss the items and decide which items would be best for each stuffed animal. Invite them to look at the cat and dog care books and discuss what is needed to take care of a pet dog or cat.

Experienced Learner: Pet Care/Dogs, Cats, and Fish

Provide the materials as described above, but add items for the care and feeding of fish, such as a fish bowl, fish food, fish net, plants, aquarium gravel, and books on the care of pet fish. Provide stuffed animal fish. Encourage the children to look at and discuss all of the items and decide which items are necessary for caring for which pets. Provide grocery bags for the children to use to make care packages for pretend families who might want to purchase the animals. Have them place everything necessary for each animal inside the bags.

LANGUAGE/DRAMATIC PLAY CENTER

Beginning Learner: Pet Tags and Leashes

Provide pet leashes and collars for the children to look at. Explain the importance of animals being on a leash and having an identification tag. Provide poster board circles with holes punched in them (for tags) and pieces of yarn (for a collar and leash). Invite the children to decorate their identification tag with markers and stickers and then help them tie it around the stuffed animal's neck to make a collar. Use longer yarn for a leash. (**Safety note:** Be sure to tell the children that they should never tie yarn or string around a real animal's neck. Collars and leashes are made especially for this purpose, but other materials can hurt an animal.)

Developing Learner: Designing Pet Collars

Provide small strips of poster board, colorful beads and jewels, and glue for the children to use to make a collar for their stuffed pet. Help each child staple the collar around her stuffed animal's neck.

Experienced Learner: Pet Names

Provide poster board circles, stamps, and stamp pads for the children to use to make identification tags. Also, provide small strips of poster board for the children to use to make a pet collar. Invite them to stamp the pet's name on the poster board strip, and then decorate it using jewels and stones. When the identification tags and collars are dry, help the children staple their collar to a stuffed animal's neck.

VOCABULARY

birds, cats, cages, chinchilla, collar, dogs, ferrets, fish, guinea pigs, hamsters, identification tag, leash, mice, obedience, pet food, rabbits, snakes, spiders, training, veterinarian

Reflect

Say to the children, "Yesterday we learned about our friends and how special they are us. Today we learned about pets and all of the different kinds of animals that can be kept as pets. Tomorrow we will talk about some of our favorite toys."

Extend and Enrich

Use the following ideas to extend and enrich what children know about their pets.

- Invite the children to make paper plate snakes. Place a paper plate (with a hole cut out of the center) on an old record player and turn it on. Have a child hold a marker against the plate as it spins to make spiral designs. When the design is complete, the child (or teacher) cuts the paper plate around and around in a spiral pattern until she reaches the top. Put a piece of yarn in the hole and tie. The snakes are fun to hang from the ceiling.
- Find pictures of different animal footprints. See if the children can match the animals to their footprints.
- Tie small bundles of broom bristles together with yarn and encourage the children to dip the bundles in paint to make "cat whisker" paintings.
- Explain to the children that cats are excellent climbers and have excellent balance. Cats always seem to land on their feet. Provide balancing activities for the children to try.
- Create a pet shop in the dramatic play center where children can sell pets and pet accessories.
- Provide a variety of doll clothes for the children to use to dress up their stuffed animals.

My Toys

Morning Circle

Prior to this activity, send a note home inviting the children to bring in one of their favorite toys to celebrate "a few of my favorite things" play day. Be sure that families write their child's name on the toy. (**Safety note:** Remind parents and children that no weapon-type toys are to be brought to school.) Just for fun, bring a favorite toy from your childhood to show the children. At group or morning circle time, engage the children in a "show and tell" discussion of their toys. Encourage the children to demonstrate how their special toy works and tell why it is their favorite. Read *The Velveteen Rabbit*, which is about a little boy who had a favorite toy that lived in a playroom with lots of other toys.

Storytime

The Velveteen Rabbit by Margery Williams

Daily Center Activity Ideas

ART CENTER

Beginning Learner: Ball Painting

Provide a variety of small balls (such as golf balls and ping-pong balls), paint, and paper. Invite the children to place the paper in a small box or tub and use a spoon to place a small amount of paint in the corner of the box. Add a small ball and show the children how to tilt the box in all directions to roll the paint-covered ball across the paper.

Developing Learner: Toy Prints

Provide a variety of small toys, such as Legos, geometric shapes, trucks, cars, and small blocks. Pour a small amount of paint on cookie sheets or paper plates. Encourage the children to select a small toy, dip it into paint, and make toy prints on paper.

Experienced Learner: Squirt Bottle Painting

To prepare for this activity, fill small squirt bottles with watered-down tempera paint or liquid watercolors. The children place the paper in a tub or child-size swimming pool and use the squirt bottles to squirt paint onto paper. After experimenting with this technique, invite the children to place a toy or small object such as a cookie cutter on the paper and squirt paint around it. When they remove the toy from the paper, the silhouette will remain.

MATH CENTER

■ **Beginning Learner:** Building Towers/Comparing

Provide several types of blocks, such as wooden blocks, cardboard blocks, and small stacking blocks, for the children to use to build towers. Invite them to build towers as tall as they can. Show them how to make comparisons by counting how many of each type of block it takes to make towers of the same height.

■ ■ **Developing Learner:** Building Towers/Counting

Provide wooden blocks and a die. The first child rolls the die and places that number of blocks on the floor to start building a tower. The next child rolls the die and adds that number of blocks to the tower. Children repeat the process to see how tall they can build the tower before it falls down.

■
■ ■ **Experienced Learner:** Building Towers/Measuring

Provide rulers, yard sticks, and measuring tapes for the children to measure their heights. Provide pieces of masking tape for them to mark their heights on the wall, and then encourage the children to use blocks and other building materials to build towers as tall as they are.

SCIENCE CENTER

■ **Beginning Learner:** Observing and Comparing Toys

Provide different types of toys, such as toys with wheels, building toys, tops and things that spin, and toys that move fast or slow. Encourage the children to explore the different toys and compare what they can do.

■ ■ **Developing Learner:** How Is That Made?

Provide a variety of toys made out of different materials, such as rubber, plastic, metal, and wood. Encourage the children to explore and experiment with the toys. Engage them in a discussion about the materials that are used to make each of the different toys. Provide toys that no longer work and screwdrivers that the children can use to take the toys apart. (**Safety note:** Observe the children carefully if small parts are involved.)

■
■ ■ **Experienced Learner:** Designing Toys

Provide scraps of wood, wooden spoons, colored tape, and interesting small building scraps or household objects that the children can combine to design and create their own toys. Provide an assortment of empty cardboard food containers for the children to use in their designs.

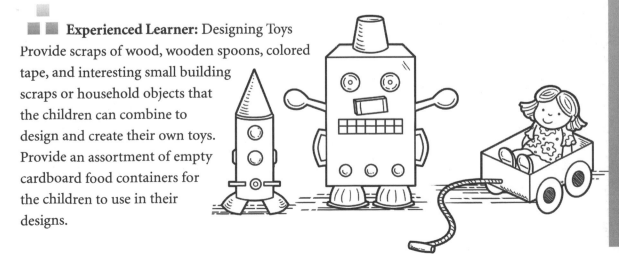

LANGUAGE/DRAMATIC PLAY CENTER

■ **Beginning Learner:** Toy Store

Provide a cash register, play money, and a variety of toys and stuffed animals for the children to use to role play setting up and working at a toy store.

■ ■ **Developing Learner:** Building and Pricing Toys

Provide toy catalogs, pictures of toys, and small building materials. Encourage the children to choose a picture of a toy and use the small building materials to build it. Provide a wagon or empty shelves for the children to place their toys on when they have finished building them. Provide crayons and paper for the children to make price tags for their toys.

■
■ ■ **Experienced Learner:** Toy Catalogs

Provide toy catalogs or toy-store ads from the newspaper. Invite the children to cut out pictures of toys to make their own toy catalog. Make sure they include prices and descriptions.

VOCABULARY

bicycles, board games, building blocks, crayons, dollhouse, dominoes, Legos, Lincoln logs, teddy bears, yo-yos

Reflect

Say to the children, "Yesterday we learned about pets and why they are special. Today we learned about our toys and how much fun we have with them. Tomorrow we will learn about our homes and why they are an important part of our lives."

Extend and Enrich

Use the following ideas to extend and enrich what children know about toys.

♦ Invite family members to bring in some favorite toys from their childhood, such as a Slinky, yo-yo, or a Spirograph, and demonstrate how they work.
♦ Invite parents for a special game day where adults and children play favorite board games from the past.
♦ Help the children design their own board games or card games.

My Home

Morning Circle

Just for fun, greet the children wearing your pajamas and looking disheveled. Tell the children to pretend that the classroom is your house and that they are visiting you there. Encourage the children to take turns knocking on the door. Answer the door and ask, "Who's that knocking on my door?" After playing this game for a while, tell the children that you are going to share a funny story with them about children who think their teacher lives and sleeps at school.

Storytime

My Teacher Sleeps in School by Leatie Weiss

Daily Center Activity Ideas

ART CENTER

To prepare for this activity, obtain a large cardboard box, such as a refrigerator box, and cut windows on three sides and a door in the front.

■ **Beginning Learner:** Painting a House
The children use tempera paints, paintbrushes, and paint rollers to paint the large box and transform it into a house.

■ ■ **Developing Learner:** Building and Decorating a House
Provide the large cardboard box as described above and have the children use paint to transform it into a house. Help the children cut pieces of construction paper to make bricks, stones, shingles, and other details for the house. The children may also want to use construction paper to decorate the inside of the box to resemble the inside of a house. Tape pieces of colored plastic to the windows to make windowpanes.

Experienced Learner: Building Smaller Houses

Provide small cardboard boxes, such as shoeboxes, cereal boxes, and empty food containers, for the children to use to make small "houses." Show the children how to stack the boxes to make multilevel houses. Provide construction paper and paint to make rocks, bricks, or stones on their houses.

MATH CENTER

Beginning Learner: House Numbers

Before doing this activity, look up each child's address and write the house or apartment number on an index card. Provide numeral stamps and stamp pads for the children to use to practice stamping their address numbers on paper.

Developing Learner: House Numbers/Sandpaper Rubbings

Follow the directions for the beginning-learner level and then trace a set of numerals from 0–10 on pieces of sandpaper and cut them out individually. Have each child look at the index card with his house number on it and choose the sandpaper numerals to match the numbers. Encourage the children to place a sheet of paper over the numerals one at a time and use a peeled crayon to rub sideways over the numerals to make a print on their papers.

Experienced Learner: Making Address Plates

Give each child a smooth scrap of wood to make an address plate for her house or apartment. Also, give each child an index card with her house number on it. Provide paints and small paintbrushes for the children to paint their house or apartment numbers on the wood.

SCIENCE CENTER

■ **Beginning Learner:** Bricks and Mortar

Provide bricks. Discuss how home builders place mortar between bricks to make the bricks stick together. Provide bricks, paintbrushes, and bowls of water for the children to paint on the bricks. Encourage the children to watch as the water on the bricks *evaporates* (dries quickly).

■ ■ **Developing Learner:** Using Tools to Build Houses

Provide Styrofoam packing squares, rubber mallets, and golf tees for the children to practice their hammering skills.

■
■ ■ **Experienced Learner:** House Construction

Provide small scraps of wood, wooden spools, craft sticks, tongue depressors, and empty cardboard food boxes for the children to "build" houses. The children can use masking tape, duct tape, clear plastic tape, or colored tape to hold their structures together. Provide the children with a variety of tapes and they can experiment to see which kinds work better.

LANGUAGE/DRAMATIC PLAY CENTER

Before doing this activity, talk about all kinds of houses that can be a home. Animals have many different types of homes, such as trees, holes in the ground, hollow logs, the ocean, and caves. People live in many different kinds of homes, too, including one-story houses, two-story houses, apartments, townhouses, igloos, tents, and mobile homes. If possible, show the children pictures of different kinds of homes to spark discussion.

■ **Beginning Learner:** Pretend Home

Cover a card table with a sheet and invite the children to pretend it is their home. Provide other props, such as flashlights, pretend food, and sleeping bags, to assist their pretend play. They may pretend to be animals or people.

■ ■ **Developing Learner:** Home Outdoors

Pitch a tent outdoors and invite children to pretend it is their outdoor home. If your room is large enough, you can put the tent inside, too. Provide dishes, cooking utensils, sleeping bags, pillows, and pretend food.

■
■ ■ **Experienced Learner:** Building a Home

Provide a variety of different building materials, such as wooden blocks, cardboard blocks, and any other materials in the classroom that the children can use to "build" different kinds of houses.

VOCABULARY

address, appliances, bathroom, bedroom, bricks, doors, hammers, home, house, kitchen, nails, roof, rooms, stairs, walls, windows

Reflect

Say to the children, "Yesterday we learned about toys and how much fun they are to play with. Today we learned about our homes and how special they are to us. We also learned that there are many different types of structures that people call 'home.' Tomorrow we will focus on our bodies and the special things that are found on the outside of our bodies."

Extend and Enrich

Use the following ideas to extend and enrich what children know about their homes.

- Teach older children how to hold and use tools, such as a hammer and nail or a screwdriver. Provide a variety of tools and discuss how each is useful in building a house or for completing household projects.
- Introduce various gadgets found around the house, including potato mashers, hand mixers, handheld vacuum cleaners, alarm clocks, and portable telephones and discuss the uses of each and how they are helpful tools around the house.
- Provide a variety of kitchen gadgets with which the children can paint.
- Introduce the concept of chores and jobs around the house (unloading the dishwasher, sorting clothes for the laundry, setting the table, and taking out the garbage). Provide materials for the children to practice some of these tasks.
- Provide graham crackers, icing, and tongue depressors for the children to use to practice spreading "mortar" on bricks.

Things on the Outside of My Body

My Hair

Morning Circle

Just for fun, wear your hair in a funny hairstyle and greet the children at the door. Rub a balloon filled with air on carpet or fabric, and then rub it on your hair to show the children the effects of static electricity. Your hair will stand up and out, which is guaranteed to delight the children! Let the children experiment with the balloon on their hair. This is a great introduction to the story *Crazy Hair Day* by Barney Saltzberg. Share the story with the children and laugh with them at all of the funny hairstyles that appear in the book. After storytime, discuss with the children how important hair is for protecting our heads (from the sun in the summer and the cold in the winter).

Storytime

Crazy Hair Day by Barney Saltzberg

Daily Center Activity Ideas

ART CENTER

Beginning Learner: Paper Wigs

Talk to the children about the little boy in the story. Explain that they are going to make their own funny hair creations. Provide shredded paper and other collage materials for the children to glue to a paper plate. When they are finished, use a hole punch to punch a hole on each side of the paper plate and tie yarn through the holes to make a hat. Tie the yarn under the children's chin and let them wear their hair creation home.

Developing Learner: Painted Hair

Some of the children in the story sprayed their hair funny colors. Show the children these pictures. Provide paper, crayons, and spray bottles with different colors of watered-down paint. Have children draw a face on their paper, put the drawing in a plastic tub, and spray "hair" around the face drawing to make a funny hair design.

Experienced Learner: Yarn Braids

Provide an inexpensive sun visor for each child and balls of different colors of yarn. (**Note:** Sun visors can be purchased at craft stores.) Let the children select several colors of yarn. Show them how to use the yarn to make braids that resemble hair braids. Each child should make two braids. Help the children tie the ends with yarn or ribbon to secure the braids. Use hot glue to attach the hair braids to their sun visors (adult only).

MATH CENTER

■ **Beginning Learner:** Practicing Numerals in Squishy Bags

Place plastic numerals inside resealable plastic bags filled with clear hair gel. Seal with tape, if necessary. Invite the children to trace the numerals and enjoy the squishy feeling of the bags.

■ ■ **Developing Learner:** Drawing Numerals in Hair Gel

Provide a tray of hair gel for children to use to practice drawing their numerals. (**Safety note:** Make sure children do not get any gel in their mouths or eyes, and have the children wash their hands immediately after doing this activity.)

■
■ ■ **Experienced Learner:** Number the Hair

Give the children colored chalk to practice writing really large numerals (0–10) on the sidewalk or playground. Encourage them to draw faces on the sidewalk with 10 strands of hair. Have them number each strand of hair. Next, provide spray bottles filled with water for the children to spray their numerals. The water will erase them.

SCIENCE CENTER

■ **Beginning Learner:** Shampoo Bubbles

Fill the water table with water and a small amount of tear-free, scented, colored shampoo. Provide water wheels, water toys, and hand beaters for children to use to make bubbles.

■ ■ **Developing Learner:** Making Shampoo

Do the activity as described for the beginning learner. Provide small empty bottles with caps for the children to use to make their own "shampoo."

Experienced Learner: Making Scented Shampoo

Give each child a small empty bottle with a cap. Pour a small amount of scented flavorings such as orange and lemon, and food coloring mixed with water into separate bowls. Add eyedroppers to each bowl. Encourage the children to choose the scents and colors they like and use the eyedroppers to add the scent and color to their bottles. When the scents and colors have been added, add enough clear shampoo to each bottle to fill it. Screw the caps on tightly. Provide white labels and encourage the children to think of a name for their shampoo. Write the names on the labels and attach them to the bottles.

LANGUAGE/DRAMATIC PLAY CENTER

Beginning Learner: Hair Salon and Barber Shop

Provide props including a blow dryer and curling iron (without the cords), hair curlers, barrettes, hair clips, combs, brushes, empty spray bottles and shampoo bottles, and dolls with hair. Invite the children to use the props to play beauty salon and barber shop.

Developing Learner: Working with Wigs

Provide the props described for the beginning-learner activity. If available, add wigs and wig stands for the children to pretend to style hair. Provide fashion and hairstyle magazines to inspire the children's "work."

Experienced Learner: Wash and Curl

Provide baby dolls with hair, containers of water and shampoo, and towels for the children to practice washing hair. Also provide combs and brushes for the children to use to style hair.

VOCABULARY

bald, beard, beauty, brush, comb, follicle, hair, hair dryer, hairspray, head, headband, mustache, root, scissors, shampoo, style

Reflect

Say to the children, "Today we learned about our hair and how it helps to protect our heads from the sun and cold. Tomorrow we will learn about our eyes and how important they are in helping us see and enjoy the world around us."

Extend and Enrich

Use the following ideas to extend and enrich what children know about their hair.

- Show the children a violin bow and discuss how it is made from horse hair. Brainstorm other things in our world that are made from or with animal hair.
- Explain that rubber bands are an important tool in helping to create many different hair styles. Provide various colors and sizes of rubber bands and geo-boards for the children to use to make designs.
- Read the fairy tale *Rapunzel.*
- Encourage the children to examine hair samples under a microscope.
- Plan a wacky hair day where the children come to school wearing creative hairstyles.
- Discuss facial hair with the children, including sideburns, beards, and moustaches.

My Eyes

Morning Circle

When the children come to circle time, give each child a handkerchief or scarf to use as a blindfold. Blindfold the children who wish to participate and discuss how they feel. What do they "see?" (**Safety note:** The children who are blindfolded must remain seated to ensure their safety.) When the blindfolds are removed, talk about all of the different things they can see and emphasize how important their eyes are in helping them discover and learn about their world. This activity provides a good opportunity to talk about blindness and impaired vision. Explain that some people need to wear glasses or contact lenses to help them see. If there are children in the class who wear glasses, encourage them to share their experiences. Talk about animals' unique ways of "seeing." For example, bats use *echolocation* as a method of knowing where an object is because their eyesight is not very good. On the other hand, hawks, eagles, and seagulls have excellent eyesight. Seagulls, for example, can spot a small shrimp or fish in the water and swoop down and pick it up very quickly with their feet.

Storytime

Close Your Eyes by Kate Banks

Daily Center Activity Ideas

ART CENTER

Provide several pairs of eyeglasses with different prescriptions for the children to try on and see how their vision changes when they look through the lenses. Also provide several pairs of sunglasses for the children to try on for comparison. (**Safety note:** Monitor this activity closely to ensure that the glasses do not break.)

■ **Beginning Learner:** Drawing with Eyeglasses
Provide paper and markers and ask the children to draw a picture. Have them put on a pair of prescription glasses or sunglasses and create a new picture. Discuss their experiences after making both pictures.

■■ **Developing Learner:** Magnified Art
Provide paper and watercolors and several different magnifying glasses or magnifying sheets. Encourage the children to paint a picture, and then encourage them to use a magnifying glass to look at their picture. Ask them what they see and how the picture looks different to them. Encourage them to pay special attention to the details of their picture when magnified.

■ ■ Experienced Learner: Colored Lenses

Provide sheets of colored acetate (like those used for report covers). Encourage the children to hold the sheets up to the light and look through them. Provide several pairs of glasses and use tape to place a small piece of colored acetate paper over the lenses. Encourage the children to wear the glasses and experience things through colored lenses. Have them draw a picture and then cut small pieces of the colored acetate to place over parts of their picture. Have them secure the corners of the acetate with tape. Discuss how their pictures look with and without the colored acetate.

MATH CENTER

■ Beginning Learner: Wiggle Eye Sort

Provide a variety of wiggle eyes in different sizes and colors. Invite the children to sort the wiggle eyes by color or size. Discuss how many children have blue eyes, brown eyes, and green eyes.

■ ■ Developing Learner: Colored Kaleidoscopes

Provide kaleidoscopes. Invite the children to hold them up to the light and spin the wheel to discover and explore the colors, shapes, and designs. Encourage them to experiment with looking at objects with both eyes and then while covering one eye. How do things look when using one eye instead of both eyes?

■ ■ Experienced Learner: Color Wheels

Provide circle cutouts and encourage the children to use markers or colored pencils to color and draw designs on their circle. When the children are finished coloring, insert a sharpened pencil through the center of the color wheel (adult only). Demonstrate what happens when the wheel is spun around the pencil. The colors appear to mix. Experiment with spinning the wheel slow and fast. Supervise the children while they are using their color wheels.

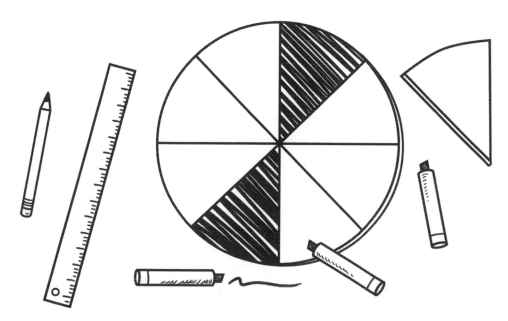

SCIENCE CENTER

■ **Beginning Learner:** Vision and Balance

Explain to the children how important their eyes are in helping them keep their balance. Have them try to stand on one foot with their eyes open. Then have them try to stand on one foot with their eyes closed. Ask them which is easier and which is harder to do. Discuss that many everyday tasks are easy to do when we can see, but these same tasks become more difficult or impossible when we cannot see.

■ ■ **Developing Learner:** Visual Aids

Provide a variety of visual aids, such as glasses with lenses, sunglasses, magnifying glasses, binoculars, opera glasses, cameras, and eye patches. Encourage the children to use these tools to explore how each one changes their vision.

■
■ ■ **Experienced Learner:** Pass the Pupil

Explain that the center of the eye is called the *pupil* and that our eyes are designed so that when light enters the pupil, it *constricts* (gets smaller), and when a room is very dark, the pupil *dilates* (gets larger). To help children understand this concept better, draw a large eye-shaped circle to resemble a dilated pupil on one side of a ball and a small eye-shaped circle to resemble a constricted pupil on the other side. Provide a flashlight. Have the children form a circle and sit on the floor. Explain that when the classroom light is on, their pupils are constricted and appear small. Encourage them to look at their classmates' eyes and notice how small their pupils are. Turn the classroom light off and turn the flashlight on. Now explain that when the classroom light is off, everyone's pupils become dilated to let more light in. Encourage the children to look at their classmates' eyes and notice how large their pupils are. Pass the ball around the circle. When the light is on, pass it with the small pupil facing up. When the light is off, pass it with the large pupil facing up.

LANGUAGE/DRAMATIC PLAY CENTER

■ **Beginning Learner:** "Wynken, Blynken, and Nod"

Read the nursery rhyme "Wynken, Blynken, and Nod" to the children. If available, show the children a wooden shoe. Make a fishing game by tracing a shoe pattern on different colors of construction paper, cutting them out, and attaching paper clips to the shoe cutouts. Make a fishing pole by tying a piece of string with a magnet on one end to a dowel rod. Children "fish" for matching colors of shoes. You may also have the children practice winking with each eye, blinking with both eyes, and then nodding their heads like the children in the poem.

■ ■ **Developing Learner:** Parts of the Eye and Eye Color

Discuss the parts of the eye, including eyelids, eyebrows, eyelashes, and pupils. Encourage the children to look at their eyes in a mirror and locate each of these parts. Talk about different eye colors. Provide colored construction paper and have each child draw and cut out an eye that matches his eye color. Help the children write their names on their cutouts and add them to a classroom graph. Using the graph, count how many children in the class have each eye color.

Experienced Learner: Eye Test

Borrow an eye chart that is used to test the vision of young children. (A good source would be a pediatrician's office. You may also print one out from the Internet.) This type of eye chart has shapes facing different directions instead of alphabet letters. Tape the chart to the wall. Discuss the importance of vision tests and how doctors use this chart to test vision. Invite the children, one at a time, to cover one of their eyes and look at the shapes on the chart. Explain how they can use their fingers to indicate the direction each shape is facing. Invite them to experiment with seeing how distance affects their vision. They can stand really close to the chart and then move a distance away from it to experience how things look different up close and far away.

VOCABULARY

blink, color blind, constrict , contact lenses, dilate, eye color, eye test, eyebrows, eyelashes, eyes, eyesight, farsighted, focus, glasses, iris, kaleidoscope, lens, lenses, nearsighted, optometrist, pupil, spectacles, vision, wink

Reflect

Say to the children, "Yesterday we learned about our hair and how it protects our head from the sun, cold, and moisture. Today we learned how important our eyes are in helping us explore and discover the world around us. Tomorrow we will learn how our noses help us recognize the smells in our world."

Extend and Enrich

Use the following ideas to extend and enrich what children know about their eyes.

- ◆ Provide "I Spy" books for the children to look at and enjoy.
- ◆ Discuss with the children animals that have very large eyes. Include in your discussion dragonflies, horseflies, and the praying mantis. Provide pictures of these and other animals for the children to compare the size of their eyes. Also provide pictures of fish, moths, and butterflies that have eye-like spots on their bodies that they use to fool predators.

My Nose

Morning Circle

If possible, bake a loaf of bread or a batch of cookies, or have another aromatic food that the children will smell and immediately recognize when they enter the classroom. Discuss how important our noses are in helping us to identify good smells, bad smells, and even dangerous smells, such as fire. Also, discuss with the children funny things that noses do such as sneeze and snore. Encourage them to make sneezing and snoring sounds. Give each child a small taste of the baked food you made or brought. As they enjoy the treat, read the book *Bear Snores On*.

Storytime

Bear Snores On by Karma Wilson

Daily Center Activity Ideas

ART CENTER

Beginning Learner: Scratch-and-Sniff Stickers
Provide a wide variety of scratch-and-sniff stickers for the children to use to make pictures. Encourage them to discover and explore the different scents and see which ones they can identify easily.

Developing Learner: Scented Markers
Provide scented markers for the children to use to make pictures.

Experienced Learner: Scented Playdough
Make playdough with the children, using a favorite recipe. Provide a variety of different scented flavorings, such as lemon, orange, peppermint, vanilla and chocolate, for the children to add to their playdough.

MATH CENTER

Beginning Learner: Feely Box
In preparation for this activity, make a "feely box" by cutting two holes in the side of a cardboard box large enough for the children to place their hands inside. Hang a small scrap of black fabric over the openings. Place pairs of objects that smell good inside the box (small candles, cinnamon sticks, small bars of soap, and so on). Make a set of picture clues for these objects. To play, the children draw a card and place each of their hands in the holes of the feely box and try to find

the matching objects. Encourage them to describe how the objects smell.

An alternate method of playing this game is to put one of the objects on the table and one in the feely box. The child chooses an object from the table and reaches inside the box to find its match.

Developing Learner: Feely Box

Prepare the feely box as described above, but do not prepare the picture clue cards. Encourage the children to reach in the feely box with both hands and find a pair of matching objects. The children describe the objects to their classmates, who try to guess what it is. When everyone thinks they know what the object is, the child removes it from box to see if they guessed correctly.

Experienced Learner: Kinds of Noses

Share pictures of different animals that have a variety of types of noses, including a crocodile, elephant, aardvark, whale (Its blowhole is actually one big nostril!), fish (Fish don't breathe with their noses), and so on. Ask the children what kind of nose each of these animals has and what they might use it for. Cut out pictures of animals and cut the noses out separately, also cut the eyes and bodies of the animals apart. Encourage the children to mix all of these animal parts up and then sort them into categories and count the number of eyes, noses, and bodies that they have. When the children have finished counting, have them assemble the noses, eyes, and bodies to create their own new and interesting animals.

SCIENCE CENTER

Before implementing this activity with the children, share the following information:

◆ The job of your nose is to filter, warm, and moisten the air that you breathe.

◆ The *cilia* or hairs in your nose act as a filter to trap dust and dirt.

◆ Your sense of taste is closely linked to your sense of smell.

■ **Beginning Learner:** Scented Jars

Prepare smell containers by soaking cotton balls in a variety of scents or flavorings, such as perfume, peppermint, chocolate, lemon, lime, and orange. Place the cotton balls inside baby food jars, put on the lids, and poke holes in the lids using a large nail (adult only). Encourage the children to smell the jars and try to identify the scents. Provide a series of cards with pictures on them that match the scents to aid in the identification process.

■ ■ **Developing Learner:** Good Smells and Bad Smells

Provide a variety of objects for the children to smell. Encourage them to rate the objects in order from those that smell the best to those that smell the worst.

■
■ ■ **Experienced Learner:** Blindfold Smell Test

Discuss with the children that their olfactory receptors are the structures in their noses that send a signal to their brains that something smells good, bad, rotten, or dangerous. Place a variety of items that have distinct smells (onion, lemon, peppermint, and so on) on separate paper plates. Blindfold the children using scarves. While they are blindfolded, pass one of the objects in front of each child's nose. Encourage them to try to identify the object by its smell.

LANGUAGE/DRAMATIC PLAY CENTER

Discuss with the children the importance of their noses in helping to give them information about whether something smells good, bad, rotten, or dangerous.

■ **Beginning Learner:** Smelly Scavenger Hunt

Have a scavenger hunt around the room to look for objects that smell good and objects that smell bad. Give each child two paper lunch sacks, one with a happy face for things that smell good and one with a sad face for things that smell bad. Encourage them to search around the room and place objects in their bags according to how they smell. When the children are finished, discuss what they found.

■ ■ **Developing Learner:** Guess What It Would Smell Like

Provide pictures from magazines of a variety of objects. Invite the children to sort the pictures into piles according to whether the object would smell good or bad.

■
■ ■ **Experienced Learner:** Good, Bad, and Dangerous Smells

Brainstorm with the children things that smell good, bad, or dangerous and write down their ideas. Provide each child with a large piece of paper that is divided into columns with the words "Things that smell good," "Things that smell bad," and "Things that smell dangerous" at the top of each column. Encourage the children to draw pictures in each column.

blow, cilia, handkerchief, noses, olfactory receptors, scent, sense of smell, snoring, tissues

Reflect

Say to the children, "Yesterday we learned about our eyes and how important they are in helping us to discover and explore the world around us. Today we learned about our noses and how they help give us information. Tomorrow we will learn about our ears and how important they are in helping us to hear sounds."

Extend and Enrich

Use the following ideas to extend and enrich what children know about their noses.

◆ Discuss the steps involved in proper nose blowing and hand washing in order to promote health.

◆ Encourage the children to taste foods while holding their noses. They will discover how their senses of smell and taste are connected.

My Ears

Morning Circle

As the children arrive to circle time, have them sit quietly and listen to the sounds around them. Encourage the children to cup their hands to their ears and see how this helps to "funnel" the sounds into the ear canal. After enjoying the silence, make a list of sounds that the children heard, including inside noises (air conditioner, fish tank motor, voices, or breathing) and outside sounds (horns honking, car motors, a fire engine, birds, or voices).

Storytime

Polar Bear, Polar Bear, What Do You Hear? by Bill Martin, Jr. and Eric Carle

Daily Center Activity Ideas

ART CENTER

Prepare by gathering a variety of stuffed animals with different ear shapes and sizes.

■ **Beginning Learner:** Animal Ear Headbands
Show the children a variety of stuffed animals and talk about the different sizes and shapes of the ears. Provide a variety of ear shapes cut from white, brown, black, gray, and pink poster board. Encourage the children to choose a set of ears and use markers to decorate them. Help the children attach their ears to a sentence strip. Staple the sentence strip to make an animal ear headband.

■ ■ **Developing Learner:** Animal Ear Headbands II
Show the children the stuffed animals. Provide different pieces of animal print paper, wallpaper, or fabric scraps and scissors for the children to cut out their own animal ears. Have them glue the ears on a sentence strip to make animal ear headbands. **Note:** If the children want their animal ears to stand up, they may have to first glue them onto a piece of cardboard or poster board to add stability.

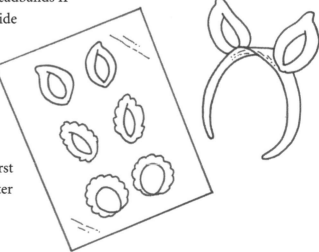

Experienced Learner: Animal Ear Headbands III

Provide animal print fabrics and cotton batting. Encourage the children to choose a fabric to make ears. Help them cut out two animal ears in whatever shape and size they want. Help them staple two sets of ears around the edges, leaving an opening on one side. Have them stuff the ears with cotton batting and staple the opening closed. Provide sentence strip headbands for the children to attach their fabric animal ears.

MATH CENTER

Beginning Learner: Sound Jars

Provide small baby food jars and sets of objects, such as pennies, marbles, and jingle bells. Encourage the children to experiment with placing one penny in a jar and shaking it to see what sound it makes. Then encourage them to put two pennies in a jar and shake it to see what sound it makes. Repeat with three pennies. Encourage the children to use other things like jingle bells and marbles to experiment with sound. (**Safety note:** Use caution as the children shake the jars to be sure they do not break.)

Developing Learner: Sound Jars

Provide the materials as described above, but make three sets of each kind of jar. For instance, one jar has one penny, one jar has two pennies, and one jar has three pennies, and so on. To play the game, blindfold a child, hand him a jar, and encourage him to shake it and guess if it has one penny, two pennies, or three pennies. Use only one set of jars at a time.

Experienced Learner: Jingle Bell Bracelets

Provide jingle bells of different sizes for the children to string onto small, thin elastic to make jingle bell bracelets. Encourage the children to experiment with making patterns on the bracelets with the different sizes of bells.

SCIENCE CENTER

Beginning Learner: Funnel Ear Experiment

Provide small funnels for the children to place up to their ears to help them listen to the sounds around them. Explain that the funnels gather sound waves and send them through the ear canal. The funnels work like the outer ear on a human. (**Safety note:** Make sure that children do not place the funnels inside their ears.)

Developing Learner: Spinning Experiment

Ask one child at a time to spin around a few times and then stop. (**Safety note:** Carefully supervise so no one gets hurt or falls down.) Discuss that they might experience a dizzy sensation. Explain that there is fluid and hairs (cilia) inside the ear that help them to maintain their balance. When people spin around or move up and down really quickly, the fluid and the hairs have to stop moving in order for them to stay balanced. Provide a glass of water or a baby food jar with water and a craft stick for the children to stir the water really quickly. Ask the children to stop stirring the water and see what happens. The water continues to spin for a few seconds just like the fluid in their ears.

Experienced Learner: Ear Drum Experiment
Explain to the children that the ear drum is a delicate membrane inside the ear, which is why we should never place anything inside our ears. To demonstrate how the ear drum works, give each child an empty paper towel tube and have them secure a piece of wax paper to one end of the tube with a rubber band. When the children place the open end of the tubes to their mouths and gently suck air in, the wax paper will move slightly. Explain that this represents how sound vibrations cause their ear drums to move inside their ear.

LANGUAGE/DRAMATIC PLAY CENTER

Beginning Learner: Picture Sounds
Read the story *Polar Bear, Polar Bear, What Do You Hear?* Give the children paper and encourage them to draw a picture of things that make a sound.

Developing Learner: I Hear a _____
Read the story *Polar Bear, Polar Bear, What Do You Hear?* Give each child a piece of paper with the words, "_____, _____, what do you hear?" written on it. Encourage the children to write their names in the spaces and then draw a picture of something they hear.

Experienced Learner: My Sound Book
Read the story *Polar Bear, Polar Bear, What Do You Hear?* Give each child a piece of paper with the words, "_____, _____, what do you hear?" written on it. Encourage the children to use these pages to make their own sound books, illustrating all the things they can think of that make sounds. Help them write the words to describe or label the pictures. Have them write their names in the first two blanks. For example, "Maddie, Maddie, what do you hear? I hear a dog."

VOCABULARY

balance, cilia, deaf, dizzy, ear canal, ear drum, earaches, earlobes, ears, earphones, earrings, hearing, hearing aids, inner ear, outer ear, shout, sound, sound waves, vibrations, whisper

Reflect

Say to the children, "Yesterday we learned about our noses and how they help to provide information about our world. Today we learned about our ears and how important they are in helping us to hear the sounds in the environment around us. Tomorrow we will learn about our toes and feet and how important they are in helping us to stand, move, run, and walk.

Extend and Enrich

Use the following ideas to extend and enrich what children know about their noses.

◆ Find a picture of a fennec fox for the children to look at. This fox has huge ears that can swivel to locate the direction of a sound.

◆ Encourage the children to play a group listening game in which one child sits in the middle of the circle with a blindfold on. Point to a child sitting in the circle. The child makes a sound and the blindfolded child must try to identify the direction of the sound.

◆ Sing the song "Do Your Ears Hang Low?" with the children.

My Feet and My Toes

Morning Circle

When the children arrive for circle time, encourage them to stand on their tiptoes and run in place, march, skip, gallop, and hop. Discuss with the children how important their feet and toes are in helping them move, run, and play. Encourage the children to put their feet out in front of them. With the children, count how many feet there are all together. This is a great introduction to the day's story.

Storytime

How Many Feet in the Bed? by Diane Johnston Hamm

Daily Center Activity Ideas

ART CENTER

Beginning Learner: Footprint Painting

Help each child take off one shoe and one sock. Use a paintbrush to apply washable tempera paint to the bottom of the child's foot. Have the child step on a piece of white construction paper to make footprints. **Note:** Provide a container of soapy water, sponges, and dry towels, and help the children wash and dry their feet. Provide a chair for the children to sit in while washing their feet. This will help them not get their clothes wet.

Developing Learner: Rainbow Feet

Place five different rows of colors of washable tempera paint (red, yellow, orange, blue, and purple) on a cookie sheet or metal tray. The children take off their shoes and socks when they are ready to paint. Be sure to support each child under the arms as he steps onto the tray with paint. Encourage each child to walk on a long sheet of white butcher paper to make sets of rainbow colored footprints. Help them wash their feet. When the footprints are dry, encourage the children to cut out their footprints and count how many they made.

Experienced Learner: Footprint Patterns

Help the children remove their shoes and socks. Provide two trays of different colors of paint. Help each child place one foot on each tray of paint and then step onto a long sheet of paper. Encourage the children to make a pattern or design as they walk across their papers. To add a twist to this activity, invite the children to use markers to draw a shape or design on the paper and then use their wet, painted feet to walk on the design.

MATH CENTER

Beginning Learner: Foot Sizes and Shapes

Have the children take off one shoe and sock. Help each child trace a bare foot onto construction paper. Cut out the children's footprints and encourage them to compare the sizes and shapes of their feet. Discuss with the children the number of toes they have on each foot.

Developing Learner: Numbering Toes

Encourage the children to take off both of their shoes and socks. Help them trace both of their feet on construction paper and cut out their footprints. Ask the children to count the number of toes on each foot and write the numeral 5 on each of their footprints. Encourage the children to compare the size of their feet with their parents' and their siblings' when they get home.

Experienced Learner: Measuring with Your Feet

Have the children take off both of their shoes and socks. Help them trace both of their feet onto construction paper. The children may also want to try to trace each other's feet. Discuss with the children the numeral 10 and encourage them to practice counting their toes from 1–10. Encourage the children to cut out the traced feet. Introduce the concept of measurement and explain that a long time ago, people used their feet as a tool for measuring things. Encourage the children to use their footprint cutouts to measure objects in the room.

SCIENCE CENTER

Talk with the children about the texture of different soles of shoes. Some shoes are smooth and slippery, and they slide on smooth floors such as tile. Other shoes are rubbery and have grooves to provide traction.

Beginning Learner: Making Shoe Rubbings

Provide a variety of shoes with different textures, shapes, and designs on the bottom. Remove the paper from a few crayons and demonstrate how to put a piece of paper on the bottom of the shoe and rub the crayon sideways to make a rubbing.

Developing Learner: Comparing Shoe Rubbings

Encourage the children to take off one of their shoes, put paper on the bottom of it, and use peeled crayons to make a rubbing. They can do the same thing with a friend's shoe, and then compare the two rubbings.

Experienced Learner: Sandpaper Shoes

Invite the children to trace their shoes onto sandpaper and cut them out. Have them rub peeled crayons directly on the sandpaper.

LANGUAGE/DRAMATIC PLAY CENTER

Beginning Learner: The Foot Book

Read *The Foot Book* by Dr. Seuss and discuss all of the things that feet can do, such as run, jump, gallop, skip, and tiptoe. Encourage the children to practice some of the movements discussed in the story.

Developing Learner: Musical Feet

Follow the directions for the beginning learner activity and then play musical chairs by arranging chairs in a circle. Suggest a movement for the children to do with their feet, such as tiptoe, and encourage them to move around the circle on tiptoes until the music stops. When the music stops, everyone sits in a chair. When the music starts again, suggest a new movement and encourage the children to practice that movement as they go around the circle. Continue the game with different movements, but do not remove any chairs.

Experienced Learner: Make Your Own Foot Book

Follow the directions for the beginning learner activity. Encourage the children to trace their feet on paper and use this tracing as the cover for their own Foot Book. Write the words "My Foot Book" on an index card for the children to copy. Encourage them to draw pictures of things that they can do with their feet. Include such things in their books as hop, skip, run, jump, and leap.

VOCABULARY

ankles, bare feet, blisters, feet, footprint, heel, hop, jump, legs, shoes, skip, socks, stomp, tiptoe, toes, walk

Reflect

Say to the children, "Yesterday we learned about our ears and how important they are in giving us information about our world. Today we learned about our feet and toes. We learned how important they are in helping us run, jump, move, and walk."

Extend and Enrich

Use the following ideas to extend and enrich what children know about their feet and toes.

◆ Make a large graph on paper and invite the children to graph their shoes by color or type.

◆ Show the children how to dip the side of their hand (formed in a fist) into paint and place it on paper to make a "baby footprint." Then, show them how to use their index finger to paint baby toes.

◆ Encourage the children to study different animals and the ways they move, including grasshoppers jumping, frogs leaping, kangaroos hopping, and snakes slithering. Have them look at pictures of animals that have unusual feet such as tree frogs (sticky feet), millipedes (hundreds of feet) and snakes (no feet).

◆ Practice tying shoes.

◆ Provide a variety of socks for the children to sort.

◆ Provide props for the children to use to role play working at a shoe store.

Things that Smell Good

Roses

Morning Circle

Before the children arrive, scatter rose petals on the path (or hallway) outside of the classroom door to spark their interest in the topic of the day. Also, spray rose-scented air freshener.

When the children arrive, ask them if they can smell the rose spray, and discuss the importance of the sense of smell. Emphasize how we use our senses to discover new things in our world. Show the children an actual small rose bush with roses in bloom. Talk about how the roses get food and water from the soil through their stems and roots. Next, show the children a cut rose on a stem and discuss the ways that this rose is different from the ones on the bush. This rose can no longer get food and water from the soil and it will no longer continue to grow because it has been cut. Examine the thorns on the stem. Ask, "How do the thorns feel?" Explain that thorns protect the flower from being eaten by animals, and the stem and thorns strengthen the rose when it is on the bush. Give each child a rose petal to hold as they listen to you read *Wanda's Roses* by Pat Brisson.

Storytime

Wanda's Roses by Pat Brisson

Daily Center Activity Ideas

ART CENTER

Beginning Learner: Rose Collage/Stickers
Provide a variety of rose or flower stickers for the children to make a collage on white paper.

Developing Learner: Rose Collage/Photos
Provide pictures of roses from magazines or calendars and invite the children to glue the pictures on construction paper to make a collage.

Experienced Learner: Paper Rose Garden
Provide a variety of magazines or calendars with flowers and garden pictures, and invite the children to cut out flowers and glue them on paper to make a rose garden collage. Offer crayons and markers so the children can add stems, petals, leaves, and other details to their pictures.

MATH CENTER

■ **Beginning Learner:** Stop to Count the Roses

Prior to this activity, cut the petals off of synthetic or silk roses or other pretend flowers and scatter the petals outside on the playground. Give the children small sacks and take them outside to find rose petals as they take a nature walk. Encourage them to count their petals as they pick them up.

■ ■ **Developing Learner:** Sorting Rose Petals

Prior to this activity, ask a local florist for petals from different-colored roses or for roses that are getting too old to sell. Scatter the rose petals outside on the playground. Prior to taking the children outside, show them a healthy rose on a stem and a rose that is wilting. Show the children how easily the petals fall off of the wilting rose and discuss the delicate nature of flowers. This demonstrates how important it is to be careful when handling roses. Give the children paper sacks and take them outside to collect the rose petals. When the children go inside, encourage them to count their petals and sort them by color.

■ ■ ■ **Experienced Learner:** Rose Petal Graph

Follow the directions for the developing learner activity above. Use the collected petals to complete a color graph. Give each child a piece of paper with columns drawn on them. Encourage them to sort their rose petals by color and place them in the columns by color. After they have sorted their petals, ask the children to count their petals and write the number of each color of petals at the bottom of their columns on their graph.

SCIENCE CENTER

■ **Beginning Learner:** Making Rose Water

To help the children use their sense of smell by filling the water table with water and then adding a few drops of a rose-scented potpourri liquid. (It is usually readily available at the grocery store in the candle section.) For enrichment, add eye droppers, a rotary hand beater and measuring cups. (**Safety note:** Add a small amount of liquid dishwashing soap to the mixture to discourage any children who might want to taste the rose-scented water. Supervise the children closely as they engage in this activity.)

■ ■ **Developing Learner:** Sachets

Provide dried flowers and potpourri for the children to make scented sachets. Put small scoops of potpourri onto precut squares of netting material and help children tie them with a colored ribbon. Encourage the children to close their eyes and use their sense of smell to enjoy the sachets.

Experienced Learner: Scratch-and-Sniff Stickers

Provide flower stickers for children to use to make their own scratch-and-sniff stickers. Mix lemon, lime, or strawberry gelatin with water and invite the children to use cotton swabs or small paintbrushes to "paint" the flower stickers with the gelatin. When the scented stickers are dry, have the children close their eyes, scratch the stickers, and smell the stickers to identify the different scents.

LANGUAGE/DRAMATIC PLAY CENTER

Beginning Learner: Flower Shop Role Play

Provide a variety of silk flowers in plastic pots or vases for children to use to role play working in a flower shop.

Developing Learner: Flower Arranging

Provide a variety of silk flowers, vases, cups, pots, and Styrofoam for the children to use to create their own silk floral arrangements. Add a play cash register and play money to the center to enhance the children's play. If a camera is available, photograph the children's final products to use for later role play and language development.

Experienced Learner: Tissue Paper Flowers

Provide colored tissue paper, chenille sticks, and craft sticks and demonstrate for the children how they can fold and twist the paper to make flowers and how the chenille sticks and craft sticks can be used to make stems for the flowers. Add Styrofoam cups for the children to use to hold their arrangements. Or, turn the Styrofoam cups upside down, poke the chenille stick and craft stick stems in the bottom, and the cup will stand up to display the floral arrangements.

aroma, artificial, bloom, blossom, buds, bush, color, cut, delicate, fragrance, garden, leaves, petals, rose, scent, stems, thorns

Reflect

Say to the children, "Today we used roses and other flowers to help us learn how important our noses are in helping us to smell good things. Tomorrow we will talk about another thing that smells good. It is a food that most of us love to eat. I will give you a clue. When it is cooking, it makes a sizzle and then a popping sound. Can anyone guess what it is? Yes, it is popcorn!"

Extend and Enrich

Use the following ideas to extend and enrich what children know about roses and other flowers.
- Provide flower-shaped sponges and paint for the children to make flower prints.
- Provide coffee filters, eyedroppers, and food coloring. Encourage the children to drop small drops of food coloring on their coffee filters. When dry, help the children bunch the filters together and add a green chenille stick stem to make a flower. **Note:** Combine the flowers together to make a pretty classroom window box.

THINGS THAT SMELL GOOD

Popcorn

Morning Circle

Just before the children begin to arrive, microwave popcorn and open the bag so that the smell permeates the classroom. When the children arrive, ask them to describe what they smell. Encourage the children to use a variety of descriptive words to describe the smell of popcorn. Following the discussion, fill a jar with popcorn kernels and talk to the children about what the kernels are now, and what the kernels will become when they become very hot and pop. Have the children guess how many kernels are in the jar.

Storytime

Popcorn by Frank Asch

This book is about a little bear that has a party when his parents leave for the evening. All of his guests bring popcorn, which the bear pops in a big kettle. The popcorn soon fills the entire house! Before reading this book, prepare several bowls, bags, and containers of popcorn to illustrate the idea that each person who came to the party brought a different size, type, or container of popcorn. Pour it all together, and then place small servings into small cups for the children to enjoy. (**Safety note:** Popcorn can be a choking hazard so supervise closely as the children eat the popcorn.)

Daily Center Activity Ideas

ART CENTER

▪ **Beginning Learner:** Popcorn Paint

Provide white paint and blue construction paper and encourage the children to paint popcorn pictures.

▪ ▪ **Developing Learner:** Popcorn Bowls

Help the children cut out popcorn bowl shapes from poster board and glue the cutouts on colored construction paper. Write the word "popcorn" on a card and suggest that the children write the word on their bowl shapes, offering help as necessary. Have the children glue Styrofoam packing "peanuts" on the bowl shapes so that it looks like popcorn is spilling out of the bowls

■
■ ■ **Experienced Learner:** Designing a Popcorn Bag

To prepare for this activity, roll down the tops of brown paper lunch bags to resemble a cuff. Show the children a few popcorn bags from movie theaters and explain that they are going to create their own popcorn bags. (**Hint:** Ask managers of your local movie theaters for empty popcorn bags.) Encourage the children to use paint and collage materials to create their popcorn bags. When the bags have dried, fill them with popped popcorn or send the bags home for the children to enjoy a popcorn treat at home.

MATH CENTER

■ **Beginning Learner:** Popcorn Toss

Provide a large laundry basket, white socks rolled into balls, and several sizes of Styrofoam balls. Show the children how to toss the socks and Styrofoam balls into the basket. Encourage the children to experiment with their "popcorn" balls to see which sizes are easier to throw.

■ ■ **Developing Learner:** Kernel Count and Guess

Provide a muffin tin with numerals inside the muffin cups, tweezers, and unpopped popcorn kernels. Encourage the children to look at each numeral and then try to use the tweezers to place that number of kernels into the muffin tin cup. **Note:** If children have trouble using the tweezers, let them use their fingers. A fun twist on this activity is to provide plastic soap holders with suction cups on the bottom for the children to play a counting game. Invite them to count the kernels as they place them on each suction cup.

■
■ ■ **Experienced Learner:** Popcorn Ball Toss

Collect several ping-pong balls. Use a black marker to write the word "pop" on some of the balls and the word "corn" on the others. Provide two laundry baskets, one with the word "pop" on the front and one with the word "corn" on it. Place the ping-pong balls in a wicker basket or tub and encourage the children to draw a ball from the basket and toss it into the correct laundry basket. Have them count the balls as they throw them.

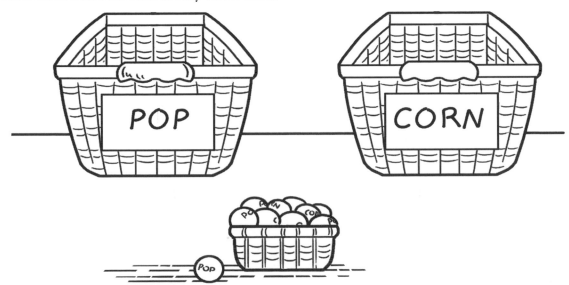

SCIENCE CENTER

Use a hot air popper to pop popcorn for all levels. The popcorn pops out of the top and goes into the air. The children love to watch this, but use extra caution and make sure children are seated far enough away from the popper so that hot kernels cannot reach them. This is a wonderful activity that engages all five of the children's senses as they explore the sights, sounds, smells, taste, and texture of popcorn as it pops and as they eat it. Be sure to place a clean sheet underneath the popper so that the children can scoop up the popcorn and eat it.

Beginning Learner: Popcorn Textures

Place deer corn in the sand table for the children to explore using measuring cups, spoons, and colanders to enrich the experience. Next, add sand and small pebbles or seeds to the kernel mixture for the children to sort and sift.

Developing Learner: Flavored Popcorn

Provide popped popcorn and a variety of flavorings, such as butter, cinnamon and sugar, and cheese flavoring. Give each child a small plastic bag of popcorn and encourage them to choose the flavoring that they would like to add to their popcorn. After adding the flavoring and closing the bag, show the children how to shake the bag to mix the flavoring and popcorn. Eat the popcorn at snack time.

Experienced Learner: Charting Popcorn Preferences

Provide popped popcorn and a variety of flavorings as described in the developing learner section. Encourage the children to taste the variety of flavorings and indicate their preferences on a classroom chart. When everyone has indicated their preferences, count how many children liked each flavoring. Add the flavoring and close each bag. Invite the children to shake the bags to mix the flavorings and popcorn.

LANGUAGE/DRAMATIC PLAY CENTER

Beginning Learner: Beginning Letters and Sounds

Provide a plastic bowl and popcorn-shaped pieces of paper with uppercase alphabet letters written on them. Play a game with the children similar to "Hot Potato." Play music and encourage the children to pass the bowl around while sitting in a circle. When the music stops, the child who is holding the bowl reaches inside and tries to find the first letter of her name. The music begins again, and the children pass the bowl. Repeat until everyone has had a turn.

Developing Learner: Writing Exercise

Prepare for this activity by writing the word *popcorn* on a sentence strip. Provide stamps, stick-on letters, or markers for the children to use to practice writing the word *popcorn* on paper or paper lunch bags.

■ ■ Experienced Learner: Words that Rhyme With *Pop*

Discuss the word *pop* and encourage the children to generate ideas for words that rhyme with pop (such as *bop, cop, drop, flop, hop, mop, prop, stop,* and *top*). Write each rhyming word that the children think of on two strips of paper and place the strips in a popcorn bowl or plastic bowl. When all of the ideas have been added to the bowl, the children take turns removing a strip of paper from the bowl, reading the word (with help, as needed), and then reaching into the bowl again to find the matching word.

VOCABULARY

flavoring, kernels, pop, popcorn, seeds, sizzle, snack

Reflect

Say to the children, "Yesterday we learned about roses and what a wonderful fragrance they have. Today we learned about popcorn and how great it smells while it is cooking. Tomorrow we will learn about pizza and how great it smells while it is cooking and how good it tastes."

Extend and Enrich

Use the following ideas to extend and enrich what children know about popcorn.

◆ Make popcorn balls to bring home. Pop popcorn with the children. Mix the popcorn with marshmallow cream. Have children wash and then butter their hands and roll the mixture into a ball. Place the popcorn balls in plastic bags.

◆ Some grocery stores sell colored popcorn kernels that are great for sorting in a muffin tin by color. Show the children a variety of popcorn poppers such as a hot air popper, a popper that uses oil and a pan that would be used to cook popcorn on the stove. Also show the children the jiffy pop popcorn that is commercially available at the grocery store. Discuss how each of these machines works to make popcorn.

Pizza

Morning Circle

Bake pizza prior to the children's arrival or bring a
pizza to school. Just for fun, greet the children at the
door wearing an apron and a chef's hat and carrying a pizza box. Show the children the pizza
box and ask them to guess what is inside. Encourage the children to brainstorm what kind of
pizza they think is in the box. After listing all of the possibilities, open the box and show the
children the pizza. Next, encourage the children to have fun brainstorming all of the toppings
that they think would taste good on pizza. Give each child a small piece of pizza to enjoy while
they listen to you read the story.

Storytime

What Do You Want on Your Pizza? by William Boniface

Daily Center Activity Ideas

ART CENTER

■ **Beginning Learner:** Paper Pizza

Provide a red construction paper circle for the dough of the "pizza" and small pieces of
construction paper to represent pizza toppings, such as pepperoni, cheese, hamburger, and
peppers. Encourage the children to choose the toppings they want on their pizza and glue them
to the pizza dough circle.

■ ■ **Developing Learner:** Cardboard Pizza and Tomato Glue

Provide a 12" circle cut from white poster board, tagboard, or cardboard for each child. Add red
food coloring to glue for the children to paint on their circle as pizza sauce. Provide various
colors of construction paper and invite the children to cut out "toppings" for their pizza (brown
for hamburger, red for pepperoni, yellow and orange for cheese, black for olives, and so on).
Encourage the children to paint the red glue on the "crust" and add their toppings.

■
■ ■ **Experienced Learner:** Small, Medium or Large Pizza

To prepare for this activity, contact a local pizza parlor and ask them to donate pizza boxes,
enough so that each child will get one. Provide three sizes of cardboard circle patterns. Let the
children choose whether they want to trace a small, medium, or large pizza shape. Have the
children trace their chosen size onto cardboard or poster board and then paint their circle with
red colored glue (as described above in the developing learner section). Encourage the children
to tear or cut colored construction paper to make toppings to glue onto their pizza.

MATH CENTER

■ **Beginning Learner:** Sorting Circles

Provide small, medium, and large circles cut from cardboard and three sizes of pizza boxes (donated from a local pizza parlor). Encourage the children to take turns sorting the circles into the correct size pizza boxes.

■ ■ **Developing Learner:** Number of Ingredients on Your Pizza

Cut out small, medium, and large circles from cardboard. Use index cards to draw or glue pictures of pizzas with different toppings. Cut out shapes for pepperoni, cheese, peppers, and any other toppings from construction paper. Give the children the index cards and cardboard circles and ask them to assemble the pizza shown on the "menu." The children look at the cards and put the same number and type of items on their pizza.

■ ■ **Experienced Learner:** Number of Ingredients on Your Pizza

Provide a circle of felt or fun foam on a round pizza pan for the crust. Cut felt or fun foam pieces to represent peppers, mushrooms, olives, pepperoni, and cheese and place the ingredients into individual bowls. Encourage the children to roll a die and then take the correct number of ingredients from each bowl and add it to their pizza crust to assemble a pizza.

SCIENCE CENTER

■ **Beginning Learner:** Toasted Muffin Pizzas

Show the children pizza ingredients, such as English muffins or hamburger buns, pizza sauce, and cheese. Discuss with the children which of the ingredients tastes better warm or cold, cooked or uncooked. Show the children how to spread pizza sauce on an English muffin and sprinkle cheese on top. Cook the mini pizzas in a toaster oven. When the pizzas come out of the oven, encourage the children to notice the difference in their cooked pizza as compared to the pizza when they first put it in the oven. Children may eat the pizzas for snack, or you can place the pizzas on small paper plates, slide them into plastic bags, and let the children take them home.

Developing Learner: Bread Dough Pizzas

Explain that when making pizza, the dough does not taste good until it is cooked. Provide bread dough and invite the children to use rolling pins to flatten the dough. Have them add sauce, cheese, and any toppings to make individual mini pizzas. Cook the pizzas in a toaster oven. When the pizzas are done, discuss the way they look compared to when they were not cooked. Discuss how the dough has risen and changed colors from tan to brown. After the pizzas cool, the children can enjoy eating them for snack.

Experienced Learner: Charting Pizza Preferences

Provide a variety of pizza ingredients, such as several flavors of sauces, cooked pepperoni, and several kinds of shredded cheese, olives, and mushrooms. Encourage the children to taste small amounts of the ingredients and graph on a chart the ones they like and the ones they dislike. The children choose their favorite ingredients and use them to assemble their own mini pizzas. Discuss the ingredients the children chose for their pizzas. Cook the pizzas in a toaster oven, let cool, and enjoy as a special snack.

LANGUAGE/DRAMATIC PLAY CENTER

Beginning Learner: Pizza Shop

Provide pizza restaurant flyers and menus, coupons, pizza boxes, a play telephone, and a note pad for children to role play working at a pizza shop. Encourage the children to experiment with carrying the pizza boxes in funny ways. See if they can come up with their own funny ideas!

Developing Learner: Pizza Shop/Making Menus

Provide the props described above in the beginning learner section, as well as paper, glue, and scissors for children to make their own restaurant menus. Also, provide dishes and play food.

Experienced Learner: Pizza Shop/Cooks and Servers

Provide the props described in the beginning learner and developing learner sections, but add playdough, aprons, and round pie tins or round cookie sheets. Set up two parts of a pizza restaurant—the kitchen and the front of the restaurant. Children can make the pizzas in the kitchen and take orders in the front section. Provide a cash register, play money, menus, and a telephone, as well as dishes, placemats, tables, and chairs.

VOCABULARY

cheese, coupons, crust, dough, ingredients, meat, mushrooms, pan, pepperoni, peppers, pizza, pizza cutter, oven, sauce, toppings

Reflect

Say to the children, "Yesterday we used our noses and our senses of smell to discover the wonderful smell that popcorn makes as it pops. Today we used our noses to smell the pizza, and we learned how to make our own pizzas. Tomorrow we will use our noses to learn about gingerbread."

Extend and Enrich

Use the following ideas to extend and enrich what children know about pizza.

◆ Take a trip to a local pizza parlor.

◆ Discuss and vote on the children's favorite kind of pizza and then call and order a pizza and have it delivered to the class for a special snack.

◆ Make "cookie pizzas" using sugar cookie dough and round pizza pans. Have the children spread the dough on the pans and add toppings, such as sprinkles, colored sugar, and chocolate chips. Bake the cookie pizza in the oven and let the children eat it for snack.

Gingerbread

Morning Circle

Before the children arrive, cut out small gingerbread man shapes from brown construction paper. Tape the cutouts to the floor with masking tape to make a trail from the front door to the circle area. Greet the children at the door and encourage them to follow the gingerbread man trail to the circle area. Show them a large gingerbread man cookie (either a real one or a paper cutout) and a gingerbread house made from a milk carton and graham crackers. (Frost a quart-size milk carton and attach graham cracker squares to the sides and top.) Read *The Gingerbread Baby* by Jan Brett. Discuss how the boy in the story made the gingerbread cookie, but, because he was impatient and couldn't wait for it to finish baking, he opened the oven and the gingerbread baby ran away. Discuss how the boy arrived at the perfect solution for catching the gingerbread baby by making a gingerbread house.

Storytime

The Gingerbread Baby by Jan Brett

Daily Center Activity Ideas

ART CENTER

■ **Beginning Learner:** Gingerbread babies
Make a recipe of homemade playdough and add ginger flavoring. Provide rolling pins and cookie sheets and encourage the children to roll the dough and make their own gingerbread men.

Playdough Recipe

2 cups water, 2 tbsp. oil, 2 cups flour, 1 cup salt, and 4 tsp. cream of tartar. In a pan on the stove, mix the water and oil and then add the flour, salt, and cream of tartar. Cook the mixture on low heat until it becomes sticky. Then, pour the playdough onto a surface where it can be kneaded until it becomes smooth.

■■ **Developing Learner:** Icing the Gingerbread Babies
Cut gingerbread baby shapes from brown construction paper. Mix glue with food coloring for the children to use to "ice" their cutouts. Provide buttons and collage materials for the children to use to decorate their gingerbread babies.

Experienced Learner: Gingerbread Baby Necklace

Cut out gingerbread baby shapes from poster board for the children to use as stencils. Encourage the children to trace the stencils onto brown construction paper and cut out a set of gingerbread baby shapes. Provide a hole punch, yarn, and small beads. Encourage the children to punch holes in their gingerbread babies and string them on yarn, separating each cutout with a bead, to make a gingerbread baby necklace.

MATH CENTER

Beginning Learner: Gingerbread People/Sizes

Cut out small, medium, and large gingerbread people from sandpaper. Provide the sandpaper cutouts, paper, and peeled crayons for the children to use to make gingerbread people rubbings.

Developing Learner: Gingerbread People/Matching

Make sets of sandpaper gingerbread people in three sizes as described for the beginning learner, and sets of three sizes of gingerbread house shapes. Invite the children to choose a house and a matching size gingerbread man. Invite them to make rubbings using peeled crayons and paper. When they are done, invite them to use markers and crayons to add details to their pictures.

Experienced Learner: Gingerbread People/Ordering and Patterns

Cut out gingerbread shapes from sandpaper (five small, five medium, and five large). Have the children mix up the gingerbread shapes and then practice their seriating skills by ordering them from small to large. Also encourage them to sort them by size. Show the children how to use the shapes to make patterns, such as small-small-large, small-small-large, and so on.

SCIENCE CENTER

Beginning Learner: Will Gingerbread Baby Float or Sink?

Cut out gingerbread baby shapes from various materials, such as sandpaper, construction paper, brown poster board, brown leather, and paper bags. Invite the children to place the different shapes into a pan of water to see which material floats and which material sinks. Encourage the children to make predictions about what they think will happen. Discuss with them the possibility that the paper items will become soaked with water and begin to sink and the leather gingerbread baby might float or sink depending on its thickness.

Developing Learner: Will Gingerbread Baby Float on a Raft?

Provide a variety of materials, such as brown fabric pieces, construction paper, cardboard, and so on, and gingerbread baby patterns (large and small) for the children to trace and cut out. Encourage the children to choose materials that they think will float in water. Let them experiment with the shapes to see which ones float and which ones sink. Discuss that the gingerbread baby in the story was a cookie and that when he jumped into the icy river, he would have fallen apart without something to float on. Demonstrate this idea by placing a gingerbread cookie in water. Next, give each child an ice cube to put under their gingerbread baby to simulate a flotation device like a raft. The children can predict what they think will happen and then test their predictions.

Experienced Learner: Will Gingerbread Baby Float on Salty Water?

Cut out gingerbread babies from a variety of materials (as described in the developing learner section). Let the children experiment with adding substances to the water such as oil, soap, salt, and food coloring to see if they help the gingerbread babies sink or float. Suggest things for the children to try, such as wrapping their gingerbread babies in plastic wrap to see if it protects them. Have them place small objects such as paperclips on top of the gingerbread babies to see how many they can carry before they sink. Provide foil for the children to use to make small boats for the babies.

LANGUAGE/DRAMATIC PLAY CENTER

Beginning Learner: Scented Dough

Prepare a playdough recipe and add cinnamon to give it a scent. Provide gingerbread man cookie cutters, rolling pins, and cookie sheets. Encourage the children to use the scented playdough and cookie cutters to make gingerbread man cookie shapes.

Developing Learner: Gingerbread Man Cookies

Purchase gingerbread man cookies from a bakery. Provide icing and sprinkles for the children to use to decorate their own gingerbread cookie to enjoy at school or take home for a special treat.

Experienced Learner: Paper Gingerbread Houses

Prepare small empty milk cartons by gluing the tops closed with hot glue (adult only). Cut out rectangles from brown construction paper to represent graham crackers. Invite the children to use thick white paint ("icing") to glue the paper rectangles to the milk cartons to make gingerbread houses. Have the children decorate their houses as desired using collage materials that represent candy.

VOCABULARY

baking, cinnamon, cookie, cookie sheet, gingerbread, gingerbread baby, gingerbread house, gingerbread man, house, oven

Reflect

Say to the children, "Yesterday we learned about pizza and how good it smells while it is baking in the oven and how good it tastes when it is ready to eat. Today we learned about gingerbread and how it is used to make cookies and breads and how good it smells when it is baking. Tomorrow we will learn about cookies and how good they smell while they are baking and how good they taste when they are ready to eat."

Extend and Enrich

Use the following ideas to extend and enrich what children know about gingerbread.

◆   Provide small containers of water and boats for children to use for pretend play to help get the gingerbread baby reach safety.

◆   Follow a recipe or use a box mix to make gingerbread with the children.

Cookies

Morning Circle

In advance, send home a note asking the children to bring an empty box or package from their favorite kind of cookie. Also, record a doorbell chime using a tape recorder. Repeat and tape the sound many times so there is a continuous doorbell sound. Greet the children at the door, carrying a tray of cookies. Have the doorbell sound playing as the children arrive. In circle time, hold up each cookie package, talk about what kind of cookie comes in that package, and whose favorite cookie it is.

After the discussion, provide a notebook with clear plastic sleeves. The children can cut the front covers or labels from their cookie packages and slide them into plastic sleeves in the notebook to make an environmental print book. Place the book in the language center for the children to enjoy. Share the story *The Doorbell Rang* by Pat Hutchins with the children. Then, read it a second time and encourage the children to chime in and say, "And the doorbell rang."

Storytime

The Doorbell Rang by Pat Hutchins

Daily Center Activity Ideas

ART CENTER

■ **Beginning Learner:** Cookie Sheet Painting
Tell the children that they are going to use a cookie sheet in a unique way. Provide cookie sheets, paper, paint, and a marble. Use white construction paper to cut out a large, round cookie shape for each child. Encourage the children to place their cookie cutouts on the cookie sheet and use a spoon to drop a small amount of paint in the corners of the cookie sheet. The children place a marble in one corner of the cookie sheet and tilt the cookie sheet. Allow the marble to roll through the paint in the corners and across the cookie to make interesting designs.

■ ■ **Developing Learner:** Paper Cookie Cutouts
Show the children a variety of cookies, such as chocolate chip, oatmeal, and sandwich cookies. Provide a large sheet of white construction paper and sheets of colored construction paper. Encourage the children to tear or cut the colored construction paper to make their own cookie shapes and decorate them using markers. Invite the children to glue their "cookies" on the white construction paper "cookie sheet."

Experienced Learner: Sugar Cookie Collage

Give each child a paper plate and tan construction paper to use to make a plate full of sugar cookies. Encourage the children to cut out cookie shapes and glue them to their paper plates. Provide collage materials for the children to use to make "sprinkles" for their sugar cookies. Give the children pieces of colored cellophane or plastic wrap to place over their plates of cookies.

MATH CENTER

Note: Just for fun, play the doorbell recording used in morning circle during this counting activity.

Beginning Learner: Counting Cookies

Provide a tray of small cookie shapes cut from construction paper and a paper plate for each child. Each child takes a turn practicing one-to-one correspondence skills by taking a construction paper cookie shape off of the tray and giving one to each child sitting at the table until all of the cookies are gone. How many cookies does each child have? Does every child have the same number of cookies?

Developing Learner: Sorting Cookies

Give each child a small plastic bag filled with different colors of construction paper cookies. Encourage the children to develop categories to sort their "cookies" and count the number of each type of "cookies" that they have. Give each child a piece of paper. Show the children how to make a simple graph indicating how many of each kind of cookie they have in their bags.

Experienced Learner: Counting and Dividing Cookies

Provide a tray of cookies made from construction paper, a plate for each child, and a bell to simulate the doorbell in the story. Each child takes a turn placing the tray of cookies on the table in front of them. They pretend they are getting ready to eat the cookies when the teacher or someone in the group rings the bell. A new child comes in and sits at the table and gets a plate. The child whose turn it is begins dividing the cookies until both children have the same number. Just as these two children are beginning to "pretend" to eat their cookies, the bell rings and a new child comes in and sits at the table and gets a plate. The first two children begin dividing their cookies between the three of them until all three children have the same number of cookies. Continue to play the game until everyone has had a turn participating in the counting and dividing of cookies.

SCIENCE CENTER

■ **Beginning Learner:** Digging for Treasure

Provide each child with a large chocolate chip cookie and a toothpick. The children use the toothpick to "dig" out the chocolate chips, like they are excavating on a treasure hunt. When all of the chips have been removed from the cookie, the children can enjoy eating their cookie as a treat.

■ ■ **Developing Learner:** Mixing Ingredients

Choose a cookie recipe for a favorite cookie and purchase the ingredients. Provide each child with a small mason jar to hold their dry cookie ingredients. Help the children measure the dry ingredients and layer them in their jars. Give each child a recipe card to attach to their dry ingredients so they can make their cookies at home.

■
■ ■ **Experienced Learner:** Making a Cookie Pizza

Provide cookie dough (either commercially prepared or homemade), toppings (chocolate candies, chocolate chips, raisins, and so on), and round cookie sheets or pizza pans for the children to use to make giant cookie pizzas for the class to enjoy. Show the children how to press the dough into the pan and begin adding the toppings until they achieve the desired result. Bake in the oven and cut into triangle pieces.

LANGUAGE/DRAMATIC PLAY CENTER

■ **Beginning Learner:** Decorating Cookies

Prepare a tray of cookies (either purchased or homemade), white icing, and food coloring for the children to use to decorate a cookie for themselves. Help the children mix food coloring to make different colors of icing. Provide sprinkles and confetti for the children to use to decorate their cookies.

Developing Learner: Cookie Lollipops

Make sugar cookies, but before baking them, insert a craft stick into each cookie to make a handle (adult only). Provide toppings, candies, sprinkles, and icing for the children to use to decorate their cookie "lollipops." Encourage the children to decorate several cookie lollipops. Give each child a small piece of Styrofoam. When they are finished decorating their cookies, show the children how to insert their sticks into the Styrofoam to make a "cookie bouquet" to share with their families.

Experienced Learner: Recipe Book

Help the children make a class recipe book that contains the children's recipes and cooking tips and ideas for making their favorite cookies. Work with each child as she dictates the ingredients, mixing and measuring procedures, and cooking tips that she believes are necessary to make her favorite cookie. Encourage the children to illustrate their pages. Combine the "recipes" into a class book for everyone to enjoy.

VOCABULARY

bake, cookie cutters, cookie jar, cookie sheet, cookies, crumbs, dough, flavors, goodies, icing, ingredients, oven, sweets

Reflect

Say to the children, "Yesterday we learned about gingerbread and how good it smells when it is baking in the oven. Today we learned about cookies and how fun they are to bake and how good they taste when they are done. We finished our study of things that smell good. We have been learning about our sense of smell and how it helps us to gather information from our environment. Next, we will learn about our sense of hearing and how our ears help us to hear sounds in our world."

Extend and Enrich

Use the following ideas to extend and enrich what children know about cookies.

◆ Plan a parent participation activity in which each child brings in one dozen of her favorite cookies on a plate. Let everyone swap cookies in a cookie exchange party. This is a fun holiday activity.

◆ Use animal cookies for a counting or sorting activity.

◆ Plan a field trip to a bakery or the bakery section of the grocery store.

◆ Encourage the children to go to the grocery store with their parents and count how many different kinds of cookies there are in the bakery or snack aisle.

Daily Preschool Experiences

Things that Make Loud Sounds or Quiet Sounds

Musical Instruments

Morning Circle

When the children arrive, give each child a musical instrument. Invite them to have a musical parade and march around the room making music. After the parade, let the children play their instruments by themselves. Discuss the names of the instruments and the sounds they make. Experiment as a group with making "loud" music and "quiet" music.

Storytime

Animal Orchestra by Scott Gustafson

Daily Center Activity Ideas

ART CENTER

■ **Beginning Learner:** Fingerpainting to Music

Put fingerpaint on the table for the children to paint with. Play classical or orchestral music while the children are painting. If the children make pictures they want to save, place a piece of white paper over their "table art" and lift it carefully to reveal a copy of their picture.

■ ■ **Developing Learner:** Fast and Slow Painting

Provide paints at the easel and play music for the children as they paint. Vary the music to include fast music and slow music. Provide several sizes and types of brushes and other painting instruments for the children to experiment with.

■
■ ■ **Experienced Learner:** Musical Murals

Attach a long piece of paper to the wall for the children to paint a class mural. Provide a variety of materials for the children to paint with, such as rollers, brushes, sponges, and feathers. Play a variety of classical and orchestral music for the children to listen to as they paint.

MATH CENTER

Beginning Learner: Sound Patterns

Provide empty oatmeal canisters or coffee cans with plastic lids for the children to tap on the plastic lids and experiment with making different sound patterns. Show them how to make loud sounds and quiet sounds and make a series of sound patterns for the children to listen to and then repeat. Encourage them to count the number of sounds that they hear as you play them.

Developing Learner: Loud Bodies, Quiet Bodies

Encourage the children to take turns using their bodies to make loud sounds such as stamping their feet and quiet sounds such as lightly clapping their hands. As one child makes a series of sounds, have the other children count the number of sounds that they hear.

Experienced Learner: Musical Cards

Provide a variety of musical instruments and a deck of playing cards with the king, queen, and jack removed. Encourage the children to take turns drawing a card and then choosing an instrument and playing it the number of times represented on the card that they drew. Have each child place the card on the table in front of them. When all of the children have had a turn drawing a card and playing their instrument, they play their instruments at the same time but make only the number of sounds indicated by the card on the table in front of them.

SCIENCE CENTER

Beginning Learner: Matching Sounds

Make sets of sound canisters by filling film canisters with objects, such as pennies, marbles, jingle bells, rice, beans, and sand. Place the tops on the canisters. Encourage the children to shake the containers to find the two that match. (**Safety note:** Supervise closely to ensure young children do not put any of the small items in their mouths.)

Developing Learner: Paper Plate Tambourines

Give each child two paper plates and a variety of materials that make sounds, including pennies, marbles, and jingle bells. Staple the edges of the plates closed (adult only), leaving a small opening to insert the objects. After the children fill the plates, staple the remaining opening shut (adult only). The children shake their plates and make sounds.

THINGS THAT MAKE LOUD SOUNDS OR QUIET SOUNDS

UNIT 5

Experienced Learner: Guess the Sound

Provide empty film canisters and the objects described for the beginning learner. Have the children select a partner. Encourage one child to choose an object or a combination of objects and place them in a film canister and replace the lid. The child's partner shakes the canister and tries to determine what objects are inside. When the child thinks that he knows, he fills an empty film canister with objects to make an identical sound canister. Then, shake the two canisters. Do they sound the same or different? Encourage the children to remove the lids and compare the contents of each. Have the partners fill a canister and repeat the activity.

LANGUAGE/DRAMATIC PLAY CENTER

Beginning Learner: Exploring Instruments

Provide a variety of musical instruments for the children to experiment with to make sounds and music.

Developing Learner: Exploring Instruments II

Provide a variety of musical instruments for the children to experiment with to make sounds and music. Discuss the names of the instruments with the children and encourage them to practice making different sounds with their instruments. Let the children play their instruments by themselves or together.

Experienced Learner: Orchestra

Provide a variety of musical instruments for the children to experiment with to make music. Arrange chairs in the same way as an orchestra. Provide a music stand, sheet music, and a CD or tape of music for the children to enjoy. Discuss the names of the instruments with the children and encourage them to make comparisons between the sounds that each instrument makes. Encourage the children to play by themselves and then together as a group. If you have a tape recorder, tape their musical creations.

VOCABULARY

drums, loud, music, music staff, noise, notes, piano, quiet, sound, tone, tune, violins

Reflect

Say to the children, "Today we learned about musical instruments and the sounds that they make. Tomorrow we will learn about thunder and lightning and the sound thunder makes during a thunderstorm."

Extend and Enrich

Use the following ideas to extend and enrich what children know about musical instruments.

- Fill glasses with different amounts of water. Encourage the children to use a spoon to lightly tap the glasses to make different sounds.
- Show the children pictures of different musical instruments and play CDs with those instruments playing. A wonderful choice is Sergei Prokofiev's "Peter and the Wolf." Each character in this musical story is represented by a different instrument.

Thunder and Lightning

Morning Circle

To prepare for the day's activities, use the recipe in the book, *Thunder Cake* by Patricia Palacco to make a special cake. (Do not ice the cake because the children will help make icing as one of their activities in the science center). When the children arrive, greet them at the door wearing an apron and a chef's hat. Put some flour on your face, too. Show the children the cake and then read the story of how this cake came to be. After reading the story, discuss how the process of making the thunder cake calmed the little girl's fears of thunderstorms.

Storytime

Thunder Cake by Patricia Polacco

Daily Center Activity Ideas

ART CENTER

■ **Beginning Learner:** Chocolate Squishy Bags

Put brown fingerpaint into a gallon-size resealable plastic bag and seal the bag shut. Tell the children that the brown paint is like the chocolate frosting in the story. Encourage the children to draw with their fingers on the outside of the bags. The paint inside the bag will move to produce interesting pictures.

■■ **Developing Learner:** Chocolate Fingerpainting

Mix brown fingerpaint with shaving cream and place it on trays. Encourage the children to enjoy finger painting with the "chocolate frosting." The children can make designs, write their names, or make pictures. If they want to save their creations, place a piece of paper carefully on their finished product and lift it off.

Experienced Learner: Making Thunder Cakes

Provide small cups of real chocolate frosting, large sugar cookies, and craft sticks for the children to decorate their own small "thunder cakes." Encourage the children to draw pictures and designs on their cookies or practice writing their names in the chocolate frosting. The children can enjoy their cookies as a special treat or take them home to enjoy.

MATH CENTER

Explain to the children that in the story *Thunder Cake*, the little girl's grandmother tells to her that when she sees lightning, she should start counting, and when she hears the thunder she should stop counting. This lets her know how close the storm is.

Beginning Learner: Counting Thunder

Provide a flashlight to make lightning, and a small piece of sheet metal (or a metal pan or trashcan lid) and a wooden spoon to make the thunder sound. Flash the flashlight and encourage the children to begin counting. After a few seconds, strike the metal can or lid with the wooden spoon to make the thunder sound. Encourage the children to practice their counting skills (1–5). Let each child have a turn counting and making the thunder sound.

Developing Learner: Counting Thunder/Stopwatch

Provide the materials described for the beginning learner. Add a stopwatch. Invite the children to take turns using the flashlight to make lightning and the metal pans and spoons to make thunder. Encourage the children to explore using the stopwatch to find out how many seconds there are between the flash of lightning and the sound of the thunder. Ask the child holding the stopwatch to count out loud as the seconds pass.

Experienced Learner: Counting Thunder/Card Game

Provide a flashlight, metal pan, wooden spoon, and stopwatch. Divide the children into pairs. Have one child make "lightning" with a flashlight and the other child make thunder sounds by striking a lid or pan with a wooden spoon. Provide index cards with the numerals 1–10 written on them. Mix up the cards so they are in random order. The child who is going to make the thunder sound draws a card. The child with the flashlight makes the lightning, and the other child waits the number of seconds indicated on the card, and then makes the thunder sound. Continue the game until all of the cards have been drawn.

SCIENCE CENTER

Beginning Learner: Making Butter

Provide whipping cream, baby food jars, and an ice cube for the children to make butter. Pour whipping cream into each baby food jar to fill it half way, add an ice cube, and secure the lid tightly to the jar. Invite the children to shake their jars until butter forms. Talk about the changes in the ingredients as they are shaken. Provide crackers and butter knives and help the children spread the butter on their crackers.

Developing Learner: Chocolate-Dipped Strawberries

Provide chocolate and a warming pot to melt the chocolate. Talk about the changes in the chocolate as it melts, pointing out that the heat turns the solid chocolate into a liquid. Explain that it is the same substance, but it looks different. Invite the children to dip strawberries into the cooled melted chocolate.

Experienced Learner: Making Chocolate Frosting

Help the children make chocolate frosting from a commercially prepared mix or a recipe from a cookbook. Help the children measure and mix the ingredients to make the frosting. Talk about the different ingredients and how they combine to form the frosting. The children can use this frosting on their own thunder cakes.

LANGUAGE/DRAMATIC PLAY CENTER

Beginning Learner: Gathering Ingredients

Provide empty egg cartons, milk jugs and milk cartons, wrappers from chocolate, empty sugar bags, and empty flour bags. Put out play food, bowls, spoons, and dishes for the children to pretend to make "thunder cakes."

Developing Learner: Milking a Cow

Find a picture of a cow in a coloring book and enlarge the picture onto poster board. Fill a surgical glove with water and white paint to resemble milk. Poke a small hole in each finger of the glove and attach it to the cow figure to resemble the udders on a real cow. Invite the child to sit in a chair and gently squeeze the udders to practice milking a cow.

■■ Experienced Learner: Scavenger Hunt

Hide empty containers of ingredients, including egg cartons, milk cartons, chocolate icing or chocolate chip packages, bags of sugar and flour, three plastic tomatoes or pictures of tomatoes, and strawberry baskets. Give the children scavenger hunt sheets with pictures of the hidden ingredients and the number of each item they need to find. When the children find the items on their sheets, they mark them off. When they have found all of the ingredients, help them make a picture rebus recipe card for how to make a thunder cake. (**Note:** The recipe for making thunder cakes is in the back of the storybook.) Encourage the children to consult the book to help with the rebus recipe writing.

VOCABULARY

clap of thunder, crash, lightning, lightning bolt, loud, thunder

Reflect

Say to the children, "Yesterday we learned about musical instruments and all of the different sounds they make. Today we learned about thunder and lightning. We also had fun learning how to make thunder cakes. Tomorrow we will learn about pots and pans and the loud sounds they make when banged together."

Extend and Enrich

Use the following ideas to extend and enrich what children know about thunder and lightning.

◆ Lead the children in a research project to discover and discuss other names for grandmother. The grandmother in the story *Thunder Cake* is named Babushka.

◆ Talk about the names the children call their grandmothers and make a list.

◆ Generate a list with the children of things they could do during a thunderstorm if they become frightened.

◆ Gather supplies from the classroom and encourage the children to experiment with making their own thunder and lightning sounds.

Pots and Pans

Morning Circle

To prepare for this activity, collect pots and pans and their matching lids. When the children arrive, greet them with a stack of aluminum pie tins and metal spoons. Give each child a pie tin and a spoon and encourage them to bang the two together as they move in a circle. During circle time, show the children a variety of pots and pans and their lids and discuss how they fit together in pairs. Demonstrate the sound that two lids make when they are banged together. Read *Pots and Pans* by Patricia Hubbell to the children.

Storytime

Pots and Pans by Patricia Hubbell

Daily Center Activity Ideas

ART CENTER

Beginning Learner: Painting Circles

Provide lids from pots and pans as well as other small round objects, such as baby food jars and plastic lids, for the children to dip into paint and paint circle shapes on paper.

Developing Learner: Circle Collages

Provide colored construction paper and various sizes of pot and pan lids for the children to use as stencils. Encourage the children to place their lids on construction paper, trace them, and cut them out. Provide glue and large sheets of butcher paper for the children to make circle collages.

Experienced Learner: Interlocking Circles

Provide various sizes of pot and pan lids for the children. Invite the children to trace around them on construction paper to make circle pictures. Demonstrate how to overlap the circles to create interlocking circle patterns. Encourage the children to use markers, crayons, or watercolors to fill in and decorate their circles to create abstract art.

MATH CENTER

■ **Beginning Learner:** Matching Lids

Provide a variety of at least 12 different sizes of pots and pans with lids and place them on a carpeted surface. Invite the children to match the lids to the pots and pans.

■ ■ **Developing Learner:** Pots and Pans Hide and Seek

Place a variety of pots and pans and lids on a carpeted surface. Hide an object in one pot and replace the lid. The children play hide and seek by taking off the lids until they find the hidden object. Have them continue the game and hiding objects for a friend to find.

■
■ ■ **Experienced Learner:** Pots and Pans Concentration

Use pots and pans to set up a concentration game by hiding pairs of objects in pans and replacing the lids. The children take turns trying to find the matching pairs of objects.

SCIENCE CENTER

■ **Beginning Learner:** Pot and Pan Sounds

Provide pots and pans with lids and wooden and metal spoons. Encourage the children to experiment with banging, clanging, hitting, and tapping them to make loud sounds.

■ ■ **Developing Learner:** Comparing Pot and Pan Sounds

Provide pots, pans, lids, wooden spoons, metal spoons, and aluminum cans (some full and some empty) for the children to use to make loud sounds. (**Safety note:** When using empty cans, tape the rough edges with masking tape.) Encourage the children to experiment to determine if small pans or large pans make louder sounds, if empty cans or full cans make louder sounds when struck with a spoon, if the pots and pans make louder sounds when struck with metal spoons or wooden ones, and if small or large pot lids make louder sounds when they are banged together.

■
■ ■ **Experienced Learner:** Musical Patterns with Pots and Pans

Encourage the children to experiment with pots, pans, and lids as described for the developing learner and then arrange them in a desired order. Invite them to create their own musical patterns by arranging and rearranging the pots and pans and tapping on each of them different numbers of times. When the children achieve a desired sound pattern, have them make numeral cards to place in front of each pot, pan, and lid to indicate how many each should be tapped or played to reproduce their musical creation. Encourage the children to try reproducing each other's musical creations. Provide a tape recorder for the children to record their creations.

LANGUAGE/DRAMATIC PLAY CENTER

■ **Beginning Learner:** Sounds from the Story

Share the book *Pots and Pans* by Patricia Hubbell with the children and discuss the words from the story, including *grab, clang, ching, cling, rat-a-tat-tat, clash, boom, bam, bang, clap, clink, jumble, rumble,* and *tumble.* Encourage the children to use the pots and pans and their lids and wooden and metal spoons to re-enact the sounds in the story.

■ ■ **Developing Learner:** Things You Cook in a Pot

Encourage the children to look through magazines and cut out pictures of foods that they think are cooked in a pot. Provide a pot shape cut from gray construction paper for the children to glue their foods on.

■
■ ■ **Experienced Learner:** Rhyming Words

Lead the children in making a list of all of the words they can think of that rhyme with the word *pot.* Next, ask them to list the words that rhyme with *pan.* Write the words on a poster chart. Encourage the children to use the words from the list and combine them to make sentences. Write the children's sentences on paper and combine the sentences to make silly stories.

VOCABULARY

aluminum, bam, bang, big, boom, can, clang, cling, crash, cooking, handle, hot, lid, match, pan, pot, small, spoon, stove, top

Reflect

Say to the children, "Yesterday we learned about lightning and the loud sound of thunder. Today we learned about pots and pans and the loud sounds they make when they are banged together. Tomorrow we will learn about the wind, which makes a quiet sound. Can you think of other things that make a quiet sound?"

Extend and Enrich

Use the following ideas to extend and enrich what children know about the loud sounds pots and pans make.

- Have a soup day. Ask parents to send in a vegetable. Have the children wash and cut the vegetables into small pieces. Put the vegetables into a crock pot to make soup.
- Share the story of Johnny Appleseed with the children and talk about how he wore a cooking pot on his head when he traveled. When he stopped to make his meals, he used the pot to cook in. Have the children place a cooking pot on their heads and practice walking on a balance beam like Johnny Appleseed.

DAY 4

Wind

Morning Circle

Obtain a child-safe fan and a variety of objects that are lightweight enough to move when the fan blows on them (feathers, facial tissue, tissue paper, paper confetti, balloons, and so on). Place the fan in the circle area and turn it on. Place the lightweight items on the floor. When the children gather for circle, talk about all of the things that are moving on the ground because of the "wind" created by the fan. Discuss the sounds that the wind makes when it blows. Discuss how the sounds are different depending on whether the wind is blowing loudly or quietly. Encourage the children to practice making their own wind sounds.

Storytime

The Wind Blew by Pat Hutchins

Daily Center Activity Ideas

ART CENTER

Beginning Learner: Windsocks

Give each child a piece of 15" x 12" poster board or construction paper. Roll the paper into a tube shape and provide strips of colored crepe paper streamers for the children to glue, tape, or staple to the bottom of the tube shape. Assist the children with making a handle for their windsocks by punching holes in the top of each windsock and adding yarn. Encourage the children to decorate the outsides of their tube shapes with stickers, markers, or crayons.

Developing Learner: Making Paper Kites

Cut diamond kite shapes from construction paper or bulletin board paper, one for each child. Put out crepe paper streamers, markers, paints, and crayons for children to use to decorate their kite shapes. Help them make a handle on the back of the kite so their arm will fit through. Go outside and invite the children to fly their kites by running and letting the streamers blow in the wind.

Experienced Learner: Ready-Made Kites

Purchase commercially available kites. Encourage the children to use markers and stickers to add decorations and details to the kites. Take the children outside so that they can experiment with flying their kites. (**Note:** This would make a good parent-involvement activity. Invite parents to come in and participate in a kite-flying day.)

MATH CENTER

■ **Beginning Learner:** Sail Boat Speed

Fill a small water table, container, or child-size swimming pool with a small amount of water and provide small toy boats with sails. Invite the children to blow on the sails to make the boats move through the water. Have them count how long it takes for their boats to move across the water from one side to another.

■ ■ **Developing Learner:** Sail Boat Races

Provide the materials described for the beginning learner and invite the children to engage in sailboat races. Divide the class into teams and have them race their boats against each other to see which boats are the fastest. Encourage the children to blow on the sails of the boats to move them across the water. Provide a stopwatch or timer to see how long it takes each boat to get across the water. Show the children how to fold paper accordion-style to make fans, which can be used to make wind to move the boats faster. Encourage the children to experiment with different ways to create wind. Talk about measuring time with the timer or stopwatch.

■
■ ■ **Experienced Learner:** Soap Boats

Give each child a bar of mild soap (such as Ivory™) and a spoon, and demonstrate how to use a spoon to carve out the center of the soap to make a "boat." Help the children cut triangles from poster board, wallpaper, fabric, or construction paper to make sails for their boats. Attach the sails to toothpicks or craft sticks and push the stick sails into the soap. Encourage the children to blow on their soap boats to make them move. Can they think of other ways to make wind to help the boats move faster? Talk about measuring speed and distance. Encourage the children to use their boats at home in the bathtub.

SCIENCE CENTER

■ **Beginning Learner:** Make Your Own Wind

Place two strips of masking tape on the floor to make a finish line and a starting line. Collect a variety of balls, such as ping pong balls, tennis balls, baseballs, golf balls, and basketballs. Ask the children which balls they think will be the easiest to blow across the floor to the finish line. After they make their guesses, let them experiment with the balls to test their guesses. After a series of tests, give each child a ping pong ball and stickers or markers to decorate it. Have the children get behind the starting line. Say, "Go." Encourage the children to blow their balls towards the finish line.

Developing Learner: Fans

Provide small objects (such as cotton balls, strings, feathers, and tissues), a small fan, and paper folded into fans. Invite the children to experiment with moving the small objects. Make a start and finish line on the floor. Encourage the children to choose an object and experiment with trying to get their object across the finish line. Encourage the children to experiment with finding out which objects are the easiest and hardest to move.

Experienced Learner: Wind Predictions

Provide the objects found in the story *The Wind Blew*, including an umbrella, a balloon, a hat, a kite, a shirt, facial tissue, a handkerchief, a wig, envelopes and letters, a flag, two scarves, and newspapers. Also, provide a fan and encourage the children to make predictions based on how hard or how easy it will be to move each object. Create a chart that shows their predictions. After experimenting with the objects, the children can use a crayon to mark on the chart whether or not their predictions were correct.

LANGUAGE/DRAMATIC PLAY CENTER

Beginning Learner: Act Out the Story

Provide some of the props from the story *The Wind Blew*, including an umbrella, balloon, kite, shirt, handkerchief, wig, letters, flag, and several scarves, as well as clothes the characters wore in the story (an overcoat, a top hat, overalls, an apron, a black robe, a hat, and coat). Encourage the children to use the props to act out events in the story.

Developing Learner: Order of Events

Share the story with the children by doing a brief picture walk through the book so the children can see the order of events in the story. Provide all of the props as listed for the beginning learner. Encourage each child to choose a character from the story and then gather props needed for the character. Encourage the children to reenact the events in the story in the order in which they occurred. Encourage the children to take turns playing different characters.

Experienced Learner: Story Cards

Make a set of picture cards using the pictures from the story. Encourage the children to place the cards in sequential order to retell the story. Make copies of some of the pictures from the story and use them to make small books for the children. Invite the children to color and assemble the pages so that they can have their own small book to retell the story.

VOCABULARY

air, air currents, blow, blustery, breeze, weather forecaster, weather vane, west wind, wind, wind speed, wind force

Reflect

Say to the children, "Yesterday we learned about pots and pans and the loud sounds that they make. Today we learned about the wind and how it makes things like kites and trees move when it blows. Sometimes the wind makes a soft sound when it blows through the trees, and sometimes it makes a loud sound when it blows during a storm. Tomorrow we will learn about the very quiet sound that is made when we whisper to someone."

Extend and Enrich

Use the following ideas to extend and enrich what children know about the wind.

◆ Take the children outside on a very windy day and encourage them to observe what is happening to the leaves on the trees, the leaves on the ground, the flags on flag poles, the movement of the clouds, people's clothes, and hair. Also encourage the children to listen to the sounds the wind makes when it blows.

◆ Plan a parent-participation day in which parents and children bring a kite and go to a local park for kite flying.

Whispers

Morning Circle

Lead the children in playing a whisper game. Ask the children to sit in a circle on the floor. Whisper a word or phrase to the child sitting next you. The child whispers what he heard to the person next to him. The secret is passed around the circle until it reaches the last child. The last child tells the class what he heard. Ask the children if the secret changed as it was passed around the circle. If it did, ask them why they think it happened. Talk about when it is appropriate to use a quiet voice, such as in a library or church, when someone is sleeping, and in a classroom when someone else is talking. Make a list of the children's ideas.

Storytime

Curious Creatures: Whispers in the Woods by Jean Christie

Daily Center Activity Ideas

ART CENTER

Beginning Learner: Whisper Phones
Cut the bottoms off Styrofoam cups. Encourage the children to use markers and stickers to decorate their cups. Invite the children to hold the cups to their ears and ask a friend to whisper a message inside the cup.

Developing Learner: Whisper Phones/Painting
Prior to this activity, cut out the bottoms of large Styrofoam cups, one for each child. Provide acrylic paint, paintbrushes, and paint smocks. Encourage the children to use the paint to make designs on their cup. Allow the cups to dry before the children handle them. Invite the children to choose a partner, hold the cups to their ears, and take turns whispering messages inside the cups.

Experienced Learner: Tin Can Phones

To prepare for this activity, cut out one end of a few cans and use an ice pick to poke a hole in the other end of the cans (adult only). Thread waxed string through the hole in the end of each can and secure with a knot on the inside of the can. Give each child two empty cans. Have them cover their cans with white contact paper and decorate using markers or stickers. Divide the children into pairs. One child holds his can to his ear, and the other child stretches the string out and does the same. One child whispers a message into his can while the other child holds her can to her ear to listen. They take turns whispering and listening to messages. (**Safety note:** Use tape to cover the rough edges of the cans to ensure the safety of the children.)

MATH CENTER

Beginning Learner: Sounds/Counting

Provide pictures of a variety of objects, including clouds, a worm, a rabbit, a horn, machines, a whistle, a bird, a lion, and so on. Discuss these pictures with the children and encourage them to make the sounds that each object makes. Play a game in which a child chooses a picture, rolls a die, and makes the sound of the object on the picture the number of times shown on the die. Continue the game until everyone has had several turns rolling the die and making sounds.

Developing Learner: Sounds/Sorting

Provide the pictures described for the beginning learner. Encourage the children to sort the pictures in order from things that are loud to things that are quiet. Next, encourage the children to sort the pictures in reverse order from things that are quiet to things that are loud. Ask them to count the number of objects in each category. Make a chart with the words "loud" and "quiet" at the top. Ask the children to place the pictures under one of the words. After all of the objects have been sorted, encourage the children to count the number of pictures in each column and write that number at the top of each column.

Experienced Learner: Sounds/Recognizing Numerals

Ask the children to use index cards and markers to draw pictures of things that make loud sounds and things that make quiet sounds. When they are done, have them place the cards in a pile on the table. Ask the children to take turns spinning a spinner with numerals on it and choosing a card from the pile of sound cards. The child who spins looks at the numeral on the spinner and makes the same number and type of sound as the object on the card.

SCIENCE CENTER

Beginning Learner: Muffled Sounds

Provide ear phones, ear plugs, and ear muffs for the children to try on. Discuss how these things affect their ability to hear clearly. Introduce the concept of *muffled sounds.*

Developing Learner: How Low Do Sounds Go?

Record a variety of sounds on a tape recorder. Play the sound tape for the children and demonstrate how the volume control on the tape recorder works to make sounds quieter and louder. Play a game with the children to see how low the volume can go before they can no longer hear the sounds. Play the tape, and gradually reduce the volume. Ask the children to raise their hands when they can hear the sounds and lower their hands when they can no longer hear the sounds. Play the game again, and when the volume is loud, the children stand up and when it is quiet the children sit down.

Experienced Learner: Loud and Quiet

Have children look through magazines to find pictures of things that make very loud sounds and those that make very quiet sounds. Ask them to use the pictures to make a graph. Make two columns at the top of the paper: "Loud Sounds" and "Quiet Sounds." The children glue their pictures under the correct headings.

LANGUAGE/DRAMATIC PLAY CENTER

Beginning Learner: Whisper a Story

Using a whisper voice, record the story for the day or one of the children's favorite stories. Invite the children to listen to the recording and follow along in the book.

Developing Learner: Recording Whispers

Provide a tape recorder so the children can experiment with making very quiet sounds and whispers.

Experienced Learner: Match the Voices

Provide a tape recorder so the children can record a story or whisper messages for their friends. When the tape is finished, encourage the children to listen to the recorded messages and identify the voices of the children who made them.

VOCABULARY

clear, library, low, peaceful, quiet, secret, soft, whisper

Reflect

Say to the children, "Yesterday we learned about the wind and the soft and quiet sounds that it makes as it blows through the trees. Today we learned about the quiet sound we make when we whisper something to someone."

Extend and Enrich

Use the following ideas to extend and enrich what children know about whispers and quiet sounds.

- Purchase commercially available whisper phones from a teacher supply store. Encourage the children to use the whisper phones to experiment with listening to their own whispering voices.
- Share with the children the story *Rumble in the Jungle* by Giles Andreae and David Wojtowycz and compare it to the story selection for the day. This story has wonderful language and vocabulary for the children to enjoy.

Things Found in the Country

Life on the Farm

Morning Circle

To prepare for this activity, cut out two road shapes from brown bulletin board paper, long enough to reach from the classroom door to the circle area. Label one road "The Country Road" and one road "The City Road." Draw a large arrow on two pieces of poster board and write, "This way to the city" on one, and "This way to the country" on the other. When the children arrive, greet them at the door while holding a suitcase and tell them that you are going on a trip but you can't decide whether you want to go to the country or the city. Have the children choose one of the roads and follow the sign to the circle. When the children arrive in Morning Circle, discuss things found in the country and things found in the city. Read the story *The Town Mouse and the Country Mouse* by Jan Brett and talk about why the country mouse was happiest in the country and the city mouse was happiest in the city. Ask the children to share any experiences they have had with visits to the country or to large cities.

Storytime

The Town Mouse and the Country Mouse by Jan Brett

Daily Center Activity Ideas

ART CENTER

■ **Beginning Learner:** Mouse's Invitation
Help the children fold a piece of paper in half and make invitations for the mice. They can make an invitation for the country mouse to visit the city or vice versa. Invite them to use stickers, crayons, and markers to decorate their invitations.

■ ■ **Developing Learner:** Mouse House
Provide a cardboard house shape for the children to use as a stencil. Let them trace the house stencil onto colored construction paper and cut it out. Help them cut a flap in the front of the house so that the door appears to open. Encourage the children to glue the house shape onto white construction paper and then decorate it to make an invitation for the city mouse to visit the country or the country mouse to visit the city.

■ ■ ■ Experienced Learner: Mouse House Poem

In preparation for this activity, engage the children in helping to create a simple poem such as the following two poems by Kay Hastings:

An invitation from a simple country mouse,
Please come for a visit at my simple country house.
We will explore the country where there is a lot to do.
I am looking forward to a visit from you.

An invitation from a fancy city mouse,
Please come for a visit at my fancy city house.
We will explore the city where there is a lot to do.
I am looking forward to a visit from you.

When the children have finished creating the poem, make a copy for each child. Provide a house-shaped stencil and two pieces of construction paper. Encourage the children to trace two house shapes and cut them out. Help the children staple the two house shapes together on one side to form a book cover. The children can glue the poem inside the "book" and then use markers, crayons, and pieces of construction paper to decorate the house shapes to resemble either country-mouse houses or city-mouse houses.

MATH CENTER

To prepare for this activity, provide doll clothing and other items that the children can sort as belonging to the city mouse (such as a dressy shirt, high-heeled shoes, a fancy hat, and a taxi cab) or the country mouse (such as overalls, tennis shoes, a straw hat, a truck, and farm animals).

■ Beginning Learner: Sorting Mouse Items

Encourage the children to look at the objects described above and sort them according to what would belong to the country mouse and what would belong to the city mouse. Provide two suitcases for sorting the items.

■ ■ Developing Learner: Sorting Mouse Items/Counting

Invite the children to sort the objects as described for the beginning learner. When they are finished, give them a die and two suitcases. Have them take turns rolling the die and putting that number of items in either the country mouse or the city mouse's suitcase to help each mouse pack for the visit.

Experienced Learner: Sorting Mouse Items/Venn Diagram

Provide the objects listed for the developing learner. Include objects that could belong to either mouse, such as a variety of dollhouse furniture, a pet dog or cat, and a toothbrush. Draw a Venn diagram on a piece of poster board (draw two circles overlapping in the middle and write "country mouse" above one circle and "city mouse" above the other circle). Encourage the children to sort the objects depending on whether they think the item belongs to the country mouse, the city mouse, or to either mouse. Let them place the item directly on the Venn diagram where they think it belongs. Encourage the children to count the number of objects in each area.

SCIENCE CENTER

Beginning Learner: Country Mouse/City Mouse Maze

Make a maze on the floor using masking tape. Use construction paper to make a house for the country mouse at one end of the maze and a house for the city mouse at the other end of the maze. Encourage the children to walk the maze to get from one house to the other. When they have finished, encourage them to walk the maze in reverse.

Developing Learner: Make Your Own Maze

Draw a simple maze on paper and put a picture of the country mouse's house on one end and the city mouse's house on the other end. Show the children how to use a crayon to follow the path from the country mouse's house to the city mouse's house. Encourage the children to draw their own mazes.

Experienced Learner: Mouse House Board Game

Use poster board and dot stickers or purchase mouse stickers to make a simple board game. Make a game board that has a path (dots or stickers) from the city mouse's house to the country mouse's house. Encourage the children to roll a die and move that number of spaces. If possible, use small mice (such as cat toys) as game pieces.

LANGUAGE/DRAMATIC PLAY CENTER

Beginning Learner: Pretend Tea Party

Provide kitchen play equipment such as play furniture, play dishes, a tablecloth, and play foods for the children to use to role play a tea party.

Developing Learner: Real Food Tea Party

Provide tea party accessories such as a table, fancy tablecloth, a play fancy tea set, and fancy finger foods (fruits cut into fancy shapes, fancy cookies, and juice) and a less formal tablecloth, less fancy dishes, and less fancy snack foods (crackers, plain cut fruit, and juice). Provide two small tables so the children can set up a country tea party and a city tea party. Invite them to role play having both a fancy city tea party and a country tea party.

Experienced Learner: Make Tea Party Snacks

Help the children make tea party snacks. Provide ingredients to make finger sandwiches (cream cheese and bread, or peanut butter, jelly, and bread), toothpicks and cubes of cheese and fruits (pineapple cubes, strawberries), and ingredients to make lemonade. The children will enjoy having a tea party with their friends.

VOCABULARY

country, crops, farmer, field, hay, hoe, plow, rake, straw, tractor

Reflect

Say to the children, "Today, we began learning about things that are found in the country. Tomorrow, we will learn about some of the animals that are found in the country on a farm."

Extend and Enrich

Use the following ideas to extend and enrich what children know about things found in the country.

- Invite parents to a "Town Mouse and Country Mouse Tea Party." Ask everyone to dress either very casual (like the country mouse) or very fancy (like the city mouse). Help the children prepare foods for the tea party.
- Make mouse ear headbands with the children, and then paint their noses black using face paint.
- Have the children use shoeboxes to make "town mouse" houses and "country mouse" houses. Provide construction paper and collage materials for the children to use to make furnishings for their houses.

Farm Animals

Morning Circle

Prior to this activity, gather small toy farm animals, such as a pig, cow, horse, sheep, dog, and chicken. Just for fun, greet the children wearing a farmer's hat and overalls. Give each child a toy farm animal to bring to circle. When everyone is at circle, sing, "Old MacDonald Had a Farm." As each animal's name is called, the children holding that animal stand up and make the sound of the animal. After you and the children sing the song, engage them in a discussion about farms. Ask them if anyone has ever visited a farm, and if so, have them describe the animals they saw.

Storytime

Old MacDonald Had a Farm by Carol Jones

Daily Center Activity Ideas

ART CENTER

Before doing this activity, show the children several different skeins of yarn in different colors and textures. Explain that sheep are sheared in the spring and their wool is removed in one large piece called a *fleece*. Show the children examples of wool fabric. Explain that the sheep's wool is washed in a big tub to remove dirt and grease and then combed (or *carded*) to straighten the fibers. Next, the wool is spun into yarn, which is knitted or woven into fabric.

■ **Beginning Learner:** Lint Animals

Show the children lint from the lint basket of a clothes dryer. Encourage them to feel the lint and notice the fibers and colors that are in it. Make copies of pages from a farm coloring book of different farm animals. Invite the children to glue dryer lint on their pictures. (**Note:** Before this activity, send a note home encouraging parents to send in lint from their dryers at home so that there is a wide variety of colors and textures.)

■ ■ **Developing Learner:** Yarn Balls

Provide skeins of yarn and show the children how to wind the yarn around a cardboard card (size of a playing card). When the card is full, slide the yarn off

of the card, tie it in the middle, and cut the yarn on both ends to form a pompom or yarn ball. Encourage the children to make several yarn balls using different colors of yarn.

Experienced Learner: Yarn Ropes

Cut different colors and textures of yarn into 36" pieces. Help the children make yarn ropes. Ask each child to choose eight strands of yarn in any color. Help them tie the yarn pieces together in a knot on each end. Have them choose partners. Each child holds the knot on her end of the rope and begins twisting the yarn. (**Note:** The children must twist in opposite directions.) When the rope is twisted tightly, take both of the knotted ends in your hands and they will begin to spin together. When the rope is twisted, tie both ends together in a knot.

MATH CENTER

Make a game board for the children by placing stickers of farm animals on a piece of poster board to form a trail. Provide a die and toy farm animals for game pieces.

Beginning Learner: Farm Animal Board Game (1 die)

Encourage the children to roll the die and move the number of spaces indicated on the die around the game board. When they land on a farm animal, they name the animal and make that animal's sound.

Developing Learner: Farm Animal Board Game (2 dice)

Invite the children to play the game as described for the beginning learner, but use two dice.

Experienced Learner: Make Your Own Game

Provide stickers of farm animals and folders for the children to use to make their own game boards. Show them how to draw a path for their game board and place their stickers along the path. Provide each child with a die, or help them make a spinner using a small paper plate and a brad. Help them write numerals on the spinners. Encourage the children to play their games.

SCIENCE CENTER

Before doing this activity, talk about foods that are made from milk. Provide clean, empty containers from dairy products such as cheese, yogurt, ice cream, and pudding and show the children how to read the labels to see if milk is included in the list of ingredients.

Beginning Learner: Making and Tasting butter

Help the children pour whipping cream into baby food jars until they are one third full. Explain that the whipping cream is at room temperature and will turn into butter much faster if it is cold. Add an ice cube to each jar. The children shake their jars until the whipping cream turns into butter. Let them add a small amount of salt to the butter and spread the butter on a cracker to taste. Discuss with the children how butter is made and show them different kinds of butter from the grocery store: stick butter, and whipped butter. Provide crackers and encourage the children to taste the different kinds of butter and see which one they like the best.

Developing Learner: Making Milkshakes

Explain to the children that milk from a cow is white or light tan. Show them flavoring such as chocolate and strawberry and explain that the flavorings can be added to milk to change both its color and its flavor. Provide small cups of milk and encourage the children to taste it. Add a small amount of strawberry flavoring to the milk and invite the children to taste it. Next, add a small amount of chocolate flavoring to plain milk and invite the children to taste the chocolate milk. Ask them which flavor of milk is their favorite. Explain that flavorings can also be added to ice cream to make milkshakes. Provide a blender and vanilla ice cream. Encourage the children to add scoops of ice cream to the blender and also add small amounts of the flavoring of their choice. Turn on the blender to mix the milkshake. When finished, pour the milkshake in cups for the children to enjoy.

Experienced Learner: Making Ice Cream

Gather ingredients for ice cream (use any no-cook ice cream recipe), one large and one smaller coffee can (both with lids), rock salt, and crushed ice. Help the children follow the recipe and mix the ingredients in a bowl. Pour the mixture into the small coffee can and secure the lid with tape. Place the smaller can inside the larger coffee can and fill the larger can with crushed ice and rock salt. Explain to the children that the ice alone would make the mixture inside the can cold, but not cold enough to freeze. When salt is added to the ice, the temperature drops and the mixture becomes much colder. Secure the lid of the larger can with tape. Encourage the children to sit on the floor and roll the can back and forth for about 15 minutes. The ingredients inside the small can will thicken and become ice cream. When the ice cream is ready, remove the smaller coffee can from the larger one. Wipe off the salt and ice before opening the can. Spoon the ice cream into bowls for the children to enjoy.

LANGUAGE/DRAMATIC PLAY CENTER

Beginning Learner: Cheese, Please

Show the children a jug of milk and a variety of products made from milk including ice cream, pudding, yogurt, and milk chocolate. Also show the children a variety of cheeses and discuss how cheese is made from milk. Recite the nursery rhyme, "Little Miss Muffet" and explain that "curds and whey" is a cheese-like substance that is formed when milk curdles and separates.

Developing Learner: Kinds of Cheese

Provide a variety of cheese, such as American, Swiss, cheddar, and mozzarella, as well as cheese graters. Help them grate the cheese onto plates. Encourage them to taste the different cheeses and decide which one they like the best. Let the children sprinkle some of their favorite cheese on a piece of bread. Toast the bread and cheese in a toaster oven (adult only). When the cheese toast has cooled, the children can enjoy eating it as a special treat. **Note:** If a toaster oven is not available, provide slices of different kinds of cheese, bread, and cookie cutters for the children to make shape sandwiches. If desired, also provide a canister of pressurized processed cheese food, such as Cheez-Whiz™ and crackers, for the children to taste.

Experienced Learner: Making Pudding

Provide instant pudding and milk. Show the children baby food jars (for shaking the ingredients), a mixing bowl and hand mixer, and a blender. Discuss how these three different methods could be used to make pudding. Decide with the children which method to try first. Provide mixing cups, the pudding boxes, and spoons and help the children follow the directions and mix the pudding. When the pudding is finished, provide small plastic cups and plastic spoons for the children to use for tasting. Try all three methods, and have them compare which method works the best and is the fastest.

VOCABULARY

chickens, cows, dogs, ducks, eggs, goats, hay, horses, livestock, pigs, sheep, straw

Reflect

Say to the children, "Yesterday, we learned about ways that life in the country and life in the city are different and ways that they are the same. Today, we learned about animals that live on farms and the important things they provide, such as yarn from sheep and milk from cows. Tomorrow, we will learn about farmers and all of the important jobs they do.

Extend and Enrich

Use the following ideas to extend and enrich what children know about farm animals.

- Borrow an incubator and obtain eggs from a farm for the children to participate in observing the eggs hatch over time.
- Have a baby chick, duck, or rabbit visit the classroom.
- Make a "Pin the Tail on the Donkey" game for the children to enjoy.

Farmers

Morning Circle

In preparation for this day, send home a note asking parents to let their children come to school the next day dressed as farmers. Suggest that they wear flannel shirts, overalls, work boots or similar shoes, a straw hat, or any other items that they think farmers may wear. Paint a large appliance box to look like a barn and place it in the middle of the circle before the children arrive. When the children arrive, greet them at the door dressed as a farmer and give each child a small pail or bucket with a paintbrush and a sponge. Ask them to "paint" the barn using their sponges and paintbrushes. During circle time, discuss the many important jobs that farmers do, including caring for the animals, growing fruits and vegetables, and taking food to the market to sell. Talk about the difference in farms of the past where the farmer did everything himself and the farms today where a lot of the work is done by machinery.

Storytime

Who Took the Farmer's Hat? by Joan Nodset

Daily Center Activity Ideas

ART CENTER

Beginning Learner: Paint a Farmer's Hat

Help the children make a farmer's hat. Place three sheets of newspaper on top of each other and then place them on a child's head. Wrap masking tape on top of the newspaper, around the crown of the child's head, to form the head section of the hat. Next, help the children to form the brim of the hat by folding up the edges of the hat and stapling it in place. Provide brown paint for the children to use to paint their farmer's hats.

Developing Learner: Make Your Own Farmer's Hat

Give each child a sturdy farm hat to use as a form. Encourage them to place three sheets of newspaper on top of the hat and wrap masking tape around the crown of the hat to form their own newspaper hats. When the shape is complete and secured with tape, remove it from the hat form and show the children how to roll the sides up to form a brim. Invite the children to tear construction paper into small pieces and glue the pieces to their hat to decorate it.

Experienced Learner: Farmer's Hat with Fringe

Show the children an example of a straw hat that has rough edges, as well as pieces of hay or straw so they can feel it and compare it to the material that the hat is made from. Help the children make a farmer's hat as described for the developing learner. But, instead of folding the sides up, show them how to use scissors to fringe the edges of their hat to make it look like the sample hat. Provide hay or straw for the children to glue to their hat.

MATH CENTER

Beginning Learner: Hat Toss/Counting

Turn over several of the classroom chairs so that the legs of the chairs are facing the ceiling. Have the children count the legs of a chair and point out that there are four legs on each chair. Encourage the children to take turns trying to toss the straw hats so that they land on a chair leg. When all of the hats have been tossed, ask the child to count how many hats actually landed on the legs of the chairs. Children receive one point for each hat that reached the target. Provide score cards for the children to record their points.

Developing Learner: Beanbag Toss/Number Match

Write the numerals 1–5 on index cards and place them inside five straw hats. Write the numerals 1–5 on a stack of index cards, one numeral per card. There may be many cards with the same number on them. Ask the children to take turns drawing a numeral card from the stack and throwing a beanbag into the hat that has the same numeral.

Experienced Learner: Animal Toss/ Number Match

Place five straw hats upside down on the floor and put a numeral card (1–5) inside each hat. Provide small toy farm animals from *Who Took the Farmer's Hat?* by Joan Nodset. Encourage the children to try to toss the correct number of animals into the correct hat as indicated by the numeral inside.

SCIENCE CENTER

Beginning Learner: Paper Plate Bird Nests

In the story *Who Took the Farmer's Hat?*, the end of the story shows a bird that has used the farmer's hat as a nest. Try to find an actual bird's nest or purchase one from a craft store. Show the nest to the children and talk about the materials that birds find in nature to weave together to make a nest for their eggs. Discuss how tightly woven the nest is and the very delicate work that the birds have done to make a home for their eggs and their baby birds. Encourage the children to tear brown shredded construction paper or a paper bag into strips and glue the strips to a paper plate to look like a nest. Add jelly beans for bird eggs.

Developing Learner: Paper Bag Bird Nests

Show the children an actual bird's nest or one that has been purchased from a craft store. Talk about the materials used for the bird's nest and how the tightly woven materials form what looks like the bottom of a basket. Show the children several wicker baskets and ask them to notice the bottom section and how it forms a bowl shape. Tell the children they will be making their own bird's nests, and they should try to make the same type of bowl or basket in their nests so that the "eggs" will be safe and secure. Give each child a brown paper lunch bag. Demonstrate how to roll the sides of the paper bag down until the sides reach the inside bottom of the bag to form a basket or bowl shape. Provide shredded paper for nesting material. Encourage the children to add the nesting material to the "nest" and then wad paper into tiny shapes for eggs.

Experienced Learner: Edible Bird Nests

Show the children pictures of bird's nests from magazines and an actual nest from nature or one purchased from a craft store. Discuss how the bird stacks and weaves tiny pieces of grass and straw together to form a strong structure that will hold the eggs. Show the children a wicker basket so they can see how the pieces of wicker are stacked and woven together to make the basket strong. Explain that they are going to use food to make a bird's nest. Show them dry chow mein noodles and talk about how the noodles resemble the tiny pieces of grass and straw from an actual bird's nest. Show the children butterscotch pieces or chips and explain that when melted, the chips act as a "glue" to hold the pieces of the nest together. Melt the butterscotch pieces in a warming pan and let the children add the noodles. Have them take turns stirring the mixture. Drop the mixture by spoonfuls onto wax paper to make "nests." When the nests cool, provide raisins or speckled jelly beans for the children to add as eggs. The children can eat their bird's nest treats or take them home to enjoy.

LANGUAGE/DRAMATIC PLAY CENTER

Beginning Learner: Retelling the Story

Make picture cards of the different characters from the story *Who Took the Farmer's Hat.* Give each child a picture card and then retell the story. Whenever you mention a character in the story, the child holding that card stands up and shows her card. After the story, encourage the children to use all of the cards to retell the story to their friends. Toy animals are also fun to use to retell the story.

■ ■ **Developing Learner:** I Took the Farmer's Hat

Write the question, "Did _____ take the farmer's hat?" on a piece of paper. Make a copy for each child. Encourage the children to fill in the blank with their name and then draw a picture of themselves with the farmer's hat.

■
■ ■ **Experienced Learner:** Make a Farmer's Hat Book

Give each child three sheets of white paper that have been cut in half. On the top of each piece of paper write, "Did the _____ take the farmer's hat?" Staple the sheets together to form a book. Encourage the children to fill in the blanks with animal names from the story or names of their classmates and then illustrate the pages of their book.

VOCABULARY

cattle, cow, crops, farmer, field, harvest, hat, hay, hoe, horse, land, pig, plant, rake, sheep, straw, tractor

Reflect

Say to the children, "Yesterday, we learned about the animals that are found on a farm. Today, we learned about farmers and the many jobs they have on the farms to raise the animals as well as plant and grow the crops. Tomorrow, we will learn more about some of the fruits and vegetables that are grown on a farm."

Extend and Enrich

Use the following ideas to extend and enrich what children know about farmers and the work they do on a farm.

- Share some favorite children's songs such as "Old MacDonald Had a Farm" and "BINGO."
- Sing the song, "The Farmer in the Dell" and have the children act out the different parts of the song.

Fruits and Vegetables Grow on Farms

Morning Circle

Before the children arrive, arrange chairs in a circle (one for each child). When the children arrive, greet them with a child-size wheelbarrow full of pretend fruits and vegetables that are grown on a farm, such as lettuce, cucumbers, broccoli, okra, squash, apples, cantaloupes, onions, potatoes, tomatoes, and corn. Invite each child to choose one of the fruits and vegetables and carry it to morning circle. Ask the children to place their fruit or vegetable on a chair. Play musical chairs. Turn on the music and invite the children to walk in a circle around the chairs. When the music stops, each child sits in a chair and holds the fruit or vegetable in her lap. Go around the circle and ask each child to name the fruit or vegetable she is holding. The children stand up, put the food back on the chair, and start over when the music begins. Repeat several times.

Storytime

Tops and Bottoms by Janet Stevens

Daily Center Activity Ideas

ART CENTER

To prepare for these activities, cut off the inedible parts of fresh vegetables and fruits, including okra, broccoli, squash, carrots, potatoes, celery, bananas, oranges, and so on. Save the edible parts of the vegetables to make soup.

■ **Beginning Learner:** Fruit and Vegetable Prints
Provide the incdible parts of different vegetables and fruits (such as peach pits, carrot tops, cucumber ends, orange peels, and so on) and encourage the children to dip them into paint and place them on paper to make prints.

■ ■ **Developing Learner:** Paper Soup Pot

Cut out a cooking pot shape from construction paper for each child. Invite them to use inedible parts of vegetables (see beginning learner) to make prints on the pots to resemble a pot of soup.

■ ■ **Experienced Learner:** Vegetable Painting

After reading the story *Tops and Bottoms*, provide the tops and bottoms of different vegetables for the children to experiment painting with. Provide the color of paint that matches each vegetable and encourage the children to use the actual color of each to paint their pictures.

MATH CENTER

For this activity, send home a note asking parents to send in a vegetable such as corn, potatoes, peas, carrots, tomatoes, okra, squash, broccoli, or any other vegetables suitable for soup. You may also purchase the vegetables yourself.

■ **Beginning Learner:** Scrubbing Vegetables

Provide vegetable brushes and pans of water to scrub the vegetables. Count the vegetables with the children as they scrub them. Make soup with the clean vegetables.

■ ■ **Developing Learner:** Cutting Vegetables

Provide vegetables, plastic knives, and a cooking pot. Help the children cut the vegetables into small pieces. Provide recipe cards with a picture of each vegetable and the number of pieces to cut for the soup. Encourage the children to choose a recipe card and place that number of vegetable pieces in the pot. Help the children add canned tomatoes and water to the pot, and then place the pot of soup on a warming tray or on the stove to cook. When the soup has cooked, place a small amount in cups or bowls for the children to enjoy when it has cooled.

■ ■ **Experienced Learner:** Making Vegetable Soup

Provide several cookbooks with recipes for making vegetable soup. Read through the recipes with the children and discuss the ingredients and measurements needed to make each kind of vegetable soup. Choose one of the recipes and provide the vegetables, spices, and other ingredients. Talk about the different measurements and show them measuring cups and spoons. Help the children scrub the vegetables, cut them into small pieces, and add the required amount of each ingredient. Cook the soup in a crock pot. When it is finished cooking, the children can enjoy the soup at snack.

SCIENCE CENTER

■ **Beginning Learner:** Shucking Corn

Show ears of corn and let the children experience pulling back the corn husk to reveal the strings inside, called silk, and the kernels of corn on the cob. Explain that when you poke one of the kernels of corn, a liquid comes out. Provide samples of things made from corn, such as cornmeal, corn flakes, and cornstarch, and discuss how corn is used to make these products. Provide ears of fresh corn and demonstrate how to shuck corn. Give the children their own ears of corn to shuck and pans of water for them to scrub the corn. Invite the children to take their corn home and ask their parents to boil it for them for lunch or dinner.

■ ■ **Developing Learner:** Cutting Corn Off of the Cob

Show the children pictures of corn growing in a field and real ears of corn in the husk. Discuss the different parts of the corn as described for the beginning learner. Give each child an ear of corn and have her try to pull the kernels out with her fingers. Then, ask them to try cutting the kernels off of the cob using plastic knives, supervising them closely. When they are finished, invite them to put the kernels into a small plastic bag to take home for their parents to cook for them. Show the children popcorn kernels and have them compare those kernels to the ones from the cob.

■ ■ **Experienced Learner:** Shelling Peas

Provide fresh beans, peas, or black eyed peas in their shells. Talk about how the shell of the bean or pea acts as a protective covering for the bean or pea inside. Discuss that when eating green beans, people eat both the shell and the bean inside the shell, but with black eyed peas, people eat only the pea. Also talk about how beans grow and how they are picked on a farm. Whatever pea or bean you choose, also provide a cooked sample for the children to taste. Show the children how to shell the beans or peas. When they have finished shelling their beans or peas, the children may put them into plastic bags to bring home.

LANGUAGE/DRAMATIC PLAY CENTER

■ **Beginning Learner:** Grocery Store

Provide play fruits and vegetables, shopping baskets, grocery bags, cash registers, and play money for the children to use to role play working at a grocery store.

■ ■ **Developing Learner:** Shop, Weigh, and Pay

Provide actual fruits and vegetables and play scales, grocery bags, cash registers, shopping baskets, and play money for the children to role play working at a grocery store. The children can use the scales to weigh the fruits and vegetables. Provide stickers for the children to put on the produce to represent the identification stickers placed on fruits and vegetables at a real grocery store. When the children have finished their role play for the day, let them help cut the fresh vegetables and fruits into pieces and enjoy them for a healthy snack.

■
■ ■ **Experienced Learner:** Farmer's Market

Provide actual fruits and vegetables for the children to pretend to take to the farmer's market. Also provide small child-sized wagons and play wheelbarrows for transporting produce, sun bonnets, sunglasses, wicker baskets, and small tables to display the fruits and vegetables. Encourage the children to take turns being the farmer who sells the produce and the shopper who buys it. Also provide poster board and markers for the children to make signs for the produce stand. At the end of the day, let each child choose a fruit or vegetable from the farmer's market that they would like to take home to eat as a healthy treat.

VOCABULARY

beans, corn, cotton, crops, fruits, garden, germinate, grow, harvest, okra, plant, peas, potatoes, seeds, sow, turnips, vegetables, wheat

Reflect

Say to the children, "Yesterday, we learned about farmers and what an important job they have. Today, we learned about the fruits and vegetables that the farmer plants, grows, and sells on his farm. Tomorrow, we will learn about barns and scarecrows."

Extend and Enrich

Use the following ideas to extend and enrich what children know about the fruits and vegetables grown on the farms.

◆ Share *Growing Vegetable Soup* by Lois Ehlert with the children.

◆ Have fun reading the old folk tale *The Enormous Turnip* and then invite the children to role play the events of the story. There are many updated versions of this folktale available.

Barns and Scarecrows

Morning Circle

Greet the children with your face painted like a scarecrow and wearing a vest and scarecrow hat. As the children arrive, play square dance music. When all of the children have arrived, demonstrate some simple square dance steps like the ones that the scarecrow is doing in the book *Barn Dance* by Bill Martin Jr. and John Archambault. After square dancing, share the story with the children. This is a fun story about a scarecrow and

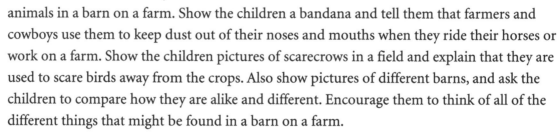

animals in a barn on a farm. Show the children a bandana and tell them that farmers and cowboys use them to keep dust out of their noses and mouths when they ride their horses or work on a farm. Show the children pictures of scarecrows in a field and explain that they are used to scare birds away from the crops. Also show pictures of different barns, and ask the children to compare how they are alike and different. Encourage them to think of all of the different things that might be found in a barn on a farm.

Storytime

Barn Dance by Bill Martin Jr. and John Archambault

Daily Center Activity Ideas

ART CENTER

■ **Beginning Learner:** Bandanas

Make bandanas with the children. Give each child a triangle of muslin or other cotton material (large enough to fit around their neck as a bandana). Provide farm-themed cookie cutters and paint and encourage the children to dip the cookie cutters in paint and then make designs on their bandana. When the paint has dried, help the children tie their bandanas around their necks.

Developing Learner: Scarecrow Vests

The scarecrow in the story wears overalls with fabric patches. Tell the children that they are going to make their own vest with patches like the ones in the story. Cut large paper bags into vests, one for each child. Cut scraps of fabric with pinking shears. Invite the children to glue the fabric scraps on their paper bag vests and then use markers to add designs. Help them cut fringe around the bottom edge of their vests.

Experienced Learner: Beaded Bandanas

Provide triangles of cotton muslin as described for the beginning. Demonstrate how to use scissors to cut strips of fringe about ½" thick along the edges of the fabric. Provide beads for the children to place on their fringed pieces. After the children add beads, help them tie a knot at the end of the fringed pieces to secure the beads. Let children add designs to their bandanas using watercolor markers.

MATH CENTER

Beginning Learner: Farm Animal Counting

Provide a toy barn, farm animals, and a die. Have the children take turns rolling the die and then placing that number of farm animals into the barn.

Developing Learner: Corn Counting Spinner

Provide deer corn, tweezers, a muffin tin, and a spinner with the numerals 1–5. Have the children take turns spinning the spinner and using the tweezers to place that number of deer corn kernels in the muffin tin.

Experienced Learner: Corn Counting Cards

Make yellow playdough using any simple playdough recipe (add yellow food coloring to make it yellow). Remove the green husks from fresh ears of corn. Have the children make a "fresh ear of corn" by rolling yellow playdough and placing it on two corn husks. Write the numerals 1–5 on index cards and place the cards in a pile. The child draws a numeral card from the pile and then presses that number of deer corn kernels into the playdough corn cob. Have the children take turns drawing cards and practicing their counting skills as they push the corn kernels into the playdough.

SCIENCE CENTER

Beginning Learner: Barn Painting

Provide small scraps of wood and wood shingles. Remove the labels from some crayons and show the children how to place paper on the wood and rub with a crayon to make barn rubbings.

■ ■ **Developing Learner:** Barn Door Painting

Provide scrap pieces of wood that resemble a barn door for the children to paint. Encourage them to paint designs on the wood with brushes. Encourage them to notice the grain of the wood as they paint and talk about the different textures.

■

■ ■ **Experienced Learner:** Barn Building

Provide scraps of wood, child-safe hammers, and nails for the children to use to build a barn. (**Safety note:** This activity needs to be closely supervised. Children should wear safety goggles when using tools, and adults should hammer each nail into the wood securely before the children begin to use their hammers.) The children can paint their "barns" when they are finished.

LANGUAGE/DRAMATIC PLAY CENTER

■ **Beginning Learner:** Scarecrow Faces/Shapes

Show the children the pictures of the scarecrow from the story. Ask them to pay special attention to the details on the scarecrow's face. Provide construction paper shapes (such as circles and triangles) and ask the children to make scarecrow faces on the table. After experimenting with making different scarecrow faces, let the children choose one to have painted on their face. Use face paint to paint the children's faces. Take pictures of the children with their faces painted and wearing their scarecrow vest costumes (made in the Art Center).

■ ■ **Developing Learner:** Scarecrow Faces/Designing

Invite the children to look at the scarecrow faces in *Barn Dance* for design ideas. Encourage them to draw scarecrow faces on paper and choose one to have painted on their face. Paint the children's faces to match their drawing. Provide handheld mirrors so the children can see themselves.

■

■ ■ **Experienced Learner:** Stuffing a Scarecrow

Read *The Little Scarecrow Boy* by Margaret Wise Brown to the children. Discuss the materials that are used to make scarecrows. Provide materials for the children to use to stuff a class scarecrow, including overalls, a flannel shirt, a straw hat, hay and straw, and rubber bands to secure the clothes. Help the children stuff a grocery bag with newspaper to make a head for the scarecrow. The children can use markers to decorate a face for the scarecrow. Use boots for the scarecrow's feet. The children will love to put the stuffed scarecrow in the reading center and have their pictures taken with him while they pretend to read him one of their favorite stories.

VOCABULARY

animals, barn, cattle, troughs, farm machinery, grain, hay, horse stables, pig sties, storage, straw

Reflect

Say to the children, "Yesterday, we learned about fruits and vegetables that are grown on a farm. Today, we learned about the barn on the farm and why it is so important to life on the farm. We also had fun learning about scarccrows and the important purpose that they serve in protecting the crops.

Extend and Enrich

Use the following ideas to extend and enrich what children know about the important role of barns on a farm.

◆ Plan a scarecrow dress-up day and ask the children to wear overalls, flannel shirts, and straw hats.

◆ Teach the children a simple square dance and play music as they practice their moves.

◆ Put straw or hay in the sand table or in a child-size swimming pool for the children to experience.

◆ Set up a barnyard bowling event. Prepare by placing white socks over the tops of 10 empty, 2-liter plastic bottles to make the bowling pins. Tape pictures of farm animals to the bowling pins. The children roll a ball toward the pins to see how many they can knock down.

◆ A great scarecrow book to share with the children is *The Lonely Scarecrow* by Tim Preston.

◆ Invite the children to make corn husk dolls by placing two husks from fresh corn long ways and two husks crossways. Help the children secure the husks by tying a piece of yarn in the middle and wrapping it back and forth over the area where the husks meet. The children can use scraps of fabric and yarn to make clothes for the dolls and yarn for the head and hair.

Things Found in Nature

Leaves and Trees

Morning Circle

Take the children outside on a nature walk. Give them small brown bags to store nature items that they find on their walk. While walking, encourage the children to notice the leaves on the trees and the ones that have fallen on the ground, as well as the twigs and branches that have fallen from the trees. Invite the children to pick up leaves, twigs, acorns, and any small nature objects that they find on their nature walk. When the children return to the classroom, discuss the items that they found and then share the story, *Fall Leaves Fall* by Zoe Hall.

Storytime

Fall Leaves Fall by Zoe Hall

Daily Center Activity Ideas

ART CENTER

Beginning Learner: Fall Painted Leaves

Give each child a brown construction paper tree trunk shape. Provide red, yellow, and orange tempera paint and small sponges cut into rectangles. Encourage the children to glue their tree trunks on construction paper and then dip the sponges into one color of paint at a time to paint "leaves" on their trees.

Developing Learner: Leaf Rubbings

Have the children choose two of their leaves from the nature walk and then show them how to use unwrapped crayons to make leaf rubbings.

Experienced Learner: Fall Painted Trees

Paint the children's arms from wrist to elbow with brown paint and then have them place their arms on paper to make the trunk of a tree. Show the children how to dip their hands in yellow paint and make yellow handprints for leaves, and then repeat the process using orange paint and red paint to make fall-colored handprint leaves on their trees.

MATH CENTER

■ **Beginning Learner:** How Many Leaves?

Prepare for this activity by cutting out five tree trunk shapes from brown construction paper and gluing them onto white construction paper. Write one numeral from 1–5 on each tree trunk. Provide actual or silk leaves for the children to place on the trees. Ask the children to place the tree trunks in numerical order (1–5) and then look at the numeral on each tree trunk and place that number of leaves on the corresponding tree.

■ ■ **Developing Learner:** How Many Leaves? II

Prepare the activity as described for the beginning learner but make 10 tree trunks and number them from 1–10. Encourage the children to play the game as described for the beginning learner, but provide more leaves for the children to use to count and place on the tree trunks.

■

■ ■ **Experienced Learner:** Leaf Books

Cut white construction paper in half and give each child 10 pieces. Encourage the children to cut out 10 tree trunk shapes from brown construction paper and glue one shape on each piece of white construction paper. Have the children write one numeral on the top of each page (from 1–10). Provide numerals for the children to look at as they write. Ask them to put their pages in order by number and then glue either real leaves or silk plant leaves on each page according to the numeral at the top of the page. When they are finished, help the children use a hole punch to poke two holes in each page. Give each child two metal rings to put through the holes to make their own leaf counting book. Substitute yarn if you do not have metal rings.

SCIENCE CENTER

■ **Beginning Learner:** Thirsty Flowers

Demonstrate the concept of how trees and plants get their food, water, and nutrients through their roots. Place a white carnation in a glass of water and then add food coloring to the water. Explain to the children that it will take several days before they notice that the carnation is absorbing the water through its petals and leaves. Give each child a white carnation and a small glass. Help them add food coloring and water to the glass and then watch this experiment over several days. Talk about what they observe.

■ ■ **Developing Learner:** Preserving Nature Items

Make nature books using the items that the children collected on their nature walk. Give the children small, plastic bags and ask them to place a leaf, stick, or flower inside a bag and seal it shut. When the children are finished placing their nature items into bags, help them use a hole punch to make two small holes in the left-hand side of each bag (with the zipper part on the right hand side—this will act as a stiff edge that will assist the child with turning the pages). When they are finished, help them tie yarn or ribbon through the holes and make a knot or bow to keep their bags together. **Note:** Use clear contact paper instead of plastic bags, if desired.

■
■ ■ **Experienced Learner:** Plant "Tattoos"

Discuss how important sunlight is for trees and their leaves. Provide a small potted plant for each child. Give the children stickers and encourage them to put a sticker on one or two of the plant's leaves. Place the plants on a sunny windowsill. In a week or so, carefully remove the stickers. The spot underneath the sticker should be yellow to show that the spot was not getting sunlight. The leaf could not make chlorophyll in that spot so it turned yellow.

LANGUAGE/DRAMATIC PLAY CENTER

■ **Beginning Learner:** Raking Leaves

Provide real fall leaves (or fake leaves purchased from a craft supply store), garden gloves, trash bags, and small rakes. Invite the children to walk in the leaves before they start raking. Encourage them to listen to and describe the sound that the leaves make beneath their feet.

■ ■ **Developing Learner:** Different Kinds of Leaves

Provide a variety of different kinds of leaves (magnolia, oak, evergreen, and so on) or take the children outside and encourage them to find a variety of different kinds of leaves. When the children return to the classroom, encourage them to compare the leaves and discuss their different colors, shapes, and sizes. Provide science books with pictures of different leaves and encourage the children to try to find pictures in the books that match the leaves that they have found. Encourage the children to draw pictures of the leaves they found.

■ ■ ■ **Experienced Learner:** Leaf People/Leaf Stories

Provide leaves from different types of silk greenery from which the children can choose. Each child glues a leaf on construction paper and then uses markers, crayons, or colored pencils to add details to create a leaf animal or a leaf person. After their leaf creations are finished, encourage the children to dictate stories about their creations. When they are finished, they can share their stories with their friends. **Note:** The stories can be taken home or combined in a class book that the children can enjoy at school.

VOCABULARY

autumn, bark, branches, brown, evergreen, fall, falling leaves, foliage tree, grow, leaves, living, seasons, maple leaf, oak leaf, pine needle, pine tree, pinecone rake, ridges, roots, rough, smooth, soil, tree sap, tree trunk

Reflect

Say to the children, "Today we learned about leaves and trees. Tomorrow we will learn about what happens when trees fall to the ground and become 'log hotels' for small animals and other creatures."

Extend and Enrich

Use the following ideas to extend and enrich what children know about leaves and trees.

◆ Show the children pine branches and pine needles. Invite them to use a small bundle of pine needles as a paintbrush. Tie the pine needles together in a bundle using a rubber band to make them easier to use.

◆ Show pictures of different kinds of trees, and then go outside and see if the children can identify some of them.

◆ Provide logs from fallen trees so that the children can see the rings inside and examine the bark and outer covering of the tree.

Acorns and Oaks

Morning Circle

Before the children arrive in the morning, make a path of acorns on the floor that leads to the circle time area. Talk about acorns with the children. Explain that oak trees have acorns and that every acorn is a seed that might become a new tree. Engage the children in a discussion of how they think acorns and seeds get from one place to another, and talk about how planting them might result in a tree. Share the story *The Acorn and the Oak Tree* with the children.

Storytime

The Acorn and the Oak Tree by Lori Froeb

Daily Center Activity Ideas

ART CENTER

▪ **Beginning Learner:** Felt Squirrels

Prepare beforehand by gathering tan, brown, grey, and white felt. Cut out shapes that can be assembled to make squirrels, including a bodies, front feet, back feet, ears, eyes, noses and tails. Show the children pictures of squirrels. Encourage them to assemble the felt cutouts to make squirrels and glue them to paper.

▪▪ **Developing Learner:** Squirrels and Oak Trees

Provide felt cutouts as described for the beginning learner and real or silk oak leaves. Encourage the children to assemble their squirrels and glue them on paper. Invite them to glue leaves and real acorns to their pictures. Have them finish their work by drawing oak trees on their pictures.

▪
▪▪ **Experienced Learner:** Sandpaper Squirrels

Cut out squirrel patterns from sandpaper. (Use the squirrel picture in the book for a pattern.) Show the children how to place a piece of white paper over the sandpaper cutout and rub an unwrapped crayon over it to make a rubbing. Children can add features to the squirrels using crayons or markers.

MATH CENTER

■ **Beginning Learner:** Acorn Game/Probability

Provide the tops of three plastic eggs and an acorn. Hide the acorn under one of the egg tops and shuffle them around. The children try to guess which egg top the acorn is under. Play the game several times and then let a child be the one to hide the acorn and shuffle the tops. Explain to the children that they have a one in three chance of guessing correctly each time. Count how many times they guess. **Note:** Make sure to keep this noncompetitive.

■ ■ **Developing Learner:** Feed the Squirrels/Counting

Cut 10 squirrels out of construction paper (use the squirrel in the book for a pattern) and gather 10 acorns. Encourage the children to practice one-to-one correspondence by giving each squirrel one of the acorns.

■
■ ■ **Experienced Learner:** Acorn Count

Provide 11 small wicker baskets or plastic bowls and place a number card (0–10) in each bowl. Provide 55 acorns for the children to use. (If acorns are not available, substitute something similar such as pebbles or store-bought nuts.) Encourage the children to arrange the bowls in numerical order from 0–10 and then count the correct number of acorns and put them in each bowl.

SCIENCE CENTER

■ **Beginning Learner:** Hiding Acorns

Place potting soil or dirt in the sand table and provide acorns for the children to "bury" or hide in the dirt like squirrels do.

■ ■ **Developing Learner:** Planting Acorns

Provide small clear plastic cups, dirt or potting soil, and acorns for the children to plant. Provide a sunny windowsill or place where the children can place their plants to get sunlight. Provide water and eye droppers each day so the children can water their plants. Tell the children that it will take several days or even a week for their plants to begin to sprout and grow.

■
■ ■ **Experienced Learner:** All Kinds of Nuts

Provide an assortment of different kinds of nuts for the children to explore, such as pecans, walnuts, hazelnuts, pistachio nuts, and other kinds of nuts found at the grocery store. (**Safety note:** Before doing this activity, be sure no one in the class is allergic to nuts.) Provide nutcrackers and nut pickers for the children to see inside of the various nuts. Discuss the names of the nuts and what they look like on the inside. Make comparisons between the colors, textures, and even the taste of the various nuts. Encourage the children to sort the nuts by size or shape, texture, or taste. After an initial exploration, the children could make a class or individual graph of their findings to record their descriptions of the nuts.

LANGUAGE/DRAMATIC PLAY CENTER

■ Beginning Learner: Mouse Detectives

Provide a small live or silk tree to represent the oak tree in the story and footprint cutouts on the floor leading away from the tree. Hide acorns in the center and encourage the children to pretend to be either the squirrel (hiding and burying the nuts) or the mice (following the squirrel's tracks to find the hidden acorns). Provide magnifying glasses and other detective props to enhance the play.

■ ■ Developing Learner: Looking for Clues

Set up a mystery clue-finding game for the children by attaching written "clues" to a silk tree or plant or by placing the clues in the pot under the tree. Encourage the children to read the clues (with adult help as necessary) and follow them to find the hidden acorns.

■
■ ■ Experienced Learner: Mystery Story Starters

Provide the children with written story starters so they can write their own mystery detective stories. Discuss the children's ideas with them, and help them write their ideas on paper and illustrate them. When the stories are finished, encourage the children to share their mystery stories with their friends. If desired, use the stories to make a class book.

VOCABULARY

acorns, bury, bushy tail, detective, fur, ground, meadow, mystery, nature, nuts, oak, pod, squirrels

Reflect

Say to the children, "Yesterday we learned about leaves and trees and their importance in providing homes for animals. Today we learned about acorns and oak trees. Tomorrow we will learn about flowers found in nature."

Extend and Enrich

Use the following ideas to extend and enrich what children know about acorns and oak trees.
◆ Take the children outside on a nature walk where there are oak trees. Ask the children to try to find acorns. Encourage the children to use the tops from acorns and their imaginations to make fanciful art creations.
◆ Provide mouse headbands, acorns, and other props for the children to use to retell the story.

Flowers

Morning Circle

Buy a real flower for each child in the class. Greet the children carrying these flowers in a bouquet. As each child arrives, invite him to choose a flower from the bouquet and carry it to the circle time area. During circle time, show the children a bouquet of mixed flowers. Pass the bouquet around for the children to smell. Discuss the names and parts of the flowers. Ask the children to name some special occasions that people send or receive flowers, such as birthdays, Valentine's Day, Mother's Day, welcoming a new baby, and when someone is sick at home or in the hospital. After the discussion, share the story with the children.

Storytime

Flower Garden by Eve Bunting

Daily Center Activity Ideas

ART CENTER

■ **Beginning Learner:** Sponge-Painted Flowers
Provide sponges cut into flower shapes, paint, and paper. The children dip the sponge in paint and make flower shapes on paper.

■ ■ **Developing Learner:** Handprint Flowers
Provide several trays or pans of different colors of paint. Encourage the children to place their hands in the paint and then make five handprints in a circle to form a giant flower. Show the children how to use green construction paper to cut a long stem and leaves to glue to their flowers.

■
■ ■ **Experienced Learner:** Flower Gardens
Provide a variety of colors of tissue paper squares (6" x 6") and green chenille sticks for the children to make tissue paper flowers. Demonstrate how to gather four tissue paper squares in the middle and squeeze tightly around the bottom to form a flower. Show the children how to wind a green chenille stick around the bottom of the tissue paper flower. Provide Styrofoam cups to use as vases and markers or stickers to decorate the vases. Help the children poke the stems into the bottoms of the cups.

MATH CENTER

■ **Beginning Learner:** Flower Count/Matching

Cut out five stems from green construction paper and five flowers from colored construction paper. Write a numeral from 1–5 on each stem and 1–5 on each flower. Encourage the children to match the numerals on the stems with the numerals on the flowers. Invite them to glue the flowers and stems on paper.

■ ■ **Developing Learner:** Flower Count/Ordering 1–5

Cut out flower petals from construction paper and write the numerals 1–5 on them. Provide green construction paper for the children to make stems and leaves to glue on paper to make a flower garden. The children place the flowers in numerical order from 1–5.

■
■ ■ **Experienced Learner:** Flower Count/Ordering 1–10

Provide a stack of flower cutouts and construction paper for the children to make flower garden pictures. Have the children choose 10 flowers and write a numeral 1–10 on each flower. Ask them to arrange their flowers in order from 1–10 on a large sheet of construction paper and use green markers to add stems and leaves to their flowers.

SCIENCE CENTER

Before doing this activity, purchase one small terra cotta pot for each child. After this activity, let the children plant flowers in their pots and give them as gifts for special occasions.

■ **Beginning Learner:** Sponge Painting Pots

Provide terra cotta pots and small sponges cut into rectangles the size of a domino. Squeeze the rectangle sponges between clothespins for the children to use to paint their pots. Have the children dip their sponges and paint designs on their pots.

■ ■ **Developing Learner:** Decoupage Pots

Provide a terra cotta pot for each child and small squares of brightly colored tissue paper. Encourage the children to glue the squares of tissue paper on their pots to cover the entire surface. When the tissue paper has dried, encourage the children to paint a thin coat of glue and water over the tissue paper to adhere it to the pots permanently.

■
■ ■ **Experienced Learner:** Brush Painting Pots

Provide a terra cotta pot for each child and brightly colored acrylic paint or tempera paint and brushes for the children to use to paint designs on their pots.

LANGUAGE/DRAMATIC PLAY CENTER

■ **Beginning Learner:** "Planting" Flowers

Provide silk flowers and an empty window box container and Styrofoam and encourage the children to "plant" the flowers in the window box.

■ ■ **Developing Learner:** Flower Shop/Silk Flowers

Provide single stems of different colors of silk flowers and take index cards and markers and draw colored dots on the cards that represent the colors of the silk flowers. Provide plastic vases and encourage the children to pick a card with colored dots and assemble the colored silk flowers in the vases according to the dots on the index cards to make a bouquet.

■
■ ■ **Experienced Learner:** Flower Shop/Real Flowers

Provide real carnations, baby's breath and greenery, and vases for the children to practice arranging flowers into bouquets. Provide gardening magazines or pictures of flower arrangements for children to use as examples for making their arrangements.

VOCABULARY

arrangement, bouquet, daffodil, dried flowers, field, florist, flower shop, flowers, garden, grow, leaves, lily, orchid, petal, plant, pollen, rose, scent, silk flowers, stamen, stem, soil, sunflower, vase, wildflowers

Reflect

Say to the children, "Yesterday we learned about squirrels and nuts. Today we explored the wonderful world of flowers that are found in nature. Tomorrow we'll learn about beautiful butterflies."

Extend and Enrich

Use the following ideas to extend and enrich what children know about flowers.

- Provide gardening catalogs and magazines for children to cut out pictures to make a floral collage. Also provide flower stickers, if available.
- Place flower petals with different textures (roses, sunflowers, carnations, lilies) in the sand and water table for the children to explore and describe. After the exploration, encourage the children to choose some of their favorite petals and glue them to paper to create a new flower. Have them think of a name for their new flower creation.
- Brainstorm all of the places that flower designs are found, including wallpaper, clothing, furniture upholstery, tablecloths, curtains, bedspreads, and sheets.
- Arrange a single flower in a vase and encourage the children to paint a picture of the flower (still life) or dictate a story about it. Encourage the children to use descriptive words for the flower.

Butterflies

Morning Circle

Bring in a live butterfly in a butterfly habitat and a milkweed plant with caterpillars or chrysalises for the children to observe. Explain to the children that caterpillars are baby butterflies and they feed on milkweed and other weeds. Provide pictures of butterflies and discuss the varieties of butterflies and the differences in their colors.

Storytime

Waiting for Wings by Lois Ehlert

Daily Center Activity Ideas

ART CENTER

 **Beginning Learner:** Painted Butterflies

Provide white construction paper, bright colors of tempera paint, and spoons for the children to use to paint butterflies. Encourage them to spoon small amounts of tempera paint on their papers, fold the papers in half, and gently rub the papers along the crease to smear the paint on the inside. The children open their papers to reveal a beautiful design. When the paint has dried, cut the design into a butterfly shape and provide black construction paper antennae for the children to glue to their butterflies.

Developing Learner: Contact Paper Butterflies

Provide 8 ½" x 11" contact paper. Encourage the children to place small squares of colored tissue paper on the sticky side of the contact paper. When the sheet of contact paper is filled with colored tissue paper squares, help the children place the other side of the contact paper on top of the sticky side. Provide butterfly stencils and show the children how to use a black marker to trace the stencil on their contact paper and then cut on the black line to make a butterfly. Encourage them to cut out antennae from black construction paper to glue to their butterflies. Have them add a black line down the middle of each butterfly.

Experienced Learner: Colored Tissue Paper Butterflies

Provide brightly colored tissue paper rectangles (6" x 8") for the children to layer on top of each other. Show them how to layer about five rectangles and then squeeze them together to secure in the middle with a clothespin. Invite them to use their fingers to gently open the tissue paper wings of each butterfly. Provide chenille sticks for antennae, wiggle eyes, and crayons for coloring the clothespins black.

MATH CENTER

■ **Beginning Learner:** Monarch Caterpillar Patterns

Show the children pictures of monarch caterpillars, which have a beautiful black, white, and yellow pattern. Provide construction paper strips in these colors for the children to roll into paper chains to form a monarch caterpillar. Show the children how to use tape to secure their chains together to form the black/white/yellow repeating pattern found on the monarch caterpillar.

■ ■ **Developing Learner:** Eggs on Leaves

Provide green construction paper leaf shapes with the numerals 1–10 written on them (one numeral on each leaf) and tiny white pompoms to represent eggs. Encourage the children to look at the numeral on the leaf and count that number of "eggs" to place on the leaf. Provide tweezers or tongs for them to pick up the eggs and place them on the leaves. Make sure they arrange the leaves in numerical order before beginning to place the eggs.

■
■ ■ **Experienced Learner:** Pompom Caterpillars

Before the activity, make caterpillar pattern cards by drawing circles in different color patterns, such as red/yellow/red/yellow or yellow/blue/yellow/yellow/blue/yellow. Provide medium-sized pompoms in many different colors. Ask the children to choose a pattern card and then use tongs to pick up pompoms and recreate the pattern on the card. Let each child choose his favorite caterpillar pattern and recreate it with pompoms, glue, and a sentence strip. Invite the children to draw feet, eyes, and antennae using markers.

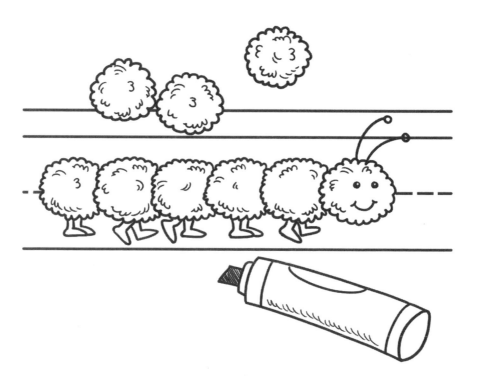

SCIENCE CENTER

Beginning Learner: Four Stages of a Butterfly

Before doing this activity, make four life-cycle picture cards: a card with a leaf and an egg on it, a card with a caterpillar crawling on a leaf, a chrysalis, and a butterfly. Use the book *Butterfly* by Susan Canizares as a helpful resource. Explain to the children that butterflies go through four stages in their life cycles. Encourage them to look at the cards, mix them up, and then put them in order to tell the story of a butterfly's life. Provide crayons and paper for the children to draw butterfly pictures.

Developing Learner: Butterfly Feeding Dish

Help the children make a butterfly feeding dish to place in the school garden. Butterflies are attracted to bright colors, especially purple, yellow, and white. Provide purple, yellow, and white flowers and fresh fruit. Invite the children to use plastic knives to cut up the fruits. Place the flowers and fruit in the feeding dish, and put it in the school garden to feed some hungry butterflies. Remind the children to check on their dish when they are outside or observe it while looking out a classroom window.

Experienced Learner: Make a Chrysalis

Provide thin green yarn or silky thread and a long pillow or soft object for the children to wrap the silky thread around to form a chrysalis. **Note:** Knee-high stockings filled with cotton batting also work well to form individual chrysalises.

LANGUAGE/DRAMATIC PLAY CENTER

Obtain a copy of the book, *Clara Caterpillar* by Pamela Duncan Edwards.

Beginning Learner: Butterfly Life Cycle Role Play

Share the story *Clara Caterpillar* with the children. Provide the props for the children to role play the four stages of a butterfly's life. Props can include a giant leaf cut from green bulletin board paper and white cotton batting that the children can roll into an egg shape, pillows in bright colors (yellow and green) that can be placed on a child's back to be a caterpillar, a piece of green shiny fabric for a child to wear to be a caterpillar in a chrysalis, and a set of butterfly wings.

Developing Learner: Butterfly Life Cycle Photographs and Storybooks

Do the activity as described for the beginning learner. Take pictures of each child as he role plays the four stages of the butterfly life cycle. When the pictures are developed, help each child put the pictures in order and glue one picture on a page to make a four-page butterfly life cycle book. Write the words *egg, caterpillar, chrysalis,* and *butterfly* on index cards and ask the children to copy the words on the top of the pages of their books. Help staple the four pages together to make a butterfly life cycle book.

Note: If there are too many children in a class to take individual photos, take pictures of the children together and use larger paper, such as poster board, for a class book.

■ ■ Experienced Learner: Words That Begin with "C"

Share the story *Clara Caterpillar* with the children. Ask the children to find as many "C" words as they can and make a list of the words they find. Help the children use the list of words to make up their own caterpillar stories. Encourage the children to illustrate their stories. Combine them into a class "caterpillar" book for everyone to enjoy.

VOCABULARY

butterfly, caterpillar, change, chrysalis, cocoon, flight, flutter, fragile, graceful, grow, leaves, metamorphosis, milkweed, net, transformation, wings

Reflect

Say to the children, "Yesterday we learned about some of the flowers that are found in nature. Today we learned about butterflies and what a wonderful part of nature that they are. Tomorrow we will learn about deer that are found in nature and what gentle creatures they are."

Extend and Enrich

Use the following ideas to extend and enrich what children know about butterflies.

◆ Provide straws and an orange for each child. Help the children poke the straw into the orange. Drink the juice, much like a butterfly uses its proboscis to drink nectar from flowers.

◆ Take a field trip to a butterfly sanctuary and observe all of the many kinds and colors of butterflies.

◆ Provide a collection of wooden beads and string for the children to make bead "caterpillars."

Deer

Morning Circle

Provide photographs or pictures from magazines of live deer. If available, show the children antlers and a deer hide. Discuss with the children different kinds of deer and the unique characteristics of deer, such as where they live, what they look like, and what they eat. After the discussion, share the story selection for the day.

Storytime

Stranger in the Woods by Carl R. Sams II and Jean Stoick

Daily Center Activity Ideas

ART CENTER

■ **Beginning Learner:** Handprint Antlers

Provide brown paint in a shallow pan. Encourage the children to place their hands into the paint and make handprints on paper to resemble deer antlers.

■ ■ **Developing Learner:** Deer Pictures/Painting

Use the deer pictures in the story to make deer heads and faces from brown or tan construction paper, and cut them out. Have the children glue their deer heads on paper. Invite the children to dip their hands into brown paint and then make handprint antlers. Let the children cut out noses, eyes, and ears from construction paper to add to their deer pictures.

■
■ ■ **Experienced Learner:** Deer Pictures/Tracing

Trace each child's left and right hand on brown construction paper. Have the children cut out their handprints. Provide brown and tan construction paper for each child to cut out a deer head and glue on her paper. Encourage the children to glue their handprints on either side of their deer heads to make antlers. Provide construction paper to make eyes, ears, and noses.

■ **Beginning Learner:** Antler Count

To prepare for this activity, find small tree limbs with different numbers of branches that could be used to resemble deer antlers. Trim the limbs so that they are small enough to use in the classroom. Place playdough in the bottom of a margarine tub and push the tree branch into the playdough so that it stands up. Make several sets of "antlers." Ask the children to count the number of branches on each antler. Encourage the children to find a magnetic numeral that matches that and the number of branches place the numeral in front of the antler. (**Note:** You may wish to use the paper deer faces from the Art Center activity with the antlers.) Position a face between two tree limbs so that it looks like a real deer.

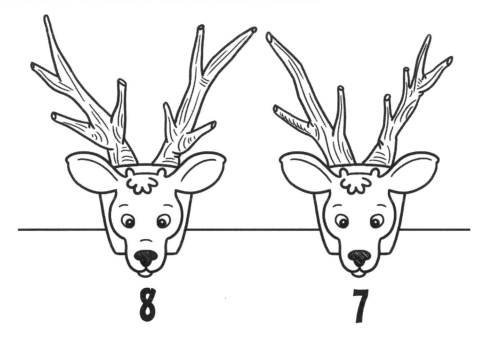

■ ■ **Developing Learner:** Antler Ring Toss

To prepare, find a sturdy tree limb with lots of branches on it. Try to find one that resembles a set of deer antlers. Secure the tree branch in a coffee can filled with rocks. Make plastic rings by cutting out the centers of large plastic margarine tub lids. Have the children try to toss the plastic rings onto the deer "antlers." Count how many times they get the rings on the antlers.

■
■ ■ **Experienced Learner:** Counting Tiptoes

Play a variation of "Red Light, Green Light." Tell the children to pretend that they are approaching a deer in the forest, so they must move very quietly and carefully. One child is the caller who turns away from the group and says, "Approach." The other children move carefully and quietly towards the caller. When the caller turns around, the children stop. The children continue until they reach the "deer." Encourage the children to keep track of the number of footsteps it takes them to reach the deer. How many did it take?

SCIENCE CENTER

Beginning Learner: Deer Corn

Place deer corn in the sand and water table for the children to explore. Add plastic measuring spoons, cups, and sifters to enhance the exploration. When the children are finished exploring the deer corn, it can be used for other activities or placed outside for the wildlife to enjoy. (**Safety note:** Supervise closely to ensure children do not put the corn in their mouths.)

Developing Learner: Fruit Tasting

Deer in the wild eat fruits such as pears, berries, and leaves. Show the children a variety of pears and discuss the fact that pears grow on trees. If desired, also provide berries and explain that berries grow on bushes or vines. Encourage the children to taste the different types of pears and/or berries. Record their preferences on a large classroom chart. At the end of the day, look at the chart to see which type of pear or berry received the most votes as the children's favorite.

Experienced Learner: Kinds of Salt

Deer enjoy eating salt. Some animals need salt in their diets to keep them healthy. Show the children examples of different kinds of salt, such as table salt, seasoned salt, and rock salt and talk about the uses for each type of salt. Provide favorite salty snacks such as pretzel rods (with salt) and popcorn. As the children taste these snack foods, explain that there are taste buds on our tongues that help us to taste salty foods. Remind the children that although the deer in the story ate salt right from the little girl's hand, people usually don't eat salt straight from the box or shaker.

LANGUAGE/DRAMATIC PLAY CENTER

Beginning Learner: Which Hand?

Explain to the children that it is often difficult and possibly unsafe to approach animals in the wild. If one does approach an animal, however, he should walk up to the animal slowly, keeping his hands behind his back or down at the side so the animal does not feel threatened. Show the children how to play the game by placing both of their hands behind their backs and then hiding an object in one hand. Have a friend guess which hand holds the object. The children take turns hiding objects and guessing which hand.

Developing Learner: Pear Alphabet Match

Make an alphabet matching game. Cut out pear shapes from construction paper and write uppercase letters on them. Make another set of pears and write lowercase letters on them. Encourage the children to match the uppercase pears to the lowercase pears.

Experienced Learner: Pear Letter Mix-Up

Provide green, pear-shaped pieces of construction paper, and have the children write one letter of their names on each pear. For example, Madison would take seven pears and use a marker to write an "M" on one pear, an "A" on the next pear, and so on. Encourage the children to mix up all of their pears, place them on the table in front of them, and spell their names. Provide sandwich bags or envelopes for the children to take home their name pears.

VOCABULARY

antler, buck, caribou, corn, deer, doe, fawn, forest, hide, horns, pear, rack, reindeer, salt

Reflect

Say to the children, "Yesterday we learned about butterflies and their life cycle. Today, we learned about deer and how they live in nature."

Extend and Enrich

Use the following ideas to extend and enrich what children know about deer.

- ◆ Encourage children to take a nature hike with their parents to look for deer footprints.
- ◆ Provide several sets of antlers and have the children compare the number of points on each.
- ◆ Provide a deer skin for the children to examine.

Things with Seeds

Strawberries

Morning Circle

When the children arrive at school, greet them at the door carrying a large basket of washed strawberries with the stems removed. Invite the children to reach inside the basket and choose a strawberry and take it to the circle to enjoy as a treat. In circle, show the children the basket of fresh strawberries and ask them what they are looking at. Lead the children in a discussion of the characteristics of strawberries. Focus on what the strawberries look like, smell like, and how they taste and feel. Also, look at the berry basket that the strawberries came in and talk about why it is made that way.

Storytime

The Little Mouse, the Red Ripe Strawberry and the Big Hungry Bear by Don and Audrey Wood

Daily Center Activity Ideas

(**Safety note:** Many of the activities for this day involve fresh strawberries, so be sure that none of the children in your class has strawberry allergies before doing the activities.)

ART CENTER

■ **Beginning Learner:** Strawberry Basket Prints

Provide empty strawberry baskets and brown paint on a shallow tray. Encourage the children to dip the baskets into the paint and make basket prints on paper. After the paint is dry, children can use crayons to draw strawberries on the prints.

■ ■ **Developing Learner:** Strawberry Fingerpaint

Mix red and white fingerpaint and add strawberry flavoring. Invite the children to fingerpaint on white paper. When the paintings are dry, help the children cut the strawberry-scented paper into large strawberry shapes and encourage them to add green construction paper stems. The children can also use a black crayon or marker to add seeds to their strawberry paintings.

■
■ ■ **Experienced Learner:** Strawberry Window Clings

Show the children how to make window clings. Give each child two sheets of contact paper about 6" x 6" and different kinds of red paper such as tissue paper, construction paper, wallpaper, and scrapbook paper. Help the children peel off the backing from one of their pieces of contact paper. Encourage the children to tear the red paper into small pieces and place them on the sticky surface of the contact paper. When the square of contact paper is filled with red paper, help the children place the other piece of contact paper on top. Have the children trace a strawberry-shaped stencil on the contact paper square and cut it out. Attach the strawberries to a window with tape.

MATH CENTER

▨ **Beginning Learner:** Counting Strawberry Seeds

Provide fresh strawberries and magnifying glasses for the children to examine the strawberries. Discuss with the children that the seeds are found on the outside of the fruit as opposed to the inside of the fruit. Talk about the number of seeds on a strawberry. There are many seeds, but encourage the children to count as many as they can. When they are done examining the strawberries, the children may eat them.

▨▨ **Developing Learner:** Comparing Fruit Seeds

Provide fresh strawberries for the children to taste. Discuss with the children that the seeds on the strawberry are found on the outside of the fruit. Show the children how they can use a toothpick to "dig" out the seeds. Provide other fruits, such as a banana, grapes, a kiwi, an apple, a watermelon slice, and oranges, and encourage the children to locate and count their seeds. After the children find the seeds, give a small taste of each fruit.

Experienced Learner: Fruit Seed Chart

Provide a variety of fruits as described in the developing learner section. Ask the children to find the seeds in each fruit. When they are finished, discuss the location of the seeds, the sizes of the seeds, and the number of seeds in each fruit. Write the names of the various fruits on the top of a chart. Have the children count the number of seeds in each fruit and write that number under the name of the fruit. After counting the number of seeds, cut the fruits into small pieces so the children can taste each one.

SCIENCE CENTER

Beginning Learner: Examining Strawberries

Provide magnifying glasses and strawberries and encourage the children to examine the strawberries. Discuss how the strawberries look and how they feel. Encourage the children to smell the strawberries and describe what they smell like. Provide small tubs of water for the children to wash the berries.

Developing Learner: Making Strawberry Jam

Provide fresh strawberries and small tubs of water for the children to wash the strawberries. Give the children potato mashers to mash the clean strawberries. Have the children add sugar to the mashed strawberries and stir. Provide crackers and plastic knives for the children to taste the strawberry jam mixture that they have made. Also provide store-bought strawberry jam for the children to taste. Compare the store-bought jam with the homemade jam mixture.

Experienced Learner: Strawberry Jam Recipe

Locate a recipe for strawberry jam in a cookbook, and make a rebus recipe poster with pictures of the ingredients. Provide the ingredients and give each child a small bowl. Encourage the children to follow the picture directions on the rebus recipe and make jam. Also provide crackers so the children can taste their jam. Provide small baby food jars so the children can take some of the jam home to share with their families.

LANGUAGE/DRAMATIC PLAY CENTER

Beginning Learner: Strawberry Shortcake

Give each child half of an unfrosted yellow cupcake or a piece of store-bought pound cake or angel food cake. Invite the children to add fresh, sliced strawberries and whipped cream to make individual strawberry shortcakes. Encourage them to describe what they are doing and tasting. Use descriptive adjectives when talking about the flavor, texture, smell, and look of the shortcakes, and encourage children to do the same.

■ ■ **Developing Learner:** Strawberry Shortcake Cookie

Provide children with a sugar cookie, a canister of whipped cream, and fresh strawberries. Help them to cut the strawberries into small pieces using a plastic knife. Encourage the children to place a few cut pieces of strawberries on their sugar cookie and squirt the whipped cream on top to make their own strawberry shortcake. After the children enjoy their strawberry shortcake treats, encourage them to use crayons and paper to make their own recipe cards to take home with them.

■

■ ■ **Experienced Learner:** Making Whipped Cream

Give each child a slice of shortcake on a plate. Encourage the children to use plastic knives to slice strawberries into pieces and place them on their slice of cake. Provide a mixing bowl, a hand beater, and whipping cream for the children to make whipped topping. Encourage the children to watch carefully as the liquid whipping cream begins to thicken. (**Note:** Whipping cream thickens much faster if the bowl, the cream, and the beater are all very cold.) Discuss how the beaters whip air into the cream and make it appear thicker as it begins to fill the bowl. Let the children add sugar to the whipped cream to sweeten it. Ask the children to taste the whipping cream before adding sugar and after to compare the tastes. Let the children add the whipped cream to their shortcakes. Provide a picture recipe card for the children to copy and take home so they can make their special strawberry shortcake treat for their families.

VOCABULARY

half, jam, jelly, juicy, red, seeds, shortcake, stem, sour, strawberry, strawberry patch, sweet

Reflect

Say to the children, "Today we learned about strawberries. We learned that strawberries have seeds on the outside, and that they taste good plain, in jam, or on top of shortcake with whipped cream. Tomorrow we will learn about sunflowers, which have lots of tiny seeds."

Extend and Enrich

Use the following ideas to extend and enrich what children know about strawberries.

◆   Show the children how to weave ribbons and strings through berry baskets.

Sunflowers

Morning Circle

Provide a large vase of fresh sunflowers or a vase of silk sunflowers. Discuss with the children the unique aspects of sunflowers. Include in your discussion the giant heads of sunflowers, their many seeds, and their long stems. Share with the children the story *Sunflower House.*

Storytime

Sunflower House by Eve Bunting

Daily Center Activity Ideas

ART CENTER

■ Beginning Learner: Paper Plate Sunflowers

Give each child a paper plate and yellow petals cut from construction paper. Encourage the children to glue the petals on the paper plates to make sunflowers. Place acorns or pecans in sandwich bags and invite the children to pound the bags using a rubber mallet. Glue the seed mixture to the middle of the yellow petals to resemble the center of sunflowers. (**Safety note:** Check for allergies before doing this activity.)

■ ■ Developing Learner: Paint a Sunflower Mural

Provide a large sheet of white art paper and yellow and green paint. Encourage the children to paint a classroom mural of sunflowers in a giant garden.

■
■ ■ Experienced Learner: Paper Sunflower Garden

Provide a paper plate and yellow petals and sunflower seeds as described for the beginning learner. Invite the children to cut out a long stem and green leaves from green construction paper to add to their giant sunflower. The children may want to glue their sunflower to a large sheet of white butcher paper or construction paper to add stability. Display the giant sunflowers to make a classroom garden.

MATH CENTER

■ Beginning Learner: Paper Sunflowers/Petal Count

Glue yellow construction paper petals to yellow paper plates and adding sunflower seeds in the middle to make 10 sunflowers. Glue a different number of petals (1–10) on each flower.

Give the children an appropriate number of sunflowers, 5 or 10 depending on their abilities. Encourage the children to put the sunflowers in numerical order according to the number of petals.

Developing Learner: Real Sunflowers/Petal Count
Provide a vase of real or silk sunflowers. Encourage the children to choose a flower and count the number of petals it has. Record the number of petals for each flower. When they are finished, have them compare the number of petals that each flower has. Ask the children to put the flowers in order from the flower with the most petals to the flower with the least petals.

Experienced Learner: Sunflower Seed Count
Provide 10 baby food jars with a small amount of unshelled sunflower seeds in each jar. Encourage the children to guess how many seeds are in each jar and record their guesses on a piece of paper under these headings: Jar #1, Jar #2, and so on through Jar #10. After they have recorded their guesses, encourage the children to open the jars and count the number of seeds inside. The children check their predictions against the actual number of seeds.

SCIENCE CENTER

Beginning Learner: Sunflower Seed Picking
Encourage the children to use their fingers or tweezers to pick out the seeds from real sunflowers. Examine the seeds using magnifying glasses.

Developing Learner: Sunflower Seed Tasting
Purchase sunflower seeds from the grocery store and let the children crack the shells and taste the seeds. Take a classroom vote to see how many children like the seeds and how many children do not care for them. Graph the results on a chart.

Experienced Learner: Classroom Bird Feeder
Help the children make a classroom bird feeder using an empty plastic milk jug. Cut a large opening around the top pouring spout, leaving the handle. Fill the jug with sunflower seeds and place it outside. Observe the birds as they enjoy a special treat.

LANGUAGE/DRAMATIC PLAY CENTER

■ **Beginning Learner:** Sunflower Names

Write alphabet letters on petals cut from yellow construction paper. Encourage the children to find the petals that have the same letters as their names. Help the children put the petals in order to spell their first names.

■ ■ **Developing Learner:** Sunflower Names II

Provide each child with a stack of yellow construction paper petals. Encourage the child to count out enough petals to have one for each letter in her first name. Help each child write one letter on each petal for each letter in her name. Show the children how to glue the petals on a piece of paper to form a flower that spells their names.

■
■ ■ **Experienced Learner:** Funny Word Combinations

Tell the children that some words are made by combining two different words together, such as the words *sun* and *flower*. Encourage the children to brainstorm a list of other words that have two parts, such as sidewalk, placemat, and doorbell. Record all of the compound words on a poster, and encourage the children to make up a story or write sentences using some of the words on the list. Invite them to draw pictures to illustrate their words.

VOCABULARY

golden, green, head, leaves, petals, rough, salty, seeds, stem, sunflower, tall, yellow

Reflect

Say to the children, "Yesterday we learned many wonderful things about strawberries. Today we learned about sunflowers and how they grow and what their seeds are used for. Tomorrow we will learn about pumpkins."

Extend and Enrich

Use the following ideas to extend and enrich what children know about sunflowers.

◆ Encourage the children to plant sunflower seeds in the school's garden or in a cup or planter box.

◆ Help the children make pinecone bird feeders by covering pinecones with peanut butter and sunflower seeds. Hang the birdfeeders outside on the playground for the birds to enjoy.

◆ Help the children use silk greenery and silk flowers to make a sunflower house like the one in the story.

Pumpkins

Morning Circle

Before doing the activity, purchase one tiny pumpkin for each child, as well as a few pumpkins of different sizes. Place the tiny pumpkins in a child-size wheelbarrow. When the children arrive at school, greet them at the door with the wheelbarrow full of pumpkins. Let each child choose a small pumpkin and take it to the circle time area. Show the children a variety of sizes of pumpkins from very small to very large. Lead the children in a discussion of the characteristics of the pumpkins, focusing on their color, size, texture, and unique traits. Share the story *It's Pumpkin Time* with the children.

Storytime

It's Pumpkin Time by Zoe Hall

Daily Center Activity Ideas

ART CENTER

■ **Beginning Learner:** Paper Bag Pumpkin Hat

Before giving a paper bag to each child, cut several inches from the top of each bag so that the sides can be rolled down. Give each child a bag, and help him to roll down the sides of the bag to make a hat. Have the children paint the outside of their hat orange and then glue green construction paper leaves to the flat bottom of the bag to make the stem and leaves. Encourage the children to wear their hats home when they have dried.

■ ■ **Developing Learner:** Papier-Mâché Pumpkin

Give each child a small inflated balloon about the size of a cantaloupe. Provide strips of newspaper and a homemade papier-mâché mixture (mix equal parts of glue and water until the mixture resembles thin cake batter). The children dip newspaper strips in the glue mixture and place the strips on their balloon. Make sure they cover their balloon with newspaper strips so that none of the balloon shows through. Let the balloons dry for at least one day. It may take several days. When the balloons are completely dry, let the children paint them orange. Encourage the children to add green leaves and stems to complete the pumpkins. The children may also want to use brown markers to draw the sections as they appear on an actual pumpkin. Provide a real pumpkin for the children to look at as they add details to their pumpkins.

Experienced Learner: Stuffed Pumpkins

Beforehand, dye knee-high stockings orange using fabric dye. Dye enough so that each child will have six orange stockings. Show the children how to stuff white cotton batting into the stockings. When all of the stockings are stuffed, help each child pull all of the toe ends of the stockings together and tie them in a knot. Then do the same for the open ends of the stockings. The filled sections tied in this way should resemble the segments of a pumpkin. Provide green chenille stems and green construction paper or green foam leaves for the children to add to the top of the pumpkin.

MATH CENTER

Beginning Learner: Pumpkin Sizes

Provide a variety of pumpkins in various sizes. Let the children practice their seriating skills by putting the pumpkins in order from largest to smallest or from smallest to largest.

Developing Learner: Pumpkin Weights

Provide a balance scale and several small pumpkins for the children to practice balancing the pumpkins to see which ones are heavier and which ones are lighter. Encourage the children to combine pumpkins on the scale and try to see what it takes to make the scale balance. Have the children weigh a really large pumpkin on a bathroom scale. Before weighing it, ask the children to predict how much it weighs.

Experienced Learner: Pumpkin Measurement

Provide pumpkins of different sizes for the children to measure. The children can use yarn or a measuring tape to find the circumference of the pumpkins.

SCIENCE CENTER

Beginning Learner: Planting Seeds

Provide each child with a small plastic cup, potting soil, and several pumpkin seeds. Encourage the children to plant and water their seeds. Observe the seeds daily; they will sprout in 7 to 10 days.

Developing Learner: Sink or Float

Provide a large tub of water and pumpkins of several sizes. Have the children predict which pumpkins will float and which ones will sink. Record their predictions on a classroom chart. The children place the pumpkins in the water to test their predictions. Record their actual findings on the same chart.

Experienced Learner: Cleaning Pumpkins

Cut off the top of a large pumpkin. Give the children spoons and bowls to clean out the inside of the pumpkin. Discuss the texture and smell of the pumpkin meat. Clean the seeds and sprinkle salt and other seasonings, if desired, on the seeds and roast them on a tray in a toaster oven.

LANGUAGE/DRAMATIC PLAY CENTER

Beginning Learner: Pumpkin Patch

Make several sizes of pumpkins by wadding up balls of orange construction paper, and twist green construction paper to make stems and leaves. Place the "pumpkins," "stems," and "leaves" on the floor in the center and encourage the children to experience crawling on the ground through the "pumpkin patch." Add a play wheelbarrow or small wagon for the children to load their "pumpkins" in to take them to market.

Developing Learner: Pumpkin Faces

Provide large Styrofoam pumpkins purchased from a craft store, golf tees, and rubber mallets for the children to use. Encourage them to pound the golf tees into the pumpkins to make their own jack-o-lantern faces.

Experienced Learner: Pumpkin Muffins

Make pumpkin muffins using a pumpkin muffin mix. You may want to cook some of the pumpkin meat from the Science Center and add it to the mix. Let the children decorate the muffins and enjoy.

VOCABULARY

blossom, carve, faces, fall, float, flowers, harvest, jack-o-lantern, meat, patch, plant, pumpkins, pumpkin muffins, pumpkin pie, roast, seeds, sink, sprout, stem, vines

Reflect

Say to the children, "Yesterday we learned about sunflowers and their seeds. Today we learned about pumpkins and how they come in many different sizes. Tomorrow we will learn about many different kinds of apples and how they grow."

Extend and Enrich

Use the following ideas to extend and enrich what children know about pumpkins.

♦ Provide a pumpkin for the children to carve in class or invite families to a pumpkin carving party.

♦ Visit a pumpkin patch. If there is not one in the area, provide pumpkins on the playground for the children to go out and "pick" a pumpkin. They can load their pumpkins into a wagon.

♦ Provide a recipe for the children to make small pumpkin pies. Or provide a pumpkin pie for the children to taste.

Apples

Morning Circle

Tell the children the following story:

Once there was a little boy who had nothing to do one day, so his mother sent him out on an adventure. She told him to go on a walk and look for something that was round, red, and had a star inside. The little boy went outside and looked for clues. He asked everyone he saw if they knew of something that was round, red, and had a star inside. Everyone he met sent him to ask someone else: the farmer, the farmer's wife, and so on. Finally, the little boy got tired. He sat down under a tree and fell asleep. When he woke up, something had fallen on the ground beside him. It was round, red, and had a star inside.

Ask the children to guess what it was. After they have generated their ideas, show them an apple. Explain that the apple is round and red, but ask the children how you can find out if it has a star inside. Cut the apple (horizontally across the middle of the apple, not vertically) to reveal a "star" inside.

Next, show the children a basket with different kinds of apples such as Red Delicious, Granny Smith, Gala, and Golden Delicious. Discuss the different colors of the apples and the parts of the apple, such as the stem, skin, seeds, and core. Encourage the children to brainstorm all of the ideas they have for things that can be made from apples, including apple pie, apple jelly, applesauce, apple butter, apple juice, apple cider, and so on. Write down the children's ideas.

Storytime

Apples by Gail Gibbons

Daily Center Activity Ideas

ART CENTER

▪ **Beginning Learner:** Apple Prints
Cut small Styrofoam balls in half. Encourage the children to dip the Styrofoam ball "apples" into red paint and make apple prints on paper.

■ ■ **Developing Learner:** Apple Prints II

Provide Styrofoam balls cut in half as described for the beginning learner, but also provide red, yellow, and green paint. Encourage the children to dip "apples" into paint and make apple prints on their paper. Provide green markers and crayons so the children can add a stem and leaves to their apple prints.

■
■ ■ **Experienced Learner:** Apple Trees

Show the children how to cut brown construction paper to make tree trunks. Have them glue the trunks on paper. Provide brown crayons and markers for the children to draw branches on their trees. Next, invite the children to choose the types of apple trees that they want to paint. Encourage them to dip half Styrofoam "apples" (as described for the beginning learner) into the color of paint of their choice and make prints on the trees.

MATH CENTER

■ **Beginning Learner:** Apple Sort

Provide a variety of different types and sizes of apples. Place all of the apples in a basket. Encourage the children to sort the apples into groups by type of apple or color.

■ ■ **Developing Learner:** Apple Sink or Float

Provide a variety of different kinds and sizes of apples and small tubs of water. Encourage the children to predict which apples they think will float and which ones they think will sink. Encourage the children to test their predictions by placing the apples in the tubs of water. Count how many sink and how many float, charting the results on a graph. Wash and slice the apples for a healthy snack. If desired, talk about the apples in terms of fractions. For example, if you slice an apple into eight pieces, explain that each slice is ⅛ of the apple and that all eight pieces make a whole apple.

■
■ ■ **Experienced Learner:** Apple Patterns

Draw different colors of apples on sentence strips or tagboard to make pattern cards; for example, red apple/yellow apple/green apple or green apple/green apple/red apple, and so on. Provide several different colors of apples and encourage the children to make apple patterns using the pattern cards.

SCIENCE CENTER

■ **Beginning Learner:** Apple Tasting

Provide several different types of apples for the children to taste, including Red Delicious, Granny Smith, Golden Delicious, and Macintosh. Cut the apples into small pieces and place them on a plate for the children to taste. The children taste the apples and decide which apple they like the best. Let them vote for their favorite by indicating their preference on a chart. Invite the children to tally the votes to see which apple is the class favorite.

Developing Learner: Things Made from Apples

Provide a variety of apple products including different kinds of apples, apple cider and apple juice, apple butter and apple jelly, and an apple pie. Provide a small amount of each item for the children to taste. Make a chart where the children can indicate which foods they think tasted sweet or tart.

Experienced Learner: Caramel Apples

Make caramel apples with the children. Provide apples, craft sticks, caramel candies, and a warming pot or microwave to melt the caramels. Encourage the children to wash and dry their apples and poke the craft sticks in the top at the stems to make handles. Remove the wrappers from the caramel candies and place them in a pot or bowl. Melt the caramels and discuss with the children how the caramels look as they are melting. They have changed from being hard to soft and smooth. Invite the children to take turns dipping their apples into the melted caramel. When the apples are coated, the children place their apples on waxed paper on a tray or cookie sheet to cool. Discuss with the children that the melted caramel will re-harden as it cools. Also provide a variety of toppings for the children to roll their warm apples in, including coconut, crushed nuts, or sprinkles.

LANGUAGE/DRAMATIC PLAY CENTER

Beginning Learner: Applesauce

Provide a blender, apples, sugar, and water. Encourage the children to use plastic knives to cut the apples into small pieces. Place the apples in the blender and let the children help with measuring small amounts of sugar and water to the mixture. Turn on the blender and mix the ingredients until it resembles applesauce. Pour the applesauce into small cups for the children to taste. Also provide commercially prepared applesauce for the children to taste and compare to their homemade applesauce.

Developing Learner: Cooked Applesauce

Set out a crock pot or electric skillet and apples, plastic knives, sugar, and water. The children use plastic knives to cut apples into small pieces. Provide a variety of apples for the children to cut. Place the apple pieces in the electric skillet or crock pot, and invite the children to use measuring spoons to add small amounts of sugar and water to the apples. Cook the mixture until it is mushy like commercial applesauce. Provide small cups or bowls and spoons for the children to taste the applesauce when it has finished cooking and has cooled.

Experienced Learner: Making Apple Pies

Provide the ingredients for each child to make a small, individual-sized apple pie. Provide small foil pie pans for each child, apples, plastic knives, sugar, cinnamon, pie crusts, and butter. Let the children help cut apples into small pieces and then mix the apples in a bowl with cinnamon and sugar. Show the children how to take small amounts of the prepared pie crust and press it into the bottom of their pie tins. Next, ask them to add the apple mixture and a small amount of butter and press a layer of pie crust on top. Bake the apple pies in a toaster oven or conventional oven. If you do not have access to an oven, place the uncooked pies in plastic bags and send them home for the children to cook with their families. Be sure to include baking directions.

VOCABULARY

apple blossom, apple bobbing, apple butter, apple cider, apple jelly, apple pie, apple tree, applesauce, candy apples, core, Golden Delicious, Granny Smith, harvest, plant, Macintosh, Red Delicious, seeds, stem

Reflect

Say to the children, "Yesterday we learned about pumpkins and all of the fun things that you can do with them. Today we learned about many different kinds of apples and how they grow. Tomorrow we will learn about many of the different kinds of foods that have seeds."

Extend and Enrich

Use the following ideas to extend and enrich what children know about apples and how they grow.
- Share the Dr. Seuss book *Ten Apples Up on Top!* with the children.
- Provide ingredients for the children to make candy apples.

DAY 5

Seeds

Morning Circle

Provide a basket of all kinds of things with seeds and a few food items that do not have seeds, including bananas, oranges, apples, lemons, cucumbers, squash, cantaloupes, watermelons, tomatoes, strawberries, pumpkins, peaches, plums, mangoes, grapes, and so on. Engage the children in a discussion of these foods and whether or not they have seeds. Divide the foods into two categories: those that the children think have seeds and those that they think do not have seeds. The children will discover in the Math Center which foods have seeds and which do not.

Storytime

How a Seed Grows by Helene Jordan

Daily Center Activity Ideas

ART CENTER

 **Beginning Learner:** Coffee Filter Flowers
Provide coffee filters, eyedroppers, and food coloring. Encourage the children to use eyedroppers to drop food coloring onto coffee filters to make flowers. Provide green construction paper stems and leaves for the children to add to their flowers.

Developing Learner: Sponge-Painted Flowers
Provide flower-shaped sponges on handles, different colors of tempera paint, and paper for the children to paint a flower garden. Have the children dip the sponges into paint and make flower shapes on their paper. Invite them to add construction paper stems and leaves.

Experienced Learner: Handprint Flower Gardens
Provide several colors of tempera paint and paper. Invite the children to place their hands into paint and then press their hands on paper to form a large handprint flower shape. Invite the children to roll small toy cars into green paint and paint a stem on their flower. Provide green markers for the children to draw leaves to complete their flower. Encourage the children to continue painting handprint flowers to make a garden.

MATH CENTER

■ **Beginning Learner:** How Many Seeds?

Remind the children of the predictions they made during circle time, regarding which fruits and vegetables they thought did or did not have seeds. Explain to the children that they will be finding out the answer with this activity. Use a knife to cut each food and show the children the seeds. Discuss how many seeds each one has, and encourage the children to count the seeds. Which fruits and vegetables have just one seed and which ones have many seeds? Discuss the color, shape and size of the seeds.

■ ■ **Developing Learner:** Seed Sort

Do the activity as described for the beginning learner, and then encourage the children to put the seeds from the fruits and vegetables in order from smallest to largest and from largest to smallest. Also encourage the children to sort the foods into categories of those with one seed and those with many seeds.

■
■ ■ **Experienced Learner:** A Giant Seed

Show the children a coconut and ask them to guess what it is and what is inside of it. Pass it around so that the children can hear the liquid inside. Use a hammer and a nail and poke the nail in the "eye" or black round space on the outside of the coconut. From this hole, pour the coconut milk into a glass. Provide small plastic cups for the children to taste the coconut milk. Have the children vote on who likes the taste of the coconut milk and who does not. Next, use the hammer to crack open the coconut and let the children taste the meat inside. Again, take a vote to see who likes the taste of the coconut and who does not. Also provide store-bought grated coconut for the children to taste and compare to the fresh coconut. (**Safety note:** Make sure that no one has a coconut allergy before doing this activity.)

SCIENCE CENTER

■ **Beginning Learner:** Planting Seeds at the Sand Table

Place potting soil and seeds in the sand and water table for the children to practice planting. Encourage them to use small gardening gloves, rakes, and shovels to plant their seeds.

■ ■ **Developing Learner:** Planting Seeds in Cups

Provide plants, or provide seeds and potting soil for the children to plant in small plastic cups. Encourage them to use eyedroppers to water their plants. Encourage the children to observe their plants every day and measure them for several days to observe their growth.

■
■ ■ **Experienced Learner:** Planting Seeds and Charting Growth

Provide packages of vegetable and fruit seeds and encourage the children to choose which seeds they would like to plant. Provide clear cups and potting soil for the children to use for planting. The children place the soil in their cup, add the seeds of their choice, and add a small amount of water. Have them write the name of what they planted on a craft stick and place it in the cup.

The children may take their plants home or leave them at school in the window and observe them for several days. Have the children chart the growth of the plants and compare the growth of different seeds planted by their classmates.

LANGUAGE/DRAMATIC PLAY CENTER

For all levels of learners, explain that the word "seed" begins with the letter "S." Talk about other words that begin with the letter "S" and see if children can come up with examples.

Beginning Learner: Giant "S"
Draw a large "S" on paper. Encourage the children to use markers and crayons to doodle on their giant "S."

Developing Learner: The Letter "S" Seed Collage
Give each child a paper with a large "S" on it. Provide a variety of different kinds of seeds for the children to glue on their letter "S" to fill it in.

Experienced Learner: Things That Begin with "S"
Discuss with the children things that begin with the letter "S" and make a list of their ideas. Give the children a large "S" stencil to trace on paper. Have them trace the "S" and then draw pictures of as many things as they can think of that begin with the letter "S."

VOCABULARY

apples, bananas, cantaloupe, dirt, flower garden, flowers, fruits, gloves, grapes, harvest, hose, leaves, oranges, peaches, peel, plants, plums, pots, seeds, shell, shovels, skin, soil, stem, vegetables, watermelon, weeds, zucchini

Reflect

Say to the children, "Yesterday we learned about all of the different kinds of apples and the things that can be made with them. Today, we learned about many different fruits and vegetables that have seeds, some of which are big and some of which are very small."

Extend and Enrich

◆ Invite families to join the children for a garden party. Let the children plant their own surprise garden by bringing in a fruit, vegetable, or flower of their choice and planting it either in pots, a garden at school, or window boxes. The children will enjoy watching to see the "surprise" things they have planted.
◆ Provide seed packages from various fruits, vegetables, and flowers so the children can explore the packages and the seeds inside.

Things Found at Night

Owls

Morning Circle

Make a tape recording of someone hooting like an owl. Repeat the owl hoot many times. Hide the tape recorder somewhere in the room and lower the lighting. Begin playing the taped owl sound when the children enter the room. Explain to the children that they will be learning about things found at night, and ask them to identify the sound. Tell them that owls rest during the day and hunt for food at night. Provide pictures of different species of owls for the children to examine, and read the story *Owl Babies*.

Storytime

Owl Babies by Martin Waddell

Daily Center Activity Ideas

ART CENTER

Beginning Learner: Paper Plate Owls

Provide small paper plates, construction paper eyes, yellow construction paper beaks, brown paint with white glue mixed in, and paintbrushes. Encourage each child to paint a paper plates and then add eyes and a beak to make an owl face.

Developing Learner: Stuffed Paper Bag Owls

Provide small lunch bags, brown paint, and construction paper to make owls. Encourage the children to paint their lunch bags brown and then cut out eyes, a beak, feet, and wings from construction paper. Have each child glue the wings to the sides of his paper bag and the feet to the bottom of the bag. To add extra stiffness to the owl body after decorating it, help the child to stuff his bag with newspaper and tape the bag closed.

Experienced Learner: Paper Bag Owls

Provide large grocery bags, brown paint, and construction paper to make large owls. Encourage the children to paint their grocery bags dark brown and cut out a beak and feet from construction paper. Encourage the children to glue craft feathers to the sides of their paper bags to make wings. Have the children glue the feet on their bags. Cut two holes in each bag to make eyes. The children can put the bags over their heads and wear them as owl costumes.

MATH CENTER

■ **Beginning Learner:** Hidden Threes

Before the children arrive, hide magnetic and foam numeral threes in the classroom. Provide several examples of the numeral three written in type and written by hand. Encourage the children to find the hidden numerals in the classroom. Add to the activity by having the children count to three, show three fingers, stand up on the count of three, and identify which classmates are three years old. Invite each child to join with two friends to make groups of three.

■ ■ **Developing Learner:** Three Times the Action

Explain to the children that the number three is an important number in the story *Owl Babies* because there are three owlets. Play Follow the Leader with the children. Choose a child to be the leader and ask him to choose an action to perform, such as jumping up and down, hopping on one foot, spinning around, and so on. The leader performs the action three times and the children follow the leader. Let the children explore the number three by having them take turns performing an action three times with the rest of the children following along. Make sure that everyone has a chance to be the leader.

■
■ ■ **Experienced Learner:** Scavenger Hunt Threes

Encourage the children to examine the cover of the book *Owl Babies*. To reinforce the concept of the number three, encourage the children to search around the room and collect three objects that are related in some way (three marbles, three blocks, three cars, or three animals). Have the children count the objects they have collected and explain how they are related. Provide sets of objects that the children can glue on paper in sets of three, such as straws, pieces of yarn, paper shapes, and pompoms.

SCIENCE CENTER

Share the following information with the children while discussing owls with them in the Science Center:

◆ Owls are amazing creatures of the night.
◆ They have excellent eyesight and hearing.
◆ They can fly without making any sound.
◆ Owls have large eyes that face forward.

■ **Beginning Learner:** Owl Eyes

Prior to this activity, locate pictures of owls. Use black and white construction paper to make several sets of large owl eyes and place them around the room. Show the children pictures of owls and point out their large eyes. Tell the children that at night, sometimes only the owl's eyes are visible to us. Turn out the classroom lights and provide flashlights. Encourage the children to use the flashlights to try to find the owl eyes around the room. When the children have located all of the eyes, move the eyes to a new location so the children can have fun finding them again.

■ ■ **Developing Learner:** Owl Nests

If possible, show the children an actual bird's nest or one that has been purchased from a craft store. Talk about the different things that might be used in nature to make a nest, and discuss how the items are closely woven together. Provide collage materials such as cotton, yarn, small sticks, grass, paper, and glue for the children to use to make a nest for an owl.

■

■ ■ **Experienced Learner:** Nature Walk

Show the children a picture of an owl. Give each child a paper bag and construction paper. Invite the children to draw a picture of an owl, cut it out, and glue it to the bag. Take the bags along on a nature walk and encourage the children to use them for collecting nature items to use to build an owl nest. Back in the classroom, have the children examine and compare their items. Give each child a small piece of cardboard to arrange and glue nesting materials to make a nest.

LANGUAGE/DRAMATIC PLAY CENTER

■ **Beginning Learner:** Animals Seen at Night

Share pictures of animals that are active at night such as owls, bats, raccoons, possums, fireflies, foxes, bobcats, badgers, rats, and skunks. Help the children to name the different animals and discuss interesting characteristics of each. Encourage the children to choose one of the pictures and take turns moving like that animal.

■ ■ **Developing Learner:** Patience and Waiting

Discuss the story *Owl Babies* and how the three owl babies waited patiently on a branch for their mother to return. Discuss the concept of patience. Ask the children to discuss times when they have had to wait patiently for their mother or father to do something. Is it hard or easy to wait? Play an "owl" version of Red Light, Green Light with the children. One child pretends to be the mother and the other children are the owl babies. The mother owl gives a direction such as, "Walk," and the owl babies walk. Then the mother owl tells them, "Wait," and the baby owls must stop. Continue playing the game until one of the owl babies reaches the mother. That owl becomes the mother. Take turns until everyone has had a chance to be the mother owl.

■ ■ Experienced Learner: What I Do at Night

Share the story *Owl Babies* with the children and discuss how the owl babies waited all night on a branch for their mother to come home. Engage the children in a discussion of things that they do at night before bedtime. Provide crayons, markers, and paper for the children to draw a picture that depicts their nighttime routine. Help them write the words: "At night I…" on their papers and then ask them to finish the sentence.

VOCABULARY

barn, branch, eyes, hoot, nocturnal, owl, owlet, patience, wings, wise

Reflect

Say to the children, "Today we talked about owls and how they are active during the night. Tomorrow we will talk about something else that is seen at night. It is the moon."

Extend and Enrich

Use the following ideas to extend and enrich what children know about owls.

- Examine pictures of different kinds of owls and discuss their differences and similarities, and where they are found.
- Share *Owl Moon* by Jane Yolen with the children.

Moon

Morning Circle

Turn off or dim the lights in the classroom and shine a flashlight on the ceiling. Ask the children if the light reminds them of anything. Encourage the children to generate their own ideas and also suggest that the light resembles the moon. Place a crescent-shaped piece of cardboard over the flashlight and ask the children to describe the new shape that appears on the ceiling. Tell the children that this shape is called a crescent moon. Explain that the moon does not always look the same because of its different phases or stages.

Storytime

Papa, Please Get the Moon for Me by Eric Carle

Daily Center Activity Ideas

ART CENTER

▪ **Beginning Learner:** Glittery Earth, Moon, and Stars
Cut out moon, Earth, and star shapes from paper. Encourage the children to use small paintbrushes to spread glue on the shapes and then sprinkle glitter on them.

▪ ▪ **Developing Learner:** Earth, Moon, and Stars Mobile
Draw earth shapes, moon shapes (full moon or crescent moon), and stars on construction paper for the children to cut out and decorate with markers. Provide yarn, a hole punch, and paper plates. Encourage the children to punch holes in the Earth, moon, and star shapes, and string yarn through the holes. Help each child punch holes in his paper plate and tie the yarn through the holes to make a mobile.

▪
▪ ▪ **Experienced Learner:** Our Earth
Provide small Styrofoam balls to represent the Earth. Show the children pictures of the Earth and discuss what the different colors represent. Provide blue and green tempera paint and encourage the children to paint the balls to represent the Earth.

MATH CENTER

■ **Beginning Learner:** Circles, Circles, Everywhere

Cut out a large circle shape from yellow construction paper to represent the moon. Encourage the children to search around the classroom to find round objects. Have the children bring their objects to circle time and discuss the various sizes of circles that they found. Have the children join hands and form a giant circle. Encourage the children to use their bodies in creative ways to form very large and very small circles. Challenge the children to look through the storybook and count all the circle shapes.

■ ■ **Developing Learner:** Rocket Ships to the Moon

Provide a variety of shapes cut from construction paper. Encourage the children to use the shapes to construct their own rocket ship and moon. Ask the children to identify the shapes they choose, and then assemble and glue their shapes on a large circle (moon) to resemble a rocket ship.

■
■ ■ **Experienced Learner:** Race to the Moon

Cut out six rocket ship shapes from red construction paper and six rocket ships from green paper. Cut out a large moon shape from yellow construction paper and place it on the floor. Place the rocket ships on the floor in a random pattern of red and green spaced apart to form a path to the paper moon. Have the children roll large dice (foam ones are great) then step on that number of rocket ships. If they land on a green rocket ship they stay put, and if they land on a red rocket ship they must take one step back. Continue playing the game until everyone reaches the moon.

SCIENCE CENTER

Share the following information with the children.
- ◆ The moon is the closest body to the Earth.
- ◆ It is a natural satellite, which means that the moon orbits or goes around the Earth.
- ◆ There are other planets in our solar system that have moons.
- ◆ It takes the moon about 28 days to go around the Earth.
- ◆ The moon appears to glow at night, but it is only reflecting the light from the sun.
- ◆ The different shapes or phases of the moon are determined by how much of the illuminated moon we can see from Earth. The moon is "waxing" when it is growing to its fullest phase and it is "waning" when it is shrinking from fullness to a small crescent phase.
- ◆ Six Apollo missions have successfully landed on the moon.

■ **Beginning Learner:** Moon Creations

Provide black construction paper, colored sand, glitter, and a small paper plate to make a night sky picture. Encourage the children to brush glue on the back of the paper plate then sprinkle it with colored sand and glitter. After the plate dries, brush glue around the rim on the front side of the paper plate and glue it on the black construction paper so that the decorated side is facing up. Provide white crayons for the children to use to add stars to their moon pictures.

Developing Learner: Phases of the Moon

To do this activity, explain the different phases of the moon.

◆ Full moon: when the moon is visible as a fully illuminated circle.

◆ Half moon: when only half of the moon appears to be illuminated.

◆ Gibbous moon: when more than half of the moon is illuminated. It appears as if one side of the moon is larger than the other side.

◆ Crescent moon: when only a sliver or small slice of the moon is illuminated.

◆ New moon: when the moon is not visible because no light is reflected on it from the sun.

Provide a grapefruit to represent the Earth, an orange to represent the moon, and a flashlight to represent the sun. Explain that the moon is about one-fourth the size of the Earth. Use the orange to demonstrate how the moon revolves around the Earth (the grapefruit). The children use the orange, grapefruit, and the flashlight to practice role playing the phases of the moon. Encourage the children to go outside at night, with supervision, and look at the moon to determine its phase. Ask them to draw a picture of the moon to bring to class the next day. Invite the children to compare and discuss their findings. For fun, visit the NASA website and access photographs of the moon's current phase to share with the children.

Experienced Learner: Phases of the Moon II

Discuss the phases of the moon with the children as described for the developing learner. Provide black and yellow construction paper for the children to create a picture showing all of the phases of the moon. Encourage the children to cut out moon shapes from yellow construction paper to represent the different and glue their moons on the black construction paper. They may wish to use gray construction paper to represent the new moon. Provide glue tinted with yellow paint and clear glitter for the children to paint on top of their pictures to give them a luminescent effect.

LANGUAGE/DRAMATIC PLAY CENTER

Beginning Learner: Letter "M" Grab Bag

Collect a variety of items that begin with the letter "M" and place the objects in a bag. Show the children a lowercase letter "m" and discuss the sound that the letter makes. Encourage the children to practice making the /m/ sound. Pass around the bag and have the children take turns reaching into the bag and removing one of the objects. The children name the object and practice making the beginning sound for that object. Talk about the children's friends in the class or their family members who have names that start with or include the letter "m."

Developing Learner: Letter "M" Search

Provide newspaper pages or magazines for the children to use to search for the letter "m." They can look for uppercase and lowercase instances of the letter "m." Encourage the children to cut out the letters that they find or use a red marker to circle them. Let the children share their letter finds with their friends.

■ ■ ■ Experienced Learner: Words That Rhyme with Moon

Talk about rhyming words. Ask the children to name words that rhyme with "moon." As the children generate a list of words, help them write their ideas on chart paper or a dry-erase board. Have the children individually dictate stories about what they would like to do if they could take a trip to the moon. They might want to write about how they would travel to the moon or what they would do when they got there. Help them write their stories on paper (or write the stories for them) and let them add illustrations. Let the children take their stories home or bind the pages together to make a classroom book.

VOCABULARY

atmosphere, crescent, dark, Earth, full, gibbous, glow, half, light, lunar eclipse, moon, new, night, orbit, phases, planets, quarter, rotation, sky, solar eclipse, sun

Reflect

Say to the children, "Yesterday we learned about owls and why they are active at night. Today we learned about the moon and its different phases. Tomorrow we will discuss our pillows and how important they are in helping us rest at night."

Extend and Enrich

Use the following ideas to extend and enrich what children know about the moon.

◆ Share the nursery rhyme, "Hey, Diddle Diddle" with the children.
◆ Janet Stevens wrote a fun version of "Hey, Diddle Diddle" entitled "And the Dish Ran Away with the Spoon." Have the children compare the two versions of the rhymes.
◆ Place playdough or clay in pie tins to represent the moon and use marbles to press craters in the moon. Another method of achieving a crater effect is to drop small rocks into wet sand. Drop small stones and marbles from different heights to see their effect on the craters.

DAY 3

Shadows

Morning Circle

As children arrive, greet them at the door while holding a flashlight. Explain that they will be learning about shadows and how to make them. Dim the classroom lights and shine the flashlight on a wall. Encourage the children to experiment with making shadows. They can use their hands to make shadow puppets or stand in front of the wall and freeze to make shadows. After this initial exploration, go outside and show the children how they can make shadows on the sidewalk with their bodies. Encourage them to experiment with making funny shadow poses on the sidewalk.

Storytime

Moonbear's Shadow by Frank Asch

Daily Center Activity Ideas

ART CENTER

■ **Beginning Learner:** Abstract Shadow Art

Place blue painter's tape on white paper in a variety of angles to create designs and patterns. Provide black paint and brushes for the children to paint the entire paper. When the painting is dry, help the children remove the tape to reveal an interesting black and white design. Provide stencils of different shapes. Assist the children with taping the stencils to white paper and provide squirt bottles filled with colored tempera paint or food coloring and water. Encourage the children to squirt the paint on top of the stencils that are taped on the paper to make interesting stencil paintings. **Note:** Stencils need to be plastic or if you make your own stencils out of poster board, cover them in clear contact paper so they won't fall apart when they get wet with paint.

■ ■ **Developing Learner:** Abstract Shadow Art II

Provide white paper, black paint, and blue painter's tape for the children to make a day- and nighttime picture. Help the children stretch small pieces of painter's tape across their paper at various angles. After the children place tape on their paper, have them cover their paper with black tempera paint. When the paint is dry, help the children remove the tape to reveal a black and white design.

■ ■ ■ **Experienced Learner:** My Shadow

Shine a light source, such as a lamp or overhead projector, on a large piece of black bulletin-board paper. Encourage each child to stand in front of the paper and freeze in a pose. Trace the child's pose using chalk. Encourage the children to cut out their shadow pictures.

MATH CENTER

■ **Beginning Learner:** Shadow Sizes

On a sunny day, take the children outside and ask them to choose partners. Encourage one child to cast a shadow on the sidewalk and have the partner copy the shadow pose. Have them take turns casting shadows and copying each other's poses. Have them stand next to each other and look at their shadows. Talk about the difference in the size of their shadows. Invite them to experiment walking forward and backward to change the shadow's size.

■ ■ **Developing Learner:** Shadow Sizes/Measuring with Blocks

Take the children outside and have them cast shadows on the sidewalk. Use chalk to trace their shadows, and then provide manipulatives such as blocks, counting bears, strips of paper, or other classroom materials for the children to measure their traced shadows.

■ ■ ■ **Experienced Learner:** Shadow Sizes/Standard Measurements

Implement the activity as described for the developing learner and then introduce the concept of standard units of measurement. Provide rulers, measuring tapes, and yardsticks for the children to use to measure their outdoor shadows.

SCIENCE CENTER

■ **Beginning Learner:** Shadow Pictures in the Sun

Provide dark construction paper (not fadeless construction paper). Ask the children to select various objects from the classroom to use to make shadow prints. Provide keys, building toys, pennies, and so on. Find a sunny place outdoors to place the papers, and then show the children how to place objects on each paper. Place rocks or small heavy objects on the corners of the papers to weight them down so they will not move. Keep the papers in the sun for several days. The sun will fade the paper and the objects will leave a shadow.

■ ■ **Developing Learner:** Projected Shadows

To do this activity at the developing and experienced levels, provide an overhead projector and objects for the children to make shadows with. Turn the lights off and encourage the children to take turns placing objects on the flat surface of the projector to make shadows on a wall.

Experienced Learner: Guess That Shadow

Implement the activity as described for the developing learner, but create a partition so that the children cannot see the objects on the overhead projector. Demonstrate this activity by placing an object on the overhead projector. Have the children guess what the object is by looking at the shadow it casts on the wall. Let the children take turns choosing an item from a basket of classroom objects to place on the projector.

LANGUAGE/DRAMATIC PLAY CENTER

Beginning Learner: Dancing Lights

Turn off the lights in the classroom and give the children flashlights. Encourage the children to lie on their backs, point their flashlights at the ceiling, and turn them on. Encourage the children to move their lights around on the ceiling and walls to make designs.

Developing Learner: Shadow Puppets

Encourage the children to use stencils to trace objects, animals, or shapes onto black construction paper. Help the children cut out the shapes and staple or tape them to tongue depressors. Provide a light source and ask the children to use their puppets to cast shadows on the wall and tell stories.

 **Experienced Learner:** Shadow Dancing

Provide a light source and hang a sheet from the ceiling. Let the children take turns going behind the sheet. Play music and encourage the children to dance to the music. The children in front of the sheet will see the dancing child's shadow. Stop the music and encourage the child behind the sheet to "freeze" until the music begins again.

VOCABULARY

dark, flashlight, light, shade, shadow, silhouette, sun

Reflect

Say to the children, "Yesterday we learned about the moon. Today we learned about shadows and all the different ways that we can make shadows indoors and outdoors. Tomorrow we will learn about bats and some of their special habits and characteristics."

Extend and Enrich

Use the following ideas to extend and enrich what children know about shadows.

◆ Talk about Groundhog Day, which occurs every year on February 2. Tell the children that some people believe that groundhogs can forecast the weather. If a groundhog emerges from its burrow and see sit shadow, then winter will last for six more weeks. If it doesn't see its shadow, the winter is supposed to end sooner. Share the story, *It's Groundhog Day* by Steven Kroll and Jani Bassett..

◆ Play "Me and My Shadow" by encouraging the children to choose a partner and mimic every move that the partner makes. Have them take turns making the movements.

Bats

Morning Circle

Prepare by cutting out bat shapes from black construction paper and attaching them to craft sticks. When the children arrive, give them the bat cutouts and encourage them to fly their bats to the circle quietly. Explain that although bats are *nocturnal* (more active at night than during the day), they don't see very well at night. Instead, they use *echolocation*, which allows them to "see" using their ears. Explain that bats eat mosquitoes, and that some people have special bat houses in their yards to encourage the bats to come and eat mosquitoes. Bats often live in caves and hang upside down by their feet with their wings crossed over their chests. Tell the children to pretend they are bats hanging quietly in a cave late at night. Dim the lights to simulate nighttime. Encourage the children to lie on their backs, cross their arms across their chests, and look at the ceiling. This will allow them to view the classroom from a different perspective. To enrich this activity, prior to the children's arrival, paint interesting designs on paper cutouts using glow-in-the-dark paint and hang the cutouts from the ceiling.

Storytime

Bats on Parade by Kathi Appelt

Daily Center Activity Ideas

ART CENTER

Beginning Learner: Hand Bats

Have the children make bat prints with their hands. First, show them how to dip their hands in black paint. Then the children place their hands on construction paper, with the heels of their hands touching and the fingers pointing out. This will make a bat print with wings. Once the bat is dried, the children can add ears and wiggle eyes.

Developing Learner: Tube Bats

Provide empty paper towel tubes and black tempera paint. Encourage the children to paint their tubes black to make the body of a bat and then cut out paper wings from black construction paper to make wings for their bats. Help them tape the wings to the tubes to make bats.

Experienced Learner: Stencil Bats

Provide black construction paper, wiggle eyes, a bat stencil, and toothpicks for the children to make their own bats. Encourage the children to trace the bat stencil on their paper and cut the shape out. Have them glue wiggle eyes on the bat's head and toothpicks on the wings to mimic bones in the bat's wings.

Beginning Learner: Bat Houses/Number Recognition

Prepare for this activity by making five bat houses out of shirt boxes. Place the lids on the boxes. On each box, cut a small slit in one of the short sides. Make sure that the slit is large enough for a paper bat to slide into easily. Write the numerals 1–5 on the outside of each box, one numeral per box. Cut out 15 bats from black tagboard. Have the children look at the numeral on the outside of each bat house and slide that number of bats into the house through the slit. When the bat houses are full, the children open the boxes and pull out the bats.

Developing Learner: Bat Houses/Size Correspondence

Prepare three bat houses as described for the beginning learner, but make one box with a small slit, one box with a medium slit, and one box with a large slit. Outline the slits using a bright colored marker to emphasize them. Now prepare three different sizes of black tagboard bats. Encourage the children to place the small bats in the box with the small slit, the medium bats in the bat box with the medium slit, and the large bats in the box with the large slit.

Experienced Learner: Bat Houses/Counting

Prepare five empty shirt boxes as described for the beginning learner, with the numerals 1–5 on each box. Cut out 25 bats from black tagboard. Place one dot sticker on five bats, two dot stickers on five bats, and so on until you have five dot stickers on the last five bats. Place the bats in a bag. Each child removes a bat from the bag, counts the number of dots on it, and places it in the bat house with the corresponding numeral on the outside.

SCIENCE CENTER

■ **Beginning Learner:** To Fly or Not to Fly

Find pictures in magazines of animals that fly and animals that do not fly. Copy and cut out the pictures. Prepare a two-column chart by drawing a line down the middle of a large piece of paper. At the top of one column, draw a cloud to represent animals that fly, and at the top of the other column, draw grass to represent animals that do not fly. Spread the pictures on a table and provide glue sticks. Ask the children to glue the pictures in the appropriate column.

■ ■ **Developing Learner:** Mammals

Tell the children that bats are the only *mammals* that fly. Explain that mammals are warm-blooded. (You may wish to explain that cold-blooded animals—such as snakes and turtles—need the sun to warm them up. Warm-blooded animals don't need the sun to keep them warm because they have a steady body temperature.) Mammals also have fur or hair, give birth to live babies (not eggs), and provide milk for their babies. Provide magazines featuring animals and encourage the children to look through them to find pictures of animals that are mammals. Let them cut out the pictures and glue them on a class poster with the word "Mammals" written at the top.

■
■ ■ **Experienced Learner:** Bats and Birds

Provide various pictures of bats and birds. Discuss with the children the characteristics of birds and bats, focusing on similarities and differences. Cut out a set of small construction paper bats and birds. Write a fact about a bat or bird on a poster and encourage the children to decide if the fact applies to a bird, bat, or both. Let the children put the cutouts next to the fact if it applies. Some facts include: bats and birds both fly; bats are born from their mother and birds hatch from eggs; birds have feathers on their wings but bats wings are bare.

LANGUAGE/DRAMATIC PLAY CENTER

■ **Beginning Learner:** Bat Caves

Cover a card table or classroom table with black fabric to represent a cave. Have the children to make bats from black construction paper to hang from yarn upside down in the cave. Encourage the children to pretend to be bats inside the cave.

■ ■ **Developing Learner:** Hunting for the Letter "B"

Send a note to parents explaining that the children will be going on a hunt for the letter "B" in the classroom. Ask them to help their children look for objects that begin with the letter "B" and send the objects to class. Make sure the objects fit into a small plastic sandwich bag and are unbreakable.

■
■ ■ **Experienced Learner:** Bat Rhymes with Rat

Discuss with the children words that rhyme with *bat*. Write the words on index cards and provide alphabet blocks for the children to spell the words.

VOCABULARY

bat colonies, bats, cave, echolocation, fly, fruit, fur, mammals, night, warm-blooded, wing

Reflect

Say to the children, "Yesterday we learned about our shadows. Today we learned about bats and all of their unique characteristics. Tomorrow we'll investigate some of the noises we hear at night."

Extend and Enrich

Use the following ideas to extend and enrich what children know about bats.

◆ Help the children trace bats onto black construction paper, cut them out, and tape them to craft sticks. Use the puppets for the following fingerplay:

Two little bats hiding in a cave,
One named Mary, and one named Dave.
Fly away, Mary; fly away, Dave,
Come back, Mary; come back, Dave.

The children place the bats behind their back and have them "fly" out of the cave.

◆ Purchase inexpensive plastic bat rings from a dollar store or party store. Give each child 10 bat rings. Have the children practice counting as they put them on and take them off again.

◆ Show the children pictures of bats and talk about all of the different kinds of bats there are.

◆ Share the book *Stellaluna* by Janell Cannon with the children, and discuss how Stellaluna the bat interacts with the bird family.

*DAY 5

Night Noises

Morning Circle

Prepare for this activity by making a tape recording of sounds such as a door shutting, creaking, and slamming; a cat meowing loudly; a dog howling or barking; running water; a person snoring; and someone walking up the stairs very loudly. Play the recording and encourage the children to identify the sounds they hear on the tape. Darken the classroom and encourage the children to listen to the taped sounds again. Are the sounds different? Explain to the children that sounds we hear at night may frighten us because it is dark, but the same sounds do not frighten us during the daytime. Share the story *Night Noises* with the children.

Storytime

Night Noises by Mem Fox

Daily Center Activity Ideas

ART CENTER

▨ **Beginning Learner:** Paper Plate Shakers

Give each child two small paper plates and encourage the children to draw designs on their plates using markers and crayons. Staple the two paper plates together, leaving a small opening at the top for the children to add materials. Provide materials such as aquarium gravel, small beads, or paper clips for the children to place inside their paper plates. When they are finished adding their materials, finish stapling the paper plates closed. Invite the children to use their paper plate shakers to make noise.

▨ ▨ **Developing Learner:** Bell Shakers

Provide each child with a foil pie tin, ribbons, and bells. Help the children use a hole punch to make holes around the edges of their pie tins. Encourage them to poke small pieces of ribbon through the holes, tie on jingle bells, and then knot the ends. The children repeat this process until they have tied bells all the way around the pie tins.

Experienced Learner: Box Shakers

Ask each child to bring an empty oatmeal box or empty plastic jar to school. Encourage the children to use markers, paint, and construction paper to decorate the outside of their boxes or jars. Provide a variety of aquarium gravel, beads, bells or other materials for the children to use to fill their jars halfway. Help the children secure the lids to their jars. Invite the children to experiment by shaking the jars to make different sounds.

MATH CENTER

To prepare for this activity, make a deck of cards with two sets of pictures of things found at night. Include things such as a flashlight, bat, raccoon, possum, candle, car with headlights on, sleeping children in their bed, stars, moon, lights in a house, bugs dancing in the light, a lighted jack-o-lantern, and so on.

Beginning Learner: Night Things/Concentration

Place a few pairs of cards on a table face down. Encourage a child to draw two cards and identify the pictures on the front of the cards. If the child gets a match, he keeps the cards; if not, he places them back where they were, face down, and continues playing the game.

■ ■ **Developing Learner:** Night Things/Old Maid

Encourage the children to deal 10 cards to each of two players and put the remainder of the cards in the draw pile. Invite the children to play a nighttime version of Old Maid by taking turns drawing cards and trying to get matches.

■
■ ■ **Experienced Learner:** Night Things/Concentration II

Encourage the children to use all of the cards to play a "nighttime" concentration game. Have the children take turns drawing two cards and trying to find a match. If a match is not found, the children return the cards and try again.

SCIENCE CENTER

■ **Beginning Learner:** Comparing Keys

Provide a collection of unused keys. Encourage the children to explore the keys and notice their similarities and differences. Provide a variety of empty keychains and encourage the children to put the keys on key chains in whatever order they choose.

■ ■ **Developing Learner:** Locks and Latches

Set out an assortment of different kinds of door locks and latches for the children to explore. If possible, mount some of the locks to boards so that they are more realistic and easier for the children to manipulate.

■
■ ■ **Experienced Learner:** Which Key Is It?

Provide three padlocks and three keys. Lock the locks and put the keys on the table. Encourage the children to experiment with finding the key that will unlock each lock.

LANGUAGE/DRAMATIC PLAY CENTER

■ **Beginning Learner:** I Spy Books

Discuss with the children that authors and illustrators often hide clues in their pictures to tell a story. Provide some child-friendly "I Spy" books and encourage the children to find the hidden pictures.

■ ■ **Developing Learner:** Hidden Pictures

Explain that the illustrator of *Night Noises* has hidden lots of details in the pictures that are not described in the story. If possible, provide a big book copy. Invite the children to play an I Spy game of trying to find the following details in the pictures: sleeping birds, a sleeping dog, a smiling moon, a dog with a party hat, a doorknob, flowers, a girl in a hat, and a lamp. Also encourage the children to find a purple checked rug and a cane. Ask, "How many times do these items appear?" (14 for the rug, 13 for the cane) Remind the children to check the front and back covers.

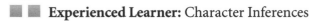 **Experienced Learner:** Character Inferences

Encourage the children to look at the illustrations in the story to learn more about the characters. Have them find the following characters and make inferences about them based on what they see. For example:

1. Lily Laceby has trouble walking. (She is shown using a cane and has a bandage on her leg.)
2. Lily Laceby likes hot tea. (She carries a teapot and places it next to her chair.)
3. Lily Laceby likes to read. (She is shown with a book in her lap.)
4. You can buy ice cream where Lily Laceby lives. (There is a sign advertising ice cream on the second page.)
5. Butch Aggie (the dog) is happy. (He is wagging his tail.)

VOCABULARY

crackle, creak, drip, drop, fantasy, make-believe, night, noises, real, scratch, squeak

Reflect

Say to the children, "Yesterday we learned about bats, which come out out at night, and how they are the only flying mammals. Today we talked about some of the noises that we hear during the night. We learned that night noises aren't scary. They are the same noises we hear during the day, but it's noisier so we don't pay any attention to them."

Extend and Enrich

Use the following ideas to extend and enrich what children know about night noises.

◆ Introduce the word *onomatopoeia*. That's what you call it when you use words that actually sound like the object or action that you are talking about. When you say the word "hiss," for instance, it really sounds like the hiss of a snake. *Night Noises* has several examples of *onomatopoeia*, such as *click, clack, crinch, crunch, shhhh, rattle, clatter, bang,* and *creak.*

◆ *Night Noises* has several surprise visitors. Give each child a brown construction paper door shape and a piece of white paper. Encourage the children to glue their doors on their papers, bending them so that they appear to be open. Have the children draw visitors behind their doors.

Things that Are Cold

Ice Cream

Morning Circle

Provide six empty, half-gallon containers of different flavors of ice cream. Use the containers to build a pyramid-type tower by stacking three on the bottom, two in the middle, and one on the very top. Place the containers so that the children can see the flavors of ice cream when they arrive at circle time. Ask them what they think came in the containers and ask them to name their favorite flavors of ice cream. After the discussion, make a modified bowling game by providing a plastic ball for the children to take turns rolling at the ice cream tower to see how many of the containers they can knock down.

Storytime

Ice Cream Bear by Jez Alborough

Daily Center Activity Ideas

ART CENTER

▪ **Beginning Learner:** Ice Cream Cones/Sponge Painting
Cut out circles from brown, pink, and white construction paper to resemble scoops of ice cream, and cut sponges into cone shapes. Encourage the children to dip the sponges into brown paint and make cone designs on their paper. When the cones are dry, invite them to glue "scoops" of ice cream on the cones to create ice cream cones. They may even want double or triple scoops!

▪ ▪ **Developing Learner:** Ice Cream Cones/Tracing
Provide glue sticks, a large piece of white construction paper, and an ice cream cone shape cut from cardboard for the children to use as a pattern. Also provide sponges cut into circle shapes and pink paint, light brown paint, and cream-colored paint. Encourage the children to trace the cone-shaped patterns on the white construction paper, dip the circle sponges into the "flavor" of ice cream that they like the best and put it on their cone pictures.

Experienced Learner: Ice Cream Sundaes

Find pictures of ice cream sundaes to show
the children. Provide yellow construction
paper for bananas, red construction paper
for cherries, dark brown construction
paper for chocolate ice cream, beige
construction paper for vanilla ice cream,
and pink construction paper for
strawberry ice cream. Also set out patterns
for bowls or sundae glasses. Encourage
each child to trace a bowl or sundae glass
on white paper and then cut scoops of ice
cream, bananas, and cherries from other
colors of construction paper to glue on the
bowl to make an ice cream sundae.

MATH CENTER

Beginning Learner: Sorting Ice Cream Flavors

Provide a bowl of different sizes and colors of pompoms (pink, white, and brown) to represent
scoops of ice cream and an ice cream scoop. Encourage the children to use the ice cream scoop
to scoop up the pompoms and sort them into bowls according to color and size.

Developing Learner: Flavor Patterns

Before doing this activity, cut out ice cream cone shapes from brown paper. Provide colored
pompoms, white construction paper, and glue. Encourage the children to glue the cone shapes
onto the white construction paper and use pompoms to create an ice cream cone with many
scoops. Have the children make patterns by alternating different "flavors" of ice cream.

Experienced Learner: How Many Licks?

Encourage the children to predict how many licks they think it will take to eat a small scoop of
ice cream. Record their predictions on a chart and put it on the table in front of them. Ask the
children to find a partner. Give one child in each pair a small scoop of ice cream on a cone. As
one partner licks the ice cream cone, the other partner counts the number of licks. Help them
count, as necessary. When the child has finished the ice cream cone, the counting partner records
the actual number of licks on the prediction sheet. The children then switch roles. Discuss how
close their predictions were to the actual number. (**Safety note:** Check for allergies before doing
this activity.)

SCIENCE CENTER

■ Beginning Learner: Root Beer Floats

Provide vanilla ice cream, root beer, straws, cups, an ice cream scoop, and spoons for the children to make root beer floats. Let the children help you scoop the ice cream into the cups. (**Hint:** Let the ice cream soften so it is easier for the children to help with this process.) Next, let them help pour root beer over their ice cream. As the children enjoy their frozen treat, talk about the carbonation of the soda. Carbonation is a process in which a gas called carbon dioxide is added to a drink to make it bubbly. Ask the children if they can think of other drinks that are bubbly. You may also want to discuss the melting of the ice cream. Explain that the root beer is not as cold as the ice cream, so the ice cream melts when the two are combined.

■ ■ Developing Learner: Ice Cream Sundaes

Provide vanilla, chocolate, and strawberry ice cream, whipped cream, sprinkles, a jar of cherries, bowls, spoons an ice cream scoop, and a container of warm water. Encourage the children to try to scoop the ice cream from the container using a room temperature ice cream scoop and then provide a bowl of warm water. Show the children how to submerge the ice cream scoop into the warm water and then use it to scoop their ice cream. Discuss with them how the warmth of the water heats the scoop and how the warm scoop melts the ice cream and makes it easier to scoop out of the container. Invite the children to decide which kind of ice cream they would like to have, and help them scoop it into their bowl. When everyone has had an opportunity to scoop ice cream into their bowl, discuss with them how the ice cream in the container looks melted. Tell the children that you are going to put the ice cream back into the freezer and take it out in a little while and see if it has refrozen and become hard again. They can top their ice cream as desired and eat.

■ ■ ■ Experienced Learner: Making Ice Cream

Provide chilled whipping cream, vanilla flavoring, rock salt, crushed ice, and zipper lock plastic bags in two sizes. Let the children help pour one cup of whipping cream and 1 teaspoon of vanilla flavoring into a zipper lock bag (double bag the ingredients). Place two cups each of rock salt and crushed ice into a larger zipper lock bag. Place the bag of ice cream ingredients inside the bag of salt and ice. Now double bag the whole thing. Encourage the children to sit on the floor or at a table and slide the bag back and forth. They may want to wear gloves because their hands will get cold. Everyone will be able to watch the ice cream as it freezes. When finished, take the ice cream bag out of the salty bag. Rinse off the salt from the ice cream bag before opening. Spoon out the ice cream into cups and bowls so the children can enjoy. (**Note:** Ingredients can be doubled or tripled to make larger quantities of ice cream depending on the number of children participating in the activity. Rock salt can be found in the most grocery stores in the same aisle as table salt. Rock salt yields the best results, but if you cannot find it, you may substitute table salt.)

LANGUAGE/DRAMATIC PLAY CENTER

■ **Beginning Learner:** Ice Cream Shop/Role Play

Give the children a small taste of chocolate, vanilla, and strawberry ice cream. Encourage them to describe the ice cream that they tasted in the math and science centers. Provide clean, empty ice cream containers, plastic bowls, spoons and ice cream scoops for the children to set up their own ice cream shop. Use pink, brown, and beige pompoms for different flavors of ice cream. Encourage the children to take turns being the customers and the employees of the ice cream shop.

■ ■ **Developing Learner:** Ice Cream Shop/Advertising

Provide crayons, markers, and construction paper for the children to make posters advertising the ice cream flavors so that customers visiting their shop will want to buy ice cream. Engage the children in a discussion of words that describe ice cream, such as *cold, creamy, smooth, soft, tasty, yummy,* and *sweet.*

■ ■ ■ **Experienced Learner:** Ice Cream Shop/Menu

Provide drawing paper, crayons, and markers, as well as a menu from an ice cream shop that lists different flavors of ice cream. Read the flavors to the children. Encourage the children to brainstorm new flavors of ice cream. Invite each child to think of a name for his own ice cream flavor and generate ideas on what the ice cream would taste like. Have the children make their own menus by drawing pictures of different ice cream flavors. Help them write the names of the flavors as well as prices on their menus. Ask them to think of a name for their ice cream shop and help them write the name in big print at the top of their menu.

VOCABULARY

cold, cone, creamy, flavor, float, frozen, melt, scoops, shake, soft, sprinkles, sticky, straw, sundae, sweet

Reflect

Say to the children, "Today we learned about ice cream and how cold, smooth, and delicious it is. Tomorrow we will learn about milk."

Extend and Enrich

Use the following ideas to extend and enrich what children know about ice cream.
- ◆ Take a class poll to find out the flavors of ice cream that the children like best. Make a graph for the children to vote on their favorite flavors.
- ◆ Plan an ice cream party and invite parents to join the fun. Provide the ice cream, and invite the children to bring their favorite toppings to share with the class.

DAY 2

Milk

Morning Circle

When the children arrive, give each child a small plastic cup of milk. Tell the children that there is a funny thing that happens when you drink milk—it sometimes gives you a "milk moustache!" Encourage the children to drink their milk and try to make a milk moustache. Provide mirrors so they can see their milk moustaches. (**Safety note:** Some children are lactose intolerant. Check for allergies before doing this activity.) Discuss with the children that milk contains vitamins and minerals, especially calcium, which makes our bones grow strong. Also explain that people aren't the only ones who enjoy drinking milk. Many animals drink their mothers' milk as babies. Tell the children that they are going to hear a story about a little kitten that thought the moon was a large bowl of milk! Read *Kitten's First Full Moon* to the children.

Storytime

Kitten's First Full Moon by Kevin Henkes

Daily Center Activity Ideas

ART CENTER

▪ **Beginning Learner:** Spilled Milk Paintings

Show the children the book *It Looked Like Spilt Milk* by Charles G. Shaw and talk about the pictures. Provide dark construction paper, small cups of white paint, and paint smocks. Help the children fold their papers in half and then open them again. Show the children how to pour "milk" (paint) on one side of the paper, fold the paper in half again, and press down on the paper. When the children open their paper, they will see what their "spilled milk" looks like.

▪▪ **Developing Learner:** Painting with "Milk"

Provide white, brown, and pink paint to represent white milk, chocolate milk, and strawberry milk. Provide paper and brushes for the children to make "milk" paintings.

▪
▪▪ **Experienced Learner:** Paint Milk in a Glass

Provide the children with three clean, pint-sized milk cartons filled with pink (strawberry), white (regular), and brown (chocolate) paint; paper; paintbrushes; paint smocks; and paper. Fill each carton with a color of paint and place a paintbrush in each milk carton. Invite each child to draw three drinking glass shapes (or trace them using a stencil) on paper and then fill the glasses with "milk."

MATH CENTER

For the beginning and developing learners, prepare by filling 10 empty, clean 2-liter bottles with a small amount of water or sand for stability. Put the cap back on the bottles and cover each bottle with a white sock. Using a black marker, write the numerals 1–10 on the socks. Provide a soft ball.

Beginning Learner: Milk Bottle Bowling/Number Recognition

Provide the materials in the preparation step and encourage the children to roll the ball to try and knock down the bottles. Ask them to identify the numerals on the bottles that they knock down and the numerals on the bottles that are still standing. Encourage the children to take turns bowling.

Developing Learner: Milk Bottle Bowling/Addition

Encourage the children to roll the ball and knock down the bottles. When some of the bottles have fallen down, help the children add the numerals on the bottles that have fallen down to get their score. Have children record their scores on index cards. Encourage them to take turns and continue bowling until their score cards are full.

Experienced Learner: Milk Bottle Game/Counting

Provide clean, plastic, one-gallon milk containers and 40 clothespins. Provide a spinner with numerals on it. Encourage the children to spin the spinner and then stand over the milk containers and try to drop the correct number of clothespins into the open top of a milk container. Encourage the children to play until each child has had several turns.

SCIENCE CENTER

Beginning Learner: Making Pudding

Provide empty, clean baby food jars, instant pudding mix, and milk. Let the children help pour a small amount of dried pudding mix into their jar, add milk, and replace the lid on the jar. Encourage the children to shake the jar until the pudding becomes solid. Talk about how shaking the ingredients in the jar, mixes them together and how the pudding seems to become thicker as it is shaken. Provide plastic spoons and eat the pudding for snack.

Developing Learner: Milk Carton Blocks

Collect different sizes of milk cartons and open their tops for easy stuffing. Help the children stuff the milk cartons with newspaper and tape the tops closed. Help the children use contact paper to cover the sides of the cartons to make building blocks. When all of the cartons have been stuffed and covered in contact paper, the children can use them to build towers. Encourage the children to experiment with different ways of stacking the blocks to make a stable tower.

■ ■ ■ **Experienced Learner:** Milk Jug Scoopers

Provide an empty, clean, plastic one-gallon milk container for each child. (You may ask parents to send in empty milk containers.) Cut each milk jug so that the top and a section of the front are removed, but the handle and bottom remain so that it looks like a scoop. Fill a child-size wading pool with white Styrofoam balls or white pompoms. Encourage the children to dip their milk jug scoopers into the pool and fill them with the pretend "milk." The children can also use their scoopers to play a tossing game with ping pong balls.

LANGUAGE/DRAMATIC PLAY CENTER

Explain to the children that a long time ago, it was not always convenient for people to go to the grocery store to buy milk. Many people had their milk delivered to their homes by people who drove milk trucks.

■ **Beginning Learner:** Milk Delivery

Show the children different sizes of milk containers, including several one-pint, half-gallon, and one-gallon empty milk cartons. Put all of the milk cartons in an empty plastic milk crate. Encourage the children to sort the "milk" by carton size and pretend to deliver milk to the houses of their classmates.

■ ■ **Developing Learner:** Milk Delivery/Taking Orders

Provide toy trucks, milk crates, empty milk jugs and milk cartons, and a telephone and order pad for the children to take orders so that they can role play being the milk delivery person of earlier days.

■ ■ **Experienced Learner:** Grocery Delivery

Today, there are grocery store companies that deliver groceries to homes if a person places an order over the phone or on the computer. Provide a computer keyboard, telephone, and a notepad for children to pretend to take grocery orders over the telephone. Also provide empty milk cartons, milk jugs, and other empty food boxes as well as brown grocery bags for children to pretend to work at the warehouse where the grocery orders are filled. They can bag the orders and other children can place the bags of groceries on wagons or in carts to "deliver" to the customer's house.

VOCABULARY

bowl, cereal, chocolate, cold, cup, glass, ice cream, milk, milkshake, pudding, refrigerator, strawberry, thick, white

Reflect

Say to the children, "Yesterday we learned about ice cream and what a special treat it is to enjoy on a hot day (or any day!). Today we learned about milk and about some of the different things that are made from milk. Tomorrow we will learn about winter and all of the fun things that we can do during that special time of year."

Extend and Enrich

Use the following ideas to extend and enrich what children know about milk and milk products.

◆ Provide grocery store advertisements from the newspaper and encourage the children to search for pictures of milk or milk products. Provide scissors so they can cut out the pictures and make their own milk collages.

Winter

Morning Circle

Gather several props to symbolize the four seasons, such as fall leaves, Styrofoam pieces (to represent snow), an umbrella or flowers, and a beach ball. Use masking tape to divide the circle area into four sections and place the seasonal props in their corresponding sections. When the children arrive, have them gather in another part of the room. Talk to them about the four seasons, and then take them to the circle area and discuss the four sections of the circle and the items in each circle. Encourage the children to stand in the section that represents their favorite season.

Storytime

The First Day of Winter by Denise Fleming

Daily Center Activity Ideas

ART CENTER

Beginning Learner: Winter Tree
Provide the children with a piece of blue construction paper and a brown construction paper tree trunk. Encourage the children to glue their tree trunk to the blue paper and use brown paint and a small paintbrush to paint limbs on the tree. Provide cotton swabs and white paint for the children to use to dot their winter picture with "snow."

Developing Learner: Painting Winter Scenes
Show the children pictures of winter scenes and snow from magazines, holiday cards, or calendars. Provide blue construction paper and white paint for the children to paint their own winter scenes.

Experienced Learner: Four-Season Wheel
Give the children paper plates and help them use black markers to divide their plates into four equal sections. Label each section with the name of one of the seasons: winter, spring, summer, and fall. Cut out arrow shapes, like the hand on a clock, from black paper. Help each child punch a hole through the center of a plate and through an arrow. Use a brad to attach the arrow to the plate.. In each section of their plates, have the children draw what they think the seasons look like. Write the words *winter, spring, summer*, and *fall* on the board, and encourage the children to copy the words onto their paper plates in the appropriate section. When the four-season wheels

are finished, the children can rotate the hand around their plates to indicate their favorite season, what the current season is, what the next season is, and so on.

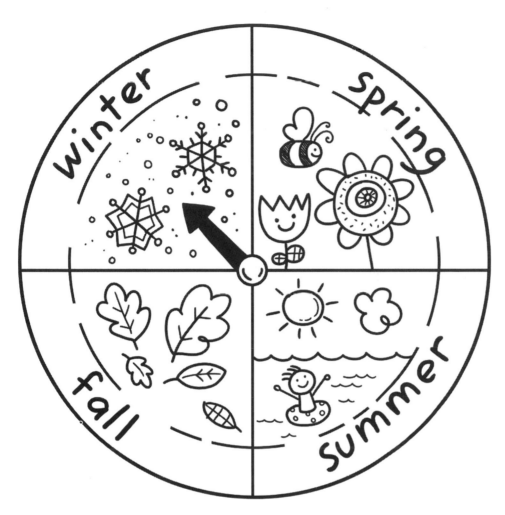

MATH CENTER

■ **Beginning Learner:** Numbers on a Calendar
Collect calendars with pictures that represent the 12 months of the year. Collect several pictures for each month. Show the children some of the pictures and discuss what seasons and months of the year the pictures depict. Show the children the squares and numerals that represent each day. Practice counting some of the squares with the children. Provide some calendar pages with squares and numerals that the children can cut and glue on paper.

■ ■ **Developing Learner:** Seasons: How Many Months in a Season?
Tell the children that there are 12 months in each year and that the months are divided into four seasons: winter, spring, summer, and fall. Write the names of the 12 months and the four seasons on index cards. Next, provide a few calendar pages with monthly pictures that represent the different seasons. Encourage the children to sort the pictures according to the four seasons and then label their piles using the index cards with the season names. Help the children sort the index cards with the names of the months on them into the appropriate season category as well. Encourage the children to move the pictures and index cards around in different ways until they are happy with the results.

Experienced Learner: Numbering the Days

Give each child an empty calendar page with boxes marked for 31 days. Also provide a completed calendar page that has the numerals 1–31 written in the boxes. Encourage the children to practice writing one numeral in each box on the empty calendar page using the completed calendar page as an example.

SCIENCE CENTER

Safety note: Check for peanut allergies. You may substitute corn syrup if any of the children are allergic to peanut butter.

Beginning Learner: Milk Carton Bird Feeder

Provide an empty half-pint milk carton for each child. Cut the milk cartons in half, keeping only the bottom parts and discarding the top parts with the spout. Use a hole punch to punch one hole near the top on two sides of the carton and thread a piece of yarn through the holes so that the bird feeder can hang from a tree when it is complete. Provide small lunch bags, birdseed, and peanut butter. Encourage the children to spread peanut butter on their milk cartons, fill a small lunch bag with birdseed, and then drop the milk carton into the bag and shake it. Remove the bird feeder from the bag and fill it with a small amount of bird seed. Hang the bird feeders outside on the playground or nearby.

Developing Learner: Pinecone Creature Feeders

Look at the pictures in *The First Day of Winter* with the children, and encourage them to notice the different creatures in the illustrations. Point out the pinecones in the story, and tell the children they are going to use pinecones to make special feeders for the little outdoor animals that need food in the winter. Provide pinecones, peanut butter, paper plates, a brown paper bag, birdseed, yarn, and plastic knives. Show the children how to spread peanut butter on their pinecones and then drop the pinecones into a small grocery bag filled with birdseed. Remove the pinecones from the bag and help the children use yarn to hang their creature feeders from a tree on the playground.

Experienced Learner

Show the children the illustrations in *The First Day of Winter*. Explain that animals often have trouble finding food in the winter because their food sources are covered with a thick blanket of snow. Give each child half of an orange, peanut butter, birdseed, and a string. Encourage the children to eat the inside of their orange. Next, invite the children to spread peanut butter inside the empty orange half and then sprinkle birdseed on the peanut butter. Help them poke tiny holes on opposite sides of the orange half and thread string through the holes. Hang the feeders from a tree on the playground.

LANGUAGE/DRAMATIC PLAY CENTER

Beginning Learner: White Blanket of Snow

Collect pictures from calendars or magazines that show lots of snow on the ground. Explain to the children that, in some places, snow falls in the winter and looks like a white blanket covering the ground. Invite the children to use cotton batting, a white blanket, and Styrofoam pieces to spread out and cover the floor of the classroom to resemble how the ground might look after a heavy snowfall. They can use the materials separately or combine them in ways to resemble a blanket of snow.

Developing Learner: Dressing for Winter

Provide an assortment of winter clothes, including heavy pants, sweaters, jackets, long underwear, winter hats, winter socks, heavy boots, and mittens. Set out a second plastic container of summer clothes, including shorts, swimsuits, sleeveless shirts, sandals, sun visors, and sunglasses. Mix the clothes together in a pile on the floor. Encourage the children to sort the clothes into two piles: one for summer and one for winter.

Experienced Learner: Warming Up by the Fire

Remind the children that in winter, people often make a fire in the fireplace to help them keep warm. Provide logs and branches for the children to arrange to make a pretend campfire. Have them tear and shred yellow, orange, and red tissue paper to make flames for their fires. Let the children lie on blankets and pillows next to the pretend fire. Have fun reading some of their favorite books or singing some of their favorite songs by the "campfire."

VOCABULARY

boots, cold, fire place, frozen, gloves, hibernation, ice, melt, mittens, scarf, snow, snow shovel, winter

Reflect

Say to the children, "Yesterday we learned about milk and how cold it feels when we drink it. Today we learned about winter and all of the special things that we can do and wear during this special time of the year. Tomorrow we will learn about ice and how it is used in many different ways to keep things cold."

Extend and Enrich

Use the following ideas to extend and enrich what children know about winter.
- Look at the story *The First Day of Winter* and use the pictures and text to provide the children with some great counting practice.

Ice

Morning Circle

When the children arrive at school, give each child a small plastic cup of crushed ice. Encourage the children to eat the ice. Ask them to pay attention to the crunching sound that the ice makes as they chew it and the chill of the ice in their mouths. See if they notice that the ice melts in their mouths and makes water. Provide a block of ice, ice cubes, and crushed ice for the children to explore. Encourage the children to come up with words to describe the different forms of ice. Discuss the concept of igloos and introduce the story for the day.

Storytime

Building an Igloo by Ulli Stetzer

Daily Center Activity Ideas

ART CENTER

Beginning Learner: Ice Painting on a Stick

Mix water and food coloring together and pour into ice cube trays. Let the ice freeze partially and then insert a craft stick or tongue depressor in each section. Place the tray back in the freezer. The children can make pictures using the frozen colored ice cube sticks.

Developing Learner: Crushed Ice Painting

Provide each child with a pie tin and a round piece of paper. Prepare a cup of crushed ice mixed with tempera paint mixed. Encourage the children to pour the mixture on their paper in the pie tin. The children shake the pie tin to move the crushed ice around, making designs on their paper. Remove their papers from their pie tins and let dry.

Experienced Learner: Block Ice Design

Provide a block of ice and small squirt bottles filled with water and food coloring (or paint). Place the block of ice in a plastic tub. Invite the children to squirt the liquid from the bottles at the block of ice and watch as the colors paint the ice, causing it to melt and drip down the sides.

MATH CENTER

■ **Beginning Learner:** Counting to 12

Provide a bowl of ice cubes, tongs, and empty ice trays. Help the children count the number of empty spaces in the ice tray. Encourage the children to use the tongs to transfer the ice cubes from the bowl to the ice trays. Talk about the number 12 with the children as they are moving the ice.

■ ■ **Developing Learner:** Paper Igloos

Share the story for the day, *Building an Igloo,* with the children. Encourage the children to look at the pictures and details in the story. Provide white construction paper, glue, and block shapes. Have them trace the blocks on their paper and cut them out to make brick shapes. The children can then assemble their own igloo structures by gluing their bricks on paper.

■
■ ■ **Experienced Learner:** Packing Peanuts Igloos

Encourage the children to look at the pictures in the book *Building an Igloo* to get ideas for constructing their own igloos. Provide packing peanuts, small watercolor paintbrushes, and water. Show the children how to "paint" a small amount of water on the packing peanuts to stick them to each other. Provide a small square of cardboard for the children to use as a base for building and then invite them to build igloos.

SCIENCE CENTER

■ **Beginning Learner:** Rescuing Frozen Toys

Place small toys such as dinosaurs, farm animals, and insects in plastic bowls. Fill the bowls with water and freeze them. When they are frozen, give a block of ice with a toy inside to each child. Encourage the children to come up with ideas on how to retrieve the objects inside the blocks of ice. Try all ideas that the children suggest.

Developing Learner: Predicting Water Levels

Provide clear plastic cups. Encourage the children to use a black permanent marker to draw a line around their cups. Fill the cups with water up to the line. Place the cups on a level surface in the freezer. Encourage the children to make predictions about what they think will happen to the water when it freezes. Will the water stay at the line, go over the line, or go under the line? Write the children's predictions on paper. When the water has frozen, take the cups out of the freezer, and encourage the children to observe what has happened to the water in relation to the line that they drew. Have them evaluate their predictions.

Experienced Learner: Melting Ice Cubes

Provide each child with a clear cup filled with water just to the brim. Give each child a large ice cube to add to their cup. Before adding the ice cube, ask the children to predict what they think will happen to the water when the ice melts. Assist the children with the experiment and with evaluating their predictions.

LANGUAGE/DRAMATIC PLAY CENTER

Beginning Learner: Sliding Ice Cubes

Provide a small toddler-size plastic slide and ice cubes. Provide a tub at the bottom of the slide to catch the ice cubes. Encourage the children to take turns letting their ice cubes slide down the slide.

Developing Learner: Ice Cube Races

In preparation for this activity, fill several ice cube trays with colored water. Also, provide a toddler-size plastic slide for the children to have ice cube races. Let each child decide what color ice cube she wants. Encourage the children to place their ice cubes at the top of the slide and when someone says "Go," the children release their ice cubes. The children watch to see which ice cube reaches the bottom of the slide first. Repeat as many times as the children wish.

Experienced Learner: Ice Cube Slalom

Provide a slide and ice cubes as described for the developing learner. Also provide different "obstacles" on the slide such as salt, baby powder, and cooking oil for the children to experiment with to see if these materials speed up or slow down their ice cubes. Discuss the different properties of the materials and why they cause different results.

VOCABULARY

block, cold, crushed, freezer, glacier, hail, ice, ice cube, iceberg, slush

Reflect

Say to the children, "Yesterday we learned about the season of winter and all of the fun things that can be done outside when it is very cold. Today we learned about ice and how very cold it feels to the touch. Tomorrow we will learn more about snow."

Extend and Enrich

Use the following ideas to extend and enrich what children know about ice.

◆ Encourage the children to conduct experiments to try to find out which will melt first in a cup: frozen water, ice cubes, or crushed ice.

◆ Show the children a magic trick. Sprinkle a few grains of salt on an ice cube. Place a piece of string approximately 3" across the area where the salt was sprinkled. Wait three seconds and then lift the string. The ice cube will be attached to the string! Explain that salt lowers the temperature of ice and freezes the string to the ice cube.

◆ Freeze colored water in round bowls. Put the colored ice in the water table. Provide droppers and food coloring. Encourage the children to squirt the food coloring on the frozen ice to create interesting patterns on the ice.

Snow

Morning Circle

Cover the classroom floor or circle area with starch packing peanuts. When the children arrive, invite them to pick up the peanuts and throw them in the air so that they fall like snow. Also provide rolled-up socks or Styrofoam balls and encourage the children to practice tossing "snowballs" into the air.

Storytime

The Snowy Day by Ezra Jack Keats

Daily Center Activity Ideas

ART CENTER

Beginning Learner: Snowstorm Painting

Provide blue construction paper, cotton swabs, and white paint for the children to paint a snowstorm picture. Encourage the children to dip the cotton swabs in white paint and paint little dots of snow all over their papers.

Developing Learner: Snowstorm Painting II

Provide a clean, empty pizza box, a marble or golf ball, white paint, and blue paper. Encourage the children to place a piece of construction paper in the pizza box and use a spoon to put a small amount of white paint inside the box. The children add the golf ball, shut the box, and take turns rolling and shaking it back and forth to create an interesting snowstorm painting.

Experienced Learner: Snow Dough

Make playdough with the children using a no-cook playdough recipe. Give each child a small sandwich bag full of rock salt to mix in with their playdough to make snow dough. Encourage the children to roll their snow dough into snowballs of different sizes. (**Note:** Rock salt can be found in most grocery stores in the same aisle as table salt. If you cannot find rock salt, you may substitute kosher salt for this activity.)

MATH CENTER

■ **Beginning Learner:** Snow Baskets/Sizes

Spread packing peanuts on the floor. Provide three containers in different sizes (small, medium, and large). Encourage the children to use their hands or small shovels or scoops to fill the three different sizes of baskets with "snow."

■ ■ **Developing Learner:** Counting Snowflakes

Invite the children to fill different sizes of cups with starch packing peanuts. Pretend that the packing peanuts are snowflakes. Encourage the children to see how many "snowflakes" they can fit into a cup. When their cups are full, help them count their "snowflakes" and use a marker to write that numeral on the outside of their cups.

■ ■ **Experienced Learner:** Timing a Snowflake Race

Provide packing peanuts and a timer. Set the timer and explain to the children that they will catch as many "snowflakes" as they can before the timer goes off. Discuss with the children how much time they think is needed, and determine the time limit. Ask each child to predict how many "snowflakes" she thinks she can gather. Have the children write their predictions on index cards. Set the timer and let the snow fun begin. Check the children's predictions.

SCIENCE CENTER

■ **Beginning Learner:** Snow Cones

Provide the children with a snow cone machine, snow cone syrup or flavored drink, ice, Styrofoam cups, a large ice cream scoop, and spoons. Gather the children around a table and let them help make snow cones. Let each child scoop crushed ice into a cup and form a snow cone. Pour flavored syrup over the crushed ice. Enjoy the snow cones for snack. While the children are enjoying their snow cone treat, show them a Styrofoam ice chest and discuss with them that the Styrofoam cup and the Styrofoam in the ice chest helps insulate the ice and keep snacks and drinks cold.

■ ■ **Developing Learner:** Which Melts Faster?

Make shaved ice ("snow") using a snow cone machine. Give each child a mitten to wear on one hand. Invite them to scoop up the "snow" with the hand wearing a mitten and use their bare hand to scoop up another scoop of "snow." Which hand is colder? Which scoop of ice will melt faster? Talk about real snow and what it feels like. Fill a tub or water table with shaved ice and invite the children to play in the "snow." (**Note:** If you live in a cold climate where there is a lot of snow, simply collect the snow needed for this activity outdoors.)

Experienced Learner: Coloring Snow

Use a snow cone machine to create snow or, if possible, collect some snow from outside. Place the snow in a water table or a large tub. Provide cups of water mixed with food coloring and droppers or pipettes. Invite the children to use the food coloring and droppers to mix colors and make designs in the snow. As the children continue to drop the food coloring on the snow, it will begin to melt and the colors will mix.

LANGUAGE/DRAMATIC PLAY CENTER

Beginning Learner: Snow Globes

Bring several examples of snow globes to the classroom. Show the children a snow globe and demonstrate how snow fills the container when you shake it. Tell the children that they are going to make their own snow globes. Provide empty baby food jars, water, clear or white plastic or metallic glitter, and small waterproof plastic objects for the children to place in their jars. Invite the each child to choose a plastic object to put into a snow globe. Help the children fill their jars with water and place their selected objects inside. Add clear glitter to the water to resemble snow. Put the lids of the jars on tightly and glue shut. Encourage the children to shake their jars and see the snow scene they have created.

Developing Learner: Snow Globe Story Starter

Provide the materials as described for the beginning learner and help the children make snow globes. Encourage the children to use their snow globes as an inspiration for dictating a story.

Experienced Learner: Story Jars

Provide each child with an empty plastic mayonnaise or peanut butter jar; white confetti or glitter to represent snow; and small toys, people figures, or animal figures. Encourage the children to select several items and place them in their plastic jars. Have them fill their jars with glitter and water and replace the lid. Encourage the children to shake their jars to see the characters inside. Tell the children that the characters inside their jars can be inspiration for telling a story. Write their stories down to accompany the story jars.

VOCABULARY

avalanche, blizzard, cold, flakes, flurries, powder, snow, snow chains, snow drift, snow plows, snow shoes, snowballs, snowman, snowstorm, snowy day

Reflect

Say to the children, "Yesterday we learned about ice and the different forms that it can take when it is frozen. Today we learned about snow and all of the fun things that you can do while playing in it."

Extend and Enrich

Use the following ideas to extend and enrich what children know about snow.

- Fill a clear bowl with colored water. Stuff a paper towel into a plastic cup and plunge the cup—with the open end down—into the bowl full of colored water. Hold it there so that the children can see that it is submerged. Carefully lift the cup out without tipping it and letting water inside. Show the children that the paper towel did not change colors and is dry. Encourage the children to repeat the process. What is happening? Answer: Air acts like an invisible lid, keeping the water from coming into the cup.
- Fill the playground area with starch packing peanuts to resemble a snowstorm. Invite the children to wear their snow boots outside to play and use plastic shovels and buckets to pick up the play "snow." Try to use biodegradable packing peanuts, which will melt into the ground with moisture.
- In the winter when it is snowing, place a container outside and catch some real snow. Have the children use a ruler to measure the snow to determine how much has fallen in a given time period.

Daily Preschool Experiences

Things Found in Cold Places

Hibernating Animals

Morning Circle

Prior to doing this day's activities, send a note home to families asking them to let their child bring a stuffed animal to class. Before children arrive, cover a long table with black fabric to represent a cave. Spread pieces of Styrofoam on the floor to represent snow and have a fan blowing to simulate a really cold environment. Dim the lights. When the children arrive, tell them that winter is almost here and they should pretend to be animals that need to find a home where the cold, wet snow will not reach them. Invite the children to crawl into the cave to stay dry. Read the story, *Time to Sleep* by Denise Fleming. Afterwards, talk about hibernation. Explain that in the winter, snow and ice cover many of the foods and plants that some animals need to eat to live, so these animals hibernate, or sleep, all winter. Other animals, such as birds, migrate to warmer places where there is food for them to eat during the winter. Frogs, snakes, bears, and skunks are some of the animals that hibernate.

Storytime

Time to Sleep by Denise Fleming

Daily Center Activity Ideas

ART CENTER

■ **Beginning Learner:** Brown Bear Painting

Cut a bear shape out of brown construction paper for each child using the bear pictures from the book *Time to Sleep* as a pattern. Provide pieces of brown fur, or felt or brown material for the children to glue on their bears. When the bears have dried, the children can add wiggle eyes and a nose, and a mouth to their bears using pieces of colored yarn or small pieces of colored material.

■ ■ **Developing Learner:** Winter Scenes

Help children trace a tree pattern on brown construction paper and cut it out. Invite them to glue the tree trunks on blue paper. Provide white paint and cotton swabs for the children to use to paint white snowflakes all over their paper for a winter scene.

Experienced Learner: Falling Leaves

In the story, *Time to Sleep*, the skunk notices that the leaves on the trees are falling to the ground. This is a sign that winter is coming. Provide white construction paper and brown, red, yellow, and orange paint. Using a paintbrush, paint the entire underside of each child's forearm, including palm and fingers, with brown paint. Have the child press his entire arm and outstretched fingers on the paper to make a tree trunk and branches. Help the children wash their arms and hands to remove the paint. The children can dip small sponges into the red, yellow, and orange paint to make leaf prints on the tree branches. Some of the leaves could even be falling down to the ground.

MATH CENTER: HIBERNATING BEARS

To do this activity at any level, ask the children to bring in their favorite stuffed bear or animal and use the "cave" you created for the morning circle activity.

Beginning Learner: Bears/Subtraction and Sizes

Ask the children to place the bears in the "cave." Gather as a group and count how many bears are in the cave. Take one away and count again. Now how many bears are there? Once the bears are all counted, have the children place them in the cave by size, either largest to smallest or vice versa.

Developing Learner: Bears/Counting

Provide a deck of playing cards and the bears or animals that the children brought from home. Place all of the stuffed animals in a large basket or in the middle of the floor. Encourage the children to draw a card from the deck and count out that number of stuffed bears from the pile or basket. Invite the children to place the animals that they count inside the cave to hibernate. The next child can take the animals out of the cave before drawing a card.

Experienced Learner: Bears/Addition

Place the animals in a basket or in the middle of the floor. Tell the children that the animals are waiting to go inside their caves to hibernate for the winter. Have a child spin a game spinner with numerals on it and identify the numeral. Ask the child to count out that number of stuffed animals and place the animals inside the cave. Invite the next child to spin the spinner

and place that number of bears in the cave. Have the child count all of the bears in the cave. Continue playing the game and adding bears until the children can no longer count that high. Then play the game by spinning the spinner and taking the bears out of the cave.

SCIENCE CENTER

Beginning Learner: Foraging for Food

Provide stuffed animals, cotton batting, and play foods such as fish, berries, and meat. Encourage the children to cover up the play food with the cotton batting and use the stuffed animals to pretend to hunt for the food buried under the snow.

Developing Learner: Bears in Their Caves

Find pictures of bears and their caves. Discuss with the children that bears often dig and make caves that they can crawl into to hibernate during the winter. Discuss what happens in the winter and how hard it is for animals to survive if they stay outside unprotected in the cold. Cover a card table or a classroom table with a piece of dark fabric to form a cave or a burrow. Place pillows in the cave and cotton batting around the cave to represent snow. Encourage the children to go inside the cave or burrow and pretend to hibernate. After the children have been inside the cave for a few minutes, remove the "snow" and replace it with leaves or flowers to represent the change in seasons. It's time for the bears to come out!

Experienced Learner: Bear Caves

Find pictures of bears and caves. Also find pictures of a snow-covered forest and different forest animals. Talk about the seasons, and then look at the pictures and discuss where the animals go in the. Discuss bears and the fact that they often make or find caves to protect them from the cold and the snow. Invite the children to make their own winter habitats that can be a safe haven for animals in the snow. Give each child a shoebox to use as their cave. Encourage the children to use construction paper, and collage materials, to make homes and burrows for their forest animals and use the batting to cover the ground with snow.

LANGUAGE/DRAMATIC PLAY CENTER

Beginning Learner: Spreading the News

In the story *Time to Sleep,* all of the animals hurry to tell their animal friends the "news" that winter is coming. Provide several newspapers and comics for the children, and explain that newspapers are a way to give information to people.

Developing Learner: Story Sequencing

Use the pictures from the story *Time to Sleep* to make a bear, a snail, a skunk, a turtle, a woodchuck, and a ladybug. Encourage the children to put the story characters in order of when they appear in the story. Let them use the book as a reference. Also encourage the children to use the characters to retell the story.

■ ■ Experienced Learner: Hibernation Stories

Have the children bring the stuffed animals that they brought from home to the center. Encourage the children to create stories about their animals preparing to hibernate. Have them dictate their stories as you write their words down on paper for them. When the stories are complete, children may illustrate them.

VOCABULARY

bears, cave, hibernation, sleep, winter

Reflect

Say to the children, "Today we learned about bears and other animals that hibernate in the winter to keep warm and safe. Tomorrow we will learn about mittens. Who knows what mittens are?"

Extend and Enrich

Use the following ideas to extend and enrich what children know about bears.

♦ Play the "whisper game" and spread news just like the animals did in the story. Sit in a circle and have one child whisper a few short words to the person seated next to him. That person then whispers the same thing to the child next to him. The last person to receive the message says it out loud to the class. Ask the children if it is the same message that they heard.

♦ The animals in the story all have special places that they plan to sleep in the winter. Discuss the different kinds of animals and where they spend the winter.

♦ Talk about when everyone sleeps at night. Show the children a clock and move the hands around the clock to the different times that people are usually in bed and asleep.

DAY 2

Mittens

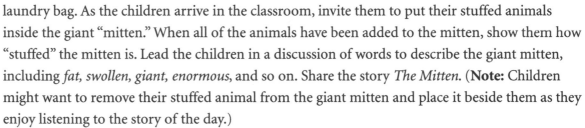

Morning Circle

Before doing this activity, send home a note encouraging the children to bring a small stuffed animal to school. Remind parents to write their child's name on the tag of the stuffed animal for easy identification. Provide a large drawstring laundry bag. As the children arrive in the classroom, invite them to put their stuffed animals inside the giant "mitten." When all of the animals have been added to the mitten, show them how "stuffed" the mitten is. Lead the children in a discussion of words to describe the giant mitten, including *fat, swollen, giant, enormous*, and so on. Share the story *The Mitten*. (**Note:** Children might want to remove their stuffed animal from the giant mitten and place it beside them as they enjoy listening to the story of the day.)

Storytime

The Mitten by Jan Brett

Daily Center Activity Ideas

ART CENTER

Show the children several sets of mittens and gloves and talk about how they are alike and different. Explain that when you wear mittens, all of the fingers fit into one opening. With gloves, each finger goes into its own compartment.

■ **Beginning Learner:** Paint Blot Mittens

Fold a piece of white construction paper in half and place the folded paper on the table. Give a folded piece of paper like this to each child. Help each child place one hand on their paper with the little finger on the fold. Make sure the fingers are touching each other to form a mitten shape. Trace the child's hand and cut out the shape, making sure not to cut through the fold. Invite the children to open up their papers and spoon small amounts of paint on different places on their mittens. Help the children fold the paper closed again. Have them use their fingers to rub gently over the top of the mittens. The paint  on the inside will spread and mix to make a design. When the children open their mittens, they will be surprised by the special design they have made. After the paint has dried, cut the mittens apart and string them together with yarn.

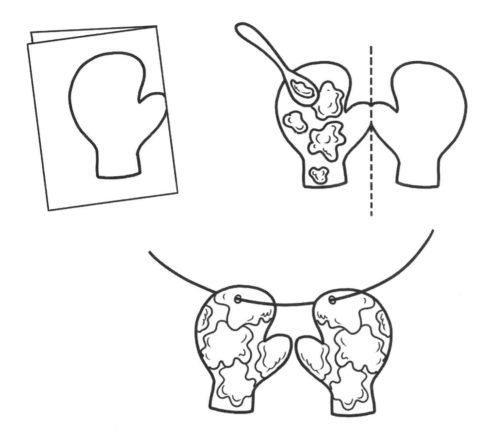

■ ■ **Developing Learner:** Decorating Mittens

Prior to this activity, trace two mittens on white cardstock for each child. Provide scissors, glue, glitter, sequins, rhinestones, yarn, ribbon, pompoms, and so on. Encourage the children to cut out a pair of mittens and use the art materials to decorate them. Allow the mittens to dry flat and then hang them on a yarn clothesline in the room for display.

■

■ ■ **Experienced Learner:** Giant Mittens

Draw two giant mittens on white bulletin board paper for each child in the class. Encourage the children to cut out both of the mittens from the bulletin board paper. Next, help the children place the mittens together and staple them (adult only) all the way around, leaving a small opening for the children to put in the stuffing. Invite the children to decorate their giant mitten using crayons, markers, dot markers, and stencils. When they are finished, help them stuff their mittens with toilet tissue or tissue paper. Staple the mitten closed.

MATH CENTER

Read the book *Three Little Kittens* by Paul Galdone.

■ **Beginning Learner:** Lost Paper Mittens

Cut out sets of mittens from wallpaper or construction paper. Hide one mitten from each set in different places in the center or the classroom, and give each child a match to the mittens that you have hidden. Encourage the children to go around the room and try to find the mates to their mittens.

◾ ◾ **Developing Learner:** Real Mitten Sets

Provide a clothesline, clothespins, and real mitten sets. Place all of the mittens in a basket and encourage the children to find the mittens and their mates and hang them beside each other on the clothesline.

◾
◾ ◾ **Experienced Learner:** Counting Animals

Put the laundry bag (giant mitten) from morning circle and the stuffed animals from the story in this center. If all of the animals from the story are not available, substitute with other forest animals. Place number cards 1–5 face down and ask a child to draw a card and identify the numeral. The child places that number of animals inside the "mitten." Let all the children have a turn, and when all of the animals are inside the mitten, reverse the game by removing animals.

SCIENCE CENTER

Prior to doing this activity, look at the pictures in the story *The Mitten* and collect a wide variety of plastic and stuffed animals from the story.

◾ **Beginning Learner:** Where Do These Animals Live?

Place all of the plastic and stuffed animals in a pillowcase. Have the children sit in a circle and take turns passing the pillowcase around the circle. Each child reaches inside the pillowcase and pulls out one of the animals and says the name of the animal and where he thinks it lives.

◾ ◾ **Developing Learner:** Animals in Cold Places

Explain that the animals in the story *The Mitten* were looking for a place to spend time during the long cold winter. When they found the mitten, they crawled inside it to keep warm and dry. Discuss with the children if they were an animal that lived in a cold place, what kind of animal would they like to be and where would they live. Provide crayons and markers, and encourage the children to draw a picture of the kind of animal they would like to be and what the cold place that they would live in would look like.

◾
◾ ◾ **Experienced Learner:** Animal Habitats

Explain that there are many different kinds of animals in the world and that they live in different types of environments. Provide many different toy plastic and stuffed animals and white cotton to represent snow. Discuss with the children how the animals in the story went inside the mitten to keep warm and dry. Show the children the animals and have them choose an animal from the group, name it and tell whether they think that it lives in a cold place or a warm place. If it lives in a cold place, have them place it on the cotton batting. If it lives in a warm place have them place it on a piece of brown construction paper.

LANGUAGE/DRAMATIC PLAY CENTER

Beginning Learner: Retelling the Story with Props

Cut out a large mitten shape from two pieces of white fabric. Sew the edges together to make a giant mitten like the one in the story *The Mitten*. Provide small stuffed animals and encourage the children to use the props to retell the story. Have them try to place as many stuffed animals as they can inside the mitten.

Developing Learner: Acting Out the Story

Write the name of each animal from the story on an index card. If possible, reproduce the pictures of the animals from the story and glue them to the index cards. Place the cards in a basket. Before reading the story, pass the basket around and ask the children to pick a card from the basket. Have them look at the card and identify what animal they have chosen. Retell the story to the children and encourage them to follow along. When a child's animal is mentioned, he pretends to be that animal. According to class size, this activity might need to be repeated more than once.

Experienced Learner: Grandmother Illustrations

In *The Mitten*, the little boy, Nicki, has a grandmother who knits him a pair of white mittens. Nicki calls his grandmother "Baba." Explain to the children that "Baba" is the Ukrainian word for "grandmother." Many boys and girls call their grandmothers many different and unique names. Ask the children what they call their grandmothers. Encourage them to write that name on their papers and draw a picture of themselves with their grandmothers.

VOCABULARY

fingers, forest, gloves, hands, knit, mittens, wool

Reflect

Say to the children, "Yesterday we learned about animals that hibernate to stay safe and warm through the winter. Today we learned about mittens and how they keep our hands warm and protect them from the cold. Tomorrow we will learn about penguins. Penguins live in very cold places, and they love it!"

Extend and Enrich

◆ Talk about the very intricate and detailed illustrations in *The Mitten* by Jan Brett. In her drawings, she provides hints or clues that relate to what is going to happen next in the story. Show the children other Jan Brett stories so they can compare the illustrations in some of her other books.

◆ Discuss that mittens are sometimes "connected" with yarn or string to keep them together and to help keep them from getting lost. Engage the children in a brainstorming session to think of other things that are "connected" in some way.

Penguins

Morning Circle

Tell the children this riddle (without telling them the title) and see if they can guess the mystery creature:

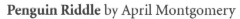

Penguin Riddle by April Montgomery
I have wings.
I am black and white
But I am never in flight.
I can walk and slide
But I love to glide.
I swim to eat
For me it is not a hard feat.

Storytime

Little Penguin's Tale by Audrey Wood

Daily Center Activity Ideas

ART CENTER

■ **Beginning Learner:** Paper Plate Penguins
To prepare for this activity, staple a small paper plate (for the penguin's head) to a large paper plate (for the penguin's body). Cut another large paper plate in half to make wings for the penguin. Staple one wing to each side of the large paper plate. Provide black and white tempera paint, wiggle eyes, and a construction paper beak. Encourage the children to paint their penguins and glue wiggle eyes and beaks on their penguins.

Developing Learner: Paper Bag Penguins

Give each child a white paper lunch bag, newspaper, and construction paper wings, feet, eyes, and beaks. Encourage the children to stuff the bag with newspaper and tape the top of the bag closed. Have the children use black paint to make their stuffed bag look like a penguin. Help the children glue on wings, feet, a beak, and eyes on their penguins.

Experienced Learner: Fingerprint Penguins

Provide a black ink pad, white and orange paint, small paintbrushes, and paper. Show the children how to make a fingerprint penguin by placing their entire index finger in the ink and then pressing it on paper to make the body of the penguin. Then have them press only the tip of their index finger into the ink and press it on top of the penguin's body to make the head. Provide small brushes for the children to use to paint the wings, eyes, and beaks on the penguins.

MATH CENTER

To prepare children for this activity, explain to them that penguins are black and white birds that cannot fly but can swim very well. They spend much of their time sitting on the ice. Show the children pictures of penguins. Point out that the penguins are black on the back and white on the front.

Beginning Learner: Counting Penguins

Give each child a cup of "penguins" (dice) and explain that the black dots on the dice are the penguins and the white part is a block of ice that the penguins are sitting on. Encourage the children to shake their cup of penguins and pour them on the table. Help the children count how many penguins are sitting on each block of ice. Continue playing until children lose interest.

Developing Learner: Copying Penguins

Give each child a cup of "penguins" (dice). Encourage the children to pour their "penguins" on the table and count the number of penguins (dots) on each block of ice (the die) as described for the beginning learner. Give each child a sheet of light gray paper. Show them how to use a white crayon to draw a square to represent the block of ice (the die) and a black crayon to color the number of penguins (dots on the die) to represent the penguins on each block of ice.

Experienced Learner: Ordering Penguins

Give each child a cup of "penguins" as described for the beginning learner. Encourage the children to shake their cup of "penguins" and then toss them onto the table. Have the children to count the number of penguins (dots) on each die and then place the dice in order from most penguins to least number of penguins.

SCIENCE CENTER

■ **Beginning Learner:** Musical Penguins

Gather pictures of different animals such as ducks, rabbits, snakes, and dogs. Discuss how these different animals move from one place to another. Show the children pictures of penguins and demonstrate how they waddle when they walk. Explain that in the winter, penguins huddle together in a tight circle to keep warm. By placing their bodies close together, they retain their own body heat and they keep the penguins close to them warm too. Play the following game to help the children see how penguins move and how they huddle. Play lively music and encourage the children to waddle around the room with their feet close together like penguins. When the music stops, they hurry to the center of the room and huddle with their arms and legs close together. They must stand very still until the music starts again, and then resume their waddling.

■ ■ **Developing Learner:** Gliding Penguins

Prior to this activity, freeze water on a cookie sheet to make a sheet of ice. Explain that penguins are very good swimmers, divers, and gliders. Because penguins frequently have to walk long distances across the ice, they often lie on their bellies and glide across the ice. Tell the children that they are going to experiment with different items to see how they "glide" across a sheet of ice. Provide small items such as dice, pennies, dominoes, and small manipulatives from the science center. Encourage the children to guess which items will glide smoothly across the ice and which ones will not glide as easily. Have the children push the items gently across the sheet of frozen ice to see if their predictions are correct.

■ ■ ■ **Experienced Learner:** Penguin Egg Transfer

Tell the children that emperor penguins protect their eggs from the harsh weather conditions by carrying them on their feet under the protection of their down feathers. The mother penguin transfers her egg to the father penguin by carefully balancing the egg on her feet and then gently rolling it onto her partner's feet. Encourage the children to find a partner, and give each pair a large plastic egg. One child balances the egg on his feet and tries to roll it gently to the feet of his penguin partner.

LANGUAGE/DRAMATIC PLAY CENTER

■ **Beginning Learner:** Penguin Walk

If available, provide the children with a couple of stuffed penguins. If you do not have stuffed penguins, substitute a variety of stuffed animals. Explain to the children that penguins carry their babies on top of their feet to protect them from the ice. The children choose a stuffed animal, place it on top of their feet, and walk around the classroom.

■ ■ **Developing Learner:** Polar Bear, Polar Bear, Penguin

Play "Polar Bear, Polar Bear, Penguin" with the children (based on the game "Duck, Duck, Goose"). Have the children form a circle and choose a child to be "IT." IT waddles around the circle like a penguin and gently touches a child's head and says, "Polar bear." IT continues touching each child's head and saying, "Polar bear," until he touches a child and says, "Penguin!" This child stands up and waddles around the circle trying to tag IT. IT tries to make it all the way around the circle to the vacated spot. The chasing child becomes the new IT. Continue the game until everyone has had a turn.

Experienced Learner: Penguin Relay Race

Divide the children into two teams for a relay race. Place two pieces of Styrofoam ("icebergs") next to each other at one end of the room to signal the turnaround point for each team. Give each team a small playground ball. The first person in line on each team places the ball between his knees and waddles down to the "iceberg" and then waddles back without dropping the ball. The child then places the ball between the next person's knees, and the relay continues until everyone has had a turn.

VOCABULARY

beak, chick, eggs, feathers, glide, ice, incubate, penguins, swim, waddle

Reflect

Say to the children, "Yesterday we learned about mittens and how useful they are in the winter. Today we learned about penguins and all of their interesting habits. Tomorrow we will learn about polar bears."

Extend and Enrich

Use the following ideas to extend and enrich what children know about penguins.

◆ Different varieties of penguins have interesting names, including Emperor, Macaroni, Rock Hopper, yellow-eyed, and Fairy Penguin, to name a few. Talk about the different types of penguins, and make a class book than includes the children's illustrations and facts about these penguins.

◆ Penguins have webbed feet. Discuss with the children other animals that have webbed feet. Talk about how their feet help them move around in the water.

◆ Explain that penguin babies have distinct voices, just as humans do. When penguins leave their babies to go and look for food, the babies make noises when the parents come back so they will recognize them. Record the children's voices and invite them to play the tapes to hear how different their voices sound.

Polar Bears

Morning Circle

Spread a large piece of fake white fur on the floor (use a white blanket if fake fur is not available). Locate as many white objects in the classroom as possible and place them on the fur. When the children arrive, invite them to discover the objects. Talk about how the objects are nearly invisible on the fur and introduce the word *camouflage*. Explain that polar bears are camouflaged in their Arctic homes because their white fur is the same color as the snow. Being hard to see increases a polar bear's chances of sneaking up on seals and other prey. Read *Polar Bear Night* by Lauren Thompson.

Storytime

Polar Bear Night by Lauren Thompson

Daily Center Activity Ideas

ART CENTER

Beginning Learner: Cotton Ball Polar Bear

Cut out polar bear shapes from large white construction paper. Give each child a piece of blue construction paper, a polar bear cutout, glue, and white cotton balls. Ask the children to glue the large polar bear onto the blue construction paper. Encourage the children to cover the polar bear with glue and then place cotton balls on it to create a soft fur coat.

Developing Learner: Handprint Polar Bear

Provide blue construction paper and white paint. Help each child place his hand in white paint and then place it on the paper to make a handprint. When the handprint is dry, turn the paper upside down or rotate it so that the fingers are pointing down (to make polar bear legs) and the thumb is pointing down or to the side (to make a polar bear head). Have each child use a marker to add an eye and dab a cotton swab with white paint to make snowflakes all around the polar bear.

Experienced Learner:
Mother and Baby Polar Bear Handprints
Have the children make a handprint
polar bear as described for the
developing learner. Next, show them
how to bend their fingers at the
knuckles and dip their palm and
fingers (still folded) into the white
paint to make a smaller handprint.
Have them make two of these
smaller handprints to represent two
baby polar bears. When the paint is
dry, invite the children to use a
marker to add eyes. Have them paint
white snow around the polar bears.

MATH CENTER

Beginning Learner: Polar Bear Family/Counting
Provide large white pompoms to represent mama polar bears, small white pompoms to
represent baby polar bears, and a muffin tin to represent dens. Encourage the children to
practice their one-to-one correspondence skills by placing one mama polar bear and one baby
polar bear together into each section of the muffin tin.

Developing Learner: Polar Bears and Fish/Numeral Recognition
Provide six pond-shaped pieces of blue construction paper and goldfish crackers for each child.
Write the numerals 5–10 on each of the cutouts. Encourage the children to count out the
number of goldfish crackers to match the numeral on each pool of water. When the children are
finished counting their goldfish crackers, they can eat them for snack.

Experienced Learner: Ice Fishing Game
Prior to this activity, cut a hole in the middle of a large piece of Styrofoam to represent a piece of
floating ice for ice fishing. Number die-cut fish from 1–10, laminate them, and attach a small
magnet strip to the back of each fish. Cut out small polar bears from white paper and draw dots
on each bear to correspond with the numerals on the fish (1–10). Create a fishing rod using a
wooden dowel by attaching yarn to the end of the dowel. Tie a large paper clip to the end of the
piece of yarn. Place the piece of "ice" in the middle of the floor and fill the hole with the fish. Put
the polar bear cutouts in a lunch bag. Have the children take turns drawing a polar bear from the
bag and counting the dots on it. The children try to catch the fish with the matching numeral. If
the child does not find the correct one on the first try, he places the fish to the side and tries
again until the numerals and the dots correspond with one another.

SCIENCE CENTER

To do this activity at all levels, provide a small food scale. Tell the children that polar bear babies weigh about one pound when they are born.

■ **Beginning Learner:** What Is a Pound?

Provide a scale and a collection of things that weigh about one pound, such as a bag of flour, sugar, sand, canned goods, packing peanuts, shredded paper, and a fishing weight. Encourage the children to explore the items and guess how much each weighs. Help them use the scale to confirm their guesses. Discuss with the children that size and weight are not always related.

■ ■ **Developing Learner:** Comparing Weights

Encourage the children to find objects in the room that they think might weigh one pound. Invite the children to weigh the objects they find to see which ones do weigh one pound, less than one pound, and more than one pound.

■
■ ■ **Experienced Learner:** One-Pound Weights

Talk about baby polar bears weighing one pound when they are born and provide one-pound items so they can feel the weight. Provide a pillowcase and items to place in the pillowcase, such as one pound of flour, sugar, rocks, and so on. Provide a bathroom scale so that the children can weigh their sacks to feel what the weight of a few baby polar bears feels like. You may also wish to explain that mother polar bears sometimes carry their cubs on their backs. They do this in the spring after they leave their den. They sometimes carry them for long distances. The children can pretend to be mother polar bears carrying their cubs over the ice.

LANGUAGE/DRAMATIC PLAY CENTER

Share some of the following information about the hibernation of polar bears. Pregnant female polar bears hibernate all winter. The female polar bear uses her long sharp claws as shovels to hollow out a long, narrow tunnel for a den. Sometimes she digs for days. The female polar bear often gives birth to a couple of cubs in the cave. They weigh about one pound each. The cubs and their mother stay in the tunnel and den all winter.

■ **Beginning Learner:** Hibernating Polar Bears

Cover a table with white material to resemble a bear cave. Pile white cotton batting ("snow") outside of the opening to the bear cave. Encourage the children to use their "paws" and "claws" to remove the snow from the entrance to the cave so they can tunnel their way through the snow and get inside the cave to keep warm.

■ ■ **Developing Learner:** Polar Bear Camouflage

Fill a small child's wading pool with soft, white materials, such as cotton batting, fake white fur, white fabric, cotton balls, and white tissue paper. Hide a picture of a seal, a toy seal, or a plush seal underneath the white materials. Encourage the children to use their "paws and claws" to play in the "snow" and pretend to sneak up on the seal.

■

■ ■ **Experienced Learner:** Polar Bear Fishing

Fill the water table with a small amount of water and lots of ice cubes. Place plastic toy fish in the icy water. Provide tongs and encourage the children to use their "paws and claws" to reach into the icy pond and catch the fish.

VOCABULARY

arctic, camouflage, carnivore, claws, cold, feet, fur, ice, polar bears, seals, swimming, webbed

Reflect

Say to the children, "Yesterday we learned about penguins. Today we learned about polar bears. Both polar bears and penguins live in cold places at the opposite ends of the Earth. Tomorrow we will begin learning about jackets and how important they are to wear when visiting cold places."

Extend and Enrich

Use the following ideas to extend and enrich what children know about polar bears.

◆ A great picture book to share with the children is *Polar Bears* by Susan Canizares.

◆ Tell the children that there are many different kinds of bears. Show them pictures of brown bears, grizzly bears, pandas (which aren't bears but people call them bears, and black bears. Discuss the similarities and differences among them.

Jackets/Coats

Morning Circle

As the children enter the classroom on a cold day, have them keep wearing their jackets or coats. After all of the children have arrived, ask them to remove their jackets and place them on the floor upside down with the collar closest to their feet. Show them how to put their jackets back on by reaching down, putting their arms in the sleeves, and then flipping their coats over their heads. After the children have finished with this activity, introduce the story for the day.

Storytime

The Purple Coat by Amy Hest

Daily Center Activity Ideas

ART CENTER

■ **Beginning Learner:** Making a Vest

Provide each child with a paper grocery bag, tempera paint, and brushes. Make the traditional paper bag "vest" by cutting up the front of the grocery bag and cutting arm holes to make a jacket. Invite the children to paint designs on their "jacket."

■ ■ **Developing Learner:** Designing a Coat

Cut out a coat shape from poster board for each child. Invite the children to decorate their "coats" using buttons, markers, crayons, and collage materials.

Experienced Learner:
Lacing a Coat
Give each child a coat shape traced onto poster board to cut out. Invite the children to use crayons and markers to draw designs on their coats. Encourage them to use a hole puncher to punch holes around the outside of the coat shape and then lace a piece of yarn around the coat.

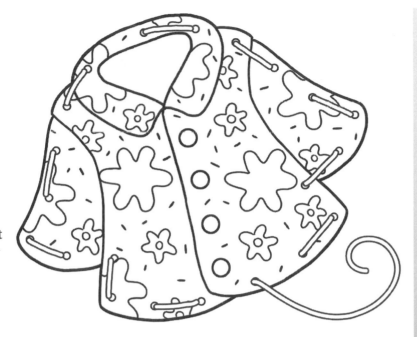

MATH CENTER

Beginning Learner: Sorting Jackets
Invite the children to bring their jackets or coats to the math center and put them in a pile. Have them sort the jackets by color or type. Encourage them to come up with different ways to sort their jackets.

Developing Learner: Zipper-Button-Pocket Count
Invite the children to bring their jackets or coats to the center. Give each child a card with either a picture of a button, a zipper, or pocket on it. Ask the children to count how many zippers, pockets, or buttons that they find on their jacket. After they have counted, have them switch cards with a friend and count a different item on their jacket.

Experienced Learner: Zipper-Button-Pocket Count II
Invite the children to bring their jackets or coats to the center and place them backwards on their chairs. Have the children fasten the jackets with the fronts facing toward them. Give each child a card with a picture of a zipper, a picture of a button, and a picture of a pocket on it. The children look at their jackets and use crayons to mark how many of each item they have on their jackets. Ask the children to go around the classroom and count the zippers, buttons, and pockets on their friend's jackets and make marks on their cards to represent how many of each they find.

SCIENCE CENTER

Beginning Learner: Button, Snap, or Zip
Encourage the children to bring their jackets or coats to the center. Help them place their coats backwards on the backs of chairs so they are convenient for the children to reach. Discuss with the children that there are many different ways to close things and keep them closed. Engage them in a discussion of things that they can think of that help things stay closed: include in your

discussion things such as locks, and latches. Show them examples of different kinds of closing devices. Then tell the children that clothes also have things on them that help them stay closed. Show them zippers, snaps and buttons. Encourage the children to go to each coat and practice zipping the zippers, snapping the snaps, and buttoning the buttons.

Developing Learner: Clothing Closures and Zippers

Discuss with the children all of the different types of closures that can be found on clothing, including buttons, snaps, Velcro, ties, ribbons, and laces. Ask the children to look at their own clothing and identify all of the types of closings they find. Discuss which types of closures are the easiest to do. Show them a variety of items that have zippers on them, including shoes, pants, shirts, sweaters, coats, pillow covers, backpacks, sports bags, purses, and zipper notebooks. Give the children magnifying glasses and have them look carefully at how the two sides of a zipper come together. Encourage the children to experiment with all of the different zippers to determine which ones are harder and which ones are easier to open and close. Also encourage them to listen to the sounds that the different zippers make as they are opened and closed.

Experienced Learner: Coats as Insulation

Provide each child with an ice cube, a large plastic cup, and a variety of insulating materials such as plastic wrap, aluminum foil, newspaper, cotton balls, strips of paper towels or cloth, and cotton. Explain that wearing a coat provides insulation for our bodies. A coat holds the warmth of our bodies in and keeps the cold air out. Insulation can be used to keep cold things cold and warm things warm. Tell the children that they are going to do an experiment to see if they can insulate an ice cube from heat. Have each child place an ice cube in a plastic bag and zip it closed. Encourage the children to use the materials to wrap around their ice cube bag and then fit the wrapped bag inside their plastic cup. When the children have placed their materials in the cup, set a timer for 30 minutes and move on to another activity. After 30 minutes, the children can remove their insulating material and check on the status of their ice cubes. Ask them to determine which insulating material worked best.

LANGUAGE/DRAMATIC PLAY CENTER

Beginning Learner: Snow Fashion

Show the children many different pieces of winter clothing such as a hat, mittens, a scarf, a coat, a sweater, boots, socks, and so on. Discuss the items of clothing and ask the children which body part is kept warm by each piece of clothing. Encourage the children to try on the different items.

Developing Learner: Weather Wheel

Before doing this activity, make a weather wheel by attaching a construction paper arrow to a paper plate using a brad. Glue pictures of a heavy coat, a windbreaker, a sweater, and a raincoat in four areas of the wheel. Provide an actual child-size heavy coat, a windbreaker or light jacket, a sweater, and a raincoat. Encourage the children to spin the wheel and describe what the weather would be like if someone was wearing the item the arrow points to. Have them put on the actual item.

■ ■ **Experienced Learner:** Coat Questionnaire

Provide each child with a piece of paper that says:

My coat has _____ pockets.
My coat has _____ zippers.
My coat has _____ buttons.
My coat has _____ snaps.
My coat has _____ pockets.

Ask the children to bring their coats or jackets to the center. Have them examine their coats and fill in the blanks with the appropriate numeral. (If they do not have one of the features listed, they put a zero in that space. When the children are finished with their coat questionnaire, encourage them to draw a picture of their jacket or coat.

VOCABULARY

book jacket, buttons, coat, denim jacket, jacket, leather jacket, life jacket, raincoat, sleeves, snaps, Velcro, warm, windbreaker, winter, zipper

Reflect

Say to the children, "Yesterday we learned about polar bears and how they keep warm in the winter. Today we learned about jackets and how they keep us warm in the winter. In our next unit of study, we will learn about things that are wet."

Extend and Enrich

Use the following ideas to extend and enrich what children know about jackets.

◆ Encourage the children to conduct a search around their home to find and count all of the different kinds of coats or jackets that their family members have.

◆ Show the children a picture of a coat of arms and talk about what it means. A coat of arms was originally a coat worn over armor to show pride in a knight's family or country. Encourage the children to design a coat of arms that represents interesting or special things about them or their families.

Daily Preschool Experiences

Things that Are Wet

Soup

Morning Circle

To prepare for this day's activities, send home a note asking families to send in one vegetable with their child so you can add it to the soup the class will be making. Suggestions include carrots, corn, beans, peas, celery, potato, squash, and okra. As the children enter the classroom, have them place their vegetables in a large kettle or cooking pot. After all of the vegetables have been placed in the pot, tell the children that they are going to hear a story about a very special man who knew how to make soup from a stone. Give each child a small stone to add to the pot and then tell the story.

Storytime

Stone Soup by Marcia Brown

Daily Center Activity Ideas

ART CENTER

■ Beginning Learner: Pot Painting

Cut out a cooking pot shape, carrots, onions, potatoes, corn, and a stone from construction paper. Give each child a pot and have them paint the pot with brown paint. When the pots are dry, invite the children to fill their pot with the vegetable and stone cutouts and glue them in place.

■ ■ Developing Learner: Stone Painting

Provide a variety of large stones (available at craft stores), tempera paint, and brushes. Encourage the children to decorate their stones to look like vegetables using different colors of paint.

■
■ ■ Experienced Learner: Rock Creatures

Provide a large variety of stones. Invite each child to choose two stones and then place them together to make an interesting shape. Use hot glue to attach the two stones together (adult only) as the child wishes. Provide wiggle eyes, feathers, beads, sequins, fabric, and other collage materials and invite the children to use the materials to transform their plain rocks into "rock creatures." Encourage the children to name their creatures and give them personalities!

MATH CENTER

■ **Beginning Learner:** Magic Stone

For this activity, you will need a large smooth stone and the tops of three plastic eggs. Write the numeral 1 on the stone using a black marker. Hide the stone under one of the egg halves and shuffle the eggs around. Encourage the children to try to guess which egg the "magic stone" is under. The children can play the game over and over to enhance their memory skills. To make the game more challenging, write different numerals on three different stones, and encourage the children to try to find the stones with specific numerals.

■ ■ **Developing Learner:** Which Stone Is Missing?

Away from the children, spray paint five stones different colors. When the stones are dry, use a black marker to number the stones 1–5. Place the stones on the table and ask the children to look at them for a few seconds. Ask them to close their eyes. When their eyes are closed, remove one of the stones. The children open their eyes and take turns guessing which stone is missing from the table. To make this game more challenging, add more stones in different colors with different numerals.

■
■ ■ **Experienced Learner:** Magic Pebble Numerals

Provide squares of cardboard with numerals written on them and a large bowl of multicolored aquarium gravel. Encourage the children to choose a numeral card, outline and fill in the numeral with glue, then cover the number with colored aquarium gravel. Have the children sort the gravel and use only one color to fill in their numeral or sort the gravel into color piles and create a design as they outline and fill in their numeral.

SCIENCE CENTER

For each of the following three levels, show the children the book *Stone Soup* and talk about the two very important ingredients that were necessary for the man to make the stone soup: a stone and vegetables.

Beginning Learner: Washing Stones

Tell the children that the man in the story carried a stone in his pocket and he placed the stone in a pot with vegetables to make soup. Explain that stones found outside are not clean and have some dirt on them. Explain that before eating unprocessed raw food, such as fruit and vegetables, it is important to wash them to remove dirt. Take the children outside on the playground and have them look for stones, or provide stones. When the children have stones, encourage them to use scrub brushes, soap and water to clean their stones for the stone soup.

Developing Learner: Washing Vegetables

Ask the children to bring the vegetable that they brought from home to the center. Discuss with the children that vegetables are grown outside in the dirt, so they are dirty and should be washed before they are eaten. Provide a tub of water and a brush for the children to scrub and clean their vegetable so it will be ready to go in the pot of soup.

Experienced Learner: Vegetable Soup

Ask the children to bring the vegetables that they brought from home to the center. Encourage them to name the vegetables and tell where and how they are grown. Explain that vegetables are usually dirty and must be washed and cleaned before they are eaten. Provide a tub of water for washing the vegetables. Talk about the outside skin of the vegetables, and discuss which skins are usually eaten and which are usually cut or peeled off. Provide vegetable peelers and plastic knives. Supervise the children closely as they peel and cut their vegetables to go into the pot of stone soup.

LANGUAGE/DRAMATIC PLAY CENTER

Beginning Learner: Alphabet Soup

Provide a cooking pot with magnetic alphabet letters in it. The children reach in the pot, one and a time, and pull out a letter. Ask them to name the letter and then return it to the pot. Challenge them to name a vegetable (or other item) that begins with each letter.

Developing Learner: Cooking Vegetable Soup

Provide a crock pot. Invite the children to cut up the vegetables they brought from home and add them to the pot. Let them choose one of the stones that they washed and place it in the pot. Add two cans of alphabet soup to the vegetables. Cook the soup in a crock pot during class for the children to enjoy later in the day. As they eat the soup, talk about the noodle letters and ask them to try to form words with them.

Experienced Learner: Soup Recipe

Prior to this activity, draw a soup pot shape on cardboard and cut it out to use as a pattern. Invite the children to trace the soup pot onto white construction paper and cut it out. Ask each child what her favorite soup is and dictate a recipe for it. Help them write their words on the soup pot cutout. Invite the children to illustrate their recipes. You may follow up by making and enjoying real soup as directed in the activity for the developing learner.

beans, broth, corn, hot, okra, pot, potatoes, rock, salty, simmer, soup, spicy, squash, stone, tomatoes, vegetables, water, wet

Reflect

Say to the children, "Today we learned about soup and the vegetables that go into it. Tomorrow we will learn about bubbles."

Extend and Enrich

Use the following ideas to extend and enrich what children know about soup and the vegetables in soup.

◆ There are many different versions of the story "Stone Soup." Select a version from one of the following authors: Heather Forest, Ann McGovern, Jon J. Muth, Tony Ross, Pete Seeger, Paul Dubois Jacobs, and Michael Hays. Compare and contrast these versions with the Marcia Brown version.

◆ Collect a variety of empty soup cans. Read the labels with the children and discuss the contents of the different kinds of soup.

◆ Provide poster board and markers. Encourage the children to vote on their favorite soup. Invite them to make posters and banners to encourage their classmates to vote for their favorite kind of soup. Have the children tally the votes to see which soup is the winner. The following day, bring in several cans of the winning soup for everyone to enjoy for snack.

Bubbles

Morning Circle

Set up a bubble machine so that bubbles are blowing when the children enter the classroom. (Inexpensive bubble machines can be purchased at some party stores. If a bubble machine is not available, blow bubbles using a wand and commercial bubble solution.) Invite the children to catch and pop the bubbles. Tell the children that bubbles can be formed many ways, such as in pancake batter as it cooks, soap in the bathtub or kitchen sink, soap in the washing machine, a bubble machine, blowing bubbles with bubble solution, blowing bubbles with bubble gum, and blowing bubbles in milk with a straw. After the children have had a chance to explore the bubbles, tell them they are going to hear a story about a factory where bubbles are made.

Storytime

The Bubble Factory by Tomie De Paola

Daily Center Activity Ideas

ART CENTER

Beginning Learner: Bubble Wrap Prints
Provide each child with a small sheet of bubble wrap, construction paper, tempera paint, and brushes. Show the children how to use tempera paint and brushes to paint their bubble wrap and then place it on white construction paper and rub it to make bubble prints.

Developing Learner: Blowing Colored Bubbles
Provide small bottles of bubbles for each child. Mix food coloring in each child's bottle. Encourage the children to use their bubble wands to blow bubbles over paper. When the bubbles land on the paper, they will make circular bubble prints. The children can take their bottles of bubbles outside for more bubble exploration on the playground. Invite them to take their bubbles home to enjoy.

Experienced Learner: Overflowing Bubble Paint
To prepare for this activity, mix three different colors of tempera paint with bubble solution and water. Place the mixtures into wide-mouth bowls. Give the children straws and invite them to stick the end of their straws into a bowl of paint and bubble mixture. Tell them to blow gently, and closely supervise to be sure that the children do not suck paint up through their straws. When a child has a bowl with colored bubbles overflowing, place a piece of white construction

paper on top of the bubbles to make a print. The children repeat this process using each of the three different colors of bubble solution. When the children have finished blowing their bubbles, discard their straws.

MATH CENTER

■ **Beginning Learner:** Bubble Wrap/Count the Pops
Give each child two pieces of bubble wrap, one with large bubbles and one with small bubbles. Encourage the children to pop the bubbles with their fingers. Ask them which bubbles are harder to pop. Encourage the children to find creative ways to pop the bubbles. Have them count the bubbles as they pop them.

■ ■ **Developing Learner:** Bubble Wrap/Comparing Times
Give each child two squares of bubble wrap, one with large bubbles and one with small bubbles. When you say "Start," set a timer and encourage the children to see how long it takes them to pop all the large bubbles. When everyone's large bubbles have been popped, stop the timer and write the time on an index card. Fold the card in half so that it will stand up. Place the index card on the table in front of a piece of large bubble wrap. Have the children repeat the exercise using the small bubble wrap. Write the time it took to pop all of the small bubbles on another index card and fold it in half. Place that card in front of the small bubble wrap. Compare the times. Which bubbles took more time to pop and which bubbles took less time?

■ ■ **Experienced Learner:** Bubble Wrap/Time Limits
Give each child two squares of bubble wrap, one with large bubbles and one with small bubbles. Ask the children to choose a time limit of so many seconds and predict how many large bubbles they think they can pop in that amount of time. (Help them choose appropriate time limits.) Write each child's prediction on an index card and set it in front of them. Set the timer or stopwatch for each child, and tell the children to pop as many large bubbles as they can until the allotted time for their prediction runs out. When the timer stops, help them count how many large bubbles they popped. How close is this number to their predictions? Repeat for small bubbles.

SCIENCE CENTER

To do this activity at any level, provide colored water and dishwashing liquid. For longer-lasting bubbles, add glycerin. Glycerin is a liquid that can be found in the pharmacy section of some supermarkets and at most drug stores.

■ **Beginning Learner:** Making Bubbles
Place dish detergent, water, and food coloring in the water table. Provide rotary beaters and whisks for the children to experience the bubbles.

Developing Learner: Making Bubble Wands

Show the children how to twist and form chenille sticks into simple shapes to make bubble wands. Invite them to use their bubble wands in the water table with the colored water and dishwashing detergent. Encourage the children to use the wands to blow bubbles. Ask the children if different shaped make different shaped bubbles.

Experienced Learner: Catching Bubbles

As the children explore bubbles in the water table as described for the developing learner, challenge the children to try to catch their bubbles using their hands. Ask them to think of other things they could use to catch the bubbles, such as straws, funnels, strings, baskets, and so on. Encourage the children to try to catch the bubbles without popping them. Have them put a little dishwashing liquid on the tips of their fingers and then try to touch a bubble without popping it.

LANGUAGE/DRAMATIC PLAY CENTER

Beginning Learner: Bubble Pop

Begin to blow bubbles in the classroom. Ask the children to follow your directions and pop the bubbles with different body parts. For example, when you call out, "Head," the children should use only their heads to pop all of the bubbles. Call out other body parts for the children to use. (**Safety note:** Make sure there is plenty of room for the children to move around and that the floor does not get too slippery. This would be a great activity to do outside.)

Developing Learner: Bubble Story Starters

Provide empty, clean bubble solution bottles. Write story starters on pieces of paper, such as "I wish I could…," "My favorite animal is…," "When I grow up…," "I want to go to…," and so on. Fold the strips of paper into small pieces and place them in the bubble containers. Encourage the children to shake a bubble bottle and then pour one of the story starters into their hands. Read what is written on the piece of paper, have the child answer the question, and then pass the bubble bottle to the next person.

Experienced Learner: Speech Bubbles

Provide white paper and markers. Show the children examples of cartoons with speech bubbles that appear above the character's heads to indicate what they are thinking about or what they are saying. Provide a piece of paper and encourage the children to draw a picture that tells a story. Help them draw speech bubbles above their characters, and then help them fill in the bubbles with words.

VOCABULARY

blow, bubble blowers, bubbles, colors, float, pop, soapy, sudsy, wand, water, wet

Reflect

Say to the children, "Yesterday we learned about soup and the vegetables that can be added to it. Today we learned about bubbles and how fun they are to make and to pop. Tomorrow we will learn about puddles and how they are formed after the rain falls."

Extend and Enrich

Use the following ideas to extend and enrich what children know about bubbles.

◆ Take the children outside on a windy day and provide them with materials to blow bubbles. Repeat the activity on another day when it is not windy. What happens to the bubbles when there is little or no wind? Remind the children of their windy bubble blowing experience. Have them compare the two experiences.

◆ Encourage the children to imagine that they are bubbles that have been blown by a child and are floating away. Where would they go? What would they do when they got there? Have them dictate their stories to you and illustrate them.

◆ Demonstrate how to insert a straw into a bubble without popping (make sure the straw is wet). Provide bubble solution, bubble wands, and a straw for each child to try this activity.

Puddles

Morning Circle

When the children arrive, greet them at the door wearing rubber boots, a rain hat, a raincoat and an umbrella. Engage the children in a discussion of where they think you are going or what you are getting ready to do. Fill a small child-size wading pool with about an inch of water. Step into the water with your boots so that the children can hear the "splish, splash" sounds that your feet make when they hit the water. Encourage the children to listen to the sound and think of their own words to describe the sound. Provide a child-size pair of rain boots and give each child an opportunity to step in the "puddle" to make her own splashing sound.

Storytime

Puddles by Jonathan London

Daily Center Activity Ideas

ART CENTER

Beginning Learner: Rain Boot Painting

Provide a child-size pair of rain boots, a small tub of watered-down brown paint ("mud"), and a long piece of white paper on the floor. Encourage the children to step in the "mud" and then walk on the white paper to make muddy boot prints.

Developing Learner: Rain Paintings

Fill spray bottles filled with colored water or watered-down washable paint. Place pieces of white paper in a child-sized swimming pool. Encourage the children to use the spray bottles and spray the paint on the paper to create rain paintings.

Experienced Learner: Splish-Splash Splatter Painting

Prior to doing this activity, use a funnel to fill several balloons with sand. Place a plastic shower curtain or plastic tablecloth on the floor. Put a sheet of white construction paper inside a plastic tub and put the tub on the plastic. Fill pie tins with paint and place them nearby. Encourage each child to dip a sand-filled balloon into one of the trays of colored paint and then drop it into the tub with the paper in it to make a splatter picture. Let them repeat this process until they have reached the desired effect on their papers.

MATH CENTER

Beginning Learner: Concept of Middle

Explain that puddles are small pools of water often found on sidewalks and on streets after it rains. They are found in the middle of a dry place on the ground. Ask the children what they think the word *middle* means. Have them form a circle, and tell them that they are the "dry ground." The children take turns standing in the middle of the circle, holding a bowl of water, to form a "puddle." To further explore the concept of middle, ask the children to name things that are in the middle of their bodies, such as their nose (which is in the middle of their face), their belly button (which is in the middle of their stomach), and so on.

Developing Learner: Beanbag in the Middle

Remind the children that the story was about puddles, which are small pools of water in the middle of a dry area. Discuss the concept of *middle* as a positional word with the children. Provide a hula hoop, a set of numeral cards from 1–10, and a variety of beanbags. Have the children sit in a circle around the hula hoop ("puddle"). Select a child to begin the activity by drawing a numeral card. The child identifies the numeral and then tries to toss that number of beanbags into the middle of the hula hoop.

Experienced Learner: Hopscotch Numerals

Tell the children that they often have to hop, skip, or jump to make it over a puddle to keep their shoes and clothes dry. Make a hopscotch board on the floor with masking tape (or do the activity outside and use chalk to make the hopscotch board). Write a numeral in each of the hopscotch squares. Show the children how to hop on one foot and then on two feet down the hopscotch board. Encourage them to take turns hopping on the hopscotch board. Have them name the numerals as they land on them with their feet.

SCIENCE CENTER

Beginning Learner: Evaporation

Provide a chalk board, small buckets of water, and paintbrushes. Encourage the children to use paintbrushes to paint a small amount of water on the chalk board and then watch how quickly it evaporates and disappears. Explain to the children that the water has "evaporated." It has turned into tiny droplets, so tiny that you cannot see them, and is now floating in the air.

Developing Learner: Pebbles in a Puddle

Provide plastic or Styrofoam plates, tablespoons, a black permanent marker, small pebbles, and water. (**Note:** It's important to use plates that will not absorb water for this activity.) Each child puts two tablespoons of water in the middle of her paper plate to create a puddle. Ask the children to use a black marker to trace around the puddle. Give each child two pebbles and ask her to place the stones in the middle of her puddle. Encourage the child to describe what happens to the puddle when she adds the pebbles.

■■ **Experienced Learner:** Water Evaporation

Provide the same materials as listed above for the developing learning activity, as well as a timer. Take the children outside on a sunny day to conduct this evaporation experiment. Have the children place their plates in sunny location, add two tablespoons of water to the middle of the plate, add two pebbles to the puddle, and draw a black circle around the puddle. Invite the children to play on the playground, but call them back to observe the puddles every 15 minutes. Ask them to describe what happens to the "puddles." Explain that the puddles are beginning to evaporate in the sun, which is what happens when the sun comes out after it rains. Ask the children to predict what they think would happen to the puddles if they left their plates in the sun all day.

LANGUAGE/DRAMATIC PLAY CENTER

■ **Beginning Learner:** Puddle to Ocean

Put a small amount of water in the water table to represent a puddle. Add two toy frogs or ducks. Provide eyedroppers and a cup of water for the children to use to add small amounts of water gradually to increase the size of the puddle to a pool, a pond, a lake, and finally, an ocean! Have them talk about the size of each body of water as they make the puddle bigger.

■■ **Developing Learner:** Frogs (or Ducks) in the Puddle

Provide the materials used for the beginning learner. Invite the children to add water to the water table so that the two small ducks or frogs are sitting in the middle of a puddle. Have them continue adding water until the animals are sitting in a pool, then a pond, then a lake, and an ocean. Ask the children to pretend to be the small frogs or ducks and complete the following sentences:

Sitting in a puddle I see _____.
Sitting in a pool I see _____.
Sitting in a pond I see _____.
Sitting in a lake I see _____.
Sitting in an ocean I see _____.

Ask the children to name the two frogs or ducks. Encourage them to choose rhyming names such as *Fred* and *Ted* or *Will* and *Bill*. Help the children make a list of the words that rhyme with the names that they choose. Write their words on a classroom chart. Ask the children to underline the letters that are the same in each rhyming word.

■■ **Experienced Learner:** If I Saw a Puddle…

Give each child pieces of white construction paper. Help the children draw and cut out shapes that resemble of small bodies of water. Write a story starter sentence each puddle shape such as, "If I saw a puddle I would…" Encourage the children to complete the sentence by writing the words or dictating them to you to write. Invite them to illustrate their sentences on the puddle shapes.

VOCABULARY

evaporate, puddle, rain, shrink, splash, splish, step, stomp, wet

Reflect

Say to the children, "Yesterday we learned about bubbles and how fun they are to make and pop. Today we learned about puddles and how much fun they are to step in after it rains. Tomorrow we will learn about the rain and how it falls in drops, showers, and sometimes in storms."

Extend and Enrich

Use the following ideas to extend and enrich what children know about puddles.

◆ Introduce the children to the consonant blend sound *dle*, as in *puddle* and *middle*.

◆ Encourage the children to think of words that have the *ble* blend sound, such as *trouble*, *bubble*, and *stumble*.

◆ Encourage the children to explore a rain puddle after a shower or a storm. Check to see if any creatures are living in the puddle.

DAY 4

Rain

Morning Circle

As the children arrive, play a tape recording of rain sounds. Have the children sit in a circle, close their eyes, and listen to the sounds of the rain. Use a rain stick to imitate the sound of rain. Pass the rain stick around the circle so that all of the children have an opportunity to make their own rain sound. Demonstrate other ways to make rain sounds using your body; for example, rub your hands together to create a rain shower sound, snap your fingers to make soft rain sounds, and tap on your knees fast to make loud rain sounds. Reverse the order and the sound of the rain shower subsides.

Storytime

Listen to the Rain by Bill Martin Jr. and John Archambault

Daily Center Activity Ideas

ART CENTER: RAIN PAINTING

Beginning Learner: "Rain" Painting with Eyedroppers
Provide eyedroppers, bowls of water mixed with food coloring, and coffee filters. The children place their coffee filters on a tray and use eyedroppers to drop colored "rain" on the filter. The colors will blend together to form beautiful new colors.

Developing Learner: Color-Absorbing Towels
Provide thick paper towels and bowls of water mixed with food coloring. Have the children fold or roll their paper towel into any shape they wish and then dip the corners of their paper towel into the different colors until the entire towel is covered. When the children open up their towels, they will discover all of the new, beautiful rainbow colors that have run together.

Experienced Learner: "Rain" Painting with Turkey Basters
Provide bowls of food coloring or watered down tempera paint, turkey basters, and thick paper towels. Place paper towels in a plastic tub. Help the child stand on a stool or short classroom chair. The child holds the turkey baster full of paint above the tub of paper towels and drops small amounts of paint onto the paper towels. The child continues until the paper towels are covered in colors.

MATH CENTER

Beginning Learner: Matching Raindrops

Prior to doing this activity, cut out two raindrop shapes from each page of an old wallpaper sample book (if you do not have a wallpaper book, use decorative scrapbook paper or gift wrap). If possible, laminate the raindrops for future use. Play a memory game by placing the raindrop pairs face down on a table. Decide how many raindrops to use depending on the children's abilities. Have the children take turns turning over two at a time to find a match. If a child turns over two patterns that do not match, she turns them face down again and another child has a turn.

Developing Learner: Counting Clouds

Prior to doing this activity, cut out 10 clouds from white poster board and label them with a different numeral from 1–10. Place the clouds face down on the floor or table. Provide a small bucket or tub of cotton balls. Encourage the children to turn over one cloud at a time, identify the numeral, and place the correct number of cotton balls on the cloud.

Experienced Learner: Counting Raindrops

Prior to doing this activity, cut out 20 clouds from white poster board. Draw 1–20 dots on each cloud (one dot on the first cloud, two dots on the second cloud, and so on up to 20). Cut out 20 raindrops from light blue construction paper and write a different numeral from 1–20 on each raindrop. Encourage the children to count the number of dots on each cloud and find the raindrop with the numeral that matches the dots on the cloud.

SCIENCE CENTER

■ **Beginning Learner:** Rain on a Glass

Have the children fill a glass half full with water. Help them put plastic wrap over the top of the glass and secure it with a rubber band. Place the glass in the refrigerator. After several hours, take the glass out of the refrigerator. There will be a layer of water droplets on the plastic wrap. Place the glasses on a table and observe. After a while, the water droplets will begin to fall from the top of the glass, creating a mini "rain shower."

■ ■ **Developing Learner:** Indoor Rain

Provide two pots with handles. Fill one pot with ice cubes and put hot water in the other. Hold the cold pot a few inches above the hot pot. After a minute or so, water droplets will start to form on the bottom of the cold pot and "rain" down into the pot below. Explain to the children that this process is called "condensation and precipitation."
(**Safety note:** Be sure that the children do not get too close to the pan of hot water.)

■
■ ■ **Experienced Learner:** Rain Band

If possible, provide a tape recording of a thunderstorm. If no recording is available, encourage the children to use descriptive words to describe thunder and lightning. Tell the children they are going to make their own thunderstorm sounds. Provide a variety of disposable aluminum baking pans (pie tins, cookie sheets, and cake pans), wooden spoons, a child-sized watering can, water, and a water table. Place the pie tins in the water table and use the watering can to pour water over the pie tins to create the sound of rain. Give a few of the children the wooden spoons and the foil cake pans and have them bang the spoons against the cake pans to create thunder sounds. Ask several other children to use the foil cookie sheets to make thunder sounds by holding them on one side and moving the cookie sheet back and forth, like a bird flapping its wings. (**Note:** Encourage the children to experiment with other classroom objects to see if they can make storm sounds in other ways.)

LANGUAGE/DRAMATIC PLAY CENTER

■ **Beginning Learner:** Dressing for a Shower

Show the children a raincoat, an umbrella, a rain hat, and a pair of rain boots. Discuss with them how each item protects different body parts from getting wet. Demonstrate how an umbrella works and discuss why we like to keep dry during a rain shower. Encourage the children to take turns putting on the rain gear and pretending to dress for rain.

■ ■ **Developing Learner:** Rain Gear Relay Race

Provide two sets of the rain gear described for the beginning learner and place each set in a different suitcase. Divide the children into two teams. Each team has one suitcase. When you say, "Go," the first child from each team walks quickly to the suitcase and puts on the rain gear. She then walks quickly back to her team. When she reaches her team, she takes off the rain gear. The next child walks quickly to the suitcase and puts the items back inside and returns to the line.

The game continues with the children alternately dressing and putting back the rain gear until one team has all of its members finish the race.

Experienced Learner: Wet-Weather Self-Portrait

Provide the props described for the beginning learner, an unbreakable mirror, markers, and paper. Encourage the children to take turns dressing up in the rain gear. Invite them to look at themselves in the mirror as they wear the rain gear. After finishing, ask them to draw pictures of themselves dressed in the rain gear with a rainy day background. Have them dictate a sentence about their picture. (**Note:** If available, use a digital camera to take pictures of the children in their rain gear. They can use the pictures as inspiration in their drawings.)

VOCABULARY

clouds, drizzle, puddles, rain, rain boots, rain showers, raincoat, umbrella

Reflect

Say to the children, "Yesterday we learned about puddles, the accumulation of rain or water on the ground. We learned that puddles can grow in size or evaporate. Today we learned about rain and how it falls in light showers or strong thunderstorms. Tomorrow we will learn about water in the bathtub and all of the fun things there are to do in the bathtub."

Extend and Enrich

Use the following ideas to extend and enrich what children know about rain.

◆ A great resource about rain is Franklyn M. Branley's book *Down Comes the Rain*.

◆ Have the children make their own rainsticks by filling toilet paper tubes or paper towel tubes with beads, or other collage materials that will make a sound, and sealing the ends with duct tape.

Bath Time

Morning Circle

Greet the children wearing a bath robe and slippers. Put "dirt" (use anything that looks like dirt) on your face and cheeks, and make your hair look a little messy. Ask the children why they think you are dressed that way and what they think you are getting ready to do.

Storytime

Beasty Bath by Robert Neubecker

Daily Center Activity Ideas

ART CENTER

■ **Beginning Learner:** Muddy Faces

Show the children pictures of children playing in mud. Talk about how messy mud is and how it gets on hands, faces, and clothes when children play in it. Provide brown paper grocery bags, brown paint, brushes, and construction paper cutouts of eyes, noses, and mouths. Cut out facial shapes (the size of a paper plate) from brown grocery bags. Have the children wad the brown bag face in a ball until it is wrinkled and then smooth it out. Ask them to paint watered-down brown paint on the paper bag circle to resemble a dirty face. Invite them to glue precut eyes, a nose, and mouth on their painted face after the paint dries.

Developing Learner: Grow a Mud Face

Show the children pictures of children playing in mud. Talk about how mud gets all over the children, including their faces. Provide Styrofoam cups, brown paint, potting soil, grass seed, brushes and markers. Have the children paint the outside of the cups brown so that they look muddy. When the paint has dried, encourage the children to fill their Styrofoam cup with potting soil and then sprinkle a small amount of grass seed in the cup. The children can use markers to draw faces on their cups. Put the cups on a sunny windowsill, and when the grass seed begins to grow, it will look like hair.

Experienced Learner: Grow a Mud Face II

Provide empty vegetable cans and construction paper. Have the children cut construction paper and wrap it around their cans. Then have each children cut shapes for eyes, a nose and mouth and glue them on the can to make a face. Next, provide seeds and potting soil for the children to plant in their cans. When the seeds begin to grow, the plants will resemble hair.

MATH CENTER

Beginning Learner: Ordering Radishes

Tell the children that many foods grow in the ground (in dirt). Talk about what happens to dirt when it rains—it turns into mud. Radishes are a kind of vegetable that grows in the ground, and when it rains, they get really muddy. Tell the children they are going to play a counting game using pretend radishes. Cut out 10 radish shapes from red construction paper and use a black marker to write the numerals 1–10 on the radishes. Have the children put the radishes in numerical order from smallest to largest and from largest to smallest.

Developing Learner: Seed Planting

Prepare for this activity by gathering three containers, potting soil, seeds, and water. Place soil in the first container and label it with the numeral 1. Put seeds in the second container and label it with the numeral 2. Put water in the last container and label it with the numeral 3. Write directions for the children to follow to plant seeds. For example:

Step 1: Put five spoonfuls of soil from container #1 in the bottom of the cup.

Step 2: Put three spoonfuls of seeds from container #2 on top of the soil.

Step 3: Use the spoon to mix the soil and the seeds together.

Step 4: Pour four spoonfuls of water from container #3 over the soil and seed mixture.

(**Note:** Use clip art or pictures for the spoons, seeds, soil, and water to make a rebus recipe.)

Experienced Learner: Mud Pie Brownies

Provide a recipe and mix for the children to make brownies. Let the children measure and mix the ingredients. Pour the mixture in a baking pan and help the children count and sprinkle mini chocolate chips into the mix before placing it into the oven. When the brownies have cooled, cut them into small pieces and enjoy for snack.

SCIENCE CENTER

To do this activity at any level, provide a variety of items for the children to use to experiment with the concepts of sink and float. Include items such as a bar of soap, a sponge, a rock, a marble, a rubber duck, and a plastic boat.

Beginning Learner: Sink or Float

Provide a dish tub with water and encourage the children to place the items in the water to see if they sink or float.

Developing Learner: Sink or Float/Predictions

Place a variety of sink or float items on the floor. Before the experiment begins, gather the children around the items. Pick up each item and ask the children if they think it will sink or float. Chart their predictions on a large poster board. After the children experiment with all of the items, discuss the results and whether or not their predictions were correct.

Experienced Learner: Sink or Float/Choosing Variables

Put out two tubs of water. Ask the children to walk around the room and choose manipulatives to place in the water. Have them bring their objects over and discuss with the class what they think might happen. The children take turns performing the experiment. Discuss what happens with each object. Were their predictions right?

LANGUAGE/DRAMATIC PLAY CENTER

Beginning Learner: Exploring Bath Toys

Provide bath toys for the children to explore with in the water table. If desired, the children may add water-safe baby dolls that can "take a bath" with the toys.

Developing Learner: Bathtub Names

Provide bathtub alphabet letters, a tub of water, and cookie sheets. Encourage the children to dip the letters in the water to get them wet and then place them on the trays to spell their names.

Experienced Learner: More Bathtub Words

Provide the alphabet letters, cookie sheets, and a tub of water as described for the developing learner. Write some bath-time words on index cards, including *bath, dirt, soap, wash, clean,* and *water.* Have the children place the bathtub letters on the tray to spell the words.

VOCABULARY

bath, bathtub, cure, dirt, mud, shampoo, soap, sponge, towel, toys, washcloth, water

Reflect

Say to the children, "Yesterday we learned about rain and how wet it feels. Today we learned about bath time and how important it is to take a bath when you get very dirty. Tomorrow we will begin learning about things that are wet, wiggly, and squirmy."

Extend and Enrich

Use the following ideas to extend and enrich what children know about bath time.

◆ Paint washable brown paint on dolls from the dramatic play center and invite the children to wash them off in tubs of water. Encourage them to wash the dolls with washcloths and let the "babies" play with bath toys.

◆ Ask the children to draw a picture of their favorite tub toy and dictate a sentence or two about why it is their favorite.

◆ Make mud pies using mud (or playdough). Provide aluminum pie tins, water, and dirt (or playdough).

Things that Are Wet, Wiggly, or Squirmy

Fish

Morning Circle

Prior to the children's arrival, cut out small, medium, and large fish shapes from poster board. Make one very large fish ("Big Al") and put it aside (use the cover of the book as your inspiration for decorating him). Put masking tape on the back of the other fish and tape them to the floor in a line, leading from the classroom door to the circle time area. Cut out a very large fish bowl from blue bulletin board paper and place it in the circle area. When the children arrive, have them follow the fish shapes to the giant fish bowl. Ask each child to pick up the last fish he lands on and place it in the fish bowl. When all of the children have arrived and placed a fish in the bowl, the fish bowl will be full. Add the "Big Al" fish to the bowl and tell the children that they are going to hear a story about a scary-looking fish who becomes the "hero" of all of the other fish. Remind the children what a hero is before beginning the story.

Storytime

Big Al by Andrew Clements

Daily Center Activity Ideas

ART CENTER

■ **Beginning Learner:** Fancy Fish

Cut out large fish shapes from construction paper. Use different colors of construction paper and shiny paper to cut out small "fish scales." Encourage the children to glue scales all over their fish cutouts.

■ ■ **Developing Learner:** Stuffed Fish

Prior to doing this activity, cut out two large fish for each child from white bulletin board paper. Help the children staple the two fish together, leaving a large enough opening to stuff the fish. Provide the children with tissue paper, watercolors, paintbrushes, and paint smocks. Encourage them to paint both sides of their fish with the watercolors. When the fish are dry, ask the children to stuff their fish with tissue paper. Staple the opening of each fish. Hang the stuffed fish from the ceiling using fishing line.

■
■ ■ **Experienced Learner:** Fish Prints

Prior to doing this activity, cut out large fish shapes from bubble wrap. Provide the bubble wrap fish, a variety of paint colors, white construction paper, paintbrushes, and paint smocks. Encourage the children to paint the bubble wrap fish and then place a piece of paper on top of the fish and press down to make a print. When the children peel off their paper, they will be amazed at the cool design the bubble wrap leaves on the fish. (**Note:** Bubble wrap can be found at local grocery, office supply or packing supply stores.)

MATH CENTER

For all levels of learners, cut out 10 fish shapes (20 for experienced learners) from construction paper. Also cut out a large pond shape from blue bulletin board paper. Attach paper clips to five of the fish. Make a fishing pole by attaching yarn to one end of a small wooden dowel and tying a magnet to the end of the yarn.

Beginning Learner: "Shape-Fish"

Make two sets of "shape -fish" by drawing five different shapes (circle, square, rectangle, star, and triangle) on the five fish with the paper clips. Then draw the same shapes on the other five fish (without paper clips). Place the five fish with paper clips in the pond and put the other set of fish (without paper clips) next to the pond, face down. Encourage the children to use the fishing poles to fish in the pond. Ask them to identify the shape on the fish that they catch and then flip over the other fish until they find a matching shape.

Developing Learner: "Number-Fish"

Write the numbers 1–5 on the fish with the paper clips and the same numbers on the other five fish. Place the fish with the paper clips in the pond and the other set of fish next to the pond, face down. Encourage the children to identify the number on the fish that they catch, and then have them look next to the pond to find the fish with the matching number.

Experienced Learner: "Dot-Fish"

For this activity, you will need 20 fish cutouts. Put dot stickers on 10 of the fish—one dot on the first fish, two dots on another fish, and so on until the tenth fish has 10 dots on it. Attach paper clips to the dot fish. Write the numbers 1–10 on the other 10 fish. Place the "dot-fish" in the pond and place the other fish next to the pond. Encourage the children to catch the dot-fish using the fishing pole, count the dots on the fish, and then find the matching "number-fish" next to the pond.

SCIENCE CENTER

Beginning Learner: Ocean in a Bottle

Prior to doing this activity, send a note home to families asking them to send in one empty water bottle. Make sure to have extra water bottles for children who forget to bring in bottles. Show the children pictures of underwater and ocean scenes, and discuss the sea creatures and other objects in the pictures. Tell the children that they are going to make their own "ocean in a bottle." Provide a small pitcher of water, a funnel, blue food coloring, and ocean fish confetti (available at craft stores). Ask the children to place some of the confetti in their water bottle. Next, help them place the funnel in the top of the water bottle and carefully pour the water into the bottle. Let the children add a few drops of blue food coloring to make the water blue. Screw on the lid and secure it tightly. If possible, use hot glue to secure the lid (adult only). Invite the children to move their bottles back and forth and watch the "fish" swim in the "ocean."

Developing Learner: Puzzle Fish

Gather pictures of large fish. Remind the children that the fish in the story *Big Al* was very large and looked a little scary. Show the pictures to the children and discuss the shapes, sizes, and colors of the fish. Ask the children if they think the fish in the pictures live in a river, lake, a pond, or the ocean. Talk about saltwater fish and freshwater fish. Tell the children they are going to make fish puzzles. Draw a large fish on a piece of white poster board. Make one for each child. Help the children cut out the fish. On the back of the fish, draw puzzle pieces. Invite the children to color their fish with markers. When they are finished coloring, use the puzzle piece patterns on the back of the fish to cut the pictures into puzzle pieces. Invite the children to put the fish puzzles back together.

Experienced Learner: Freshwater Fish, Saltwater Fish

Fish live in both fresh water and salt water. Provide fresh water (water from the tap), salt water (one pint of water mixed with ½ oz. of salt), and a fresh egg. Have the children predict whether or not they think the egg will float or sink in each solution. Record their predictions. Invite them to test their predictions by placing the egg in the fresh water and then in the salt water. Explain that the egg floats in saltwater because the salt makes the water denser so it holds the egg up. This is the same reason that people float more easily in the ocean than in a swimming pool.

LANGUAGE/DRAMATIC PLAY CENTER

Beginning Learner: Catch of the Day

Provide construction paper cutouts of fish in two distinctly different sizes. Discuss other words for *small* (tiny, bitsy, little) and other words for *big* (huge, giant, enormous). Provide two fishing nets, and on one net write the word *small* and on the other net, write the word *big*. Talk about the word on each net, making sure to point out that small begins with "s" and big begins with "b." Have the children sort the different sizes of fish into each net.

■ ■ Developing Learner: Camouflage Fish Collage

Cut out large fish from construction paper. Provide collage materials (such as sand, moss, shredded paper, grass, artificial greenery) and wiggle eyes. Show the children the pictures of Big Al from the story. Encourage the children to camouflage their fish cutout using the collage materials and then have them add a wiggle eye. When they are finished with their pictures, encourage them to describe their fish collage.

■ ■ ■ Experienced Learner: Big Al's Friends

After the children have heard the story of Big Al, discuss what being a friend means. Remind the children that Big Al tried very hard to make the other fish in the story be his friends, and then he did something really special for them by rescuing them from the giant net. Ask the children, "What is something special you can do for your friends?" Give each child a piece of paper that says, "I can help my friends by _____." Encourage the children to answer the question. Write their answers on their papers and then provide markers and crayons for the children to illustrate their sentences.

VOCABULARY

bait, bobber, dorsal fin, fins, fish, fish hook, fisherman, fishery, fishing rod, gills, lure, net, reel, salmon, scales, shark, tackle, tail, trawl, tuna

Reflect

Say to the children, "Today we learned about fish, which are wiggly and squiggly and fun to watch. They are also good to eat. Tomorrow we will learn about octopuses, some of which are giant creatures that live in the deepest ocean. Octopuses are wet, wiggly, and kind of squirmy."

Extend and Enrich

Use the following ideas to extend and enrich what children know about fish.
◆ Provide a variety of fishing worms for the children to sort and categorize.
◆ For a creative writing exercise, have the children plan a fishing trip and write about all of the things that they would take with them in their boat. Provide boat cutouts and have the children draw the items they would take.
◆ Invite the children to sit in large plastic tubs and pretend they are floating in boats. Encourage the children to design and make sails and paddles. They could sit in their pretend boats and practice paddling across pretend blue water.

Octopuses

Morning Circle

Prior to doing this day's activities, make a giant octopus using a large outdoor trash bag. Place three helium balloons in the trash bag, and use masking tape to close the bag at its base, forming the head of the octopus. Cut the remaining part of the bag into eight sections to form the arms. Tape each arm to the floor so that the octopus, whose head will rise due to helium balloons, will look like it is floating. When the children arrive at circle time, they will be excited to see the visiting octopus.

Storytime

How to Hide an Octopus and Other Sea Creatures by Ruth Heller

Daily Center Activity Ideas

ART CENTER

▪ **Beginning Learner:** Handprint Octopus
Provide tempera paint, paper, and wiggle eyes for the children to use to make a handprint octopus. Paint the children's hands (palms and fingers, but not the thumbs) and have them place their two hands right next to each other to make the body and eight arms. Another option is to paint one of the child's hands (palm and fingers, not the thumb) and help the child make a print. Then paint the child's other hand in the same way, and help him put his painted palm almost on top of the palm print on the paper to complete the body and all eight arms. The children can add wiggle eyes after the paint dries.

Developing Learner: Paper Bowl Octopus

Provide paper bowls, white and gray paint, a stapler, wiggle eyes, and white crepe-paper streamers. Have the children paint the outside of their paper bowls with a mixture of white and gray paint. When the paint is dry, help them staple eight streamers to the sides of the bowls to resemble octopus arms. The children glue wiggle eyes to the bowl to complete the octopus.

Experienced Learner: Paper Bag Octopus

Give each child a brown or white lunch bag, green paint, paintbrush, toilet paper, giant wiggle eyes, a 2-liter soda bottle, and tape. Ask the children to place the lunch bag over the bottle and paint the bag green. After the bags have dried, remove them from the soda bottles. Have the children tear off two handfuls of toilet paper and stuff it in the bottom of the lunch bag. Close the bag and wrap tape around the neck of the bag to create a head. Make sure to leave about three inches of bag below the head. Cut the ends of the bag to create the eight arms. Spread the arms apart for the octopus to sit up.

MATH CENTER

Beginning Learner: More or Less than Eight?

Show the children a picture of an octopus and pictures of other animals. Talk about the octopus and how many legs it has. Ask the children to look at the pictures of the different animals and count the legs on each animal. Ask them if each animal has more or less legs than the octopus.

Developing Learner: Octagon Octopus

Tell the children that *octa-* means eight and that an octopus has eight arms. Explain that an octagon is a shape that has eight sides. Give each child an octagon shape on green construction paper to cut out, eight 12" green construction paper strips, two small white octagon cutouts, and glue. Invite the children to cut out the large green octagon and glue the paper strips to it. Encourage the children to glue the small octagons on the octopus for eyes. Ask them to count the sides of the octagon and the arms on the octopus.

Experienced Learner: Eight Steps

Place a hula hoop on the floor to represent an octopus's head. Use colored tape or masking tape to make eight lines on the floor extending from the hula hoop to represent the octopus's arms. Encourage the children to walk on the eight arms by trying to take only eight steps on each of the eight lines. Encourage them to experiment with taking small steps or larger steps until they can walk each of the eight sides by taking only eight steps.

SCIENCE CENTER

Discuss that an octopus is unique because it has its own ink sac, which it uses to create an ink cloud to protect itself from predators. The following activities will help the children learn about this creature's natural defense mechanism.

Beginning Learner: Squirting Octopus Ink

The day before doing this activity, prepare four or five batches of clear, unflavored gelatin. Pour the gelatin into bowls and allow it to set overnight in the refrigerator. Release the gelatin from the bowls and place it in the water table or in dish tubs. Provide eyedroppers or pipettes and black paint that has been thinned to look like ink.. Encourage the children to use the droppers to squirt the "ink" on and inside the gelatin.

Developing Learner: Octopus Art/Blow Paint

Show the children a picture of an octopus and talk about how it has eight arms. Encourage the children to notice the shape of its head. Help the children cut out octopus heads from construction paper. Have them glue the heads in the middle of a large sheet of white construction paper. Give each child a straw to blow through. Ask the children to feel the air coming out of the other end of the straws. Mix black paint with water so that it looks like ink. Invite the children to put eight large drops of paint around the head of the octopus and then carefully use their straws to blow the "ink" to make arms. (**Safety note:** Make sure children blow out through the straw, not in. For sanitary purposes, make sure each child disposes of his straw when he is finished with it.)

Experienced Learner: Suction Cup Art

Show the children a picture of an octopus from a science or nature magazine. Try to find one that shows the suckers on the underside of the arms. Discuss how the octopus closes its arms together and the suckers help it to capture its prey. Provide soap dishes that have suction cups (found in grocery stores) or some other small suction cups. Invite the children to experiment with the suction cups to see how they stick to table tops and other surfaces. Ask the children to draw their own octopus on paper and then dip the suction cups into black paint to make suction cups on the arms of their octopus.

LANGUAGE/DRAMATIC PLAY CENTER

For all levels of learners, read *How to Hide an Octopus and Other Sea Creatures* before doing the activity.

Beginning Learner: Retelling the Story

Provide the children with plastic or stuffed animals from the story. Invite them to use the animals to retell the story.

Developing Learner: Favorite Sea Creatures

Ask the children look at the pictures of the animals in the story and name them. Engage the children in a discussion of how the animals are alike and how they are different. Then have the children choose their favorite sea creature. Invite them to draw a picture of the sea creature and its home in the sea.

■
■ ■ **Experienced Learner:** My Octopus Story

Encourage the children to dictate a story about what would happen if they needed to hide an octopus. Ask questions such as, "What would it look like? Where would it stay in your house? What would you feed it? What would your family say?" Encourage the children to illustrate their stories.

VOCABULARY

arms, camouflage, eight, ink, invertebrate, octopus, suckers

Reflect

Say to the children, "Yesterday we learned about fish and how the make-believe fish called Big Al tried to camouflage himself so the other fish would not be afraid of him. Today we learned about another amazing creature of the sea called the octopus. Tomorrow we will learn about worms."

Extend and Enrich

Use the following ideas to extend and enrich what children know about the octopus.

◆ Encourage the children to visit an aquarium or fish market that has fish and other sea life such as squid, lobsters, shrimp, and octopuses so they can see these creatures and learn more about them.

◆ Use masking tape or colored tape to make a giant figure eight on the classroom floor. Have the children walk the outline of the eight and count how many steps it takes them to walk the whole numeral.

Worms

Morning Circle

In preparation for this activity, purchase earthworms (or night crawlers) at fishing/bait stores or pet stores, or find them outdoors in flower beds. Place several inches of damp soil into a small aquarium and place the worms on top of the soil. Cover the aquarium with a dark piece of material. The dark environment will encourage the worms to begin tunneling. When the children arrive for the day, discuss the fact that worms create tunnels as they work their way through the soil. Encourage the children to observe the worms in their environment. Discuss the worms and what they are doing. Encourage the children to notice how the worms wiggle as they move. Invite the children to lie on their stomachs on the floor and pretend to be wiggling worms. Read the story *Wiggling Worms at Work* by Wendy Pfeffer.

Storytime

Wiggling Worms at Work by Wendy Pfeffer

Daily Center Activity Ideas

ART CENTER

Beginning Learner: Fingerprint Worm

Provide a brown ink pad and paper and encourage the children to press their fingers into the ink and then make overlapping fingerprints to make worms. Have them draw dirt and tunnels around the worms.

Developing Learner: String-Painted Worms

Give each child a 12" piece of brown yarn and a piece of white paper folded in half and then opened, so that there is a fold line. Place brown paint on a tray or in a pie pan. Encourage the children to dip their piece of yarn into the brown paint and place it on one side of the paper. The children fold the paper in half (at the fold), but before folding the paper together, make sure they keep one end of the yarn in their hand and the other end on the paper. When the paper is folded closed, have them pull out the piece of yarn from the paper. The yarn will leave a long worm-shaped design on their paper. The children will love doing this activity over and over again, and will delight in seeing their creations.

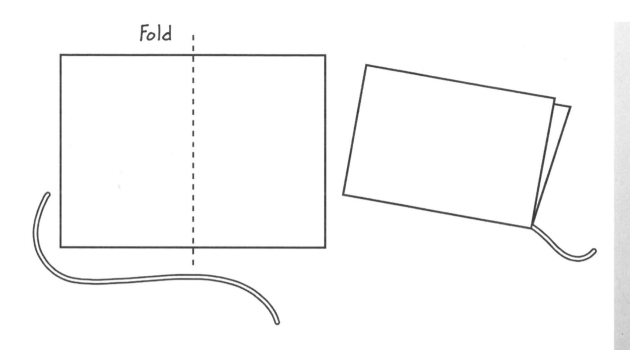

Fold

■ ■ **Experienced Learner:** Pipe Cleaner Worm
Provide brown beads and brown pipe cleaners or chenille sticks. Encourage the children to string the brown beads on the pipe cleaners to make worms. Cut the lengths of pipe cleaners to different sizes so that the children can make a variety of worms.

MATH CENTER

■ **Beginning Learner:** Fishing Worms/Sorting
Provide a variety of rubber fishing lures that look like worms. These can be purchased at a sporting goods store. Invite the children to sort them into categories by size or color. (**Safety note:** Be sure that the lures do not contain hooks.)

■ ■ **Developing Learner:** Fishing Worms/Counting
Place the fishing lures described for the beginning learner into a tub of water. Provide an aquarium net, a bucket, and a numeral die. Have the children take turns rolling the die. The child identifies the number he rolls, and then uses the net to scoop out the appropriate number of worms from the water and places them in the bucket. Place the fishing worms back in the tub of water for the next child's turn.

■ ■ **Experienced Learner:** Inchworm Measuring
Tell the children that there is a worm called an inchworm, but it is really a caterpillar. Provide 1"-long construction-paper worm shapes. Encourage the children to use the "inchworms" to measure different items in the classroom. Have them record their findings on a classroom chart. For example, the desk is 20 inchworms long, the book is five inchworms long, my foot is six inchworms long, and so on.

SCIENCE CENTER

Share some of the following information with the children as they are learning about worms in the science center:

◆ Worms have been called "underground farmers." They burrow through the soil, making holes that allow air and water to seep into the ground, which is what a farmer does with a plow.

◆ Worms eat decaying plant matter, soil, and debris such as fungus and mold. The debris is passed through the worm's digestive system and then expelled in tiny pellets called worm castings. The worm castings are high in nutrients and provide good "food" for the soil and plants.

Beginning Learner: Worm Observation

Provide a tub of worms in the sand table and clear plastic cups. The children may pick up the worms with their hands or use clear plastic cups to scoop up dirt and worms and observe them through the side of the cup. For children who do not wish to touch the worms, provide a container with worms and dirt for them to observe. (**Note:** Remind children to wash their hands after handling the worms.)

Developing Learner: Worm Farm

Give each child a small, clear plastic jar or container. Invite the children to create their own worm habitats by putting soil in the jars and gently adding worms. Help them to place a small square of wax paper over the opening of the jar and secure it with a rubber band. Poke air holes in the wax paper. Invite the children to observe their worms through the sides of their containers. Have them tape black construction paper to the outside of their jars to simulate the darkness underground. Ask them to compare the worms' activity level in each environment (dark or light).

Experienced Learner: Worm Farm II

Provide a plastic jar or plastic tub filled with dirt and earthworms. Invite the children to observe the worms with magnifying glasses and handle them, if desired. Explain to the children that when the worms first come out of a cold refrigerated environment (in the bait shop), they are very lethargic, but as they heat up they become more active. Share an informational book about worms to help them to gain more facts and information as they observe the worms in the classroom. Provide paper, markers, and crayons for the children to make their own worm observation and fact books. Invite them to record what they observe and learn as they watch the worms. When the activity is over, place the worms outside in the school garden.

LANGUAGE/DRAMATIC PLAY CENTER

■ **Beginning Learner:** Bait Shop

Provide a variety of rubber worm-shaped fishing lures, resealable plastic bags, a play cash register, and play money. The children pretend to work at a bait shop, taking customer orders and packaging the "worms." The children set the prices and exchange money.

■ ■ **Developing Learner:** Dirt Dessert

Tell the children that they are going to make a pretend "dirt and worm" dessert. Show them a finished dessert before they begin to make their own. Provide clear plastic cups, chocolate pudding, chocolate cookies, resealable plastic bags, gummy worms, and spoons. Each child places two cookies in a plastic bag and crush them with his fingers or with a rolling pin. Children make the dessert by spooning ¼ cup of chocolate pudding into their cups, adding half of their crushed cookies, 1–2 spoonfuls of chocolate pudding, and then the remainder of the crushed cookies on top. Top off with a gummy worm.

■
■ ■ **Experienced Learner:** Dirt Dessert with Recipe

Provide the items as described for the developing learner to make a dirt dessert. In addition, give each child a large index card with the recipe for making a dirt dessert. Help the children illustrate their recipe directions by drawing pictures to represent the ingredients.

VOCABULARY

burrow, casting, dirt, earth, earthworm farm, ground, segments, slink, squirm, wiggle, worms

Reflect

Say to the children, "Yesterday we learned about the amazing octopus and what a wonderful sea creature it is. Today we learned about worms and how they live and work underground. Tomorrow we will learn about ducks and what funny little creatures they are as they waddle and wiggle around the pond."

Extend and Enrich

Use the following ideas to extend and enrich what children know about worms.
◆ Encourage the children to find earthworms in their yard at home, at a park, playground, or other outdoor area.

Ducks

Morning Circle

When the children arrive, tell them that they will be learning about ducks. Explain that baby ducks always follow their mother everywhere she goes and that they often walk in a line. Pretend to be the momma duck and show the children how to waddle like ducks by squatting on the ground and wobbling to and fro with necks stretched high. Encourage the children to quack like a duck all the way to the circle area. Show them a picture of a goose and a duck. Discuss their similarities and differences and then share the story for the day.

Storytime

Duck and Goose by Tad Hills

Daily Center Activity Ideas

ART CENTER

▨ **Beginning Learner:** Duck Feet
Cut out webbed-foot shapes from white paper plates to represent duck feet. Make two for each child. Invite the children to paint the webbed feet with orange paint. When the paint is dry, help the children tape the feet on top of their shoes so they can practice waddling like a duck.

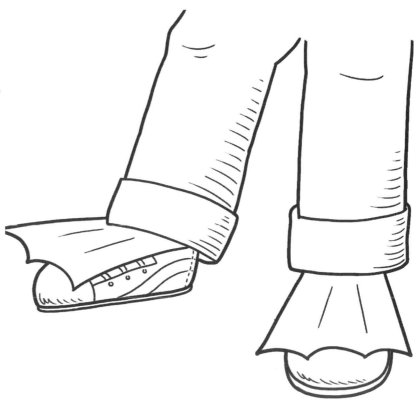

Developing Learner: Little Ducklings

Provide white paper plates, yellow feathers, wiggle eyes, orange construction paper beaks, and glue. The children glue feathers on their paper plates to make them look like duck faces. Have them add wiggle eyes and beaks.

Experienced Learner: Baby Ducklings in Their Nest

Provide paper plates, shredded paper, yellow cotton balls, glue, and plastic eggs. Invite the children to shred paper and glue it to paper plates to create nests. To make baby ducks, the children place one yellow cotton ball inside each of the plastic eggs. The children carefully place the eggs in the nest.

MATH CENTER

Beginning Learner: Ducks in a Row/Ordering

Remind the children that baby ducks following their mother appear to walk in a line or row. Write the numerals 1–5 on the bottom of five toy bathtub ducks. Place a small amount of water in a small wading pool and add the ducks. Encourage the children to take turns choosing ducks from the "pond" and placing the ducks in numerical order by looking at the number on the bottom.

Developing Learner: Duck Eggs/Matching and Counting

Provide ducks in a "pond" as described for the beginning learner. Place a large piece of green paper "grass" near the pool. Add a shredded paper "nest" and plastic eggs. Have the children choose a duck from the pond and look at the numeral on the bottom of it. Ask them to go to the "grassy patch" where the eggs are and count out the number of eggs to match the number on the bottom of the duck.

Experienced Learner: Duck Book/Numeral Recognition

Give each child 10 pages of white paper, a duck stamp, and yellow paint. Help the children write the numerals 1–10 at the top of each page (one numeral on each of their 10 pages). The children dip the duck stamp in the yellow paint and make a duck print on each page. Ask them to draw a nest and the number of eggs to match the numeral at the top of each page (page one would have one egg, page two would have two eggs, and so on up to 10).

SCIENCE CENTER

Beginning Learner: Water Off a Duck's Back

Provide a collection of feathers gathered from nature walks or natural feathers purchased at a craft store, paper towels, a pitcher of water, magnifying glasses, and eyedroppers. Encourage the children to use a magnifying glass to examine the colors and textures of the feathers. Invite them to place a feather on a paper towel and drop water from an eyedropper on their feather. What happens? Discuss why the water runs off and the concept of "waterproof." Explain why this is an important characteristic for ducks.

Developing Learner: Egg to Duck

If possible, find a book about the life cycle of a duck to share with the children. Talk about how ducks hatch from an egg and grow into an adult duck. Provide sequence cards showing the steps of the journey, and invite the children to place the picture cards in sequential order.

Experienced Learner: Rubbery Eggs

Provide several hard-boiled eggs, plastic cups, vinegar, and plastic wrap. Invite the children to examine the eggs, noting their weight and feel, as well as the smell, texture, and color of the shell. The children place one egg in the plastic cup with vinegar, cover it with plastic wrap, and place it in the refrigerator. (If it is not possible to leave it in a refrigerator, leave it out on a table.) Every day, the children observe the egg and notice any changes. Change the vinegar every day and replace the cover on the cup. After several days, remove the egg from the vinegar and rinse it off. Ask the children to examine the egg and compare it to a hard-boiled egg that was not in vinegar. Ask them to note the changes in its shell from its original state. The shell will have become rubbery. Explain to the children that the acid in the vinegar has eaten the shell of the hard-boiled egg and made it disappear.

LANGUAGE/DRAMATIC PLAY CENTER

Beginning Learner: Walk Like a Duck

Show the children a picture of a duck that shows the details of its feet. Show the children a set of flippers and point out how they are similar to the foot of a duck. Invite the children to put on the flippers and walk around the classroom. Explain that a duck's foot is webbed, which helps to propel the duck through the water just as flippers help people move through the water. Invite the children to pretend they are swimming, moving the water with their "webbed feet." Cut out webbed foot shapes from orange construction paper, one pair for each child. Use rubber bands to attach the duck feet to the top of the children's shoes. The rubber bands will help keep the duck feet from falling off. Encourage the children to walk around the room pretending to be little ducks.

Developing Learner: Uppercase and Lowercase Ducks

Prior to doing this activity, cut out a large duck and small duck for each child. Write each of the child's names on his two ducks, using uppercase letters on the large duck and lowercase letters on the small duck. Scatter the ducks around the room, and encourage the children to find both of their ducks.

Experienced Learner: Alphabet Eggs

Prior to doing this activity, gather plastic eggs and a permanent marker. On each egg, write an uppercase letter on the top of the egg and the same lowercase letter on the bottom of the egg. For example, write "A" on the top of an egg and "a" on the bottom. Continue until all of the letters of the alphabet are represented. Separate the tops and bottoms of all the eggs, and place the egg halves in a basket. Encourage the children to dump out the eggs and find all of the matching letters and put the eggs back together.

VOCABULARY

brood, down, duck, duckling, egg, feathers, feet, flock, hatch, paddle, quack, swim, water, webbed, wing

Reflect

Say to the children, "Yesterday we learned about worms and what how they wiggle and squirm underground mixing the dirt and making tunnels. Today we learned about ducks and how they waddle and paddle their way through the water. Tomorrow we will learn about whales and what giant and majestic sea creatures they are."

Extend and Enrich

Use the following ideas to extend and enrich what children know about ducks.

◆ Obtain an incubator and fertilized eggs. Invite children to observe the eggs as they hatch and as the chicks grow. You can get fertilized eggs at some farm supply stores. You can also check with a local 4-H group or agricultural extension service.

◆ Obtain a variety of eggs from the grocery store or a farm for the children to compare.

◆ Share the folk tale "The Ugly Duckling" with the children.

DAY 5

Whales

Morning Circle

Before doing this activity, purchase
a small plastic wading pool. Fill
it with items such as seashells,
starfish, sand, plastic seaweed or
aquarium plants, and plastic
ocean animals to create a seascape
in the pool. Pour a very small
amount of water into the baby
pool. As the children arrive, let them take turns using a small fishing net to scoop up different
treasures from the "seascape." Talk about whales with the children and explain that there are
many different types of whales. If possible, show them pictures of whales.

Storytime

The Whales by Cynthia Rylant

Daily Center Activity Ideas

ART CENTER

For all levels of learners, cut out a whale shape from the middle of a piece of poster board to use
as a stencil. The beginning and developing learners use the stencils, and the experienced learners
use the whale cutout.

■ **Beginning Learner:** Stencil Whales/Watercolors
Help the children clip a large piece of paper on the easel, and then use clothespins to hang the
whale stencil over the paper. Encourage the children to use watercolors to paint inside the cutout whale shape. Carefully remove the stencil. The children can paint an ocean scene around the
watercolor whale.

■ ■ **Developing Learner:** Stencil Whales/Sponge Painting
Provide the children with a stencil of a whale, sponges, clothespins, blue watercolor paint, and
gray and black tempera paint. The children use blue watercolors to paint their paper. When it is
dry, help them place the stencil on the paper. The children dip a sponge (attached to a
clothespin) in gray and black paint and use it to fill in the whale.

■ ■ ■ Experienced Learner: Negative Space Whale

Provide cutouts of a whale, drawing paper, pencils, painter's tape, and tempera paint. Help the children use painter's tape to attach their whale cutout to their paper. Show them how to dip the eraser-end of a pencil into paint and use it to make dots all around the whale cutout, covering all the white space on their paper. When dry, the children carefully remove the stencil from their paper to reveal a white whale.

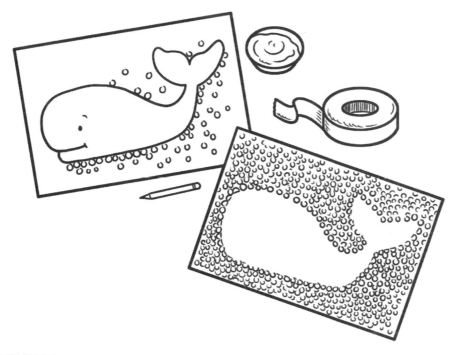

MATH CENTER

■ Beginning Learner: How Long Is a Whale?

Discuss with the children that the blue whale is the largest animal on Earth. It is approximately 90 feet long and weighs 120 tons. Tape a piece of 90' long rope to the ground so that the children can visualize the whale's length. Invite the children to walk the length of the rope to experience the whale's large size.

■ ■ Developing Learner: Would a Whale Fit in Your Bathtub?

Discuss with the children that the blue whale weighs an average of 120 tons. Ask the children to compare the size of blue whale with other large animals. (It's a good idea to have a reference book handy so you can provide information about the size of other animals they mention. Have the children walk the length of the rope to get an idea of the blue whale's actual size as described for the developing learner. Invite the children to line up building blocks and other materials along the length of rope. As the children work, ask them questions about the whale's size. "Do you think a blue whale would fit in your bathtub?" "Would the whale fit in your car or in your house?"

Experienced Learner: A Whale Is 90 Rulers Long

Talk about the length of the blue whale. Show the children what 12" looks like using a ruler, tape measure, or the floor tiles (if they are 12"). Explain that there are 12" in one foot, so a blue whale would be 90 ruler-lengths long. Give each child a 90' length of yarn. Have them tape one end to the ground at one end of a large area (indoors or outdoors) or hallway. The children hold the other end of their yarn and walk until they reach the end of the 90'. Have them tape the remaining end of the yarn on the floor. The children now have a full-length whale measurement. Invite them to practice their measuring skills by measuring the yarn using Unifix cubes or other classroom materials.

SCIENCE CENTER

Beginning Learner: Whale Exploration

Provide a small plastic tub of water or a child-size wading pool with a small amount of water in the bottom. Provide toy whales for the children to explore with in the water.

Developing Learner: Baleen Whales

Tell the children that the blue whale is a baleen whale. Baleen whales are unique because they have no teeth. Instead of teeth, they have *baleen plates* in their mouths, which are made out of the same material as fingernails and hair. Baleen whales feed on tiny animals and plants called plankton, which are filtered through the baleen in their mouths. To demonstrate how this process works, do this activity with the children. Provide a deep container such as a plastic fish aquarium, aquarium nets, and decorative aquarium rocks. Fill the aquarium with water and place the aquarium rocks in the bottom. The children use nets (the "baleen") to sweep through the water and scoop up the rocks ("plankton").

Experienced Learner: Whale Blubber

Explain that whales have a large layer of fat called blubber that protects them from the cold water. To demonstrate how fat keeps them warm, have the children put on disposable plastic or latex gloves and cover one of their gloves with vegetable shortening. Invite the children to place both of their hands into a bucket of ice water. When they remove their hands from the ice water, ask them to describe which hand feels colder. The shortening protects the hand from the cold the same way the whale's blubber protects the whale from the cold.

LANGUAGE/DRAMATIC PLAY CENTER

Beginning Learner: What's in the Sea?

To prepare for this activity, fill a plastic jar (the size of a mayonnaise jar) with sand. Add small toy sea creatures and any other item that relates to the sea. Place the lid on the jar. The children roll the jar and identify all the objects that they see.

Developing Learner: Whale Tale Game

Gather the children into a circle to play a "whale tale" game. Start the game by whispering a fact or something funny about a whale into the ear of the child sitting next to you. That child whispers the same message into the ear of the child sitting next to him, and so on until everyone has heard the message. The last child to receive the message says it out loud to everyone. Let the children take turns starting the secret game.

Experienced Learner: "What's in the Sea?" Story

Prepare a jar with sand and small toy sea creatures (the same way as for the beginning learner). As the children roll the jar, invite them to look at the sea creatures inside the jar and create stories about them. Encourage the children to dictate their ideas to you and then illustrate them.

VOCABULARY

algae, baleen whales, blowhole, blubber, calf, large, ocean, plankton, whales

Reflect

Say to the children, "Yesterday we learned about ducks and how they waddle and paddle around ponds. Today we learned about whales. They are the largest creatures found in the world today."

Extend and Enrich

Use the following ideas to extend and enrich what children know about whales.
- Have the children brainstorm words that rhyme with whale, such as *tail, sail, mail, fail, hail, jail, nail,* and *pail.*
- There are two different kinds of whales: baleen whales and toothed whales. The toothed whales include killer whales and beluga whales. Baleen whales include blue whales, gray whales, and humpback whales. Provide pictures of the different whales and talk about their similarities and differences.
- Discuss with the children the importance of the whale's blowhole and how it acts as the whale's nose. Explain that even though whales live in water, they are mammals and not fish.

Things that Are Very Small or Very Big

Beetles

Morning Circle

Before greeting the children, put on a safari hat and hold a net with a plastic beetle in it. As the children arrive, swing the net wildly in the air and say, "I just caught this bug. I think it is a beetle. Let's look at it together." Provide several magnifying glasses for the children to examine the bug. Ask them to pay special attention to the beetle's legs, wings, and eyes. Before reading the story *The Very Clumsy Click Beetle,* use a plastic bug toy to make a clicking sound and ask the children what they hear. Demonstrate how to use your tongue to make a clicking sound and invite the children to practice making a clicking sound with their tongues. Share the story with the children and discuss the lessons learned. Explain the concepts of persistence and patience, and talk about how the little beetle never gives up. Ask the children to talk about times when they have had to be persistent or patient.

Storytime

The Very Clumsy Click Beetle by Eric Carle

Daily Center Activity Ideas

ART CENTER

▪ **Beginning Learner:** Beetle-Shaped Nature Collage
Prior to doing this activity, cut out large beetle shapes from brown construction paper for each child. Use the pictures in the book as a reference, if needed. Take the children outside and give them paper bags to collect nature items, such as sticks, leaves, twigs, seeds, and tree bark. Back inside, have the children take out their collection and discuss their finds. Encourage them to glue their nature items on their beetle shape.

▪▪ **Developing Learner:** Designing a Beetle
Provide a large outline of a beetle on heavy paper (one for each child), a watered-down glue mixture, paintbrushes, markers, and shades of brown, black, and gray tissue paper. Invite the children to paint the glue mixture on the beetle outline and attach torn pieces of tissue paper to the different sections of the beetle. When the children have finished adding tissue paper, have them use markers to draw six legs and antennae on the beetle.

■ ■ Experienced Learner: Egg Carton Beetle

Before doing this activity, explain to the children that beetles have three body sections: a head, thorax (middle), and abdomen (end). The beetle's six legs are connected to the thorax. Cut egg cartons into four pieces each piece should have three connected compartments like a bug).Give each child a piece of egg carton. Provide chenille sticks, brown or black tempera paint, wiggle eyes, a hole punch, and brown tissue paper. Encourage the children to paint their egg cartons, then let them dry. Help the children punch holes through the middle section of their beetles, and then help them thread their pipe cleaners through the holes to create legs. Provide tissue paper for the children to use to make wings to add to their beetles. Help them attach wiggle eyes and small pipe cleaners to the front of the egg carton for antennae.

MATH CENTER

■ Beginning Learner: Insect Counting Books

Fold two or three pieces of construction paper together to form a "book." Write the numeral 1 on the first page, the numeral 2 on the second page, and so on until a numeral 5 is added to the last page. Provide insect stickers for the children to use to make their own insect counting books. Have them put one sticker on page 1, two stickers on page 2, and so on.

■ ■ Developing Learner: Hide and Seek Insects

Hide a stuffed or toy insect somewhere in the room. Show the children a sand timer and explain how it works. Turn over the sand timer and ask the children to find the hidden "insect" before the sand runs out. As an alternative, make an insect headband by twisting two chenille sticks on a headband. Glue half of a Styrofoam ball to the end of each stem. The "insect" hides and the children try to find her before the sand runs out. Let all the children have a turn being the "insect" or hiding the toy insect while the rest of the children go seek.

■ ■ Experienced Learner: Insect Sort

Prior to doing this activity, discuss some of the differences between insects and other animals. Talk about how insects have six legs and three body parts. They wear their skeletons on the outside of their bodies. This hard covering protects the insect and is called an exoskeleton. Some insects have wings and some do not. Some insects have two eyes, whereas some have as many as five. Provide a collection of stuffed and toy animals of all different kinds, including mammals, frogs, snakes, sea creatures, and insects. Encourage the children to identify the creatures and animals and then sort out the insects from the other creatures.

SCIENCE CENTER

While the children are working in the science center, remind them that the beetle's body (as well as all other insects' bodies) consists of three segments: the head, the thorax, and the abdomen. Six legs are always attached to the thorax of the beetle.

Beginning Learner: Bug Jars with Stickers

Give each child a small plastic jar with a lid and sheets of bug stickers. Invite the children to use the bug stickers to decorate their "bug jars." As they are working, explain that bugs play a very important role in nature, and therefore,. should be returned to their homes unharmed whenever we capture them for a closer look. Provide extra bug stickers, markers, and paper for the children to make pretend bugs to add to their bug jars.

Developing Learner: Bug Jars/Coloring Insects

Find small pictures of insects in coloring books and reproduce enough pages for the children to color. Show the children the insect pictures and discuss each insect. Talk about their names, what role they play in nature, and where they can be found. Focus on the unique characteristics of each insect, such as the location of their eyes and the shapes of their bodies. Discuss the importance of leaving harming these creatures. Invite the children to color the insect pictures, cut them out, and add them to their bug jars (see beginning-learner activity).

Experienced Learner: Making Insect Field Guides

Locate pictures of insects such as ants, ladybugs, grasshoppers, crickets, roaches, bees, wasps, butterflies, flies, dragonflies, and moths. Make copies of the pictures and give a copy to each child. The children can color the pictures and cut them out. Also provide nature magazines and invite the children to cut out pictures of insects and bugs they have seen in nature. Help each child staple several sheets of white paper together to make a book. Have the children glue their insect pictures on the pages of their books. Write the names of the insects on index cards and encourage the children to copy the appropriate words in their books. The children can use their books as "field guides" when they are outside looking for insects.

LANGUAGE/DRAMATIC PLAY CENTER

Beginning Learner: Acting It Out

Provide props for the children to act out the story *The Very Clumsy Click Beetle.* Look at the pictures in the book to give you ideas. For example, provide a yellow ball for the sun, a silk flower, a small pile of rocks, green construction paper cut into grass shapes, brown paper cut into a tree shape, and a beetle. Read the beginning of the book until you get to the part where the click beetle falls out of the tree and lands on his back. Have the children use the props to act out the story as you read it to them. Make sure the children take turns using the different props as you read the beginning of the book.

◾◾ **Developing Learner:** Acting It Out/Making Props

To prepare for this activity, encourage the children to help create the animals from the story so they can be used to retell the story. Cut out two beetles from construction paper and paint them to look like the beetles in the story. To make the worm, stuff a knee-high stocking with cotton batting. Paint the bottom of a paper bowl green and add a head, feet, and a tail to make the turtle. Cut out a snail from gray construction paper. Cut out a mouse from gray felt. Draw a picture of a boy and cut it out. Read the first part of *The Very Clumsy Click Beetle,* and stop when you get to the part when the click beetle falls out of the tree and lands on its back. Ask the children to act out the second half of the story as you read it. Give each child a story prop. Continue reading the story and stop at the point where each of the props is mentioned. The child with that prop acts out her part of the story. Have the children switch props and read the story again.

◾

◾◾ **Experienced Learner:** Acting It Out/Stick Puppets

Read the story to the children. Provide construction paper, scissors, markers, craft sticks, and tape. Encourage the children to use the book as inspiration for making their own stick puppets to retell the story. Let them choose their favorite characters from the story and cut out the shapes from construction paper. Have them use markers to add details to the characters. When the story characters are complete, help the children tape them on craft sticks. Read the story again and encourage the children to use their puppets to act out the story.

VOCABULARY

abdomen, adult, antenna, beetle, colony, egg, feeding, flying, grub, head, insect, larva, pupa, swarm, thorax

Reflect

Say to the children, "Today we learned about beetles, which are very small and hard to see unless you are looking for them. Tomorrow we will talk about another type of insect, ants."

Extend and Enrich

Use the following ideas to extend and enrich what children know about beetles.

◆ Encourage the children to lie on their backs on the floor like the clumsy click beetle from the story. Play music and the children wiggle like the click beetle; stop the music and the children freeze.

◆ Provide musical instruments and other objects that could be used to make a "clicking" sound. Encourage the children to experiment with the different instruments.

Ants

Morning Circle

Prior to the children's arrival, drop pretend "crumbs" (small wadded-up pieces of paper) to make a crumb trail to the circle area. When the children arrive, greet them at the door wearing giant glasses and very large men's shoes. Tape a pretend ant or bug on a stick and show it to the children when they come in the door. (Look at the pictures in the story *Hey, Little Ant* for ideas.) Encourage the children to pretend to be ants and follow the trail of "crumbs" to the circle area. Give each child a small plastic ant to hold in their hand as they listen to the story.

Storytime

Hey, Little Ant by Phillip M. Hoose

Daily Center Activity Ideas

ART CENTER

Beginning Learner: Tiny Paper Ants
Draw an anthill shape on paper for each child. Show the children how to tear black construction paper into small pieces and glue the pieces on their anthill shape to make ants on their anthills.

Developing Learner: Shoe Painting
Discuss with the children that in the story, the little boy places his shoe over the ant, and it looks as if he might step on the ant. The ant is very small, so the boy's shoe appears to be huge from the ant's perspective. Let the children experiment with making giant footprints. Provide a large men's shoe, paint, and paper. Encourage the children to paint the bottom of the large shoe and then place their hand in the shoe. Have them "walk" their hand in the shoe across the paper to make giant shoe prints. Provide a variety of shoes in different sizes from which the children can choose. Invite the children to use black crayons to draw tiny ants beneath their shoe paintings.

Experienced Learner: Shoe Painting with Laces
Provide the materials described for the developing learner for the children to use to make shoe prints, but stuff the men's shoe with newspaper so that it will fit on the child's foot. Pour black paint on a cookie sheet and roll out a long piece of white bulletin board paper. Ask the children to remove one of their shoes. Help them place the large men's shoe on their foot and then support them under the arms as they step on the cookie sheet with the paint. Help the children

step off the cookie sheet and onto the long piece of bulletin board paper. Have them take several steps, making shoe prints along the way. Help each child take off the shoe and put on her own shoe. When the shoe prints have dried, the children can cut out the prints and use a hole punch to punch holes where the shoelaces would be. Provide black yarn for the children to lace through the holes.

MATH CENTER

Beginning Learner: Sorting Shoes
The little boy in the story is thinking about using his shoe to squash the little ant. Place a variety of pairs of shoes in a basket and encourage the children to sort the shoes into categories, such as by color, size, and type.

Developing Learner: Anthill/Counting
Use the pictures from the book as patterns for making ants and potato chips. Cut out 10 potato chip shapes from yellow construction paper. Use a marker to draw one dot on one potato chip, two dots on another chip, and so on until you have 10 dots on the last chip. Place the potato chip shapes in an empty chip canister or chip bag. Provide 55 small plastic ants. Place a red-and-white checked tablecloth over a table and put the ants in the middle of the table. The children take turns reaching into the chip can and pulling out a chip. The child counts the dots and puts that number of plastic ants on the chip.

Experienced Learner: Anthill/Counting
Cut out 10 anthill shapes from black construction paper. Use a white crayon to write a numeral from 1–10 on each anthill ("1" on one anthill, "2" on the second anthill, and so on). Provide 55 plastic ants. Encourage the children to look at the numerals on the anthills, say the numeral, and then count out that number of ants and place them on the anthill.

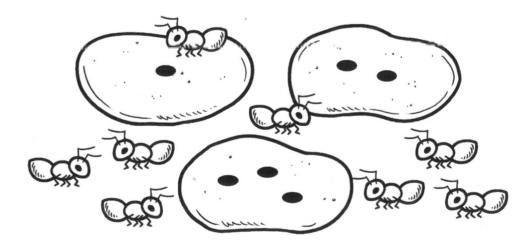

SCIENCE CENTER

Share some facts about ants while the children are working in this center. Ants are small and strong for their size. There are more ants on Earth than any other creature; and they can live underground, above ground in earthen mounds, and in trees. Ants live in well-organized colonies, with every ant performing a particular job. The head of the colony is the queen, which can be identified by her large size. Her only job is to lay eggs.

Beginning Learner: Observing an Ant Farm

Purchase a commercially available ant farm and establish it a few days prior to doing this activity. Explain that some of the ants in the colony are responsible for cleaning the colony, some are responsible for taking care of the queen and the babies, and some of the ants are the food gatherers and protectors of the colony. Have the children observe the ant colony and notice the different jobs that the ants are doing. Ask the children what job they would like to do have if they were ants. Provide paper and crayons for the children to draw pictures of anthills and ants as they observe the ant farm.

Developing Learner: What Are the Ants Saying?

Set up a colony of ants as described for the beginning learner. After the children have observed the ant colony for several days and identified the jobs that the ants are performing, place an obstacle in one entrance of the colony (drop a grain of rice into the ant farm to block the entrance). Encourage the children to watch what happens. "Do the ants appear to be communicating with one another?" "Are they reorganizing?" "How has their behavior and activity changed?" Invite the children to draw a picture of ants at work. Ask them to dictate to you what the ants in the picture are saying and doing.

Experienced Learner: Which Ant Job Would You Do?

Explain that all ants have important jobs to do in the colony. Some ants are the workers, some are the guards, some are the nurses, some are hunters, and one is the queen. To prepare for this activity, make a chart with four columns and write Worker, Guard, Nurse, Hunter, and Queen at the top of each column. Draw an outline of an ant on a piece of paper and make a copy for each child. Have the children cut out their ants and write their names on them. Discuss the different ant jobs listed on the chart. Ask the children which job they would like to have if they were ants. Have each child put his ant cutout in the appropriate column. Count all of the ants in each column and discuss the results.

LANGUAGE/DRAMATIC PLAY CENTER

Beginning Learner: Ants at the Picnic

The boy in the story says that he doesn't like ants because they always carry off the picnic food. Provide a red-and-white checkered tablecloth and pretend food and dishes for the children to have a picnic. Encourage them to use plastic ants to pretend to take the food away.

■ ■ **Developing Learner:** Working Together

Explain that ants must work together in groups to do certain jobs, such as carrying something heavy. Have the children place blocks in cardboard boxes and then work together as a group to move or carry the box. Let them place different objects in the box and work together to move the box of heavy items.

■

■ ■ **Experienced Learner:** Having a Picnic with Real Food

The little boy in the story doesn't like ants because they take foods from people having a picnic. Provide picnic-type foods, such as bread, cheese, apples, and juice for the children to prepare for a picnic. Help them make cheese sandwiches and use plastic knives to cut the apples. Place the food in a picnic basket, and take the children outside for a picnic on the playground. As the children enjoy the picnic snack, tell them to be aware of ants and see if any come to take their food.

VOCABULARY

abdomen, antenna, ants, army, colony, egg, head, larva, pupa, queen, swarm, thorax, trails, workers

Reflect

Say to the children, "Yesterday we learned about the very clumsy click beetle and how he had trouble flipping his body over when he would land on his back. Today we learned about ants and all of the different jobs that they do living in an ant colony. Tomorrow we will learn about bees and the helpful work that they do in our environment."

Extend and Enrich

Use the following ideas to extend and enrich what children know about ants.
- The game Ants in the Pants™ is a great activity for developing motor skills.
- Play a freeze game with the children. Have them dance like they have "ants in their pants" while the music is playing and when the music stops, they freeze.

Bees

Morning Circle

Bees communicate with each other by copying each other's movements. Play some active music to resemble the high activity level of bees. When the children arrive, ask them to join you in the circle for a game of Follow the Leader. When all of the children have arrived, ask them to pretend they are bees. Tell them that honeybees drink nectar from flowers. When a honeybee finds a good patch of flowers, it will return to the hive and tell all the other bees where to find the flowers. They do this by dancing a certain way, and then all the other bees follow that dance. Encourage the children to join hands and form a very large circle. Choose one child to be the "hunter bee" and have that child stand in the middle of the circle. The hunter bee makes an action with her body and all of the other children mimic that action. Have the hunter bee choose another child to replace her in the middle of the circle. Play the game until everyone has had a turn to be the leader.

Storytime

Buzz Bumble to the Rescue by Lynn E. Hazen

Daily Center Activity Ideas

ART CENTER

■ **Beginning Learner:** Bumblebees

Cut out a small circle and a medium circle from yellow construction paper for each child. Provide black paint, brushes, wiggle eyes, glue, and wing shapes cut from wax paper. Encourage the children to use the yellow circles to make a bee's body and then use black paint to paint stripes on the bee. The children can glue two wiggle eyes on the small yellow circle. Help the children glue the wax paper wings to the sides of the bee's body.

■ ■ **Developing Learner:** Bumblebees II

Provide yellow construction paper circles, black markers, half sheets of black tissue paper, scissors, glue, and pipe cleaners. Have the children use markers to draw black lines on the yellow circle. Help the children fold the circle in half and cut two slits in the center of the fold, one inch apart. The children cut out black tissue paper wings and insert them through the slits, with help as needed. Have them glue chenille sticks to the bee to make antennae and use markers to draw a face on the bee.

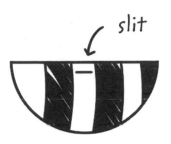

■■ ■ **Experienced Learner:** Footprint Bee

Provide yellow and black paint, paintbrushes, scissors, half sheets of black tissue paper, glue, chenille sticks, and white paper. Pour yellow paint on a cookie sheet and unroll a long piece of white bulletin board paper on the floor next to the paint. Have the children take off one shoe and sock. Support the children under their arms as they step onto the pan of yellow paint and then step onto the white paper to make a yellow footprint. After the footprints are dry, the children can cut them out and paint black stripes on the footprints to make bees. Have them draw a face with markers and glue black tissue paper wings and chenille stick antennae to the bee.

MATH CENTER

■ **Beginning Learner:** Baby Bees/Numeral Recognition

Cut out 10 large "momma" bees and 10 smaller "baby" bees. Use the bees in the book *Buzz Bumble to the Rescue* as a model. Write the numerals 1–10 on the momma bees (one numeral per bee) and draw dots on the baby bees (one dot on one bee, two dots on another bee, and so on). Invite the children to take turns matching the momma bees with the baby bees.

■ ■ **Developing Learner:** Flower Board Game/Numeral Recognition

Write the word "start" at the bottom of a piece of white poster board and the word "finish" at the top of the poster board. Draw a picture of a bee at the starting point and a hive at the finishing point. Make a trail start to finish using flower stickers. Provide a die and board game pieces. Have the children take turns rolling the die and moving the number of spaces indicated on the die until they reach the beehive. (**Note:** This game could be played with 3 or 4 players at one time. If there are more children, then make several game boards.)

■■ ■ **Experienced Learner:** Make Your Own Flower Board Game

Show several different board games and tell the children they are going to make their own board game. Give each child one quarter of a piece of white poster board. Have them use crayons to draw a path on their poster boards, and then place flower stickers on the path to make the game board spaces. Help them write "start" and "finish" on their game boards. Help each child write the numerals 1–10 on a piece of paper and cut them out to make game cards. They can make game pieces by putting flower stickers on small pieces of poster board. To play the game, the children put the cards in a pile and draw a card. The child moves that number of spaces on the game board using her game piece. Encourage the children to take turns playing on the game boards that their friends have made.

SCIENCE CENTER

■ Beginning Learner: Honey

Find pictures of bees in science and nature magazines; if possible, try to find pictures of bees working on a honeycomb. Show the pictures to the children and talk about the different jobs that bees have, from the queen to the worker bee. Explain that bees leave the hive to get nectar from flowers, and then they come back to the hive to turn the nectar into honey. Provide honey and bread for tasting. (**Safety note:** Check for food allergies before doing this activity.)

■ ■ Developing Learner: Beeswax Rubbings

Collect pictures of bees and their honeycombs from science magazines and show the pictures to the children. Talk about the honeycombs and point out the little compartments in the comb where the honey is stored. Show the children honeycomb cereal and discuss how the circles form different little sections or compartments. Tell the children that beeswax is a substance that is formed in the honeycomb, and things such as candles are often made from this wax. Provide the children with beeswax candles or sheets of beeswax for the children to look at and explore. Provide paper and crayons for the children to draw honeycomb designs.

■ ■ ■ Experienced Learner: Show Your Scent

Explain to the children that bees recognize other bees by their scent. Guard bees are stationed outside the hive to keep bees that do not belong to that hive from entering. To prepare for this activity, collect empty film canisters (one for each child in the class). Soak cotton balls in four different scents, such as peppermint, orange, lemon, and cinnamon. Place a scented cotton ball in each empty film canister. Give four children film canisters, each with a different scent in it. These children are the guard bees. Station them in different areas of the room to guard their "hives." Pass out the rest of the film canisters to the remaining "bees." The children "buzz" around the room and approach a guard bee. The guard bee smells the other bee's film canister "scent" and if it matches her own scent, she lets that bee into the hive. If it does not match her scent, she sends the bee on her way to locate her own bee hive. Continue until all of the bees have arrived safely in their hives. Switch jobs.

LANGUAGE/DRAMATIC PLAY CENTER

■ Beginning Learner: Busy Bees Role Play

As a member of the hive there are many jobs to be done. There are three levels of bees: workers, drones, and the queen. Worker bees tend to and feed the young bees (larvae), make honey, produce wax, gather nectar, guard the hive, build the honeycomb, and feed the queen and drones. The queen's job is to lay eggs every day for her entire life. Drones help the queen by fertilizing her eggs. Provide props for the children to be either the queen bee, the drone bee, or the worker bee. Include props such as crowns, pretend shields for the guards, play food to feed the other bees, and cotton batting for eggs. Encourage the children to use the props to pretend to be bees busy at work in the hive.

Developing Learner: What Job Would You Do?

Tell the children about bees and their different jobs (refer to the beginning learner section for details). Encourage the children to discuss what job they think they would most like to have if they were a bee. Have them draw a picture of a bee doing the job they have chosen

Experienced Learner: Famous Bees

In the story *Buzz Bumble to the Rescue*, Buzz rescues the little bee, becomes famous, and gets his picture on the front of the "National Bee-Graphic" magazine. Take a photo of each child using a Polaroid or digital camera or use pictures you already have. Encourage the children to think of the name of a magazine that they would like to have their picture on the cover. Provide slick white paper and encourage the children to use markers to decorate the paper for their magazine cover. Help the children glue their photo to the "cover" and write the name of the magazine.

VOCABULARY

abdomen, adult, antenna, bees, beeswax, bumble, buzz, drone, egg, guard, head, hive, honeycomb, larva, mandibles, pollen, pupa, stinger, swarm, thorax, wings, worker

Reflect

Say to the children, "Yesterday we talked about ants. We learned about all of the fascinating things that they do in their colonies underground. Today we talked about bees. Ants and bees are both insects and they live in highly organized groups. They are both also very small. Tomorrow we will learn about a very large animal, the elephant."

Extend and Enrich

- Help the children make a beehive by cutting off the top half of a paper grocery bag and filling the bottom part with yellow crepe paper to look like honey. The children use toy bees or make their own bees and use them to fly in and out of the hive.
- Provide yellow and black construction-paper strips for the children to use to make paper chains. Show them how to loop a strip, tape both ends together, and then loop another strip through the circle and tape it closed. Encourage the children to practice making and extending patterns.
- Obtain a recording of Rimsky-Korsakov's "Flight of the Bumblebee" and play it for the children. Ask the children why they think the composer named this music after the bumblebee.

Elephants

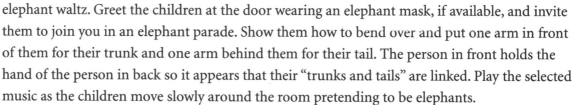

Morning Circle

Prior to the children's arrival, select a song that
has a slow beat such as an elephant march.
Children's tapes or CDs that have songs to accompany a
unit of study on the circus often have an elephant march or
elephant waltz. Greet the children at the door wearing an elephant mask, if available, and invite
them to join you in an elephant parade. Show them how to bend over and put one arm in front
of them for their trunk and one arm behind them for their tail. The person in front holds the
hand of the person in back so it appears that their "trunks and tails" are linked. Play the selected
music as the children move slowly around the room pretending to be elephants.

Storytime

Seven Blind Mice by Ed Young

Daily Center Activity Ideas

ART CENTER

Beginning Learner: Paper Plate Elephant Masks
Give each child a paper plate. Draw and cut out two eye holes and a nose hole from their paper
plates. Staple each child's plate to a craft stick. Provide gray paint, paintbrushes, elephant ears
cut from gray paper, long strips of gray construction paper for trunks, and tape. Show the
children how to accordion-fold a long strip of paper so that it resembles an elephant trunk. Have
the children paint their plates gray. When the paint has dried, help the children tape their ears
and trunks on their plates to complete their masks.

Developing Learner: Paper Bag Elephant Masks
Provide a paper grocery bag for each child. Cut out two holes for eyes and one hole for a nose
from each bag. Set out gray paint, paintbrushes, gray construction paper, and a stapler.
Encourage the children to paint their entire bags gray. Help each child cut out ears and a long
trunk from gray construction paper, and then staple the ears and trunk to the bag to make a
mask.

Experienced Learner: Elephant Skin
Before doing this activity, use the elephant from the story to make an elephant pattern on
cardboard. Cut open large paper grocery bags to make large sheets of brown paper and give
one sheet to each child. Demonstrate how to roll a bag into a ball and soak it in water. Have

the children unroll their bags and smooth them out. The wrinkled paper will resemble the wrinkled skin of an elephant. Invite the children to paint the wrinkled paper (wet or dry) with gray paint and allow it to dry. Encourage the children to trace the elephant pattern on their wrinkled paper and cut it out. Invite them to use markers to add eyes and other features, such as toes, to their elephants.

MATH CENTER

▪ **Beginning Learner:** Colorful Mice/Patterns
Cut out mice from red, green, yellow, purple, blue, gray, and orange construction paper, using the pictures of the mice from the story as a guide. Cut out five mice for each color. In the story, the mice go exploring to try to figure out what the mysterious creature is. There is a picture toward the back of the book in which all of the mice are lined up on the elephant's head. Use a paper grocery bag to make an elephant like the one in the story. Encourage the children to use the construction-paper mice to make color patterns on the elephant's head.

▪▪ **Developing Learner:** Mouse Matching Game
In preparation for this activity, use your index finger to make a print on paper and then use a marker to add ears to form a mouse print. Make a set of index cards with one mouse, two mice, three mice and so on until there are 10 mice on the final card. One another set of 10 index cards write the numerals 1–10 with one numeral on each card. Mix the numeral cards and the mouse fingerprint cards and have the children play a game counting mouse prints and matching the cards with the numeral cards.

▪
▪▪ **Experienced Learner:** Two-Ring Elephant Circus/Addition
Prior to doing this activity, cover a table with butcher paper and draw two large circles on the paper. Provide toy elephants and dice. The first child rolls one die and places that number of elephants in the first circle. She then rolls the other die and places that number of elephants in the second circle. The child counts the elephants in the first circle and the second circle to see how many elephants there are all together. Let all the children have a turn.

SCIENCE CENTER

Share some of the following information about elephants as the children work in the Science Center:

◆ Elephants are the largest mammals on land.

◆ Elephants have three very distinguishing features: their ears, which help them stay cool; their tusks, which are really teeth that grow throughout the elephant's lifetime; and their unique trunks.

Beginning Learner: How Much Do You Weigh?

Cut out a baby elephant from poster board or bulletin board paper and write "800 pounds" on it. Tell the children that an elephant about the same age as they are weighs 800 pounds! Provide a scale, poster, and index cards. Help the children weigh each other and write their weights on an index card. Have each child give you her card, and write down each child's weight on a large poster. Add the weights together. Does the weight of the whole class equal the weight of one baby elephant?

Developing Learner: Elephant Ears and Cooling

Explain to the children that elephants flap their large ears to cool themselves. Provide large pieces of gray fabric cut into elephant ear shapes and a tub of warm water. Dip a fabric ear shape in the water and wring it out. Invite the children to feel the ear and notice its warmth. Shake out the fabric and hold it in front of a fan. Have the children touch the ear again. Does it still feel warm? Let the children experiment with their own pieces of gray fabric and a tub of water. Encourage them to place the ear in water, wring it out, and flap it around. The breeze they create makes the ear cool to the touch.

Experienced Learner: Elephant Trunks and Water

Provide a 12" piece of ¼" clear plastic tubing and a tub of water with 4" of colored water in it. Have the children place one end of the tubing in the tub of colored water and slowly dip the other end in the water. They will see bubbles rising from the end of the tube. When all of the bubbles are out of the tube, ask one child to place a thumb over one end of the tube and lift that end out of the water. When the child releases her thumb, the water will flow out just like it flows from an elephant's trunk. Explain that this action is called "siphoning."

LANGUAGE/DRAMATIC PLAY CENTER

Beginning Learner: Making Gray

Talk about the color gray. Provide a bowl of black tempera paint, a bowl of white tempera paint, paintbrushes, and paper. Explain that elephants are a unique shade of gray, and tell the children that they are going to experiment with making the color gray. Have them put a small amount of black paint on their paper and then a small amount of white paint. Invite them to use their paintbrushes to mix the two colors until they get a shade of gray. Encourage the children to smear the gray color all over their papers.

■ ■ **Developing Learner:** Shades of Gray

Provide black tempera paint and white tempera paint in muffin tins (one tin for each child), paintbrushes, and spoons. Cut out elephant shapes for each child. Invite the children to use spoons and paintbrushes to mix white paint into black paint and black paint into white paint to make different shades of gray. When they have shades of gray that they like, encourage them to use to paint their elephant shapes.

■

■ ■ **Experienced Learner:** Elephant's Trunk and Words

Provide strips of gray construction paper. Show the children how to accordion-fold the construction paper to resemble an elephant's trunk. Help them write the letters E, L, E, P, H, A, N, and T on each section of the accordion fold. Have them brainstorm a list of words that start with each of the letters in the word "elephant." Write their ideas on chart paper. Invite them to choose words from the list and write one word on each section of the accordion trunk that starts with each letter of the word "elephant."

VOCABULARY

African elephant, Asian elephant, bull, circus, cow, ear, floppy, forest, savanna, tail, trunk, tusk, white elephant

Reflect

Say to the children, "Yesterday we learned about bees. Today we learned about elephants, which are the largest of all of the land animals. They live on the continents of Asia and Africa. Tomorrow we will learn about another large animal that is now extinct, the dinosaur."

Extend and Enrich

Use the following ideas to extend and enrich what children know about elephants.

◆ The story *Seven Blind Mice* has great pictures of elephant body parts. Enlarge some of the pictures from the book, and use them to discuss the unique features of the elephant's body.

◆ Elephants have long tails that they use to swat away flies. Find a picture of an elephant and enlarge it on a copy machine. Make a fabric tail and play Pin the Tail on the Elephant with the children.

THINGS THAT ARE VERY SMALL OR VERY BIG

Dinosaurs

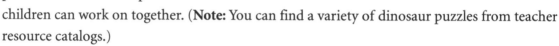

Morning Circle

Prior to the children's arrival, cut out enough giant dinosaur footprints (the size of a man's shoe) to reach from the classroom door to the circle area. Tape the footprints to the floor. Place a few dinosaur puzzles in the circle area. As the children arrive, encourage them to step on the footprints to get to the circle area and work the puzzles in the circle. For variety, provide small individual puzzles as well as floor puzzles that several children can work on together. (**Note:** You can find a variety of dinosaur puzzles from teacher resource catalogs.)

Storytime

How Do Dinosaurs Say Goodnight? by Jane Yolen and Mark Teague

Daily Center Activity Ideas

ART CENTER

Beginning Learner: Dinosaur Rubbings
Cut out dinosaur shapes from corrugated cardboard. Invite the children to place a piece of paper over the shape and rub unwrapped crayons all over the paper. This will leave an interesting design.

Developing Learner: Dinosaur Stencil Paintings
Cut out large dinosaur stencils from poster board. Provide sponges, clothespins, and paint. Attach pieces of paper to the paint easel. Use clothespins to attach the dinosaur stencils to the easel at the top of the papers. Encourage the children to use sponges to paint inside the stencils. Carefully remove the stencils from the easels to view each child's painting.

Experienced Learner: Clay Dinosaurs
Provide pictures of dinosaurs, air-dry clay, paint, and paintbrushes. Invite the children to form their own dinosaurs using the clay. Allow the clay to dry. Let children paint the dinosaurs as desired.

MATH CENTER

■ Beginning Learner: Dinosaur Count

Write the numerals 1–10 on large plastic eggs. Provide small toy dinosaurs. Ask the children to pick an egg, look at the numeral, and place that number of toy dinosaurs inside the egg.

■ ■ Developing Learner: Dinosaur Concentration

Prior to doing this activity, use dinosaur stickers to make pairs of matching cards (place matching stickers on pairs of index cards). Mix up the cards and place them face down on the table. Have the children take turns turning two of the cards over to see if they can find a dinosaur match. Play the game until all of the cards have been matched.

■
■ ■ Experienced Learner: Dinosaur Bingo

Make BINGO cards using dinosaur stickers. Provide toy dinosaurs as the objects to cover the stickers on the card. Call out the name of a dinosaur and if the child has that dinosaur sticker on her card, she covers it with a toy dinosaur. The children try to cover all of the dinosaurs in a row or the whole card to get BINGO.

SCIENCE CENTER

■ Beginning Learner: Mix-and-Match Dinosaurs

To prepare for this activity, make copies of a variety of dinosaur pictures from coloring books. Cut the pictures into thirds (the head, the middle, and the tail). Invite the children to color the pictures and then mix and match the dinosaur parts to create their own new dinosaurs.

■ ■ **Developing Learner:** Dinosaur Excavation

To prepare for this activity, place plastic toy dinosaurs in muffin tins, mix plaster, and pour the plaster into the muffin tins on top of the dinosaurs. Allow the plaster to set. When the plaster is hard, remove each piece from the muffin tins. Hand out rubber mallets and golf tees. Show the children how to tap the plaster lightly using their mallets and golf tees to knock the plaster off and reveal the dinosaur fossils. (**Safety note:** Children must wear goggles when working with the plaster.)

■
■ ■ **Experienced Learner:** Dinosaur Fossils

Explain that *paleontologists* make plaster casts of fossils found in the field so that the plaster cast can be handled to run tests and the original imprint is preserved. Provide clay, plastic dinosaurs, and plaster for the children to make their own dinosaur fossils. Have them press dinosaur toys into 1" thick clay and then remove the dinosaur from the clay, leaving an imprint. Pour plaster into the impression. Allow the plaster to set until it is hard. The children gently remove the plaster from the clay to reveal a plaster cast of a fossil.

LANGUAGE/DRAMATIC PLAY CENTER

■ **Beginning Learner:** How Do You Say "Goodnight?"

After reading *How Do Dinosaurs Say Goodnight?*, discuss the children's nighttime routines. Ask them what they do as they prepare to say goodnight to their families. Provide drawing paper, crayons, and markers. The children illustrate the answer to "When I say goodnight, I _____."

■ ■ **Developing Learner:** Dinosaur Names

Discuss with the children the many different dinosaur names they may have heard. Share the book with them, and explain that the illustrator has cleverly placed the dinosaur names throughout the story. Provide several copies of the book and encourage the children to look at each page and try to find the dinosaur names.

■
■ ■ **Experienced Learner:** Dinosaur Letter Hunt

To prepare for this activity, write the word "DINOSAUR" in uppercase letters on the outside of envelopes. Make one envelope for each child in the class. Write the letters D, I, N, O, S, A, U, and R on small index card squares. Prepare enough letter cards for each child to have one of each letter. Tape the letters around the room where the children can find them. Give each child an envelope with the word DINOSAUR on it and tell them that they are going on a dinosaur hunt. The children go around the room and find all the letters in the word "dinosaur." Have them place the letters in their envelopes.

VOCABULARY

Ankylosaurus, Allosaurus, Apatosaurus, Dimetrodon, Diplodocus, dinosaur, egg, extinct, fossil, paleontologist, prehistoric, pterodactyl, reptile, skeleton, Stegosaurus, Triceratops, Tyrannosaurus rex

Reflect

Say to the children, "Yesterday we learned about elephants. They are the largest animals on land. We also learned how they keep cool and how they eat. Today we learned about dinosaurs. They were also are very large. Scientists have found many dinosaur bones and fossils."

Extend and Enrich

Use the following ideas to extend and enrich what children know about dinosaurs.

◆ Use the story *How Do Dinosaurs Say Goodnight?* as an inspiration for learning how to say "goodnight" in other languages. Share some of words with the children, and invite them to practice saying goodnight in other languages.

◆ Place plastic dinosaurs, large plastic eggs, paintbrushes, and sifters in the sand table for the children to use to conduct their own dig.

Things that Are Round

Eggs

Morning Circle

Before the children arrive, use blocks to build a "wall" like the one Humpty Dumpty sat on. As the children enter the classroom, hand each child a plastic egg. Invite the children to take turns placing their eggs on the wall. See if they can make them stay on the wall. Read *Humpty Dumpty* after everyone has had a chance to participate in the wall activity. (**Safety note:** Check for any egg allergies before doing any of the activities involving real eggs. Also, make sure children wash their hands after handling eggs.)

Storytime

Humpty Dumpty (any favorite version)

Daily Center Activity Ideas

ART CENTER

To do this activity at any level, provide hard-boiled eggs for the children to decorate.

Beginning Learner: Dyeing Eggs

Provide hard-boiled eggs, food coloring, and vinegar. Mix food coloring and vinegar in cups for the children to use. Invite the children to choose a color and then gently dip their eggs into the cup. After the eggs have been in the food coloring and vinegar mixture for a short period of time, the children use a spoon to remove the eggs and place them on a paper towel to dry. (**Note:** The longer the eggs are left in the mixture, the darker the color will be.)

Developing Learner: Magic Painted Eggs

Provide hard-boiled eggs, white crayons, watercolors, and brushes. Encourage the children to draw on their eggs with the white crayons to make a design, and then use the watercolors to paint the entire egg. The children will be amazed when a magic design appears!

Experienced Learner: Dotty Eggs

Show the children examples of polka-dotted fabric and discuss how the dots are arranged on the fabric. Tell the children that they are going to make their own polka dot patterns on eggs. Provide hardboiled eggs, small dot stickers, and food coloring mixed with vinegar in cups. Invite the children to cover their eggs with the dot stickers and then dip or paint the eggs with the dye and vinegar solution. When the egg has dried, have the children remove the stickers to see their design. Tell the children that the round spaces left where the dot stickers were is called *negative space* because there is no color there.

MATH CENTER

Beginning Learner: Counting Eggs from 1–5

Provide plastic eggs for the children to manipulate and count. Write the numerals 1–5 on index cards, and encourage the children to place that number of eggs beside each card.

Developing Learner: Counting Eggs from 1–10

Provide plastic eggs for the children to manipulate and count. Write the numerals 1–10 on index cards, and encourage the children to place that number of eggs beside each card. When the eggs are next to the numeral cards, provide small objects such as pennies, and encourage the children to count that number of objects and place them in each egg.

Experienced Learner: Card Game with Eggs

Provide large plastic eggs, pompoms or cotton balls, and a deck of playing cards. Invite each child to pick a partner. One partner draws a card from the deck and places that number of cotton balls or pompoms inside the egg. Encourage the children to do this without letting their partner see how many objects they place inside the egg. The other partner opens the egg and counts the number of pompoms inside. Have them switch roles.

SCIENCE CENTER

Beginning Learner: Egg Roll

Give each child a hard-boiled egg. Have the children pick partners and sit across from each other. Discuss what they think will happen when they roll their egg. "Will it roll like a ball? Will it roll straight or will it wobble?" The children roll their eggs to their partners and test their assumptions. Talk about the results.

Developing Learner: Sink or Float Eggs

Provide hard-boiled eggs and a tub of water. Discuss with the children that eggshells are *porous*, which means they have little holes called pores in them. This is so air can get in and out. If the egg was fertilized and there was a baby chick inside, it would breathe this way. Ask the children if they think their egg will sink or float. Record their guesses on a graph. Invite the children to test their assumptions by placing their eggs in the water. Graph and discuss the results.

Experienced Learner: Bubbling Eggs

Provide hard-boiled eggs and a clear container of warm water. Discuss with the children that eggshells are porous, which means they have little holes called pores in them to allow air to get in and out. Have the children gently drop their eggs into the warm water to see if bubbles form on the outside of the egg. Ask the children why they think bubbles form. Explain that the air inside the egg is trying to get out. Try placing other items or objects in the warm water to see if the same process happens. Graph the results.

LANGUAGE/DRAMATIC PLAY CENTER

◼ **Beginning Learner:** Humpty Dumpty's Wall

Provide blocks and plastic eggs filled with paper confetti. Read the story of *Humpty Dumpty* and show the children a picture of the wall in the story. Invite the children to use blocks to build Humpty Dumpty's wall. At the top of the wall where "Humpty" will sit, put a small dot of playdough or clay. Place the egg on the playdough, to hold the egg in place, and encourage the children to help Humpty Dumpty have a great fall! Make sure you have plenty of eggs filled with confetti because the children will want to repeat this activity often! (**Note:** You may substitute real eggs, blown out and washed, if you wish. To do this, make a hole in both ends of the egg with a pin. Make one hole larger than the other. Blow in the smaller hole so that the insides of the egg come out of the other end. Wash the egg, let it dry for a day, then fill the egg with confetti.)

◼ ◼ **Developing Learner:** Humpty Dumpty's Wall II

Provide a variety of building materials and plastic eggs filled with paper confetti. Read the story of *Humpty Dumpty* and show the children pictures of the wall in the story. Discuss the way the wall looks in the picture, and encourage the children to use various building materials to make walls of different heights. Have them draw a face on their plastic eggs using a permanent marker and then place the eggs at the top of each wall. Use playdough to hold the egg in place. Sit the egg in the playdough and encourage the children to help Humpty Dumpty have a great fall!

◼
◼ ◼ **Experienced Learner:**
Comparing Humpty Stories

Provide several versions of the story of Humpty Dumpty. Read the different versions of the story and compare them. Ask the children if the outcome of the story is always the same. Encourage the children to notice the differences in the illustrations of Humpty Dumpty, the wall, and the king's horses and the king's men. Give each child a copy of the rhyme to illustrate.

VOCABULARY

boiled, brown, eggs, hard, oval, porous, raw, round, shell, white, wobbly, yolks

Reflect

Say to the children, "Today, we learned about eggs. We learned how they roll and that they are porous. Tomorrow, we will talk about donuts and their shape."

Extend and Enrich

Use the following ideas to extend and enrich what children know about eggs.

- Discuss with the children the different types of animals that lay eggs. Have them find or draw pictures of those animals.
- Give each child a piece of white paper cut into an egg shape and squares of colored tissue paper. Mix vinegar and water in cups. Encourage the children to paint their egg shape with the vinegar and water mixture and then place the squares of tissue paper on the wet paper. The tissue paper will bleed and leave beautiful colors. The children can leave the tissue paper on the paper or peel it off while it is still wet.
- Bring in several different kinds and sizes of eggs from a grocery store for the children to explore. Talk about brown eggs and white eggs and the different sizes and grades listed on the egg cartons.
- Spin a hard-boiled egg and a raw egg to see which one spins faster. Try this experiment with the eggs on their sides, and then repeat with the eggs on their ends to see which way the eggs spin faster and whether or not it makes a difference.

Donuts

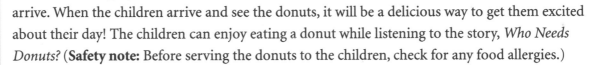

Morning Circle

Stop by a donut shop or bakery on the way to
school and pick up an assortment of mini donuts or
donut holes. Display the donuts on a table before the children
arrive. When the children arrive and see the donuts, it will be a delicious way to get them excited
about their day! The children can enjoy eating a donut while listening to the story, *Who Needs
Donuts?* (**Safety note:** Before serving the donuts to the children, check for any food allergies.)

Storytime

Who Needs Donuts? by Mark Alan Stamaty

Daily Center Activity Ideas

ART CENTER

■ **Beginning Learner:** Paper Donuts

Cut out donut shapes from white paper. Invite the children to decorate their "donuts" using
colored glue for icing, confetti for sprinkles, and brown-tinted glue for chocolate.

■ ■ **Developing Learner:** Cutting Out Donuts

Give each child a piece of paper with a donut shape drawn on it. Invite them to cut out their
donuts and decorate them using colored glue for icing and confetti for sprinkles.

■
■ ■ **Experienced Learner:** Tracing Donuts

Provide a round donut-shaped template for tracing, pencils, scissors, colored glue for icing,
several colors of construction paper, white paper, and a hole punch. Have each child trace the
donut template onto white paper, cut it out, and decorate it as desired. Invite the children to use
a hole punch to make their own confetti sprinkles.

MATH CENTER

■ **Beginning Learner:** Circle Shapes

Provide small glazed donuts for the children. Talk about the circular shape of the donut. Point
out the two parts of the donut—the donut itself is a big circle and the hole in the middle is a
smaller circle. This is a good time to explore the concepts of *inside* and *outside*. Place the
children's donuts in plastic bags for them to take home as a special treat.

Developing Learner: Donut Fractions/Half

Demonstrate the concepts of half and whole. Show the children a glazed donut and tell them it is a "whole" donut. Use a plastic knife to cut the donut in half. Explain that the donut is now two halves. Place the two donut halves together, and explain that it is whole again. Invite the children to find other objects in the classroom that could be divided in half and then put back together.

Experienced Learner: Donut Fractions/Quarters

Show the children a glazed donut and tell the children it is a "whole" donut. Demonstrate the same activity as for the developing learner by cutting the donut in half and explaining that the donut is now in two halves. Then, cut the two halves in half. Explain that the donut is now in four quarters and that each piece is ¼ of a donut. Place the quarters back together so that the donut is whole again. Provide a round circle of paper (or a paper plate), pencils, and scissors for the children to make their own fractional parts.

SCIENCE CENTER

Beginning Learner: Donut Holes

On your way to school, purchase donut holes for the children to use. Provide plates, straws, cinnamon, sifters, and a large tub. Show the children a sifter and explain that it is a special kitchen tool used to *sift* things, such as flour and sugar. Pour a bit of cinnamon and a cup of sugar into the sifter and invite the children to take turns sifting the cinnamon and sugar into a large bowl. After each child has had a turn sifting, pour the mixture onto a large cookie sheet. Give each child a few donut holes, a plate, and a straw. The children use the straw as a handle and roll the donut hole around in the cinnamon and sugar. Encourage the children to make a few more and take them home to enjoy as a special treat.

■ ■ **Developing Learner:** Icing a Donut

Provide small plain cake donuts, icing in a small bowl, and sprinkles. Show the children the icing and discuss that it is thick and, therefore, hard to stir. Then, melt the icing in a microwave for about 10 seconds or heat it in a crock pot. Discuss with the children that the microwave works by making the particles inside of the food move around very fast. The friction of the particles rubbing together causes food to heat up. Show the children the melted icing and discuss its texture. When the icing has cooled a little bit, pour it on a plate so the children can dip the tops of their donuts into the icing. Show the children a chocolate bar and a vegetable grater. Discuss with the children that the grater is a tool that takes large food ingredients and shaves them into smaller pieces. Closely supervise the children as they take turns moving the chocolate bar across the grater to make chocolate shavings. Invite them to place some of the chocolate shavings on top of their donuts. Place their donuts into plastic bags and send them home for the children to enjoy for breakfast the next day.

■
■ ■ **Experienced Learner:** Cinnamon Twist

Show the children a round donut and discuss its shape with the children. Tell the children that donuts come in many different shapes. Show the children a twisted pretzel rod and ask them to look closely at how the rod is actually two pieces of pretzel twisted together. Explain to the children that they are going to practice making their own twisted shapes. Provide refrigerated biscuit dough, cinnamon, sugar, melted butter, a large tray or cookie sheet, and a toaster oven or regular oven. Give each child a portion of the biscuit dough. Ask them to roll out two "snakes," and then show them how to twist the two snakes together and then form the twisted shapes into a round circle shape. Show the children a stick of butter before melting it in a microwave. When it is melted, compare the consistency of both. Invite the children to use a clean brush to brush melted butter on their twisted dough and then roll their buttered dough on a tray of cinnamon sugar. Place each twist on a cookie sheet and bake according to package directions.

LANGUAGE/DRAMATIC PLAY CENTER

Write the following fingerplay on a large piece of poster board.

Five Fat Donuts by Kay Hastings

Five fat donuts
Big and round,
One fat donut
Fell to the ground.

Four fat donuts
Big and round,
One fat donut
Fell to the ground.

Three fat donuts…
Two fat donuts…
One fat donut…

No fat donuts
Big and round,
No fat donuts
Fell to the ground.

■ **Beginning Learner:** Donut Fingerplay

Do the fingerplay with the children, using fingers or plastic play donuts from the dramatic play area.

■ ■ **Developing Learner:** Stand Up for Donuts

Give each child a large donut shape cut out from construction paper. Invite the children to decorate their donut cutouts using markers. When they are finished, have the children sit on the floor and begin to recite the poem. For the first verse, have five children stand up and hold their donuts up. For the second verse, one child pretends to fall to the ground. Continue until there are no more "donuts" standing. Continue until everyone has had a chance to participate.

■
■ ■ **Experienced Learner:** Donut Finger Puppets

Teach the class the fingerplay and point to the words when reading the poem. Provide construction paper, craft sticks, and tape. Invite the children to cut out five circles to make their own donut on sticks. Tape each "donut" on a stick. Have the children use their props when saying the poem.

VOCABULARY

cake, circle, donut shop, glazed, hole, icing, round, soft, sprinkles, sticky, sugar, sweet, whole, yummy

Reflect

Say to the children, "Yesterday, we discussed eggs and we did some fun 'Humpty Dumpty' experiments. Today, we discussed donuts and how they are round on the outside and on the inside. Tomorrow, we will discuss buttons, and we will have lots of fun exploring their various uses."

Extend and Enrich

Use the following ideas to extend and enrich what children know about donuts.

◆ Take a field trip to a donut shop, if possible, or a grocery store bakery. If this is not possible, invite an employee of a bakery or donut shop to come to class.

◆ Set up a donut shop in the dramatic play area. Provide boxes, aprons, and rolling pins for the children to use in their play.

Buttons

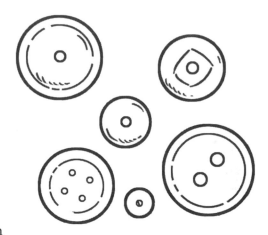

Morning Circle

Provide a button box like the one from the story
The Button Box. (This could be an old shoebox
covered with buttons on the top.) Fill the box with
buttons. As the children enter the classroom, "accidentally" drop the button box so that the
buttons spill onto the floor. Ask the children to help you gather up all the buttons and put them
back in the button box. When all the buttons have been placed back in the box, ask the children
if they have any idea what the story might be about today.

Storytime

The Button Box by Margarette S. Reid

Daily Center Activity Ideas

ART CENTER

 **Beginning Learner:** Foam Button Necklaces

Prior to doing this activity, cut out small circles from colored foam sheets (found at craft stores)
to resemble buttons. Punch holes in the middle of the circles so the children will be able to string
them on a piece of yarn. Using foam circles in place of real buttons is a great solution for the
beginning learner because buttons can be a choking hazard for young children. Show the
children a real button and talk about its shape. Help the children create their "button" necklaces.

Developing Learner: Real Button Necklaces

Provide buttons of various sizes and colors and yarn for the children to make button necklaces.
Discuss the different shapes and sizes of the buttons. The children may even want to use the
buttons to create a pattern for their necklace.

Experienced Learner: Clay Button Necklaces

Provide the children with air-dry clay, a pencil, string, buttons, and paint (optional). Encourage
the children to examine the buttons and choose a few of their favorites. Ask the children to roll
the clay into a small ball and use their thumbs to flatten the balls into button shapes. Help the
children use the pencil to poke large holes in the middle of their "buttons." Allow the clay
buttons to dry (they may need to dry overnight, depending on package directions). The next day,
the children can paint their buttons. When dry, the buttons can be strung to make a button
necklace.

MATH CENTER

■ **Beginning Learner:** Sorting and Counting Buttons

Provide the button box used during morning circle for the children to examine. Encourage them to dump the buttons on a table and touch the buttons. Sit with the children and begin to count out a few buttons for them. Depending on their knowledge and skill level, some of the children may be able to count out buttons too. To introduce the concept of one-to-one correspondence, make sure the children touch each button as they count. (**Safety note:** Buttons can be a choking hazard. Supervise closely.)

■ ■ **Developing Learner:** Hanging Buttons

Hang long pieces of yarn from the ceiling so that they reach all the way to the floor. Provide a tub or bucket of buttons and ask the children to see how many buttons they can string on the yarn and how high they can go. Explain to the children that if they let go of the string, all their buttons will come crashing down to the floor. This makes a great partner activity.

■
■ ■ **Experienced Learner:** Counting Dots and Buttons

Provide buttons, plates for sorting the buttons, and a die. Have the children roll the die, count the number of dots on the die, and then count out that number of buttons onto their plates.

SCIENCE CENTER

To do this activity at any level, provide a large amount of buttons, a water table or tub, and spoons or nets.

■ **Beginning Learner:** Sink or Float Buttons

Provide red, green, and blue buttons in a variety of sizes as well as bowls or cups in the same three colors. You will also need a tub of water or a water table and small aquarium nets. Mix the colored buttons together and place them in the tub of water. Encourage the children to "catch" the buttons in their net and then sort the buttons by color into the various bowls. Discuss which buttons sink and which ones float.

■ ■ **Developing Learner:** Button Predictions

Have the children examine the buttons ahead of time and what they think will happen if they are put in water. Write their ideas down on a piece of paper. Take the buttons to a tub of water or a water table and provide cups, spoons, and a small aquarium net. Place the buttons in the tub and encourage the children to stir, pour, and catch them. Let the children explore the movement and what happens to the buttons. "Do they sink? Do they float?" Discuss the results.

■
■ ■ **Experienced Learner:** Charting Buttons

Give each child a few buttons. Provide plastic cups, clear tape, and a tub of water. Draw a vertical line down the center of a piece of chart paper and write "Sink" at the top of one column and "Float" at the top of the other column. Invite each child to dip his cup into the tub of water and then drop a button into the cup of water. "Does it sink or float?" The child removes the button and dries it off. Help the child tape the button in the appropriate column of the chart.

LANGUAGE/DRAMATIC PLAY CENTER

▪ **Beginning Learner:** Letter "B" Hunt

Make cutouts of the letter "B" or write the letter "B" on cards. Hide the cutouts or cards in the classroom and have the children hunt for them. When they find a "B," have them put it in the button box.

▪ ▪ **Developing Learner:** Finding Objects that Begin with "B"

Invite the children to go around the classroom and find objects that begin with the letter "B." Give a few hints before they begin their hunt.

▪
▪ ▪ **Experienced Learner:** Brainstorming "B"s

Invite the children to sit in a circle to form a "writing circle." In the middle of the circle, place a large piece of paper with a giant uppercase "B" on it. Remind the children that the title of today's story began with the letter "B." Ask the children to think of as many "B" words as they can. Write the words on the paper as the children call out their ideas.

VOCABULARY

button, holes, needle, pants, round, sewing, shape, shirt, size, small, thread

Reflect

Say to the children, "Yesterday, we talked about donuts and made paper donuts. Today, we discussed buttons and explored whether they can sink or float. Tomorrow, we will talk about rocks and the many places they are found."

Extend and Enrich

Use the following ideas to extend and enrich what children know about buttons.

- ◆ Invite the children to make giant flowers by stapling or gluing large petal cutouts around a paper plate. For the center of the flower, the children glue on many colorful buttons.
- ◆ Have the children make playdough prints by pushing buttons into playdough and talking about their different designs and shapes.
- ◆ Provide materials for the children to make their own button boxes out of shoeboxes or empty food containers.

Rocks

Morning Circle

To prepare for this activity, place one stone for each child in individual lunch bags and staple them closed. As the children enter the classroom, give each child one of the "mystery bags." Invite them to shake the bags and try to guess what is inside. After they have guessed, let them open the bags and pull out their rocks. Encourage the children to hold their rocks while you read the story *Hunwick's Egg*.

Storytime

Hunwick's Egg by Mem Fox

Daily Center Activity Ideas

ART CENTER

Beginning Learner: Painting Rocks

Provide acrylic paint, brushes, and cotton swabs. Encourage the children to paint their rocks. Have the children wear paint smocks and remind them to be careful using the acrylic paint. This type of paint works best for the rocks, but it will stain clothing. Allow 1–2 days drying time.

Developing Learner: Painting with Pebbles

Provide a shoebox, pebbles, paper that fits inside the shoebox, and bowls of paint. Place a few of the pebbles into the paint. Have the children use a plastic spoon to cover the pebbles with paint. Place the piece of paper in the bottom of the shoebox, and help the children retrieve the pebbles. Place them in the shoebox. Place the lid on the box, and encourage the children to shake the box back and forth. Remove the lid and admire the interesting design on the paper.

Experienced Learner: Rock Creatures

Provide acrylic paint, brushes, paint smocks, wiggle eyes, chenille sticks, and construction paper. Take the children outside to look for large rocks. Bring the rocks into the classroom and encourage the children to use their imagination to turn their rocks into different animals, creatures, or insects. Make sure to protect clothing from acrylic paint and allow 1–2 days to for the paint to dry.

MATH CENTER

For all levels of learners, make a "mystery box" by taping the sides of a cardboard box closed and cutting a hole in the top of the box large enough for a child's hand to fit inside. Place rocks and plastic eggs inside the box.

Beginning Learner: Rocks and Eggs/Counting
Remind the children that in the story, Hunwick finds a mysterious "egg" that is really a rock. Encourage the children to reach inside of the box and pull out either a rock or an egg. Divide a piece of poster board in half and write "Egg" at the top of one column and "Rock" at the top of the other column. Have the children place their rock or egg in the appropriate column. When all of the rocks and eggs have been pulled out of the box, help the children count how many they have of each.

Developing Learner: Rocks and Eggs/Adding
Glue a picture of a rock on one index card and a picture of an egg on another card. Provide two dice. Put one die on the rock picture card and one die on the egg picture card. The children take turns playing the game. The first child rolls the die on the rock picture card. He counts the number of dots on the die and reaches inside the box and pulls out that number of rocks. Next, the child rolls the die on the egg card and pulls out that number of eggs. Ask the child to count the total number of rocks and eggs together. The child returns the eggs and rocks to the box and the next child has a turn.

Experienced Learner: Rocks and Eggs/Numeral Recognition
Make egg numeral cards by gluing a picture of an egg to a card and writing the numeral 1. Repeat with two eggs on the second card with the numeral 2, and so on until you have 10 egg numeral cards. Do the same thing with rock pictures so that you have 10 rock numeral cards. Place all 20 cards face down in a pile on a table. Encourage the children to take turns drawing a card and then reaching in the box to try to find the number and type of item that is pictured on the card.

SCIENCE CENTER

Beginning Learner: Rock Exploration
Provide three different kinds of small rocks (small pebbles, aquarium gravel, play gravel, and so on) in the sand table, sand sifters, and aquarium nets. Encourage the children to explore the rocks by sifting and scooping them.

Developing Learner: Sorting Rocks
Provide large rocks (found outside or purchased from a plant nursery), scrub brushes, and a water table. Encourage the children to scrub and clean their rocks. Invite them to sort their rocks by size and color.

Experienced Learner: Sorting Rocks II

Provide containers for sorting, and a variety of rocks, pebbles, stones, gravel, and so on. Label each container with a different heading, such as smooth, rough, colored, big, and small. Have the children sort the rocks into the appropriate container.

LANGUAGE/DRAMATIC PLAY CENTER

Beginning Learner: Letter "R" Hunt

Make index cards with the letter "R" written on them and hide them throughout the classroom. Show the children what the letter "R" looks like and ask them to hunt for all of the cards. Be sure to remember how many cards are hidden and help the children keep count as they find the cards.

Developing Learner: Words that Rhyme with "Rock"

Encourage the children to form a circle for group time. Explain that rhyming words are words that begin with different sounds but end with the same sound. Provide a few examples to get the children started. Ask them to brainstorm words that rhyme with "rock" and write the words on a poster.

Experienced Learner: Pet Rock Stories

Encourage the children to look at the rock creature, animal, or bug they made in the Art Center earlier. Ask the children to name their creatures and encourage them to dictate a letter or story (a few sentences) to you about their creatures. Invite them to illustrate their stories and bring them home with their creature.

VOCABULARY

bumpy, classify, dig, gravel, ground, hard, minerals, pebbles, rocks, rough, sift, smooth, sort, stones

Reflect

Say to the children, "Yesterday, we talked about buttons and made button necklaces. Today, we talked about rocks and classified them by size and other characteristics. Tomorrow, we will talk about one more thing that is round—the sun."

Extend and Enrich

◆ Bury rocks in mud and have the children dig for them.
◆ Scatter colored aquarium gravel on the playground. The children will love finding this cool treasure!

Sun

Morning Circle

Purchase an inexpensive pair of sunglasses for each child. These can be found at many discount or party stores. Put on a recording of the song "Mr. Sun," and greet the children when they arrive. Wear the sunglasses and give each child a pair of sunglasses to wear during story time. Introduce the story for the day.

Storytime

Sun Up, Sun Down by Gail Gibbons

Daily Center Activity Ideas

ART CENTER

Beginning Learner: Sun Catchers

To prepare for this activity, cut colored tissue paper into 1" squares and cut clear contact paper into 8 ½" x 11" sheets. Tape the contact paper to the table, sticky side up. Invite the children to stick their tissue paper squares to the sticky paper. When they have covered their contact paper with tissue paper, help them place another 8 ½" x 11" sheet of contact paper on top of their tissue paper. Place the sun catchers in a window in the classroom for the children to see their beautiful creations.

Developing Learner: Sun Catcher Mosaics

Cut colored tissue paper into 1" squares and contact paper into 8 ½" x 11" sheets. Tape the contact paper to the table, sticky side up, the same way as for the beginning learner. Encourage each child to stick tissue paper squares to the contact paper to make a design such as a sun, a flower, the first letter of a name, a heart, or shapes. When the children have completed their designs, place another sheet of contact paper on top. Hang the sun catchers in the window for the children to see.

Experienced Learner: Wax Paper Sun Catchers

Provide wax paper, cups of glue, brushes, scissors, and colored tissue paper. Help the children tape the wax paper to the table. The children brush glue all over the piece of wax paper. The children cut the tissue paper into strips, squares, or shapes and attach them to the sticky wax paper. When the tissue paper has completely dried, hang the artwork in the window. The children will be amazed at the beautiful colors that appear from the sunlight.

MATH CENTER

■ **Beginning Learner:** Temperature Circles

Discuss with the children that the sun is referred to as being hot. Also tell the children that there are various degrees of hot from very hot to lukewarm. Show the children a red circle and a blue circle and ask them to identify the colors. Discuss that red is often used to signal that something is hot and blue is often used to signal that something is cold. Explain that "warm" is a temperature between hot and cold. Introduce the concept *between*. Place the red circle on the floor to represent "hot" and the blue circle on the floor to represent "cold." Place another circle with the word "warm" written on it between the two circles. Add red food coloring to a tub of warm water and blue food coloring to a tub of cold water. Let the children explore the different temperatures as they feel the water with their hands.

■ ■ **Developing Learner:** Gauging Temperature

Discuss with the children that the sun is referred to as being very hot but there are varying degrees of hot that range from "scalding" to "lukewarm." Show the children a baby bath thermometer and discuss the markings on the thermometer. Explain that the markings or readings on the thermometer change when placed in hot, cold, or warm water. Provide a tub of warm water, a tub of cold water, and two baby bath thermometers. Invite the children to place the thermometers in each tub and check the temperature readings. The color strips on a baby thermometer will change colors as the temperature goes up.

■
■ ■ **Experienced Learner:** Graphing Temperatures

Show children several examples of thermometers and discuss the numerals on the thermometers and how to read them. (**Safety note:** Use caution when showing the thermometers to the children.) Provide a tub of lukewarm water, a tub of cold water, a pitcher of ice water, a pitcher of very warm water, and two baby bath thermometers. Let the children place the thermometers in each tub and get a reading of the current temperatures. Record their findings. Next, have them add some of the ice water to the cold water and some of the very warm water to the lukewarm tub. Have the children check the readings again. "Did the temperatures change? Did the number go up or down?" Have the children record their findings using a graph.

SCIENCE CENTER

■ **Beginning Learner:** Melting Ice

Tell the children that when the sun comes out after a snow or ice storm it causes the ice and snow to thaw. Provide a bowl of crushed ice and a cup of warm water for each child. Have the children pour the warm water over the ice. What happens? Where did the ice go? Discuss with the children the difference between hot and cold and what happens when heat is added to something frozen.

■ ■ **Developing Learner:** Melting Ice II

Give each child a bowl of crushed ice, and salt. Before doing this activity, ask the children what they think will happen when they pour salt over their ice. Conduct the experiment and then discuss the children's observations.

■
■ ■ **Experienced Learner:** Which Ice Melts Faster?

Provide bowls filled with a variety of ice, including crushed, cubed, shaved, and block. Take the children outside and talk about the sun's heat. Invite the children to make a hypothesis of what happens to ice when it is left in the sunlight. What will happen to the ice? Which kind of ice will melt faster? Which kind will take longer? Write down each child's hypothesis and then observe the ice.

LANGUAGE/DRAMATIC PLAY CENTER

■ **Beginning Learner:** Sunshine Writing Circle

Ask the children to wear their sunglasses from the morning circle activity. Give each child a large piece of paper and crayons or markers. Have the children sit in a group and talk about things they like to do outside in the sun. Write their ideas on their paper and invite them to illustrate their ideas.

■ ■ **Developing Learner:** Sunny Words

Draw a large sun on a piece of poster board, including the rays on the outside of the sun. In the middle of the sun, write the word "sun." Invite the children to put on their sunglasses and get ready to brainstorm. Ask the children to think of words that relate to the word *sun*, for example, hot, big, yellow, sky, and so on. Write their responses on the sun's rays.

■
■ ■ **Experienced Learner:** Words that Rhyme with "Sun"

Cut out a large circle and six large triangles from yellow bulletin board paper to represent the sun and its rays. Staple the rays to the outer edges of the sun. Write the word "sun" in the middle of the circle. Invite the children to name words that rhyme with sun. Write their responses on the rays and display in the classroom when finished.

VOCABULARY

big, bright, circle, eclipse, heat, hot, light, rays, rotate, round, sky, sunny, sunshine

Reflect

Say to the children, "Yesterday, we discussed rocks and how they are round. Today, we learned about the sun and how it is round and hot."

Extend and Enrich

Use the following ideas to extend and enrich what children know about the sun.

◆ Place a flat leaf on a piece of construction paper and leave it out in the sun. See what happens to the paper the next day when you remove the leaf.

◆ Have the children paint a sun at the art easel.

Daily Preschool Experiences

Things that Are Sticky

Jam

Peanut BUTTER

Glue

Morning Circle

Place a few objects on a table, such as feathers, yarn, and paper. Show the children a bottle of glue and ask them what it is used for. Ask the children to think of descriptive words for glue. Write their ideas on chart paper. Pour some glue on your hand and pick up some of the objects on the table to demonstrate how sticky the glue is. Read the story *Spence Makes Circles*, which is about a little boy and what happens to him and his cat when he tries to make circle pictures.

Storytime

Spence Makes Circles by Christa Chevalier

Daily Center Activity Ideas

ART CENTER

▪ **Beginning Learner:** Yarn and Glue Collage

Cut yarn into 12" strips and pour glue into a bowl. Encourage the children to dip the yarn into the glue, scrape off the excess glue with their fingers, and adhere the yarn to a piece of paper to make a yarn and glue collage. As the children do this activity, encourage them to discuss how the sticky yarn feels.

▪▪ **Developing Learner:** Dried Glue Necklaces

To prepare for this activity, mix glue and paint together and pour the mixture into glue bottles. Place wax paper on a tray or on paper plates and invite the children to squeeze the glue bottles to create shapes on the wax paper. They may use a single color or mix the colors to get a different design. Provide glitter for them to add to wet glue designs, if desired. Allow 48 hours for the glue shapes to dry. When the shapes are dry, they should peel off the wax paper easily. Use a hole punch to punch a hole in each glue shape. Let children string their shapes on yarn to make necklaces or hang them in a window as sun catchers.

▪▪▪ **Experienced Learner:** Refrigerator Magnets

Prepare the materials described for the developing learner but also provide cookie cutters. Invite the children to choose several cookie cutters and arrange them on wax paper. Have the children drizzle the colored glue mixture (described above) inside the cookie cutter shapes. Allow the creations to dry, remove the cookie cutters, then peel the shapes from the wax paper. Provide magnetic tape for the children to add to the back of their creations to make refrigerator magnets.

MATH CENTER

▢ Beginning Learner: Circle Collage

Show the children the book *Spence Makes Circles,* and remind them that in the story, the little boy was trying to make circle pictures using glue. Provide large pieces of white paper, a variety of sizes and colors of circles cut from construction paper, and glue sticks. Invite the children to make a circle collage using the various circles. Discuss the different sizes of the circles.

▢ ▢ Developing Learner: Concentric Circle Collage

Show the children the book *Spence Makes Circles,* and remind them that in the story, the little boy was trying to make circle pictures using glue. Provide large paper; small, medium, and large circles cut from construction paper; and glue sticks. Discuss the different sizes of the circles. Encourage the children to glue their circles on top each other to make a concentric collage. Show the children how to glue the largest circle on first, then the medium circle, and finally, the smallest circle.

▢ ▢ ▢ Experienced Learner: Circle Collage with Stencils

Provide large white paper, circle stencils in various sizes, a variety of different kinds of paper such as wrapping paper and wallpaper, markers, pencils, scissors, and glue sticks. Encourage the children to trace different sizes of circles onto different kinds of paper and cut them out. Invite them to glue the circles onto their large paper in interesting ways to make a circle collage. Provide magazines and encourage the children to find and cut out as many circle-shaped objects as possible. The children may add these magazine pictures to their circle collages.

SCIENCE CENTER

▢ Beginning Learner: Gak

Make Gak by combining 2 cups of glue and 1 ½ cups of warm water in a bowl. Add food coloring or a small amount of paint to reach desired color. In another bowl, mix 1 cup warm water with 2 tablespoons of borax. Combine the two mixtures together. There will be an instant chemical reaction. Continue mixing the ingredients until all of the water is absorbed into the glue. The children will love this! (**Safety note:** Make sure that the children do not put the borax in their mouths. Borax can be toxic in substantial amounts. Also, be aware that Gak is extremely hard to remove from clothing and carpet.) Place Gak on trays and invite the children to stretch, pull, touch, and squish the Gak in their hands. Encourage them to notice the squishiness and stickiness of the Gak.

Developing Learner: Glue and Water

Discuss with the children the concepts of liquids and solids. Pour a container of water into a tub. Discuss how it pours out quickly. Next, squirt glue from a bottle of glue onto paper and discuss how slowly the glue comes out of the bottle. Tell the children that they are going to conduct an experiment by mixing these two elements to make something new. Fill the water table with glue and water. Encourage the children to use their hands and wooden spoons to stir the water and glue together. Add food coloring or tempera paint to the mixture, if desired. Ask the children to describe what the mixture feels like. Discuss that the mixture is thicker than the water, but not as thick as the glue.

Experienced Learner: Making Colored Glue

Give each child a small bottle of white glue and a small funnel. Explain that funnels are used to help liquids go into a container. Help the children place the funnel in the glue bottle, drop a small amount of food coloring into the funnel, and put the lid back on the bottle. Invite the children to turn their bottles upside down and shake them to mix the food coloring and the glue for a few minutes. Provide paper and small paintbrushes and let the children paint a picture using the colored glue. The children can also use the glue to outline a coloring book picture. When the glue is dry, it will leave a textured outline on the paper.

LANGUAGE/DRAMATIC PLAY CENTER

Beginning Learner: Circle Shape Hunt

Cut out circles from paper and give one to each child. Sit in a circle with the children and have them name things that are round or shaped like a circle. Encourage them to go on a treasure hunt in the classroom and find things that are round or shaped like a circle and bring them back to the circle. Discuss what they found. Show the children a piece of Velcro and explain that the two sides of the Velcro are different and they are made to stick together. Allow the children to place Velcro strips on the back of the round objects and stick them to a piece of Velcro on the table or the floor. When you are finished with the activity, remove the Velcro and have the children return the objects.

Developing Learner: Magnets

Show the children several magnets or objects that have magnets or magnetic tape on the back of them. Discuss how the magnets "stick" to certain surfaces and makes things "stick" together. Provide magnetic letters and cookie sheets for the children to use to spell their names and other simple words. You can also add magnetic tape to pictures cut from magazines or to felt cutouts and encourage the children to use the pictures to tell stories on a magnet board.

Experienced Learner: Sticky Foods

Provide one large construction paper circle for each child, scissors, magazines, and glue sticks. Ask the children to cut out pictures of foods that are "sticky" from magazines. Have the children glue the pictures of sticky foods on their large circles. The children dictate words to describe the different foods that they found.

glue, slick, squeeze, sticky, thick, wet, white

Reflect

Say to the children, "Today, we learned about glue, which is very sticky. We use it for art projects, as well as for sticking things together. Tomorrow, we will talk about pie and how sticky and delicious it is."

Extend and Enrich

Use the following ideas to extend and enrich what children know about glue.

◆ Add glue to tempera paint to make it shiny.

◆ Give the children a variety of colored glue bottles and let them squeeze the colors on a paper plate. The next day, ask the children to describe what happened to the colors as they dried.

Pie

Morning Circle

Prior to the children's arrival, step on a tray of flour and then step on the floor to create footprints leading to the circle area. Greet the children at the door wearing an apron and carrying a freshly baked fruit pie. Ask the children to follow the footprints to the story circle. Ask the children if they can guess what made the white footprints, and tell them that you were using flour to make a pie crust for your pie. Cut the freshly baked pie into tiny slices, and give each child a small piece on a paper plate with a plastic fork. Let the children enjoy the pie while listening to the story. Encourage the children to describe how the pie looks and feels. Use the word *sticky* to describe the pie's filling as the children eat it. If desired, have children use their hands to eat the pie so they can experience the sticky sensation of the pie filling.

Storytime

I Know an Old Lady Who Swallowed a Pie by Alison Jackson

Daily Center Activity Ideas

ART CENTER

Beginning Learner: Baking Mini Pies

Provide the children with a thawed mini pie shell, new paintbrushes, food coloring, and water. (Mini pie shells are available in the freezer section of most supermarkets.) Prepare three cups of water mixed with food coloring. Encourage the children to paint their pie shells using the food coloring mixture. Bake the pie shells in an oven or toaster oven according to package direction. Remove them from the oven and allow them to cool. Encourage the children to describe what happened to their pie shell, and then fill it with pudding or canned pie filling.

Developing Learner: Baking Mini Pies II

Provide thawed mini pie shells, pipettes, and three cups of food coloring mixed with water. Encourage the children to place the pipettes in the food coloring, and then squeeze some of the food coloring from the pipette onto the pie shell to make different colors. When they are finished painting, let them use forks to make indentions and designs in their pie shells. Bake pie shells according to package directions. Remove and cool. Encourage the children to see what happened to their pie shells, and then let them fill the pies with pudding and whipped cream.

■■ Experienced Learner: Pie Dough Cutouts

Give each child a ball of pie dough and discuss how sticky it feels. Provide cookie cutters, rolling pins, trays, flour, food coloring, and new paintbrushes. Flour the trays for the children so the dough doesn't stick and encourage the children to roll out their ball of dough. Let them use cookie cutters to cut out three designs in their dough. Have the children place their cutouts on a cookie sheet, brush them with melted butter or margarine, and sprinkle with cinnamon sugar. Bake in a toaster oven or toaster.

MATH CENTER

■ Beginning Learner: Pie Sort

Place the numerals 1–5 in the bottom of foil pie pans. Cut out cardboard circles to represent pies and put dot stickers on them. Make some of the pies with one dot, some with two, some with three, some with four, and some with five. Have the children sort the pies into the correct pie pan by matching the number of dots on the pie to the numeral in the bottom of the pie pan.

■■ Developing Learner: People Pie Graph

Tell the children that they are going to make a graph using their bodies. Place a picture of a pie on the floor. Ask the children to line up by the picture of the pie if they like pie. Count the number of children standing and record the numeral on a paper graph. Next, place a picture of a pie with a large "X" across it on the floor. Ask the children who do not like pie to line up by that picture. Count the number of children standing and record that numeral on the paper graph. Talk about the results. Finally, provide pictures of different kinds of pies, and let children vote on their favorite pies using their bodies.

■■ Experienced Learner: Apple, Pumpkin, or Lemon Pie

Make a three-column chart with a picture of an apple pie in the first column, a picture of a pumpkin pie in the second column, and a picture of a lemon meringue pie in the last column. Place apples, small pumpkins, and lemons in a grocery bag. Encourage the children to sort the items into the appropriate columns on the chart.

SCIENCE CENTER

■ Beginning Learner: Making Whipped Cream

Show the children a pressurized canister of whipping cream and ask if they have ever eaten this and what did they eat with it. Squirt some whipping cream on a plate and touch it so the children can see that it is sticky between your fingers. Tell the children they are going to make whipped cream using a milk product called heavy cream or whipping cream. Let the children help pour the whipping cream into a cold metal bowl and use a rotary beater to beat the mixture until it is stiff. Discuss how the whipped cream looks compared to when it was poured out of the milk container. Explain that beating adds air to the cream making it stiff.

■ ■ **Developing Learner:** Making Pudding

Show the children a small container of pudding from the refrigerated section of the grocery store. Discuss how it looks sticky on a spoon. Tell the children that they are going to make their own sticky pudding. Provide baby food jars, milk, and instant pudding. Help the children pour a small amount of instant pudding and milk in their baby food jars. Secure the lids tightly. Encourage the children to shake their jars until the mixture turns to pudding. Give each child a mini pie shell. The children add their pudding to the pie shell and top with whipped cream.

■
■ ■ **Experienced Learner:** Making Apple Pie Filling

Show the children a can of apple pie filling. Remove a spoonful of filling and discuss how sticky it looks. Provide a crock pot, apples, cinnamon, sugar, and plastic knives. Help the children cut apples into small pieces and place them in a crock pot. Discuss that the apples do not feel sticky, but when sugar, cinnamon, and other spices are added to the mixture and it heats up, it begins to *caramelize* and the mixture becomes sticky. Encourage the children (with close supervision) to take turns stirring the apple mixture. When the pie filling is finished cooking, ask the children to notice how sticky it is. Let it cool. Give each child a mini pie shell and a spoon to add filling. The children may enjoy the apple pies as a special treat or take them home to enjoy with their families.

LANGUAGE/DRAMATIC PLAY CENTER

■ **Beginning Learner:** Pie Tasting Collage

Provide four different kinds of pies for the children to taste. As the children taste the pies, discuss the names of the pies and encourage them to compare the flavors. Draw a large circle on a large piece of poster board, and divide it into four "pie" sections. Write the names of the pies at the top of each of the four sections. The children stick a happy face sticker on the section that represents their favorite pie.

■ ■ **Developing Learner:** Make-Believe Pies

Provide magazines and pie crusts cut from construction paper. Encourage the children to look through magazines and find pictures of things that are sticky to put in their make-believe pie. Encourage them to cut out pictures of their pie ingredients and glue them to their pie shell. When their pies are complete, have them tell you what kind of pie they made, the ingredients, and how long it needs to bake in the oven.

■
■ ■ **Experienced Learner:** Rhyming Words

Ask the children to make a list of words that rhyme with "pie" and write their words on a large piece of paper shaped liked a pie. Provide small pie-shaped pieces of construction paper for the children to practice writing some of the words on. Have them write one word on each pie shape and then staple their pie pages together to make a flip book that they can read over and over.

VOCABULARY

apple, bake, blueberry, cherry, crust, filling, flour, gooey, meringue, peach, pecan, pie, rolling pin, slices, sticky, sweet

Reflect

Say to the children, "Yesterday, we talked about glue and how sticky it is. Today, we talked about pie. We talked about all of the different kinds of pie there are, and we found out which ones we like and which ones we do not like. Tomorrow, we will learn about jam and how to make it."

Extend and Enrich

Use the following ideas to extend and enrich what children know about pie.

◆ Set up a bakery in the dramatic play center.

◆ Visit a bakery to see how pies are made. Or, invite a baker to come in and describe how he or she makes pies.

◆ Provide cans of pie filling for the children to taste.

Jam

Morning Circle

Prepare a plastic bag for each child with a strawberry, blackberry, and raspberry inside. As the children arrive, give each child a baggy of berries. Encourage them to examine their berries and notice the difference in the color, size, and texture of each berry. Have a variety of berries on the table next to the book, and talk about each type of berry with the children. Show the children a jar of strawberry, blackberry, and raspberry jam and tell the children that berries are often smashed and mixed with sugar, water, and other ingredients to make jams and jellies. Enjoy sharing the story with the children.

Storytime

Jamberry by Bruce Degen

Daily Center Activity Ideas

ART CENTER

Beginning Learner: Basket Prints
Provide berry baskets, red and blue paint, and paper. Place the paint on trays and encourage the children to dip the bottom of the berry baskets in the paint and make basket prints on their paper.

Developing Learner: Scented Berry Paintings
Provide berry baskets, red and blue paint, and paper. Place the paint on trays and have the children dip the bottom of the berry baskets in the paint and make prints on their paper. Add three drops of strawberry flavoring to the red paint to add a berry aroma. When the berry paintings are dry, encourage the children to use markers to draw small raspberries, strawberries, or blueberries in their baskets.

Experienced Learner: 3-D Berry Collage
Provide berry baskets, brown paint, and construction paper. Put the brown paint on a tray and encourage the children to dip the bottom of the baskets in the paint and make prints on the construction paper. After the basket prints dry, encourage the children to cut or wad red, blue, and purple tissue paper into berry shapes and glue them onto their berry basket prints. Also provide small pieces of green and brown chenille sticks for the children to add to their berries as the stems.

MATH CENTER

■ **Beginning Learner:** Sorting Berries

Give each child a small cup of washed strawberries, blueberries, raspberries, and blackberries. Encourage the children to sort the berries according to type. When the berries are sorted, let the children eat them.

■ ■ **Developing Learner:** Berry Patterning

Provide a clean tray or plate, and a cup of washed strawberries, blueberries, raspberries, and blackberries for each child. Tell the children they will be using the berries to make a pattern. Draw a few examples of berry patterns on paper, such as ABAB, ABBA, or AABB (for example, strawberry, blackberry, strawberry, blackberry). Encourage the children to choose a pattern and use the berries in their cup to create and reproduce patterns. When they have completed their patterns, they can enjoy their work and have a delicious snack!

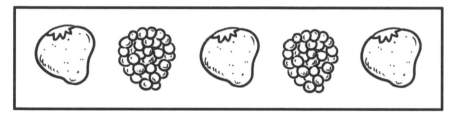

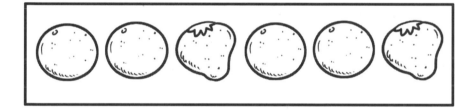

■
■ ■ **Experienced Learner:** Comparing Weights

Provide blueberries, raspberries, strawberries, and blackberries; napkins; and a kitchen scale. Encourage each child to select five berries of his choice and weigh them on the kitchen scale. Record the weight on a berry-shaped piece of paper. As the children weigh their berries, discuss with them that the smaller berries usually weigh less than the bigger berries. Encourage the children to compare the weights of their berries with that of their friends' berries.

SCIENCE CENTER

■ **Beginning Learner:** Berry Smoothie

Provide an assortment of berries, milk, sugar, and a blender. Talk about the different berries, including their names and colors. Have the children look closely at the berries and notice their similarities and differences. Have each child place a few berries, a spoonful of sugar, and a small cup of milk (or water if the child has milk allergies) in the blender. Turn the blender on and mix the ingredients. Add a couple cubes of ice and mix again. Pour the berry smoothie in a cup and enjoy.

Developing Learner: Smashing Berries

Provide an assortment of berries, rolling pins, and large storage bags. Discuss how the berries look and ask the children to describe them. Invite the children to place berries in their bag and seal it. Demonstrate how to use a rolling pin by rolling it over a ball of playdough to flatten it. Then roll over the berries in the bag to see what happens. Discuss how the berries look after they are smashed. Write down the vocabulary that the children use to discuss the changes in the berries. When they have finished smashing their berries, have them add a small spoonful of sugar to their berries, close the bag, and mix in the sugar with their fingers. The children can open their bags, pour the berries in a small cup, and enjoy eating them with a plastic spoon.

Experienced Learner: Smashing Berries II

Provide an assortment of berries, rolling pins, large storage bags, and magnifying glasses. Invite the children to place a few berries in their bag and seal it. Have them roll over the berries in the bag using a rolling pin and observe what happens. Invite the children to use magnifying glasses to take a closer look at the berries. Discuss the changes they see, such as the colors mixing together and the berries becoming liquid. Have the children add a small amount of sugar and then close their bags to continue mixing the berries and sugar. When everything is mixed together, provide cups for them to taste the berry juice.

LANGUAGE/DRAMATIC PLAY CENTER

Beginning Learner: Jam Tasting

Provide crackers, different flavors of jam, plastic knives, and paper plates. Place a plastic knife inside each jar of jam. Invite the children to spread the jam on their crackers to taste each flavor. After the children have tasted each flavor, ask them which jam they liked best and to describe the flavors and stickiness of the jam.

Developing Learner: The Letter "J"

Use masking tape to outline a giant lowercase "j" and a giant uppercase "J" on the floor. Tell the children that the words *jam, jelly,* and *jar* all start with the letter "J." Draw an uppercase "J" and a lowercase "j" on a dry-erase board. Ask the children to use their fingers to trace the letter in the air, and then take turns walking on the letters taped to the floor. After everyone has had a turn, ask them to think of other ways to move around the letters, such as jumping, hopping, placing one foot in front of the other so their feet are touching, and skipping. Give each child a piece of paper to practice drawing the letter "J."

Experienced Learner: Types of Jam

Provide sets of sentence strips with the words *strawberry, blueberry,* and *grape* written on them. Provide scented markers for the children to draw over the words.

apple, apricot, blackberry, blueberry, grape, jam, jar, jelly, orange, raspberry, sandwiches, spread, sticky, strawberry, sweet, toast

Reflect

Say to the children, "Yesterday, we talked about pies and all of their many possible flavors. Today, we talked about jam and different things to do with berries. Tomorrow, we will talk about marshmallows and how sticky they feel on your fingers."

Extend and Enrich

Use the following ideas to extend and enrich what children know about berries and jam.

◆ Make jam or jelly in class using a favorite recipe.

◆ Show the children a jar of strawberry jam or jelly and discuss how it feels and looks. Then tell them that they are going to paint with pretend strawberry jam. Mix glue into red fingerpaint so that it is the consistency of jam or jelly and invite the children to paint a picture.

Marshmallows

Morning Circle

As the children enter the classroom, ask them to wash their hands and then give each child two marshmallows. Encourage the children to touch, smell, and pull on the marshmallows to see what happens. Ask them how their hands feel when they are finished. Ask the children to wash their hands again and then get ready to listen to a fun story about Owen and his marshmallow chick.

Storytime

Owen's Marshmallow Chick by Kevin Henkes

Daily Center Activity Ideas

ART CENTER

Beginning Learner: Painting with Marshmallows

Stick straws that have been cut in half into jumbo marshmallows. Give each child a small paper plate with a small amount of chocolate syrup on it and white construction paper. Encourage the children to use the marshmallow as their paintbrush and dip it into the chocolate syrup to make fun dots and designs on their paper. When they are finished with their paintings, they can enjoy eating their marshmallow "paintbrush."

Developing Learner: Marshmallow Sculptures

Place several jumbo and miniature marshmallows into small sandwich bags. Encourage the children to use marshmallows and straws that have been cut into small pieces to make sculptures. When the sculptures are finished, the children can enjoy eating them as a special treat.

Experienced Learner: Marshmallow Chicks

Show the children the book *Owen's Marshmallow Chick,* and, if possible, show them a marshmallow chick (Peeps™). Tell the children that they are going to make their own marshmallow chicks. Provide jumbo and miniature white marshmallows, colored small marshmallows, and pretzels. Encourage the children to combine the marshmallows in interesting ways to make their own marshmallow chick or other marshmallow animals.

MATH CENTER

Beginning Learner: Sorting Colored Marshmallows

Give each child a cup of small colored marshmallows and squares of pastel construction paper that match the colors of the marshmallows. Place the construction paper on the table and encourage the children to match the colored marshmallows to the squares of paper. When they have finished sorting their marshmallows, the children can eat them as a treat or bring them home in a baggie.

Developing Learner: Counting and Sorting Marshmallows

Give each child a cup of small colored marshmallows and squares of pastel construction paper that match the colors of the marshmallows. Have the children sort the marshmallows according to color and count how many of each color they have. Have them practice writing numerals by writing how many of each color marshmallow they have on the paper squares. When they are finished, they can eat the marshmallows as a special treat or bring them home in a baggie.

Experienced Learner: Making Marshmallow Patterns

Give each child a cup of small colored marshmallows. Encourage them to use their marshmallows to make a pattern. When they are finished making patterns, they can enjoy eating the marshmallows as a special treat or bring them home.

SCIENCE CENTER

Beginning Learner: S'mores

Before starting this activity, make a s'more (marshmallow and chocolate between two graham crackers) to use as an example. Also, make a pretend campfire out of blocks ("logs") and red, yellow, and orange tissue paper ("flames"). Show the children the premade s'more and ask them what they think is in the treat. Explain that s'mores are treats that people make using toasted marshmallows, usually when they are outside around a campfire. Show them a long kebab stick with a large marshmallow on one end. If possible, melt the marshmallow so the children can observe the change in its texture and appearance. Give each child two graham crackers, a miniature chocolate bar, and a small amount of marshmallow cream. Help them place one spoonful of marshmallow cream on a graham cracker, unwrap and add their chocolate bar on top, and then put the

second graham cracker on top of the chocolate. Enjoy the s'mores around the "campfire."

■ ■ **Developing Learner:** Marshmallow Cream

Show the children a marshmallow and discuss how it feels in your hand. Start smashing and squishing it, and tell them that it is becoming very sticky (it will stick to your fingers). Tell the children that they are going to make a gooey, sticky marshmallow treat. Give each child a small bowl of marshmallow cream, a plastic spoon, and a small cup of colored marshmallows. Have the children stir the marshmallow cream. Ask them to describe the cream as they stir it. Have them stir their colored marshmallows into the marshmallow cream. Give each child two graham crackers, and invite the children to spread the marshmallow mixture on the crackers. Discuss how some of the small marshmallows got squished and mixed into the mixture and some of them remained whole. As they eat the treat, talk about the sticky texture of the marshmallows.

■
■ ■ **Experienced Learner:** Marshmallow Taffy

Purchase a small amount of colored taffy. Show it to the children and unwrap it so they can see it better. Explain that the taffy feels hard and stiff and a little sticky in your hands. Tell the children that they are going to make their own taffy using marshmallows. Make sure children wash their hands before this activity, and then give each child a small bowl of large marshmallows. Show the children how to use their fingers to pull on the marshmallows. Explain that marshmallows are beginning to turn into taffy. When the marshmallows begin to break down, drop one drop of food coloring into the bowl to give them a pastel color. Encourage the children to continue stirring the mixture until it is thoroughly mixed. Invite the children to taste their taffy. If you have enough, let them taste the store-bought taffy to compare the two versions.

LANGUAGE/DRAMATIC PLAY CENTER

Use the following recipe for Rice Krispie™ Treats for all levels of learners. The recipe serves eight.

Rice Krispie™ Treats

¼ cup butter

10 ounces of marshmallows

6 cups of crispy rice cereal

Melt butter in large pan over low heat. Add marshmallows and stir until melted. Remove from heat and add cereal. Combine until well coated. Line a 13"x 9"x 2" pan with waxed paper and press mixture into pan. When the mixture has cooled, cut into squares.

■ **Beginning Learner:** Rice Krispie Treats/Decorating Recipe Card

Prepare Rice Krispie treats with the children using the recipe above. Give each child a copy of the recipe and instructions on a 4"x 6" index card. Invite the children to turn the card over and decorate the back of the recipe card using markers to draw marshmallows, butter, Rice Krispie cereal and the finished Rice Krispie treats.

Developing Learner: Making Rice Krispie Treats

Make Rice Krispie treats with the children. Make a copy of the recipe for each child and go through it line by line as you make the treats. When melting the butter and marshmallows, supervise the children closely and make sure they stay away from the hot surface. When the treats have cooled, invite the children to use a cookie cutter to cut out a shape. Enjoy your snack!

Experienced Learner: Rice Krispie Chicks

Show the children the book, *Owen's Marshmallow Chick*. Tell the children that they are going to make their own marshmallow chick treats. Make Rice Krispie treats with the children. When melting the butter and marshmallows, supervise the children closely and make sure they stay away from the hot surface. Once the mixture has cooled just a bit, grease the children's hands with butter and spoon some of the mixture into their hands. Encourage the children to mold and shape their treats into chicks. When the treats are cool, ask the children to dictate stories about what they would do if they had a marshmallow chick for a friend. Encourage them to tell what they would do with their chick and where they would take it. Ask them if they would eat their marshmallow chick friend. Write their words on paper and have the children illustrate their stories. When the stories are complete, the children can enjoy their marshmallow chick treats.

VOCABULARY

chick, colored, fluffy, fun, hot chocolate, marshmallow, marshmallow cream, small, s'mores, sticky, sweet, taffy, white

Reflect

Say to the children, "Yesterday, we talked about jam and the different kinds of berries that can be used to make it. Today, we had a wonderful time playing with and eating marshmallows and discovering how sticky they are. Tomorrow, we will talk about peanut butter and where it comes from."

Extend and Enrich

Use the following ideas to extend and enrich what children know about marshmallows.

- Provide hot chocolate with marshmallows for the children to enjoy. Ask them to pay special attention to what happens to the marshmallows as they float in the warm hot chocolate. Introduce the words *melt* and *dissolve*. Discuss how the marshmallows go from being whole, then smaller, and then disappear because of the heat.
- Show the children a bag of small marshmallows and a bag of large marshmallows. Have them cut out pictures from magazines of marshmallows and foods with marshmallows in them. Use the pictures to make marshmallow collages.

Peanut Butter

Safety note: Prior to doing this activity, be sure that no child in the class or in other classes nearby has allergies to peanuts. Children with peanut allergies should not touch, handle, eat, or be exposed to peanuts in their environment.

Morning Circle

As children arrive, give them a small plastic bag of peanuts in the shell and ask them to take their peanuts to a large tub (for shells). As they remove the peanuts from the shell, encourage them to listen to the cracking sound of the peanuts. If desired, have them count the peanuts as they fall out of the shell. Save the nuts to make homemade peanut butter for another activity or to eat as a snack.

Storytime

Peanut Butter & Jelly: A Play Rhyme by Nadine Bernard Westcott

Daily Center Activities

ART CENTER

Before doing this activity for all levels of learners, gather ingredients for peanut butter playdough. Make sure the children wash their hands before using the dough.

Peanut Butter Playdough

(serves 1 child)

½ cup peanut butter

½ cup nonfat dry powdered milk

½ tablespoon honey

Mix until combined and make small balls for the children to manipulate.

■ **Beginning Learner:** Playing with Peanut Butter Playdough

Make peanut butter playdough and give each child a small ball of the dough. Provide sheets of wax paper on which the children can play with their dough. When the children have finished playing, they can enjoy the playdough as a treat or take it home in a plastic bag.

Developing Learner: Making Peanut Butter Playdough

Make peanut butter playdough with the children. In addition to the ingredients, provide a bowl, spoons, measuring cups, cookie cutters, rolling pins, and trays. Talk about each ingredient as you add it to the bowl. Let each child have a turn stirring the dough. When the dough is finished, give each child a small ball of the dough. Provide sheets of wax paper on which the children can play with their dough. Invite the children to smash and roll the dough with rolling pins and make different shapes and textured designs using plastic forks and cookie cutters. When the children are finished playing, they can eat it as a special treat.

Experienced Learner: Making Playdough

Bring in a bag of roasted peanuts in their shell. Let the children each have a shell to crack open and remove the peanut. Explain that peanuts are "legumes" and not really nuts. They do not grow on trees like most nuts. Peanuts grow underground. Have the children make peanut butter playdough as described for the other learning levels. Encourage them to shape their playdough into peanut shell shapes and enjoy eating when they are done.

MATH CENTER

Beginning Learner: Counting Peanuts

Provide peanuts in a bowl and paper plates. (If children have peanut allergies, use Styrofoam packing peanuts.) Let each child grab a handful of peanuts and count them on a paper plate. Ask the children to grab two handfuls of peanuts to count. Finally, use your hand to grab adult-sized handfuls of peanuts to give each child. Have them count the peanuts. Compare the amount of peanuts in one handful, two handfuls, and a large adult handful. Discuss how your hand is larger than theirs, which is why it holds more peanuts.

Developing Learner: Counting Peanuts/Recognizing Numerals

Provide peanuts, paper plates, and numeral magnets. Place a handful of peanuts on each child's plate and have the children count how many peanuts they have. Place the numeral magnets in the middle of the table and encourage the children to find the numeral that matches the number of peanuts on their plates and place that numeral on their plate. Give them another handful of peanuts and repeat.

Experienced Learner: Counting Peanuts/Rolling a Die

Place peanuts in a bowl in the middle of the table. Have the children take turns rolling a die. The child counts the dots on the die, and counts out that number of peanuts and puts them on her plate. The children continue playing until everyone has a large pile of peanuts. Have them count all of the peanuts in their pile. The children take turns rolling the die and putting that number of peanuts back into the bowl until all the peanuts are back in the bowl.

SCIENCE CENTER

Beginning Learner: Smashing Peanuts

Provide peanuts in the shell and point out the rough outer shell. Explain that the shell is not eaten but is cracked and discarded. Shell a peanut and show the children the peanuts inside. Crack open several shells to show that the number of peanuts inside the shells sometimes varies. Describe the peanuts as smooth, which is the opposite of the rough outer shell. Tell the children that they are going to smash peanuts to see how they change. Place shelled peanuts in resealable plastic bags (one bag for each child). Invite them to smash the peanuts using rubber mallets. Talk about the change in the peanuts. Eat them as a snack and ask if they taste the same when smashed.

Developing Learner: Grinding Peanuts

Show the children unshelled peanuts and talk about the texture of the outer shell. Shell a few peanuts and talk about the smooth texture of the peanut. Provide a hand-crank nut grinder with a rotary handle and shelled peanuts. You can find a nut grinder at many kitchen supply stores and in some supermarkets. Explain to the children that when the nuts are ground, they become oily and sticky and eventually turn into peanut butter. Encourage the children to take turns placing nuts in the nut grinder and turning the handle to grind the nuts into tiny pieces. Pour the ground nuts into a small cup and compare them to whole peanuts. Encourage the children to touch the nuts and feel how oily and sticky they feel. Eat them for snack and talk about the flavor.

Experienced Learner: What's the Best Way to Smash a Peanut?

Provide the children with a resealable storage bag and shelled peanuts. Encourage them to use their imaginations to figure out how to smash the peanuts. For example, they could use their hands, stomp their feet, use different objects (mallets, blocks), and so on. Encourage the children to experiment with the different objects to find out which ones work best for smashing the peanuts.

LANGUAGE/DRAMATIC PLAY CENTER

Beginning Learner: Interactive Storytelling

Read the story *Peanut Butter and Jelly* again to the children. Divide the children into two groups ("peanut butter" and "jelly"). As you read the story, the peanut butter group stands up and turns around each time it hears the word "peanut butter." The jelly group does the same thing when you say "jelly." Provide peanut butter and jelly sandwiches for the children to enjoy. Encourage the children to describe their sandwiches as they enjoy them.

Developing Learner: Making Peanut Butter

Provide a blender, peanuts to shell, oil, and sugar. Let the children shell the peanuts and place them in a blender. Add a small amount of oil and sugar and turn on the blender to mix the ingredients. The children can enjoy tasting the homemade peanut butter by spreading a layer peanut butter on a cracker and then topping it with jelly. Following is the recipe for homemade peanut butter:

Homemade Peanut Butter

2 cups roasted shelled peanuts

2 teaspoons oil

1 teaspoon sugar

Blend in a blender until smooth.

Experienced Learner: Following a Recipe for PBJs

Provide bread, jelly, peanut butter, plates, and plastic knives. Make simple rebus recipe cards for making a peanut butter and jelly sandwich. Encourage the children to follow the recipe cards to make their own sandwiches.

VOCABULARY

creamy, crunchy, gooey, jelly, nutty, peanuts, sticky, sandwich, smooth, spread, thick

Reflect

Say to the children, "Yesterday, we talked about marshmallows and how much fun they are to eat and enjoy. Today, we talked about peanut butter and how it is made from peanuts."

Extend and Enrich

Use the following ideas to extend and enrich what children know about peanuts and peanut butter.

- Find a place outside and plant raw shelled peanuts with the children. Soak the peanuts overnight prior to planting.
- Talk about other things with shells, such as animals (turtles, crabs, lobsters, shrimp, crawfish, snails, and oysters), nuts (almonds, pecans), and so on.

Things that Are Fun

Bubble Gum

Morning Circle

Chew bubble gum and begin blowing large bubbles as the children enter the classroom. (**Note:** You might want to discuss appropriate uses and places for chewing gum and blowing bubbles.) If available, provide a small gumball machine and give the children each a penny so that they can get their own bubble gum for exploration. The children will want to learn how to blow a bubble, which is very difficult at this age. As an alternative to blowing bubbles with chewing gum, provide a bottle of soap bubbles and wands for the children to make bubbles of their own. If available, provide a bubble machine for added fun. After a few minutes of bubble exploration, share the story *Bubble Gum, Bubble Gum*.

Storytime

Bubble Gum, Bubble Gum by Lisa Wheeler

Daily Center Activity Ideas

ART CENTER

▪ **Beginning Learner:** Gumball Painting
Give each child a sheet of white construction paper cut in the shape of a gumball machine (a large circle on top of a square). Provide a real gumball or a marble, paint, and a tray or shallow box. Have the children place their paper on the tray and then place the gumball on the paper. Add a spoonful of paint and invite the children to roll the gumball on the tray from side to side so the gumball rolls in the paint and makes colored designs on their "gumball machine."

▪▪ **Developing Learner:** Gumball Stencil and Tracing
Provide a gumball machine stencil (a large circle on top of a square), paper, markers, scissors, and bingo markers. Encourage the children to trace the stencil on their paper and cut it out. Invite the children to trace around the bingo markers in the center of the machine to make gumballs.

■ ■■ Experienced Learner: Contact Paper Gumball Machine

Prior to doing this activity, cut out circles, about the size of quarters, from colored tissue paper to represent gumballs. Give each child a sheet of contact paper with the paper backing still on it. Provide a gumball machine stencil (as described for the developing learner) for the children to trace onto the contact paper and cut out. Have them repeat this process on another sheet of contact paper. The children carefully peel off the backing of one of the gumball machines and fill the circular part with tissue paper circles. Help them place the other sheet of contact paper on top. Mount the gumball machine on a piece of construction paper. (**Note:** You may wish to tape the contact paper to the table so that it is easier for children to work with.)

MATH CENTER

■ Beginning Learner: Sorting Gumballs

Provide the children with colored pompoms ("gumballs") and bowls. Have the children sort the pompoms into the bowls by colors.

■ ■ Developing Learner: Counting and Sorting Gumballs

Cut out gumball machines from white paper (a large circle on top of a square or rectangle). Provide the children with colored pompoms ("gumballs"), bowls, and numeral cards (1–5 written on index cards). Encourage the children to draw a card, count out that many "gumballs," and place them in their "gumball machine." Have them also sort the "gumballs" by color and size.

■ ■ Experienced Learner: Estimating Gumballs

Provide a large mason jar of gumballs. Talk with the children about estimating. *Estimation* is a guess about the amount of something. Write down on a piece of paper each child's name and how many gumballs they think are in the jar. After everyone has made their guess, count out the gumballs and see who was the closest. Continue the game by secretly removing some of the gumballs from the jar, having the children guess again, and then recounting to see how close their guess was.

SCIENCE CENTER

■ **Beginning Learner:** Sink or Float/Rubber Balls

Show the children small rubber balls and tell them to pretend that they are gumballs. Ask the children if they think that the balls will float or sink when placed in the water table. Remind the children that objects sink or float depending on how wide and heavy they are. Provide "gumballs" and nets for the children to explore in the water table.

■ ■ **Developing Learner:** Dissolving Gumballs

Provide gumballs and glasses of water. Ask the children if they think the gumballs will sink or float when placed in water. Discuss that the inside of a gumball is often white, but the outside has a colored coating to make it more appealing. Have the children select a gumball of their choice and drop the gumballs in the water to see what happens. They will be amazed to see the water change color as the colored coating begins to dissolve. Talk about how the gumball looks different and how the color of the water has changed. Ask two children to drop two different colored gumballs into a glass of water to see what happens. Discuss color mixing with the children as the candy coatings dissolve. The gumballs can be placed in a resealable bag after the experiment and sent home with the children. (**Note:** Be sure to put a note on the outside of the bag to let parents know that there is a gumball inside and they can make the decision if it is okay for their child to chew the gum or not.)

■
■ ■ **Experienced Learner:** Sink or Float/Comparing Balls

Provide small and large marbles, a golf ball, a ping-pong ball, and a small rubber ball. Show the children the balls and discuss the differences in their sizes. Ask them if they think the objects will sink or float when placed in water. Provide a tub of water and place the marbles and balls in the water one at a time. Discuss the differences in sizes and weights of the different balls. Ask them if size and weight had an impact on whether or not the balls float or sink. Tell the children that they are going to try the same experiment using gumballs. Provide large and small gumballs and glasses of water. Ask the children if they think the large and small gumballs will sink or if they will float when placed in water. Ask them to choose either a large or small gumball and place it in the water one at a time to see what happens. Graph what happens to the different sizes of gumballs.

LANGUAGE/DRAMATIC PLAY CENTER

■ **Beginning Learner:** Find the Letter "B"

Provide colored construction paper circles, glue sticks, and a large gumball machine drawn on a piece of poster board. Have the children practice writing the letter "B" for bubblegum on each circle. Invite them to glue the gumballs on the poster board.

Developing Learner: Bubble Gum Game

Have the children gather in a circle and make fists with both hands. Children hold out their fists in the middle of the circle. Selecte one child to be the "counter." The counter goes around the circle tapping everyone's fist while saying this rhyme: Bubble gum, bubble gum in a dish. How many pieces do you wish? (Each word gets one tap.) When the counter lands on a child, that child says a number from 1–5. The counter then continues tapping around the circle and counting aloud until she gets to that number. The child the counter taps last gets to be the next counter.

Experienced Learner: Rhyming Words

Provide a giant gumball machine cut out of paper. Invite the children to cut out colored circles from construction paper and glue the circles to fill the gumball machine. Ask them to think of words that rhyme (ball/wall, car/jar). Write down the children's words on each of the "gumballs" in the machine.

VOCABULARY

blow, bubble gum, bubbles, chewing, flavor, fun, pink, sticky, wrapper

Reflect

Say to the children, "Yesterday, we discussed things that are sticky such as marshmallows and jam. Today, we talked about gum and made gumball machines. Tomorrow, we will talk about games and how many different kinds of games we can play."

Extend and Enrich

Use the following ideas to extend and enrich what children know about gumball machines.

- If appropriate, purchase a bubble gum kit and let the children make their own bubble gum in class. Make sure the children do not eat the gum in class. Send home the gum with a note to parents, explaining that they can decide whether or not their child can chew it.
- Find different types of gum and make a gum collage. This will not be edible because children need glue to make the collage. If desired, substitute royal icing to make an edible collage.
- Have children use sticks of gum and gumballs to make buildings or structures.
- Use gum wrappers to make a paper collage.

Games

Morning Circle

Welcome the children to class and invite them to sit in a circle on the floor. Tell them they will be playing a game called "I Spy." Explain that you will look around the classroom and find an object you want them to locate. Use words (color, size, shape, and location) to describe what the object looks like. The older the children, the fewer hints you need to give. Once they get the hang of it, let the children take turns as the person "spying" the object.

Storytime

Little Quack's Hide and Seek by Lauren Thompson

Daily Center Activity Ideas

ART CENTER

Beginning Learner: Blindfolded Painting/Dot Markers

Provide an easel, paper, and paint dot markers. Ask the children to close their eyes and use the dot markers to paint on their paper. When finished, have the children open their eyes and see what they created!

Developing Learner: Blindfolded Painting/Brushes

Provide a bandana, an easel, paper, paint, and paint smocks. If the children are comfortable with their eyes covered, use the bandana to blindfold them. If the children are afraid, have them close their eyes to participate in this activity. Once the child is blindfolded, dip a brush into paint and place it in the child's hand. Guide the child to the paper and tell him to paint away! When they are finished with their painting, have them remove the blindfold and see their creation.

Experienced Learner: Blindfolded Painting with Partners

Provide a bandana, an easel, paper, paint, and paint smocks. Use the bandana to blindfold the children (if they are comfortable with this). They may choose to close their eyes instead. Dip the brush into paint and place it in the child's hand. Guide him to the paper and invite him to start painting. After a few minutes of "solo" painting, let the children choose partners. The partner gives the blindfolded child clues about where to paint.

MATH CENTER

■ **Beginning Learner:** Hide and Seek/Counting Objects

Provide a child-sized plastic pool filled with shredded paper and small manipulatives from the classroom. Invite the children to take turns digging for the objects. Let them know ahead of time how many items you have hidden. When they have found all of the objects, ask them to identify and count the objects.

■ ■ **Developing Learner:** Hide and Seek/Counting Numerals

Fill a large box with shredded paper and magnetic or foam numerals from 1–10. The children take turns digging through the shredded paper for the different numerals. When they have found all of the numerals, line them up and count them together.

■
■ ■ **Experienced Learner:** Hide and Seek/Ordering Numerals

Wrap 10 small boxes (about the size of a child-size shoebox) with wrapping paper so that the top and bottom are separate. Place foam numerals inside each box (for example, in one box place all of the foam 1s, in the second box place all of the foam 2s, and so on until all of the boxes have been filled with numerals). Place the lids on the boxes and mix the boxes up so that they are in no particular order. Explain that they are going to play a game of hide and seek to find the numerals 1–10. When they have found all of the numerals, ask them to put the numerals in order from 1–10.

SCIENCE CENTER

To do this activity at any level, cut a hole in the top of a large cardboard box so a child can fit his hands inside.

■ **Beginning Learner:** Feely Box/Recognition

To prepare, place a few simple objects inside the box. Use a variety of objects with different sizes, shapes, and textures (a ball, a rock, a stuffed animal, a leaf, a piece of bark, and so on) so the children must use their sense of touch to find the "hidden" object. Remind the children that the story they heard was about a fun game of hide and seek. Explain that when you lose something, you must use words to describe the item so someone can help you find it. Describe an item in the box and let the children take turns reaching into the box to find the object.

■ ■ **Developing Learner:** Feely Box/Description

Show the children a tray of objects of different sizes, shapes, and textures and talk about them with the children. Talk about the five senses, emphasizing the sense of touch as an important tool in helping one get information about the world. After the discussion, remind the children that the story for the day was about a game of hide and seek. Place the objects from the tray in the box. Have the children take turns reaching into the box and locating an object. The child uses his sense of touch to describe the object to a friend. The friend tries to guess what object is being described.

Experienced Learner: Feely Box/Matching

Discuss the five senses, focusing on the sense of touch and how important it is in helping us to identify things that might hurt us (hot, sharp, and so on). Provide a tray of pairs of objects with different textures, such as two shells, two pinecones, two blocks, two cotton balls, and so on. Pass the objects around the table so the children can touch and describe them. Then place one of each matching object inside the box and leave the other object on the tray. Let each child choose an object from the tray and then use their hands to locate the matching object inside the box. After everyone has had a chance to do the activity this way, have the children put a sock or glove on one of their hands. Repeat the activity, and see if the glove or sock makes it harder to find the object. Talk about the difference.

LANGUAGE/DRAMATIC PLAY CENTER

Beginning Learner: Letter Hunt

Write the first letter of each child's name on sticky notes. Stick the notes all over the room before the children arrive. When they arrive, talk about the first letter of each child's name. Invite the children to find the sticky note that has their letter written on it. Each child then places her sticky letter somewhere else in the room for her friends to try to find it.

Developing Learner: Name Hunt

Write each child's name on a card and hide the cards all over the classroom before the children come in. Ask the children to look around the room to find their name cards. Have extra name cards available for children who are not familiar with recognizing their names. Children may choose to carry these cards around while looking for their names.

Experienced Learner: Name Hunt II

Provide blank index cards and markers. Invite the children to write their names on a card. Collect the cards from the children and hide them around the room. Invite the children to go around the room and locate the cards with their names on them.

VOCABULARY

basketball, board games, checkers, competition, dice, exciting, fun, hide, jacks, laughing, leader, seek, silly, soccer, softball

Reflect

Say to the children, "Yesterday, we learned about bubble gum and how much fun it is to chew. Today, we talked about games and how fun it is to play them with friends. Tomorrow, we will talk about kites and how fun they are to fly."

Extend and Enrich

Use the following ideas to extend and enrich what children know about games.

◆ Have the children sit in a circle with their hands behind their backs. Hold up an object, and then tell the children to close their eyes. Place the object in a child's hands. Have the children open their eyes, and let them take turns guessing who has the object.

◆ Provide three cups and hide a ball under one of the cups. Move the cups around and see if the children can guess where the ball is.

◆ Play favorite outdoor children's games such as "Statues," "Tag," and "Red Light, Green Light."

◆ Play BINGO. There are many versions available such as alphabet, shapes, or number BINGO.

◆ Have a game day and ask the children to bring their favorite game to school.

Kites

Morning Circle

Buy inexpensive kites and hang a few of them from the classroom ceiling. Once all of the children have arrived, take a few extra kites outside for everyone to fly kites. This would be a great activity for involving parents.

Storytime

Let's Fly a Kite by Stuart J. Murphy

Daily Center Activity Ideas

ART CENTER

■ **Beginning Learner:** Paper Bag Kites

Provide the children with a white paper lunch bag, colorful stickers, and yarn. Cut off the bottom of the lunch bags so air can pass all the way through. Have the children decorate their bags with the stickers. Punch a hole on each side of the bag near the top. Cut four 12" pieces of yarn. Thread one piece of yarn through each hole in the sack. Bring the four pieces of yarn together and tie into a knot. Take the bag kites outside for the children to run and fly their kites.

■ ■ **Developing Learner:** Cylinder Kite

Provide the children with white construction paper, colorful stickers, markers and crayons, streamers, and yarn. Bring the ends of the piece of construction paper together to form a cylinder shape. Tape it together to secure. Let the children decorate their kites. Punch four holes spaced equally apart at the top of the kite. Cut four 12" pieces of yarn. Thread one piece of yarn through each hole in the tube. Bring the four pieces of yarn together and tie into a knot. Tape the streamers to the bottom of the kite. Take the kite outside for the children to run and fly!

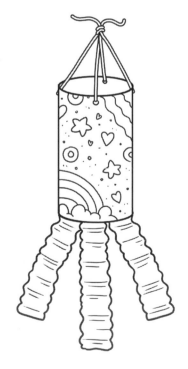

■

■ ■ **Experienced Learner:** Diamond Kite

Provide a large diamond shape cut from white bulletin board paper for each child, crayons and markers, two dowels per child, tape, and string. Let the children decorate their diamond shape (kite) with the markers and crayons. When completed, turn the kite over and form an X with the dowels. This will be the support for the kite. Secure with tape. If necessary, trim the excess off of the dowels. Tie a piece of string about 2–3 feet long to the spot where the dowels meet. Let the children take their kites outside to run and watch them fly through the air.

MATH CENTER

Beginning Learner: Diamond Art
Show the children shapes such as a square, rectangle, and triangle, and then introduce the diamond shape. Have the children count the number of sides that the diamond shape has. Show them pictures of diamond-shaped kites in magazines or storybooks. Provide a variety of sizes of diamond shapes cut from construction paper. Have the glue the diamond shapes on a piece of paper and then use crayons to add streamers to make their diamond shapes into "kites."

Developing Learner: Diamond Headbands
Show the children a variety of shapes (cut from construction paper or from the manipulative center). Ask them to name the shapes. Introduce the diamond shape and have the children count the number of sides it has. Mix all of the shapes together and have the children find the diamond shapes. Provide sentence strips, cutouts of diamond shapes in various colors and sizes, and glue sticks. Invite the children to trace a diamond shape stencil on paper and cut it out. Have the children use the diamond shapes to make a pattern and glue the shapes on their sentence strip to make a headband.

Experienced Learner: Diamond Kite Stencils
Show the children several examples of shapes such as a circle, square, and diamond-shaped kite and several kites of other shapes. Provide stencils of diamond shapes and other shapes, markers, and paper. The children choose a stencil shape to trace and cut out to make their own kite. Invite them to decorate their "kites" using markers.

SCIENCE CENTER

Beginning Learner: Wind Chimes
Show the children examples of wind chimes and gently tap the chimes with your hand so that they make music. Let the children use their hands to make the chimes sound. Plug in a small fan and position it so that the wind from the fan blows on the chimes. Ask the children if the chimes sound the same or different with this method. Discuss how the wind outside moves things. Ask the children to identify things that the wind blows, such as the leaves on the trees and on the ground, flags flying on poles, water in ponds and lakes, our hair, and so on.

Developing Learner: Fans
Provide ping-pong balls and handheld fans. Have the children place the balls on a table and use the fans to blow the ping-pong balls around on the table. Turn the fans off. Do the ping-pong balls move without the air? Repeat again. (**Safety note:** Make sure the fans have a safety guard to keep fingers safe.)

Experienced Learner: Make Your Own Wind

Provide ping-pong balls, straws, and empty toilet paper, paper towel, and gift wrap tubes. Have the children blow through the different tubes to see which one affects the balls the most. Does more air from the larger tubes make the balls move faster? Do they move farther? (**Safety note:** Since the children will be putting their mouths on the tubes, make sure that each child has his own tube and does not share their tubes or straws with others.)

LANGUAGE/DRAMATIC PLAY CENTER

Beginning Learner: Name Kites

Cut out kites from colored construction paper. Write each child's name on a kite. Spread the kites on the floor or table and ask the children to find the kites that have their names on them. Ask them if they can find a kite with a friend's name on it.

Developing Learner: The Letter "K"

Cut out a large kite shape from poster board and write a large letter "K" in the middle of it. Ask the children to think of words that begin with the letter "K." Write their answers around the "K."

Experienced Learner: Kite Writing Project

Provide markers, crayons, and colored pencils. Ask the children to draw a picture of a kite. Have them dictate to you what it would be like to be a kite flying in the sky. What would they see?

VOCABULARY

clouds, colors, diamond, flying, fun, handle, kite, wind, shape, sky, streamers, string, tail

Reflect

Say to the children, "Yesterday, we talked about games and how fun they are to play. Today, we talked about kites and their unique diamond shape. Tomorrow, we will talk about mud and discover how much fun it can be to get dirty!"

Extend and Enrich

Use the following ideas to extend and enrich what children know about kites.
- Make a kite using a paper plate.
- Make toast and use a diamond-shaped cookie cutter to cut it. Let children spread cream cheese on top and use pretzel sticks to make an X frame on the kite.

Mud

This day's activities offer lots of opportunities for exploring dirt and mud. While most children enjoy getting dirty and actively participating in this type of play, some do not. They may want to wear disposable gloves. In the event that some children do not want to participate, encourage them to watch as their friends enjoy the messy play.

Morning Circle

Give each child a quart-size resealable plastic bag filled with dirt. Ask the children what they think will happen if they add water to the dirt. Let the children help add water to their bags of dirt. Have them squish the bags to mix the water and dirt together. Talk about what happened, and introduce the story for the day.

Storytime

Mud by Mary Lyn Ray

Daily Activity Center Ideas

ART CENTER

Beginning Learner: Pretend Mud Paint

Give each child a piece of wax paper. Pour a small amount of brown and black fingerpaint on the wax paper and encourage the children to use their fingers and hands to mix the "mud" and make designs on their paper. After they have made an interesting design or picture, place a piece of white paper over the creation and lift it off to make a print of their work.

Developing Learner: Real Mud Paint

Provide white construction paper, paint smocks, newspapers, brushes, and trays or cookie sheets. Place newspaper under the trays to help control the mud. Have the children pour their mud from the morning circle activity onto the tray and use their hands, fingers, or brushes to paint a mud picture.

Experienced Learner: Mud Painting with Worms

Provide white construction paper, paint smocks, brushes, chenille sticks, glue, and trays or cookie sheets. Place newspaper under the trays to make cleanup easier. Have the children pour their mud from the morning circle activity onto the tray and use their hands and brushes paint a mud picture, the same as for the developing learner. Cut chenille sticks in half and invite the children to dip them into glue and glue them to the mud to represent worms in the mud. Allow two to three days for this artwork to dry.

MATH CENTER

■ **Beginning Learner:** Tracing Numbers in Mud

Mix water and dirt together on trays to a thinned consistency. Encourage the children to use their hands to mix the mud and use their fingers to practice tracing the numerals in the mud.

■ ■ **Developing Learner:** Matching Numbered Rain Boots

Prepare for this activity by cutting out 20 rain boot shapes from yellow construction paper. On 10 boots, write the numerals 1–10 (one numeral on each boot) and draw dots on the remaining 10 boots (one dot on one boot, two dots on the second boot, three dots on the third boot, and so on). Ask the children what kind of shoes they wear outside in the rain. Show them a pair of yellow rain boots . Tell them that boots are fun to wear in the rain, and they are good for stepping in puddles and mud after it rains. Mix the two sets of boots together and have the children find pairs of boots by matching numerals and dots.

■
■ ■ **Experienced Learner:** Muddy Number Prints

Prior to doing this activity, make a batch of homemade playdough and add food coloring or liquid watercolors to make the playdough black or dark brown like mud. Make numeral prints (instead of footprints!) in the pretend "mud." Put the playdough on trays and provide magnetic numerals. Encourage the children to take turns rolling a die. The child counts the dots on the die, finds that numeral, and uses it to make that number of prints in the "mud" on the tray.

SCIENCE CENTER

To do this activity at any level, provide dirt, water, and a water table or large plastic tub in which the children can create mud.

■ **Beginning Learner:** Pretend Worms and Dirt

Talk to the children about dirt and worms. Encourage them to describe what mud and dirt feel like and what worms feel like when they hold them. Provide dirt and plastic worms in plastic tubs, and invite children to add water to create mud. Let children explore the mud and worms. Add plastic shovels to enhance the children's play.

■ ■ **Developing Learner:** Mud Pies

Provide dirt, water, plastic worms and pretend bugs, shovels, and aluminum pie tins. Let the children add water to the dirt in the tubs to create mud. Encourage them to make mud pies by spooning the mud into the pie tins, and then mix plastic bugs and worms into the mud pies. Place the pie tins outside in the sun to "bake." Tell the children that the sun will bake the mud mixture. Explain that the heat causes the water to evaporate, drying out the mud, and making it crack. Check on the mud pies the next day to see what happened.

Experienced Learner: Real Earthworms

Provide dirt, water, a tub or water table, and live earthworms. Place the worms in the tub of dirt and add a little bit of water. Ask the children to observe the worms. The worms will begin to dig and bury themselves in the mud. Explain that worms usually bury themselves to keep cool and moist. Some children will feel comfortable enough to pick up the worms. Children who do not want to touch the worms may use crafts sticks to gently pick them up. Have a discussion about worms and their environment.

LANGUAGE/DRAMATIC PLAY CENTER

Beginning Learner: Dirt Dessert/Descriptive Words

Tell the children they are going to make a "dirt" dessert. Show them the ingredients—crushed chocolate sandwich cookies, chocolate pudding, and gummy worms. Talk about each ingredient. Help children spoon pudding ("mud") into a small cup, place a gummy worm on top of the pudding, and spoon crushed cookies ("dirt") on top. As the children eat, encourage them to use descriptive words to describe what their "dirt" tastes like and what they think real dirt and worms would taste like. (**Safety note:** Remember to check for food allergies before implementing this activity.)

Developing Learner: Dirt Dessert/Sentences

Provide chocolate sandwich cookies, chocolate pudding cups, gummy worms, plastic bags, spoons, a rubber mallet, and clear plastic cups. Place three cookies in each bag and give one to each child. Invite them to use a mallet to smash the cookies into small pieces to make "dirt." Children add the crushed cookies to a pudding cup and top with a gummy worm. Have the children dictate a sentence about their dirt dessert, describing the flavor of it.

Experienced Learner: Dirt Dessert/Recipe Cards

Provide chocolate sandwich cookies, chocolate pudding, gummy worms, plastic bags, spoons, a rubber mallet, and clear plastic cups. Prior to doing this activity, make recipe cards for the children using the following "recipe:" Place three cookies in a bag and seal. Hammer the bag 10–20 times to create "dirt." Put five spoonfuls of pudding in a cup. Place one gummy worm on top of the "mud." Pour the bag of dirt over the mud and worm. After the children eat their special snack, have them make their own recipe cards using ingredients such as real dirt, insects, and so on.

VOCABULARY

brown, dig, dirty, gooey, ground, messy, mucky, mud, slimy, splat, squish, wet

Reflect

Say to the children, "Yesterday, we talked about kites and how much fun they are to fly. Today, we talked about mud and how fun it can be to touch it and play with it. Tomorrow, we will talk about pockets and all the things we can put inside them."

Extend and Enrich

Use the following ideas to extend and enrich what children know about mud.

- Paint with chocolate pudding and then eat for snack. Have children wash their hands first.
- Bury root vegetables, such as carrots, turnips, and potatoes, in dirt and invite the children to dig for them.
- Let the children plant grass seed in plastic cups. It grows very quickly.

DAY 5

Pockets

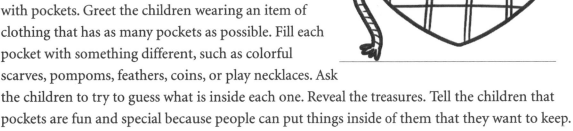

Morning Circle

In advance, ask parents to donate (or lend) old clothes with pockets. Greet the children wearing an item of clothing that has as many pockets as possible. Fill each pocket with something different, such as colorful scarves, pompoms, feathers, coins, or play necklaces. Ask the children to try to guess what is inside each one. Reveal the treasures. Tell the children that pockets are fun and special because people can put things inside of them that they want to keep. Provide a collection of old shirts, pants, and coats and encourage the children to explore the pockets on each item. Read the story *A Pocket for Corduroy*.

Storytime

A Pocket for Corduroy by Don Freeman

Daily Center Activity Ideas

ART CENTER

■ **Beginning Learner:** Design a Pocket
Give each child a pocket shape cut from construction paper, stickers, and crayons. Invite the children to decorate their pockets.

■ ■ **Developing Learner:** Design a Pocket II
Give each child a pocket shape drawn on paper, scissors, markers, stickers, and crayons. Have the children cut out their pockets and decorate them.

■
■ ■ **Experienced Learner:** Lacing Pockets
Provide a pocket stencil, colored construction paper, a hole punch, yarn, scissors, glue, and decorating supplies such as sequins, rickrack, dot markers, crayons, markers, and stickers. Invite the children to trace and cut out their own pockets. Help them use a hole punch to punch holes around the outside of their pockets and lace yarn through the holes. Children may decorate their pockets as desired.

MATH CENTER

Beginning Learner: How Many Things are in the Pocket?

Provide the articles of clothing from the morning circle activity. Hide objects, such as cotton balls, pompoms, small manipulative shapes, feathers, and foam numerals inside the pockets of the clothing. Each child chooses an item of clothing and first counts the number of pockets on the item of clothing and then counts the number of objects inside each pocket. Encourage them to do this with another item of clothing.

Developing Learner: Matching Pocket Numbers

Cut out 10 pockets from construction paper, write a numeral from 1–10 on each pocket, and glue the pockets in numerical order to a poster board. Make sure to leave the top part of the pockets open. Write the numerals 1–10 on craft sticks and ask the children to match the sticks with the pockets and place each stick inside the appropriate pocket.

Experienced Learner: Ordering Numbers of Pockets

Provide the articles of clothing from the morning circle activity. Encourage the children to count the number of pockets on each item of clothing and then put the items of clothing in numerical order from the item of clothing with the least number of pockets to the item of clothing with the most number of pockets. Next have the children count the number of pockets on their own clothing and place themselves in order according to who has the most number of pockets on their clothes and who has the least number of pockets.

SCIENCE CENTER

Beginning Learner: Sewing Pockets

Remind the children of the story *Corduroy* and show them pictures from the book of his pocket coming unsewn. Provide a variety of objects that have laces or things that are sewn onto one another. Show the children a plastic needle and thread and demonstrate how to sew something onto something else. Demonstrate how the needle goes down through the fabric and comes back up to help things stay attached to each other. Provide lacing cards and shoelaces for the children to practice their lacing skills.

Developing Learner: Concept of Inside

Tell the children that people put things *inside* pockets. Ask them to think of things that go inside other things, such as wallets inside purses, food inside mouths, and people inside houses. Discuss the opposite of inside and have the children list things that go *outside* of other things. Provide pockets cut from construction paper and encourage the children to draw things on a piece of paper that they can fit inside their pockets.

Experienced Learner: Pizza Pockets

Tell the children that people put things *inside* of pockets. Have the children brainstorm places where pockets are found (such as in a car or a purse), and things that are pockets themselves (such as a pillowcase or an envelope). Explain that *pita bread* is a pocket made from bread. Make pizzas with the children using pita bread, pizza sauce, and cheese. Provide recipe cards, spoons, and bowls. Cut the pitas in half to help the children understand the concept half. The children place sauce and cheese into their pita pockets. Heat them in an oven or toaster oven until warm.

LANGUAGE/DRAMATIC PLAY CENTER

For all of the following activities, use the clothing from the morning circle activity and uppercase magnetic or foam letters.

Beginning Learner: Pocket Letters
Place foam or magnetic letters inside the pockets of the clothing. Invite the children to look in all of the pockets to find the alphabet letters. Place the letters in alphabetical order when they have all been discovered.

Developing Learner: Pocket Letters/Finding Names
Prior to doing this activity, write each child's name on a sentence strip. Hide foam or magnetic letters in all of the pockets of the clothing. Invite the children to find a hidden alphabet letter. When they find a letter that is in their name, they cover that letter on the sentence strip with the matching magnetic letter.

Experienced Learner: Pocket Letters/Race
Prior to this activity, hide uppercase foam or magnetic letters in the pockets of the clothing used during the morning circle activity. Invite the children to choose a partner and see how fast they can find all of the letters hidden in the pockets.

VOCABULARY

buttons, coats, inside, jeans, money, pants, pocket, shirts, stuff, wallets

Reflect

Say to the children, "Yesterday, we talked about mud and how fun and dirty it is. Today, we talked about pockets and all of the types of clothing they are found on and the things you can put inside of them."

Extend and Enrich

- Talk about kangaroos and read *Do Kangaroos Wear Seatbelts?* by Jane Kurtz and Jane Manning, *Does a Kangaroo Have a Mother, Too* by Eric Carle or *I Love You, Blue Kangaroo!* Emma Chichester Clark.
- Encourage the children to look around their homes and find clothes with different types of pocket, such as aprons, coats, pants, and overalls.

Things that Are Special

THINGS THAT ARE SPECIAL

Birthdays

Morning Circle

Play a recording of "Happy Birthday" as the children enter the room. Decorate the classroom with balloons, streamers, and confetti. Just for fun, provide a cake with candles that reads "Happy birthday to everyone!"

Storytime

The Birthday Box by Leslie Patricelli

Daily Center Activity Ideas

ART CENTER

Beginning Learner: Ribbon Art

Provide gift wrap, bows, paper, paint smocks, and paint. Encourage the children to dip their bows in the paint and make prints on their paper. When they are finished, allow the paintings to dry. Children can peel off the backing from the bows and stick the bows to their paintings.

Developing Learner: Wrapping Paper

Prior to this activity paint a piece of paper and when it is dry show the children an empty box and wrap it with the wrapping paper that you have made. Invite the children to paint a piece of paper to make their own piece of wrapping paper. Provide paint, paintbrushes, and large paper. Have the children paint the paper to make their own wrapping paper. When the paper is dry, the children can bring it home to wrap a future gift.

Experienced Learner: Ribbon Collage

Provide a variety of ribbons and bows, tape, scissors, and large construction paper. Ask the children to use their imaginations to make a ribbon and bow collage. Encourage them to layer the different textures and colors, and use tape to adhere the ribbon to the paper.

MATH CENTER

■ **Beginning Learner:** Sorting Birthday Stuff

Place party hats, bows, invitations, and noisemakers in a giant gift bag. Show the children a birthday candle shaped like a numeral 2. Talk about the numeral 2. Have the children take turns holding the candle and pulling out two party items from the bag. Draw four columns on a piece of poster board. Label one column "Party Hats," one column "Bows," one column "Invitations," and the last column "Noisemakers." Encourage the children to place their items on the poster board and sort them by category.

■ ■ **Developing Learner:** Counting Birthday Stuff

Place party hats, bows, invitations, and noisemakers in a giant gift bag, as described above for the beginning learner. Provide birthday candles shaped like the numerals 2, 3, 4, and 5. Ask each child how old she is and invite her to find the birthday candle that matches her age. Talk about the numbers and ages. Have the children take turns holding the candle and pulling out the appropriate number of party items from the bag. When everything has been removed from the bag, count how many of each item there are.

■
■ ■ **Experienced Learner:** Counting Birthday Candles

Provide numeral birthday candles (0–9) and plain birthday candles. The children place the candles in numerical order and then count that number of birthday candles. Provide playdough for the children to use to stand their candles up. Children may also choose a number candle and then count that number of plain candles.

SCIENCE CENTER

■ **Beginning Learner:** Birthdays on a Calendar

Show the children a calendar and discuss the months of the year. Ask the children what month their birthday is in and find that month on the calendar. Locate the dates on the calendar, too. (**Note:** It's a good idea to have a list of the children's birthdays handy because some children might not remember when their birthday is.) Talk about the different seasons of the year as you look at the calendar. Ask children if they know what season their birthday is in.

■ ■ **Developing Learner:** Making Cupcakes

(**Safety note:** Check for food allergies before doing this activity.) Talk about the different things people eat to celebrate birthdays, such as cakes, cookies, ice cream, and cupcakes. Tell the children they are going to bake their own birthday "cakes" and decorate them. Provide cake mix, necessary ingredients, , a mixing bowl, a spoon, measuring cups and spoons, muffin liners, muffin tins, icing, sprinkles, and other decorations. Let the children help follow the directions for making cupcakes. As the children are adding and mixing the ingredients, discuss each item and encourage them to notice how they look before they are mixed together. Help the children place a muffin liner in each muffin cup. Fill the muffin tins with the cake mix. Follow the box directions for baking information. Talk about the liquid texture of the cake batter before baking.

When the cupcakes are finished baking, let them cool. Talk about the texture of the cupcake after is it baked. Encourage the children to decorate their cupcakes as desired.

(**Note:** If an oven is not available, you can still have the children make the batter, but you can bring pre-baked cupcakes for the children to decorate. Take the batter home so you can bake and freeze the cupcakes for another day.)

Experienced Learner: Cupcake Cones

Show the children a store-bought cupcake and have them describe its color, shape, size, and texture. Write their descriptive words on a poster. Provide a cake mix, ingredients to add to the mix, flat-bottomed ice cream cones, icing, sprinkles, muffin pan, and foil. Show the children one of the cones and ask them to describe its size, shape, color, and texture. Write what they say on the poster. Prepare the cake mix according to the box directions. As the children are mixing the ingredients, talk about what each ingredient looks like, and what happens when it is mixed with something else and baked. Tell them that this change from liquid to solid is called a "change of state." Line the muffin cups with the foil. Help the children fill the ice cream cones about 3/4 full with cake batter and place them in the muffin pan. Push the foil up around the bottom of the cones to prevent them from tipping over. Bake according to the package directions. When the ice cream cone cupcakes have cooled, the children can decorate them as desired. (**Safety note:** Check for food allergies before doing this activity.)

LANGUAGE/DRAMATIC PLAY CENTER

Beginning Learner: Making Birthday Cards

Provide 8 ½" x 11" sheets of colored construction paper folded in half. Have the children decorate the cards with colorful stickers and markers. If a child wants to give hers to someone special, be sure to add that person's name to the front of the card. Invite the children to dictate a message inside their cards. Have them sign their names, or try to sign their names.

Developing Learner: Signed Birthday Cards

Provide 8 ½" x 11" sheets of colored construction paper folded in half, markers, crayons, and stickers. Write "Happy Birthday" on the front of each card and have the children decorate their cards using the materials provided. Ask them if there is someone special they would like to give their card to and help them write that person's name on the card. Encourage the children to practice writing their own names by signing the card.

Experienced Learner: Making a Birthday Banner

Purchase or make a large birthday banner. Show the banner to the children and discuss the words on it. Give each child a sheet of bulletin board paper to make a birthday banner for someone they know. They can use markers, crayons, and collage materials to decorate their banner. Provide a poster or word cards with the words *Happy Birthday, mom, dad, sister, brother,* and the names of their siblings and friends for them to refer to when writing on the banner.

VOCABULARY

age, balloons, birthday party, cake, candles, cards, confetti, decorations, family, favors, friends, fun, gifts, Happy Birthday, hats, ice cream, invitations, noisemakers, party, piñata, streamers

Reflect

Say to the children, "Today, we talked about birthdays and how much fun they are to celebrate. Tomorrow, we will talk about gifts and how special it is to give a gift to a friend."

Extend and Enrich

Use the following ideas to extend and enrich what children know about birthdays.

◆ Have a class birthday party. Encourage the children to make birthday hats, noisemakers, and other decorations. Play Pin the Tail on the Donkey and eat the cake from morning circle.

◆ Give each child a roll of streamers and tape to decorate the room.

THINGS THAT ARE SPECIAL

Gifts

Morning Circle

Before children arrive, place a bunch of bananas in a box and wrap it using fancy paper. Put a variety of sizes of boxes, wrapping paper, scissors, and tape on a table in the classroom. When the children arrive, invite them to wrap the boxes. When they have finished, have them exchange boxes with one another and take turns tearing off the paper like they are opening a gift. Show the children the "mystery gift" and ask them to guess what is inside the box. Pass the gift around so everyone can shake it and make a guess about its contents. Prior to reading the story, open the box to reveal a "beautiful bunch of bananas" just like the ones in the story *Beautiful Bananas*.

Storytime

Beautiful Bananas by Elizabeth Laird

Daily Center Activity Ideas

ART CENTER

Beginning Learner: Wrapping Paper Collage
Provide a variety of wrapping paper cut into different shapes, paper, and glue sticks. Ask the children to glue the different kinds of wrapping paper onto the paper to create a collage.

Developing Learner: Design Wrapping Paper
Show the children purchased gift wrap paper and discuss the different colors and designs on the paper. Provide white paper, paint, and cookie cutters for the children to use to design their own wrapping paper. When the paper dries, invite them to bring it home to wrap a gift!

Experienced Learner: Painted Gift Boxes
Provide plain white boxes in a variety of shapes and sizes and dot markers. The children pretend that they work in the gift wrapping department of a store, but instead of wrapping the boxes, they paint dots on them. Encourage them to make different-colored polka dots all over the boxes. When the boxes are dry, the children can add colorful ribbons and bows to their presents.

MATH CENTER

■ **Beginning Learner:** Box Dice/Matching Colors

Prepare a color die using a large box and red, blue, and green construction paper. Tape red construction paper on two sides of the box, blue construction paper on another two sides of the box, and green construction paper on the remaining two sides of the box. Place red, blue, and green gift bows on the floor. Play a color matching game with the children. Have them take turns rolling the box like a die and finding all of the matching color bows the die lands on. Have the children count how many bows there are of each color.

■ ■ **Developing Learner:** Box Dice/Identifying Numerals

Cover a large box with white craft paper. Write the numerals 1–6 on each side of the box (one numeral per side). Ask the children to roll the "box die" and identify the numeral. Help them count out gift bows to match the numeral.

■
■ ■ **Experienced Learner:** Box Dice/Counting Dots

Give each child a small box. Help them cover their boxes with white paper to make dice. Show them a real die and talk about what the dots on each side represent. Provide black markers for the children to copy the dots onto their boxes to make their own dice. Let the children take turns rolling their box and counting out that number of gift bows or ribbons.

SCIENCE CENTER

■ **Beginning Learner:** Fruit or Vegetable?

Show the children a variety of fruits and vegetables, and hold up each one for the children to name and identify as a fruit or a vegetable. Make a poster with two columns. Write "Fruit" at the top of one column and "Vegetable" at the top of the other. Have the children place the fruits and vegetables under the correct columns. Show them a banana and ask them which column it belongs under. When the poster is complete, peel a banana and discuss all of the parts of the banana. Talk about how peeling a banana is similar to opening a wrapped gift. Provide small pieces for the children to taste.

■ ■ **Developing Learner:** Where Do Fruits Grow?

Draw a tree, a bush, a vine, and the ground on a large poster. Show the children a variety of fruits and talk about each one. Ask them to tell you where they think each fruit grows (on trees, underground, on vines, or bushes). Have them place the fruits on the poster where they belong. For example, an orange would go on the tree, and a blueberry would go on the bush. When all of the fruits have been sorted and discussed, cut them up or peel them so that the children can see what is inside. Discuss the color, size, and texture of each fruit and talk about the seeds. Show the children a banana and have them compare it to the other fruits. Talk about how peeling a banana is similar to opening a wrapped gift. Provide small pieces of each fruit for the children to try.

Experienced Learner: Chocolate Bananas

Show the children a bunch of bananas and have them describe their color, shape, and size. Write their descriptions on a poster. Show them chocolate chips, sprinkles, coconut, and sandwich cookies and have them describe each item. Write their descriptions on the poster. Heat chocolate chips in a microwave or in a crock pot. Discuss the change of state and how the chips changed from solid to liquid when heated. Invite the children to roll rolling pins over sealed plastic bags of sandwich cookies to crush them. Talk about the difference in appearance when crushed. Give each child a banana. Have them peel the banana and insert a craft stick in one end. Dip the banana in the chocolate and roll it in sprinkles, crushed cookies, or coconut. Place bananas on a tray and freeze for 1 hour. Enjoy them for snack. (**Note:** Write each child's name on the end of her craft stick for easy identification.)

LANGUAGE/DRAMATIC PLAY CENTER

Beginning Learner: Gifts in a Box

Give each child a small white box. Ask the children to describe the best gift they ever received. Write each child's answer on a small piece of paper to place inside the box. Have them decorate their boxes using markers and stickers. While the children are decorating their boxes, discuss how fun it is to give and receive gifts. Invite them to name all of the different kinds of gifts that they can think of (including nonmaterial gifts!).

Developing Learner: Choosing and Wrapping Gifts

Provide small white boxes and old magazines. Invite the children to cut out a picture of a gift they would like to give someone and place it in their box. Provide wrapping paper, scissors, and tape for the children to use to wrap their box. While they wrap their gifts, talk to them about the person that their gift is for and why they have chosen that person and that gift.

Experienced Learner: Remembering Special Gifts

Provide paper, crayons, and markers. Ask the children to describe the best gift they ever received or gave. Which gift was the most special to them and why? Write down their answer on a piece of paper and ask the children to draw a picture of that gift.

VOCABULARY

birthday, bows, box, from, gift, give, holiday, occasion, package, present, scissors, special, tape, thank you, to, wrapping paper

Reflect

Say to the children, "Yesterday, we talked about birthdays and how special they are to everyone. Today, we talked about gifts and how special it is to give a friend a gift. Tomorrow, we will talk about picnics and what a treat it is to go on a picnic."

Extend and Enrich

Use the following ideas to extend and enrich what children know about gifts and giving.

◆ Invite the children to use collage materials or empty food boxes and containers, craft sticks, ribbons, and paper to make a gift for their parents or caregiver and wrap it.

◆ Children draw a picture and give it to a friend. Encourage the children to tell their friend why he or she is special.

◆ Encourage the children to use plastic animals for the children to retell the story.

DAY 3

Picnics

Morning Circle

Prior to this day's activities, send home a note encouraging the children to bring a teddy bear to school the following day for a very special "Teddy Bear Picnic." Remind parents to write their child's name somewhere on the teddy bear for easy identification. If desired, children can dress their bears in special clothes for the picnic. Provide a large blanket or tablecloth and a picnic basket filled with plates, cups, napkins, and play food. Place the book *Teddy Bears' Picnic* in the picnic basket. As the children arrive, invite them to join you on the blanket for a special picnic. Read the book during the "picnic." Leave the picnic set up for the remainder of the day for children to use for dramatic play.

Storytime

Teddy Bears' Picnic by Jimmy Kennedy

Daily Center Activity Ideas

ART CENTER

■ **Beginning Learner:** Torn Paper Bears
Give each child a bear shape cut from white construction paper. Invite the children to glue torn pieces of brown paper all over their bear. When the glue is dry, the children may glue wiggle eyes to their bear and use crayons to draw a mouth and nose.

■ ■ **Developing Learner:** Torn Paper Bears II
Draw a bear shape on a piece of white paper and make a copy for each child. Have the children cut out their bears. Provide brown paper for the children to tear into small pieces. The children put glue all over their bear and then cover it with the torn brown paper. Provide materials such as wiggle eyes, pompoms, yarn, and so on for the children to use to add details to their bear.

Experienced Learner: Brown Felt Bears

Have children cut out bear shapes from brown felt. They can glue buttons, rickrack, pieces of fabric, and ribbon on the bear to make clothes.

MATH CENTER

Beginning Learner: Watermelon Measuring

Provide a large watermelon and yarn. Cut the yarn into three different lengths. Hold up each piece of yarn and have the children guess which piece of yarn will wrap around the watermelon. After the children have made their guesses, invite them to take turns using the yarn to measure the watermelon.

Developing Learner: Watermelon Estimating and Measuring

Provide a large watermelon, scissors, and yarn. Ask the children to examine the watermelon and think about its size. Each child cuts a piece of yarn that she thinks will wrap around the watermelon. Let them take turns wrapping their yarn around the melon to see if it fits. Discuss with the children that their guesses were *estimations* and that the yarn was their *measurement tool.* Show them rulers, yard sticks, and measuring tapes and discuss how each one is used to measure things. Invite the children to practice using them to measure things in the classroom.

Experienced Learner: Watermelon Length and Circumference

Provide a large watermelon, scissors, and yarn. Discuss with the children *length* (measurement from end to end) and *circumference* (measurement around the outside of an object). Have the children examine the watermelon and think about its size. Ask each child to cut two pieces of yarn, one piece to represent the watermelon's length and the other piece to represent its circumference. Let each child take a turn to check her estimations. Record the results on watermelon-shaped pieces of paper that the children can take home. Encourage the children to compare the length and circumference measurements with their friends.

SCIENCE CENTER

Beginning Learner: Investigating Seeds

Give each child a slice of watermelon on a plate and a toothpick. Show them how to use toothpicks to dissect the watermelon and locate all of the seeds. The children remove the seeds and place them on their plate. Ask questions, such as "What do they look like?" and "What color are they?" Discuss seeds and planting, and talk about how watermelons grow. The children can enjoy eating their watermelon as a special treat.

Developing Learner: Planting Watermelon Seeds

Give each child a slice of watermelon and a toothpick. Do the activity described above for the beginning learner. Make sure to talk about how seeds grow into plants. When the children are finished eating their watermelon, have them bring their seeds outside and plant them in a classroom garden or a galvanized tub. Provide soil, gloves, and small shovels. Water the plants every day.

Experienced Learner: Comparing Seeds

Provide a watermelon, honeydew melon, apple, orange, banana, kiwi, and pomegranate. Cut each of the fruits in half and have the children examine all the different kinds of seeds. Graph which fruit has the biggest seeds, which fruit has the smallest seeds, which fruit has the most seeds, and which fruit has the fewest seeds. Provide toothpicks for the children to remove the seeds from the fruit. Have children examine the seeds using a magnifying glass. Serve the fruits for snack, and talk about the taste, texture, and color of each fruit.

LANGUAGE/DRAMATIC PLAY CENTER

Beginning Learner: Going on a Picnic

Provide the blanket and picnic supplies from the morning circle activity. Encourage the children to use the items to act out the story, *Teddy Bears' Picnic.*

Developing Learner: Serving Bears

Have the children arrange the bears brought from home around a table or on the floor around a picnic blanket. Provide a picnic basket and play foods. Invite the children to fill the basket with foods that they think the bears would enjoy on their picnic. Encourage the children to use play dishes, napkins, silverware, and glasses to set a place for each bear. Let the children serve the foods to the bears and sit with them and pretend to eat. As the children are sitting with the bears ask them to describe the foods that their bear is "eating."

Experienced Learner: Inviting Bears

Encourage the children to make an invitation inviting their teddy bears to a picnic. Help each child write the words. Children can use markers, stickers, and so on to decorate their invitations. Encourage them to make envelopes and stamps for their invitations. Provide a pretend mailbox for them to mail their invitations.

VOCABULARY

ants, basket, beach, blanket, bugs, drink, food, grass, napkin, outside, park, picnic, picnic table, plate, sandwich, swing

Reflect

Say to the children, "Yesterday, we talked about gifts and the ways they are special. Today, we talked about picnics and the special foods are often eaten at a picnic. Tomorrow, we will talk about surprises."

Extend and Enrich

Use the following ideas to extend and enrich what children know about picnics.

- Have the children make placemats and glue plastic ants or put ant stickers on them.
- Ask parents to join the class for a real picnic at the park.
- Use cookie cutters to cut meat, cheese, and bread into fun shapes for sandwiches.
- Fill the sand table with sand and plastic ants.
- Place magnetic letters in a picnic basket. Children pull them out one at a time and identify them.

Surprises

Morning Circle

Before the children arrive, paint a picture on a piece of poster board. It could be something abstract or a picture of a bear to go with the story for the day. Cut the picture into several small pieces to resemble a puzzle. As the children arrive for morning circle, hand each child a "puzzle" piece.
When everyone has a piece of the painting, ask them to place the pieces on the floor to reassemble the painting. Talk about surprises with the children, and ask if they were surprised to see what the painting looks like.

Storytime

One to Ten Pop-Up Surprises by Chuck Murphy

Daily Center Activity Ideas

ART CENTER

■ **Beginning Learner:** Surprise Paintings
Give each child a shirt box, a piece of paper that will fit inside the box, and a marble. The child places the paper inside the box, drops the marble into a small bowl of tempera paint, retrieves it with a spoon, and drops it on the paper in the box. The child places the lid on the box and shakes the box back and forth. When the child is finished, she removes the lid to see the surprise painting. (**Note:** For a variation, use heart-shaped Valentine candy boxes with heart-shaped paper.)

■ ■ **Developing Learner:** Group Surprise Painting
Tell the children they are going to work together to paint a surprise painting. Place a piece of large paper on an easel. Encourage the children to take turns painting on the same piece of paper to create a surprise painting. Ask each child to tell you something special about the painting and write her words on it. Also write the names of the children who participated in the painting. Make color copies of the painting so that everyone can take one home.

Experienced Learner: Musical Surprise Painting

Have the children sit at a table and tell them they are going to work together to create a surprise picture. Place a sheet of paper in front of the first child at the table and play a recording of music. Encourage the child to begin drawing on the paper. Then stop the music and ask her to pass it to the child on her right. Place a new sheet of paper in front of the first child. Play the music and the two children begin drawing. Stop the music and the first child passes her paper to the second child, and the second child passes his paper to the child on his right. Continue this process, giving the first child new paper each time, until everyone has added something to each picture.

MATH CENTER

Beginning Learner: Surprise Color/Probability

Prior to doing this activity, fold a piece of yellow construction paper in half and place one yellow dot sticker on the inside. Repeat the process using blue paper and a blue dot sticker, red paper and a red dot sticker, and green paper and a green dot sticker. Vary the number of stickers inside each card. Also make a set of "surprise" cards, such as yellow construction paper with a blue dot sticker, blue construction paper with three red dot stickers, and so on. Mix up all of the papers and place them, closed, on a table in front of the children. A child chooses one card and guesses what color sticker is inside. Have the child open the card and count the number of stickers inside. If the child chooses one of the "surprise" cards, she says, "Surprise!"

Developing Learner: Surprise Numeral

Use a white crayon to write large numerals on pieces of white paper. Give a sheet to each child and don't tell her about the numeral written on the paper. Have the children paint over the entire paper using watercolors. The children will be surprised when the numeral appears (the waxy crayon will not absorb the paint, so the numeral will be revealed). Ask them to identify the numeral. Invite them to make their own numerals to paint over.

Experienced Learner: Counting Dots/Surprise Picture

Write the numerals 1–10 on index cards, one numeral per card, and place the cards in a "surprise box" (or bag). Give each child a dot marker and white paper. Let the children take turns reaching inside the box and pulling out a numeral card. The child identifies the numeral and then uses the dot marker to make that number of dots on her paper. Continue playing the game until each child has a page full of dots. Encourage the children to use crayons to connect the dots in some way to make a "surprise" picture for their parents or for a friend.

SCIENCE CENTER

■ **Beginning Learner:** Surprising Textures

Provide a tub of white flour, spoons, and a pitcher of water. Encourage the children to use the spoons to mix the flour. Talk about the dry texture of the flour and how it feels like powder. Add water to the flour. Encourage the children to mix the water and flour mixture. Ask the children to explain what happened to the dry flour. Were they surprised at the new texture?

■ ■ **Developing Learner:** Surprising Reactions

Tell the children that they are going to conduct a "surprise" experiment. Give each child a clear plastic cup and a tray or large paper plate. Ask them to place the cup on the tray or plate and fill it half way with baking soda. Help them pour vinegar over the baking soda and watch what happens. Tell the children when the baking soda and vinegar are combined, they produce a *chemical reaction*, which means that they have a special effect on one another and create a foaming and fizzing reaction. Ask the children to describe what they see. The children will love watching this reaction and will want to do it over and over. An extension to this activity would be to add drops of food coloring to the baking soda before pouring the vinegar on it. (**Note:** If you discuss volcanoes at any time during the year, you can use this activity to demonstrate the process.) Mold wet sand into a volcano shape on a cookie sheet and use your finger to make a hole in the top. Pour this mixture in the hole and watch as the "volcano" erupts.

■
■ ■ **Experienced Learner:** Surprising Changes

Provide dish tubs, bowls of cornstarch, and a pitcher of water. Invite the children to add cornstarch to the tub using measuring spoons and water to the tub using measuring cups. Invite the children to stir the mixture with their hands or a wooden spoon and then have them pick up the mixture in their hands. Explain that when dry cornstarch is mixed with water, it goes from a solid to a liquid. If the children hold the mixture tightly in their hands and squeeze it with their fingers, it will form into a ball and return to a solid state. But, when they open their fingers, it seems to return to a liquid state. The children will delight in watching the mixture clump together and then spread out again.

LANGUAGE/DRAMATIC PLAY CENTER

■ **Beginning Learner:** Letters in a Box

Cut a hole in a box large enough for the children to stick their hand through. Place foam or magnetic alphabet letters inside the box. The children take turns reaching into the box and retrieving a letter. Have them identify the letter and drop it in back inside the box.

■ ■ **Developing Learner:** What's Inside the Box?

Before the children arrive, place a classroom object in a large box. When it is time for this activity, tell the children there is an object from the classroom inside the box. Give them clues about the object. When someone guesses correctly, show them the item. Then, have everyone close their eyes while the child who guessed correctly places another object into the box. That child can give clues to the class about the new item.

■ ■ ■ Experienced Learner: The Best Surprise Ever

Provide paper, markers, and crayons. Ask the children to dictate a few sentences about the best surprise they ever received. Write down their words and have them illustrate their stories.

VOCABULARY

excitement, happy, party, pleased, shock, startled, surprise

Reflect

Say to the children, "Yesterday, we talked about boxes and the fun objects you can create from boxes. Today, we talked about surprises and how unexpected they are. Tomorrow, we will talk about wishes."

Extend and Enrich

Use the following ideas to extend and enrich what children know about surprises.

◆ Use art ideas from the story and invite children to splatter paint, bounce a ball with paint on it, or paint stripes on paper.

◆ Plan a surprise party for the class. Any occasion will do!

DAY 5

Wishes

Morning Circle

Before the children arrive, cut out giant duck feet from orange construction paper, enough pairs for you and for each child. Greet the children wearing the giant orange duck feet. When everyone is at circle time, give each child a pair of duck feet. Use duct tape to attach the duck feet to the top of the children's shoes. Read *I Wish That I Had Duck Feet*. Have the children walk around the classroom with their new "duck feet." When they come back to the circle, ask the children what they wished they had.

Storytime

I Wish That I Had Duck Feet by Dr. Seuss

Daily Center Activity Ideas

ART CENTER

▪ **Beginning Learner:** Funny Characters
Using construction paper, cut out all of the items listed in the story (duck feet, elephant nose, antlers, water spout, tail). Give each child a large body shape on bulletin board paper. Encourage the children to glue all of the items to the paper to create a funny person.

▪▪ **Developing Learner:** Funny Characters/Tracing
Provide construction paper cutouts of all the items listed in the story, as described for the beginning learner. Invite the children to trace each other on bulletin board paper. Roll out enough paper for one child at a time to lie on it. Pair the children and ask them to trace each other's bodies. Invite the children to add the cut-out body parts to their body tracings to create funny characters. They may use markers to draw clothes and facial features.

Experienced Learner: Funny Characters/Painting

Provide a roll of bulletin board paper; grey, blue, brown, orange, and black tempera paint; brushes; paint smocks; and markers. Roll out the paper and have the children lie down on the paper one at a time. Trace the children's bodies. Encourage them to paint the duck feet, elephant nose, antlers, water spout, and tail that the boy in the story had. Have them use markers to add clothes and facial features.

MATH CENTER

Beginning Learner: Making Sets

Explain to the children that a "set" of items is at least two items that belong together or are alike. For example, salt and pepper shakers; a knife, fork, and spoon; and a shirt and pants. Write the numeral 2 on a large piece of cardstock. Talk about the numeral 2. Ask the children to go around the classroom and find two of the same item. Encourage the children to find another "set" of items.

Developing Learner: Counting Feet

Revisit the story *I Wish I Had Duck Feet*. Ask the children how many feet the boy had. Have children sit in a circle and count all of the feet in the classroom. Take it a step further and count how many of each type of shoe there is, such as sandals, sneakers, and regular shoes.

Experienced Learner: Sorting Shoes

Invite the children to remove their shoes and place them in a pile in the middle of the floor. Have the children sort the shoes into the pairs. Discuss left feet and right feet and have the children arrange the shoes with the left feet and the right feet in the correct position.

SCIENCE CENTER

Beginning Learner: Footprint Painting

Tell the children that when animals walk through the mud, they leave muddy footprints. Tell the children that they are going to make their own muddy footprints. Provide a tray of tempera paint, two chairs, a tub of soapy water, a large piece of paper, and a towel. Place the two chairs facing one another with about three feet between them. One child sits in one of the chairs, removes her shoes, and places her feet in the tray of paint. Help the child to stand up carefully on the paper to create a footprint. (**Note:** The children will need a steady hand because their feet will be extremely slippery.) After the child has made print, help her to the other chair and have her place her feet in the soapy water to remove the paint. Use the towel to dry off the children's feet. Let each child have a turn.

■ ■ **Developing Learner:** Identifying Feet

Find pictures of different kinds of animal feet and place them on a table. Ask the children to identify the animal according to the animal's feet, paws, or hooves. For example, the children should be able to identify a zebra because its legs and feet have distinctive black and white stripes.

■
■ ■ **Experienced Learner:** Different Kinds of Feet

Provide pictures of animal feet, paper, pencils, and markers. Invite the children to look at the pictures of the animal feet and decide what kind of feet they wished they had. Ask the children to draw pictures of themselves with different types of feet.

LANGUAGE/DRAMATIC PLAY CENTER

■ **Beginning Learner:** Mystery Wish Box

Give each child a small empty box. On the top of each box write "Mystery Wish Box." Ask each child to say what she wishes were inside the box. (Children may say things such as, "I wish today was my birthday," or "I wish I was big enough to ride the roller coaster at the fair.") Write down each child's wish and have her place it inside of the box. The children can decorate their boxes using markers.

■ ■ **Developing Learner:** Rhyming Words for Wish

Form a writing circle with the children. (In a writing circle, ask each child to contribute something to the discussion and record their words.) Go around the circle and ask the children to generate words that rhyme with "wish." Record their answers on a large piece of paper. Then go around the circle again and encourage the children to dictate a sentence using one of the words on the paper.

■
■ ■ **Experienced Learner:** Making a Wish Book

Staple together a few pieces of paper to form individual books. Ask the children to create a "wish book" about things they would like to have or special wishes that they have for their friends or family members. Help them to record their responses on the pages of their books. Remind them that they can wish for things for others and that the wishes do not have to be for material items. Invite them to illustrate their books and write their names and a title on the covers.

VOCABULARY

birthday, desire, hopeful, magic, shooting star, want, wish

Reflect

Say to the children, "Yesterday, we learned about surprises. Today, we learned about wishes and how very special they are."

Extend and Enrich

Use the following ideas to extend and enrich what children know about wishes.

◆ Put books about wishes in the Library Center.

◆ Provide magazines and toy catalogues and encourage the children to cut out toys they wish for. Invite them to make a "wish collage."

◆ Teach the children the poem, "Star Light, Star Bright." Talk about making wishes on stars.

Daily Preschool Experiences

Places that Are Special

Fairs

Morning Circle

Tell the children that today they will learn about fairs. Explain that popcorn is a popular treat often available at fairs. Place a large clean sheet on the floor or on a table. Pop popcorn in a hot-air popper on top of the sheet. When the popcorn begins to pop, remove the lid and watch as the popcorn explodes out of the popper. (**Safety note:** The popcorn will be hot when it pops out of the popper. Supervise closely. Make sure children stand far back from the popper.) Scoop up the popcorn into cups and let the children enjoy it as they listen to the story.

Storytime

Night at the Fair by Donald Crews

Daily Center Activity Ideas

ART CENTER

■ **Beginning Learner:** Paint with Corn Cobs

Explain that popcorn comes from corn. Show the children an ear of corn and allow them to pass it around and feel it. Invite the children to take turns shucking the corn (removing the outer green leaves or husks) and then using a plastic knife to cut the kernels off the corn. Save the kernels for cooking later, and keep the corn cobs for this activity. Pour yellow paint on a tray and let the children roll the corn cob in the paint and make corn cob prints by rolling the cob on their paper.

■ ■ **Developing Learner:** Painting on Corn Husks

Provide several ears of corn, paint, paintbrushes, and paint smocks. Talk to the children about corn, including how it grows and how it is harvested. Have the children wash their hands and take turns removing the outside leaves or husks and cutting off the corn kernels. Save the corn kernels to cook and eat later. Each child washes and dries his own corn husk. Have them paint pictures or designs on the husks and then glue them to paper. Children use yellow markers and crayons to draw corn kernels inside their husks.

■ ■ **Experienced Learner:** Ears of Corn

Provide several pieces of green construction paper, yellow tissue paper, corn cob shapes cut from construction paper, scissors, and glue. Also provide an ear of corn for the children to explore. "What color is it?" "What does it look like on the inside?" Ask the children to cut small squares of yellow tissue paper to resemble corn kernels. Have them glue the tissue paper kernels to the corn cob shape, and then draw a corn cob shape on green paper to resemble corn husks. Children cut out the husks and attach them to the corn cob.

MATH CENTER

■ **Beginning Learner:** Beanbag Toss/Identifying Numerals

Make a typical fair game by dividing a shower curtain into nine squares (three rows up and three rows across). Number the squares 1–9. Encourage the children to toss beanbags onto the shower curtain and identify the numeral they land on.

■ ■ **Developing Learner:** Walk the Dots/Counting Steps

Prior to doing this activity, place 25 colored dot stickers in a line on the floor. Invite the children to take turns rolling a die and moving that many steps on the colored dots in the line. The first child to reach the end of the line rolls the die for the next game.

■
■ ■ **Experienced Learner:** Ring Toss/Counting

Provide 10 soda bottles or plastic water bottles and 10 rings. Invite the children to try tossing the rings around the bottles. Let each child have a turn tossing 10 rings. When each child has finished tossing the 10 rings, he counts how many bottles he successfully got rings around.

SCIENCE CENTER

■ **Beginning Learner:** Corn Textures

Provide the children with a large tub or empty sand table filled with deer corn and cups. Have the children touch, smell, and scoop the corn with the cups.

Developing Learner: Corn Observations

Show the children a fresh ear of corn and encourage them to use descriptive words to describe the color, size, shape, and texture of the corn with the husk on. Write their descriptive words on a poster. Remove the husk from the corn and have them describe the inside of the corn. Fill a large tub with fresh ears of corn. Explain that corn and other vegetables have to be washed before eating them because they are grown outside in the dirt. Encourage the children to pull the husks off ears of corn and wash them in a tub of water. Remind the children that popcorn comes from a special type of corn. Give each child an ear of corn in a plastic bag to bring home for their parents to cook for dinner.

Experienced Learner: What's Inside a Popcorn Kernel?

Provide a large bowl of popped popcorn, butter, and caramel sauce. Show the children unpopped popcorn kernels, and have them describe how the popped kernels are different from the unpopped ones. Explain that the white part of the popcorn is squeezed inside the kernel. When heated, the white part gets so big that it pops out of the hard kernel shell. Then show the children a stick or tub of butter and have them use descriptive words to talk about its color and texture. Tell the children that they are going to use the butter and popped kernels of corn to make a special treat. Have the children wash their hands, and then help them to grease their hands with butter. Explain that the butter is used in cooking to keep foods from sticking to the pan. In this case, the butter will keep the caramel from sticking to their hands. Show them caramel candies in their wrappers and ask them to compare the candies to the caramel sauce. Fold the caramel sauce into the popcorn and place a scoopful into each child's hands. Invite the children to mold and shape the popcorn mixture into popcorn balls.

LANGUAGE/DRAMATIC PLAY CENTER

Beginning Learner: Reenact the Story

Provide props of things that might be found at a fair, including stars for fireworks, a play Ferris wheel, play foods, a horse barn for the carousel, and so on. Encourage the children to reenact what happened at the fair. Ask them if they would like to go to a fair someday and what they would do there.

Developing Learner: Make a Fair Book

Invite the children to dictate a sentence or two about a fair they have been to or one they imagine going to. Invite them to illustrate their words. Combine them into a class fair book.

■■ ■ **Experienced Learner:** Animals at the Fair

Using a whiteboard or chart paper, make a chart with three columns. At the top of the first column, write "Fair," in the second column write "Zoo," and in the third column write "Circus." Have the children form a circle and ask them to think of the different kinds of animals that would be at each of these places. Go around the circle and let each child name an animal and where it could be found. Some animals can belong in all three columns, such as a monkey or elephant. Record their answers in the appropriate column. This activity could also be done using different pictures of animals.

VOCABULARY

agriculture, amusement ride, blue ribbon, booth, contest, county fair, craft, fair, fairground, game, pie, popcorn, state, vegetables

Reflect

Say to the children, "Today, we learned about special places, including the circus and the zoo. Tomorrow, we will learn about the beach and what fun activities there are to do at the beach."

Extend and Enrich

Use the following ideas to extend and enrich what children know about special places, including the circus and the zoo.

◆ Brainstorm games that might be found at a fair and help the children recreate them to play in the classroom.

◆ Have children sort different kinds of eggs, including brown, white, large, and small.

◆ Use a food scale to weigh vegetables with the children. Talk about how vegetables are judged at fairs.

Beach

Morning Circle

Provide beach towels, beach balls, and sand buckets for the children to explore as they enter the classroom. Once everyone has arrived, have the children sit on the beach towels to hear the story.

Storytime

Sea, Sand, Me! by Patricia Hubbell

Daily Center Activity Ideas

ART CENTER

(**Note:** These flip-flop paintings would make great invitations to a school beach day party.)

 **Beginning Learner:** Flip Flop Prints/Hand Stamping

Purchase a few pairs of inexpensive flip flops. Pour tempera paint onto cookie sheets or trays. Invite the children to place a flip flop on each hand, dip the bottom of the flip flops into the paint, and press them on paper to make prints.

Developing Learner: Flip Flop Prints/Walking in Paint

Purchase a few pairs of inexpensive flip flops and pour tempera paint onto cookie sheets or trays. Invite the children to put the flip flop on their foot and step into the tray of paint. Next, they step on the paper to make a print. (**Note:** Make sure the pairs of flip flops have different designs on the bottom to make cool and unique prints!) Children can decorate their dry prints as desired.

Experienced Learner: Flip Flop Prints with Sand

Purchase a few pairs of inexpensive flip flops and pour tempera paint onto cookie sheets or trays. Invite the children to choose two flip flops with different designs on the bottom and put them on their feet. Help the children step into the paint and then walk on the paper to make prints. They may want to sprinkle sand on the wet paint. When the paint has dried, help them cut out their flip flops. Use markers and crayons to draw seashells on their paintings.

MATH CENTER

Beginning Learner: Seashells/Grouping

Provide a plastic sand bucket filled with seashells. Encourage the children to take out the shells and group them according to color, size, and shape. Put a few shells together and have the children count how many shells are in the grouping.

Developing Learner: Seashells/Matching Numerals

Provide a metal tray, 10 seashells, numeral magnets 1 through 10, and a plastic sand pail. Using a black permanent marker, label each seashell with a numeral from 1–10. Place the magnetic numerals in order on the cookie sheet. Place the seashells inside the bucket and gently mix them up. Invite the children to pull out one shell at a time and match it with the magnetic numeral.

Experienced Learner: Seashells/Number Pairs

Provide a metal tray, 20 seashells, and a plastic sand pail. Sort the seashells into 10 pairs of seashells. Using a black permanent marker, label each seashell pair with a numeral from 1 through 10. Place the seashells inside the bucket and gently mix them up. Ask the children to pull out one shell at a time and make sets of two. (Shells with the numeral 1 go together, shells with the numeral 2 go together, and so on.)

SCIENCE CENTER

Beginning Learner: Seashells in the Sand

Provide a sand table, seashells, sifters, and plastic shovels. Encourage the children to dig and sift for the seashells. If there are enough shells to go around, encourage the children to take home one shell to remember their day.

Developing Learner: Sort Seashells in the Sand

Show the children a variety of seashells. Encourage them to describe the shells and discuss the differences in their sizes, shapes, and colors. Show the children pictures of animals that live in shells, such as hermit crabs, oysters, and snails. Explain that some creatures outgrow their shells and move into a new one. Provide a sand table, seashells, sifters, and plastic shovels. Encourage the children to dig and sift for the seashells and sort them by size. Provide paintbrushes for the children to dust off the shells after they find them. Have the children choose a shell to paint.

Experienced Learner: Making Shell Fossils

Provide Plaster of Paris, a large mixing bowl, water, a spatula, plastic disposable bowls, and seashells. Mix the plaster according to package directions. Pour the plaster into a small plastic bowl and allow it to set briefly. Watch carefully because it will harden quickly. Let each child choose a shell to place in the plaster. Allow the plaster to set for a few minutes and then remove the shell from the bowl. Pop the plaster from the bowl and admire the cool shell fossil. Paint the fossils if desired.

LANGUAGE/DRAMATIC PLAY CENTER

To do this activity at any level, provide a few trays and fine sand (like sandblasting sand).

Beginning Learner: Sand Drawing

Encourage the children to use their fingers to draw in the sand. Invite them to describe their picture and the texture of the sand.

Developing Learner: Sand Letters

Encourage the children to draw letters in the sand. Have alphabet letters available for the children to refer to.

Experienced Learner: Sand Names

Encourage the children to write their name and their friends' names in the sand. Provide name cards to the children for reference.

VOCABULARY

bathing suit, beach, beach ball, beach chair, beach towel, crab, fish, jellyfish, ocean, sand, sand bucket, sand castle, seashell, seaweed, shark, shovel, sun, sunburn, sunscreen, water

Reflect

Say to the children, "Yesterday, we learned about fairs and all the interesting activities to do at fairs. Today, we learned about the beach, and we counted with seashells. Tomorrow, we will learn about toy stores and talk about the toys we like to play with."

Extend and Enrich

Use the following ideas to extend and enrich what children know about the beach.

◆ Invite children to toss a beach ball in a blanket.
◆ Decorate sand pails with foam stickers.
◆ Add sand to a playdough recipe to make sandy dough.
◆ Make an "ocean in a bag" by filling a resealable bag with blue hair gel and plastic ocean confetti. (Confetti can be found at a local party or craft store.)
◆ Make an ocean dessert. Crush graham crackers (sand) and add it to a clear plastic cup. Make blue gelatin (water) and pour it on top of the graham crackers. Add a gummy fish. Refrigerate to set the gelatin, and serve.

Toy Store

Morning Circle

Prior to doing this activity, send a note home asking the children to bring their favorite stuffed animal to school. Remind the parents to write their child's name somewhere on the animal's tag. (The stuffed animals will be used in the math center for a counting activity.) Also, go to a local toy store and ask for several copies of their weekly or monthly catalogs. Scatter the catalogs on the floor as the children enter the classroom. The children will automatically begin discussing the toys that they would like to have. This will also give them a clue about the topic of the day's story. Save the catalogs for a later activity.

Storytime

Worry Bear by Charlotte Dematons

Daily Center Activity Ideas

ART CENTER

Beginning Learner: Painting with Toys
Provide toys with wheels, such as wagons, cars, and trucks, and paint on a tray. Encourage the children to drive their car or truck through the paint and then make tracks on their paper.

Developing Learner: Toy Collage
Provide the toy catalogs from the morning circle activity, magazines, paper, scissors, and glue sticks. The children cut out pictures of toys they would like to have from the catalogs and magazines and glue the pictures on their papers to make a toy collage.

Experienced Learner: Toy Box
Provide the catalogs from the morning circle activity, magazines, paper, markers, scissors, and glue sticks. Give each child a shoebox to make a toy box. The children cut out pictures of toys they would like to have from the catalogs and magazines and glue the pictures all over the shoebox until it is completely covered. This will make a special "toy box" for small toys.

MATH CENTER

■ **Beginning Learner:** Counting Animals

Gather the children and ask them to show their stuffed animal they brought from home. Invite the children to tell the class their animal's name and something special about it. At the end of sharing time, line up all of the animals and count how many animals are in the class today.

■ ■ **Developing Learner:** Worry Bear's Board Game

Prior to doing this activity, create a folder game using dot stickers and bear stickers. Arrange a path on the folder and create a starting and ending position. Provide a numeral die and bear counters to use as game-piece markers.

■
■ ■ **Experienced Learner:** Musical Chairs with Animals

Arrange a group of chairs in a circle with the seat facing out. Make sure there are enough chairs for each child and his or her stuffed animal. Everyone carries their animal as they walk around the circle. When the music stops, each child finds a chair for himself and his animal. Continue playing without removing chairs.

SCIENCE CENTER

■ **Beginning Learner:** Exploring with Duplos

Explain that many toys have multiple parts that can be taken apart and reassembled, such as blocks and other small manipulatives. Provide large Duplo blocks and encourage the children to put them together and take them apart. The great thing about the Duplo blocks is that they are much easier for smaller hands to manipulate.

■ ■ **Developing Learner:** Taking Things Apart

Provide small items that no longer work, such as old telephones, computer keyboards, clocks and cameras. Show the children the different things, and discuss what they are and their uses. Invite them to take the items apart. Discuss the names for the different parts that they remove, such as screws, hinges, and so on. (**Safety note:** Supervise closely to make sure that children do not place small objects in their mouths.) Also, explain that they should never take anything apart at home without permission.

Experienced Learner: Bubbles and Time

Remind the children that in the story *Worry Bear*, all of the toys in the toy store try to help Worry Bear in different ways. Add mild dish soap to water in the water table and add small doll clothes. This represents the laundry bear that washed the worried bear's sweater. Talk about the soap bubbles and invite the children to explore with the bubbles. Show them an alarm clock and discuss the different times of day. Talk about how the little bear did not sleep at night, but he slept during the day. Discuss nocturnal animals.

LANGUAGE/DRAMATIC PLAY CENTER

Beginning Learner: Building Toys

Provide toy catalogs, pictures of toys, blocks, and a variety of building materials such as boxes, tape, toilet paper tubes, and so on. Have the children use the toy pictures as inspiration for building some of their own toy creations.

Developing Learner: Favorite Toys

Provide a large piece of paper and a marker. Write the word "toys" in the middle of the paper. Ask the children what their favorite toy is at home. Write down the children's name with their favorite toy beside their name.

Experienced Learner: Writing a Story

Provide paper, markers, and crayons. Ask the children, one at a time, to tell a story about a time they went to a toy store. Write down their stories in their own words. When the stories are complete, the children can illustrate them.

VOCABULARY

bike, block, book, doll, game, music, puzzle, stuffed animal, toy car, toy store, toy train

Reflect

Say to the children, "Yesterday, we learned about the beach and we painted with flip flops. Today, we learned about toys and we built with Legos and Duplos. Tomorrow, we will learn about the circus and the different kinds of circus acts and performers that are found there."

Extend and Enrich

Use the following ideas to extend and enrich what children know about toys.
♦ Provide stuffed animals, toys, a cash register, and play money and encourage the children to set up a toy store.
♦ Provide books about toys in the reading center.
♦ Provide new toys in centers or rearrange some of the old ones to give them new life. Encourage the children to use some old toy favorites in a new way.

Circus

Morning Circle

Before the children arrive, tie balloons around the room, hang strips of fabric from the classroom ceiling, and hang circus posters on the walls (Posters can be printed from the Internet). Pop popcorn so the children will smell the fresh popcorn. Play circus music as the children enter the classroom. When everyone has arrived, have them look around the room and describe what they see. Ask the children where they think these things would be found. They may say things such as a zoo or birthday party. Talk about circuses with the children and list their ideas of what they might see there on a poster.

Storytime

Last Night I Dreamed a Circus by Maya Gottfried

Daily Center Activity Ideas

ART CENTER

▪ **Beginning Learner:** Make Clown Hats
Make clown hats by rolling construction paper into a cone shape, stapling or taping the ends together, and trimming off the excess paper. Provide colored dot stickers, and encourage the children to use dot stickers to decorate their own clown hat. Top each hat with a large pompom. Punch a hole in each side of the cone and attach string or elastic through the holes. This will make it easier to wear.

▪▪ **Developing Learner:** Make Clown Shoes
Tell them that they are going to make their own pair of floppy clown shoes by tracing their own feet. Trace around each child's right and left foot on large paper, but make the tracings much larger than the child's actual foot size to make giant clown shoes. Invite the children to paint and draw designs on their funny clown shoes. When the shoes are dry, have the children cut them out.

Experienced Learner: Clown Faces

Show the children a variety of clown faces and discuss how clowns apply makeup that makes their eyes, noses, and mouths look funny. Invite the children to design their own funny clown faces using a variety of colors of construction paper, scissors, and glue.

MATH CENTER

Beginning Learner: Shape Search

Provide Styrofoam packing peanuts and a variety of shapes cut out of colored construction paper (circle, square, triangle, and rectangle). Place the packing peanuts in a large tub and hide the shapes in the peanuts. Ask the children to find all of the shapes.

Developing Learner: Number Search

Provide Styrofoam packing peanuts and magnetic numerals. Place the packing peanuts in a large tub and hide the numerals in the peanuts. Ask the children to find all of the numerals. Have them put the numerals in order.

Experienced Learner: Sorting Sticky Shapes

Provide starch packing peanuts, which dissolve in water, numeral cards 1–5, and a container of water. The children take turns drawing a numeral card from the stack and using water to stick that number of peanuts together until they have a long line of peanuts.

SCIENCE CENTER

Beginning Learner: Balance/High Wire Act

Discuss the concept of balance. Show the children how to stand on one foot and balance with their arms out to their sides. If possible, show the children pictures of circus performers walking on a high wire. Tell them that they are going to practice walking on a "high wire." Using painter's tape, make a line on the floor about 6' long. Encourage the children one at a time to pretend they are walking on a high wire. Show them how to use their arms to help them balance.

Developing Learner: Balance/Scales

Provide a balance scale and have the children select items from around the room to balance on the scale. Which items balance each other and which items do not?

Experienced Learner: Balance/Spoons and More

Put markers, cotton balls, puzzle pieces, plastic cups, plastic spoons, and so on into a basket. Invite the children to choose one item at a time and try to balance the items on different parts of their bodies. They might balance a spoon on the end of their nose or balance a marker on their head. Challenge the children to see who can balance the items the longest.

LANGUAGE/DRAMATIC PLAY CENTER

Beginning Learner: Let's Join the Circus

Invite the children to dress up in costumes and dress-up clothes and pretend they are in a circus. Use the items from the morning circle activity to create a circus atmosphere.

Developing Learner: Circus Photos

Provide costumes, mirrors, circus posters, props from the morning circle activity, and a Polaroid camera. Encourage the children to use the props and pretend they are in a circus. Encourage the children to look at themselves in the mirror. Use the Polaroid to take a picture of the children's circus act and write at the bottom of the picture what they were pretending to be. This will be a great keepsake from the day.

Experienced Learner: Circus Faces

Show the children pictures of circus clowns, performers, and animals, and discuss what their faces look like. How are they alike and how are they different? Use face paint to paint the children's faces with clown, circus performer, or circus animal designs. Encourage the children to look at themselves in the mirror and talk about what they look like. Use a Polaroid camera to take a picture of the children's faces and write at the bottom of the picture what they are pretending to be. This will be a great keepsake from the day.

VOCABULARY

bear, circus, circus tent, clown, cotton candy, elephant, high wire, horse, hot dog, lion, popcorn, ring, snow cone, tiger, trapeze

Reflect

Say to the children, "Yesterday, we talked about toys. Today, we learned about the circus and we pretended to join the circus. Tomorrow, we will learn about the zoo and the different kinds of animals that live in the zoo."

Extend and Enrich

Use the following ideas to extend and enrich what children know about the circus.

- Place books about the circus in the Library Center.
- Make circus posters with the children.
- Ask parents and caregivers to donate old dance costumes or Halloween costumes for the children so they can dress up and pretend to be in a circus.
- Invite a clown to come to the classroom to demonstrate for the children putting on his or her makeup and getting dressed in the clown costume. (**Note:** A parent volunteer could come to class and demonstrate for the children how to put on simple makeup to make them look like a clown.)

Zoo

Morning Circle

Turn off the lights in the classroom to create a nighttime environment. If needed, leave a small lamp on for children who might be afraid of the dark. As the children enter the classroom, place a gorilla sticker or stamp on their hand and give them an old key. Place a locked box in the circle area and invite each child to go and try to unlock the box. An alternative idea is to give the children plastic zoo animals to play with as they enter the classroom. Before story time, ask the children to pick out their favorite zoo animal and tell the class why it is their favorite animal. It might be fun to write down the children's responses.

Storytime

Goodnight, Gorilla by Peggy Rathman

Daily Center Activity Ideas

ART CENTER

Beginning Learner: Zoo Animals

Give each child a large piece of paper, die-cut zoo animals, green construction paper (for grass), and glue sticks. Invite the children to glue the animals to the paper and then tear the green construction paper to make grass and glue it to the bottom of the paper so that it looks as if the animals are grazing in the grass.

Developing Learner: Zoo Animals II

Provide a large piece of paper for each child, pictures of zoo animals from science magazines, green paint for grass, blue watercolor for the sky and for water, and glue sticks. The children use blue watercolor to paint the sky and green paint to paint grass. They might want to use blue watercolor to add a small body of water. Ask the children to find pictures of animals and glue them to the paper either in the sky, on the ground, or in the water.

Experienced Learner: Zoo Mural

Provide a large piece of bulletin board paper; magazines; paint in a variety of "earthy" colors; real grass, dirt, and leaves; paintbrushes; paint smocks; and bottles of glue. Tell the children they are going to make a class mural, which means they will work together to create one large picture. Encourage them to work together to create different habitats. Some areas of the mural may have lots of grass and trees (jungle), while other areas may be rocky and dry (desert). When the habitat is complete, invite the children to find pictures in magazines of animals that might live in a zoo. Have them cut out the pictures and glue the animals to their appropriate habitat. Hang the mural in the classroom.

MATH CENTER

The following chant can be used for all three levels of learners:

Monkey see, monkey do
I can count to _____ (one, two, three)
Can you?

Beginning Learner: Monkey Math Chant/Counting Up

Make numeral cards from 1–5. Teach the children the "Monkey Math Chant." Hold up a numeral card and help the children to fill in the blank in the chant. When the children finish reciting the chant, encourage everyone to count aloud to the numeral on the card.

Developing Learner: Monkey Math Chant/Counting Children

Teach the children the "Monkey Math Chant." Have them take turns filling in the number and counting to it. Then have the children stand up in a line and count out that number of children to match the number in the chant.

Experienced Learner: Monkey Math Chant/Counting Dots

Teach the children the "Monkey Math Chant." Invite them to take turns rolling a die, counting the number of dots, and filling in that number in the chant. Encourage children to make their own numeral cards to count with.

SCIENCE CENTER

Beginning Learner: Zoo Animal Headbands

Provide pictures of zoo animals, sentence strips for headbands, and construction paper. Invite the children to pick a picture of an animal they would like to be. Form the sentence strip around each child's head and staple the strip together. Help the children cut out ears to correspond with their chosen animal. Talk about the ears of different animals and why some animals have large, floppy ears (elephant) and other animals have small, pointed ears (giraffe). Explain that elephants flap their ears to keep cool, while giraffes use their ears to listen for predators.

■ ■ **Developing Learner:** Zoo Animal Headbands/Camouflage

Provide pictures of zoo animals; sentence strips for headbands; construction paper; and gray, orange, and black paint. Encourage the children to pick a picture of an animal they want to be. Have them paint and decorate their sentence strips to match their chosen animal. For example, they might paint an elephant gray, add stripes to a zebra, and make spots on a giraffe. When the strips are dry, help the children cut out ears from construction paper to match their animal, and help staple the headbands together so they fit. While the children are working on their animals, talk to them about the ears of the different animals—how they are alike and how they are different. Also discuss the concept of camouflage and how this feature helps animals stay safe by blending in with their environment.

■

■ ■ **Experienced Learner:** Comparing Transportation

Show the children the clown picture in the story where the clown is being shot out of a cannon. Discuss how this is a funny way of getting from one place to another. Talk about other methods of transportation related to the circus such as riding on an elephant's back, walking across a tight rope, or riding on a unicycle. Ask the children to name all the modes of everyday transportation that they can think of, including cars, trains, buses, planes, bicycles, and so on. Invite children to draw some of these modes of transportation. While they are drawing, ask them how these ways of getting around are alike and different.

LANGUAGE/DRAMATIC PLAY CENTER

■ **Beginning Learner:** Be a Zoo Animal

Provide pictures of zoo animals. Ask the children to pick out an animal they would like to pretend to be. Encourage each child to have a turn pretending to be a zoo animal by making the animal's movements and sounds. If desired, paste the pictures on cards and have the children take turns drawing them from a bag.

■ ■ **Developing Learner:** Guess What Animal I Am

Prior to doing this activity, make zoo animal cards by placing animal stickers on index cards. If stickers are not available, glue pictures from magazines on the cards. Ask the children one at a time to select a card. Have the child pretend to be that animal and see if his classmates can figure out what animal he is. This is similar to the game Charades.

■
■ ■ **Experienced Learner:** Zoo Animal Card Game

Provide stickers, magazines, glue sticks, and index cards. Encourage the children to make three or four animal cards. Have them choose partners. Each partner draws a card from his partner and acts out the animal .

VOCABULARY

aquarium, bear, elephant, fish, giraffe, habitat, hippo, lion, monkey, petting zoo, seal, tiger, zebra, zoo

Reflect

Say to the children, "Yesterday, we learned about the circus and we dressed up as circus performers. Today, we learned about the zoo and the different kinds of habitats the animals live in."

Extend and Enrich

Use the following ideas to extend and enrich what children know about the zoo.
◆ Encourage the children to paint zebra stripes or cheetah spots at the easel.
◆ Encourage the children to bring in stuffed animals and create a school zoo.
◆ Ask the children to tell you about a trip to the zoo.

Things that Are Make-Believe

Pirates

Morning Circle

Before the children arrive, hide the book *Tough Boris* somewhere in the room. Make a "treasure map" of the classroom using brown craft paper. Make sure the clues on the map are easy to read. To make the map look antique and authentic, crumple the paper and use a lighter to burn the edges of the map. Place the map on the floor, and when the children enter the classroom, tell them that a pirate left the map for them. Encourage them to use the map to find the book. When they have found the book, show them the picture of the pirate on the front and tell them that his name is Tough Boris. Ask the children what they know about pirates, including any pirates they may have read about in books or seen in movies. Explain that although they will be talking about things that are make believe this week, there were real pirates a long time ago that rode on boats and stole treasures from people on other boats and from islands. Tell the children that they will be talking about storybook pirates like Captain Hook and Tough Boris. Read the story to the children and invite them to join you in repeating the "rough" and "tough" phrases in the book.

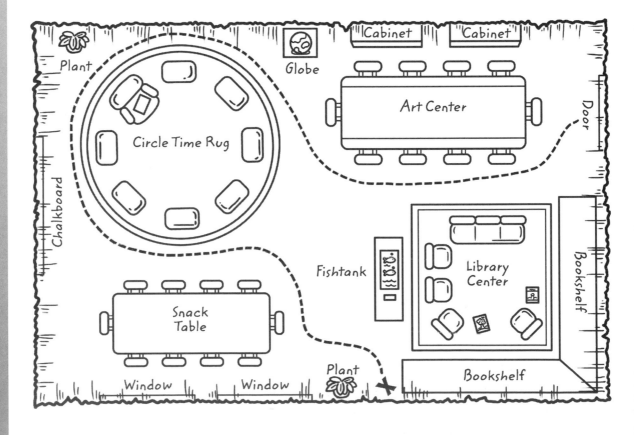

Storytime

Tough Boris by Mem Fox

Daily Center Activity Ideas

ART CENTER

Beginning Learner: Parrots with Feathers

Draw an outline of a parrot or find a picture of a parrot in a coloring book. Make copies for each child in the class. Provide feathers, paint brushes, and glue. Invite the children to cover the parrot with glue and then place the feathers on the parrot.

Developing Learner: Painted Parrots with Feathers

Draw an outline of a parrot or find a picture of a parrot in a coloring book (the same as for the beginning learner) and make a copy for each child in the class. Give the children scissors, feathers, paint brushes, watercolors, paint cups, and glue. The children cut out their parrot shapes and paint them with watercolors. When the paint has dried, the children glue feathers on their parrot.

Experienced Learner: Playdough Parrots with Feathers

Give each child a ball of playdough and feathers. Encourage the children to make a body and head of a parrot using playdough. When their playdough parrots are complete, the children can poke different colors of feathers into the body of the parrot. Provide wiggle eyes, small beads, or buttons for the children to use as eyes.

MATH CENTER

Beginning Learner: Feather Exploration

Dump a large variety of colorful feathers on the floor for the children to explore. Encourage them to toss the feathers in the air, blow on the feathers, and watch the feathers float to the ground. After the exploration, ask the children to choose their favorite color of feathers and then find as many of those color feathers that they can.

Developing Learner: Measuring Length with Feathers

Invite the children to lie down, one at a time, on the floor. Measure each child's length (height) by lining up feathers from the child's head to feet (tape feathers to the floor so they stay in place). When the child's length has been measured, have her stand up and count how many feathers were used. Make comparisons among the number of feathers that it takes to measure each child. Record each child's measurement on construction-paper feathers.

Experienced Learner: Measuring Classroom Objects with Feathers

Fill a basket with colored feathers for the children to use as measurement tools. Invite the children to use the feathers to measure different classroom objects. Give the children construction-paper feathers to record the amount of feathers used for each object.

SCIENCE CENTER

■ **Beginning Learner:** Digging for Treasure

Before children arrive, hide "treasures" such as pretend gold coins, sequins, and large rhinestones in the sand table filled with sand. Show the children a model treasure chest or toy treasure chest, if available. Explain that a long time ago, pirates used to land on islands and dig for buried treasure or steal treasures from the people on the island. Tell the children they are going dig for their own treasures like pirates did. Provide several digging tools, including shovels, and invite the children to dig for small treasures in the sand table.

■ ■ **Developing Learner:** Searching for Treasure

Wrap the outside of several different sizes of empty cardboard boxes in brown paper or paint them brown to resemble treasure chests. Fill them with shredded paper, gold coins, sequins, and large plastic craft-type rhinestones. Hide the "treasure boxes" in different areas throughout the room. Draw several treasure maps with clues for locating the treasure chests. Use brown paper and crinkle up the maps to make them look old. Encourage the children to follow the clues on the treasure maps to find the "buried treasure."

■
■ ■ **Experienced Learner:** Digging for Buried Treasure

Prior to doing this activity, dig a hole outside near the playground and place "treasures" (gold coins, sequins, and rhinestones) in a plastic container or jar. Place the "treasure chest" in the hole and cover it with dirt. Draw a "treasure map" and make copies for each child. Encourage the children to look at the map and try to locate the buried treasure. Provide small plastic shovels for them to use to dig for the buried treasure. When the children have located the treasure, open the container and give each child some of the treasures to take home.

LANGUAGE/DRAMATIC PLAY CENTER

■ **Beginning Learner:** Hunting for Treasure

Place pirate props inside of a cardboard box ("treasure chest"). Include items such as rhinestones, old costume jewelry, pretend gold coins, a pirate hat, an eye patch, and a stuffed animal parrot. Let each child have a turn digging through the pirate chest to find a hidden treasure. Encourage the children to describe what they find. After each child has found a treasure, encourage the children to use the items to role play being pirates.

■ ■ **Developing Learner:** If I Found a Buried Treasure

Give each child a copy of a picture of a treasure chest with the following sentence underneath the picture: "If I found a buried treasure, I would want to find _____ inside." Write the children's words in the blank and invite them to illustrate their sentences.

■ ■ ■ Experienced Learner: Alphabet Treasures

Place items such as rhinestones, old costume jewelry, gold coins, a pirate hat, an eye patch, and a few feathers inside of a "treasure chest" (large box). Provide a set of alphabet letters. Encourage the children to draw an alphabet letter from the pile, open the treasure chest, and look for an item that begins with that letter.

VOCABULARY

dirty, eye patch, fearless, greedy, mean, parrot, pirates, scary, scruffy, ships, skull and crossbones, thieves, tough

Reflect

Say to the children, "Today, we learned about a make-believe pirate from a storybook named *Tough Boris.* Tomorrow, we will learn about giants and read the story *Jack and the Beanstalk.*"

Extend and Enrich

Use the following ideas to extend and enrich what children know about make-believe pirates.

◆ Use brown paper grocery bags to make a pirate hat and vest for each child.

◆ Create a pirate ship using a large appliance box or a large plastic tub. Invite the children to decorate the ship and use it for dramatic play.

◆ Make Jell-o Jigglers™ in a few different colors, following the recipe on the box. Let the gelatin set, cut into squares, and serve for snack. Tell the children they are eating a "pirate snack" because the jigglers look like beautiful treasures.

Giants

Morning Circle

Cut out large footprints from poster board or large paper. Write the words "fee," "fi," "fo," and "fum" on each footprint. Place them on the floor leading from the door to the circle area for the children to follow when they arrive. Ask the children to guess what the story is for the day. Give clues if they cannot guess what it is.

Storytime

Jack and the Beanstalk by Steven Kellogg

Daily Center Activity Ideas

ART CENTER

■ **Beginning Learner:** Draw a Castle

Remind the children that in the story *Jack and the Beanstalk*, there was a castle at the top of the beanstalk. Show the children the picture of the castle in the story, and encourage them to use markers to draw a picture of a castle.

■ ■ **Developing Learner:** Create a Beanstalk

Provide green paint, green construction paper leaves, large paper, glue, paint brushes, and paint smocks. Encourage the children to paint a green beanstalk on their paper. Allow the paint to dry, and then have children glue the leaves to the beanstalk. Invite children to crumple brown tissue paper and add it to their beanstalk to represent beans.

 **Experienced Learner:** Create a Beanstalk and Castle

Provide several shades of green tissue paper and show the children how to twist the tissue paper to make it look like a beanstalk. When they are finished, have them glue their stalks on large paper. Invite the children to tear green tissue paper into leaves and vines and shape brown tissue paper into beans and glue them to their beanstalk. When they finish, have them draw a castle at the top of their beanstalk.

MATH CENTER

 **Beginning Learner:** Bean Counting

Label five clear plastic cups with the numerals 1–5 and place them in ascending order. Provide a bowl of white lima beans and ask the children to count the correct number of beans into each cup. Remove the beans when they are done and place the cups in order from 5–1. Have the children count the beans into the cups again. Invite them to arrange the cups in different numerical orders and then count the beans. (**Note:** Save the beans for a future recipe.)

Developing Learner: Bean Sorting

Provide a variety of beans such as lima beans, red beans, and black-eyed peas. Mix the beans together in a large bowl and provide plastic cups or a sorting tray. Ask the children to sort the beans. (**Note:** Save the beans for a future recipe.)

Experienced Learner: Bean Patterning

Provide a bowl of different colors and types of dried beans. Make a set of pattern cards that match the available beans. For example, draw a red bean, a black-eyed pea, a red bean, and a black-eyed pea on one card. Draw two black-eyed peas, a red bean, and a black bean on another card. Continue making cards until you have a set with different combinations of beans. Place the pattern cards and the bowl of beans on a table. Have the children take turns choosing cards and extending the patterns on each card. When they are done, encourage them to make their own patterns and extend them. Provide markers or colored pencils and sentence strips for them to make their own bean pattern cards.

SCIENCE CENTER

■ **Beginning Learner:** Find the Magic Beans

Remind the children that the mother of the boy in the story threw the magic beans out the window. Talk about what happened to the beans overnight. Discuss what happens when beans or seeds are planted in the ground, and how the beans or seeds need water and sunshine to grow. Explain that real beans or seeds take several days or weeks to grow. Fill a child-size wading pool with shredded brown paper ("dirt") and hide several large wooden beads ("magic beans"). Children can search through the "bean patch" to find the magic beans.

■ ■ **Developing Learner:** Planting Beans in a Cup

Prior to doing this activity, soak a bag of lima beans in water overnight. Provide plastic cups, lima beans, soil, plastic spoons, and a cup of water with an eyedropper. The children place a few spoonfuls of soil in the bottom of their cups, place two or three beans in the soil, and then cover the beans with more soil. Have the children use the eyedropper to water the beans. Place the bean plants in a sunny place, and invite children to observe their growth.

■
■ ■ **Experienced Learner:** Planting Beans in a Plastic Bag

Prior to doing this activity, soak a bag of lima beans in water overnight. Give each child a clear zipper sandwich bag, wet paper towels, and clear tape. The children place three beans in a wet paper towel, gently fold it, and place it in the sandwich bag. Help them write their names on their bags. Tape the bags in the classroom window and watch the beans for a few days to see what happens.

LANGUAGE/DRAMATIC PLAY CENTER

■ **Beginning Learner:** Giant Letters

Give each child a small piece of poster board or tagboard with the first letter of her name written on it. The children use their fingers to trace over their letter. Mix sand with dry tempera paint and pour it into an empty saltshaker. Encourage the children to outline their letters with glue using a small brush, and then shake the colored sand on top of the glue. Ask them to shake off the excess sand to reveal their letters.

■ ■ **Developing Learner:** Giant Class Name Collage

Provide giant letter stencils, large paper, markers, pencils, and crayons for the children to make a class name collage. Help the children use the stencils to spell their names on the giant paper. Encourage the children to trace the letters of their names with their fingers and then use markers and crayons to decorate. After everyone has a chance to see the giant class name collage, cut out each child's name so they can have them to take home.

**Experienced Learner:** Giant Story

Show the children a picture of a giant and encourage them to create a story about themselves and a giant. Write the children's dictated stories, and then encourage them to illustrate their stories.

VOCABULARY

beans, beanstalk, big, cow, giant, golden egg, large, magic, sky, tall

Reflect

Say to the children, "Yesterday, we learned about pirates and buried treasure. Today, we learned about giants and beanstalks. Tomorrow, we will learn about monsters, and we will make a monster mask."

Extend and Enrich

Use the following ideas to extend and enrich what children know about giants.

◆ Cut out a large egg shape from paper. Encourage the children to paint it yellow and sprinkle it with gold glitter.

◆ Provide green beans for the children to snap. Cook them and encourage the children to taste them.

◆ Twist pieces of green bulletin board paper to make tall beanstalks, and hang them from the classroom ceiling to enhance the children's dramatic play.

Monsters

Morning Circle

Create a not-too-scary monster mask (see Art Center below for ideas) and wear it as the children enter the classroom. Play the song, "The Monster Mash." Have a discussion about monsters, pointing out that they are make-believe. Share the story *Where the Wild Things Are* with them.

Storytime

Where the Wild Things Are by Maurice Sendak

Daily Center Activity Ideas

ART CENTER

Beginning Learner: Make a Monster Mask

To prepare for this activity, cut brightly colored furry material to fit on a paper plate. Use hot glue to attach the material to the plate. Allow the glue to dry, and then cut out two eye holes in the middle of the plate. Invite the children to choose a paper plate with the color of furry material they want. Provide ribbons and other collage materials, and invite the children to decorate their monster masks as desired. When they are finished, staple each mask to a craft stick.

Developing Learner: Monster Puppets

Provide brown paper lunch bags, crayons, markers, colored construction paper, and glue. Show the children the "wild things" from the story and invite them to create their own "wild thing" puppets using the paper bags. When the puppets are complete, have the children place them on their hands and make up their own creative monster stories.

Experienced Learner: Monster Costumes

Give each child a large brown paper grocery bag and tissue paper streamers, ribbons, construction paper, and other collage materials. Encourage the children to decorate their bags to make a monster. Have the pictures from the book available to inspire the children's designs. When they are finished, cut out two large eye holes and a large nose hole in each bag. Make sure the eye holes and nose hole line up with the children's eyes and nose when they place the bags over their heads.

MATH CENTER

Beginning Learner: Monster Face Shapes

Use the pictures from the story *Where the Wild Things Are* for ideas to cut out shapes from felt to make eyes, noses, and mouths for the children to use to make monsters. Provide regular facial features cut from felt as well as the "monster" facial features. Talk about each shape and what body part it resembles. Encourage the children to be creative as they combine the shapes to make their own monster faces.

Developing Learner: Monster Face Shapes/Counting

Cut out shapes (triangle, square, and so on) and facial features (eyebrows, noses, mouths, eyes, teeth, and hair) from felt. Give each child a large felt circle ("face"). Place the felt shapes and facial features in the center of the table. Have the children take turns rolling a die and adding that number of parts to their felt circle to make a  face. The children continue to play the game until their monster faces are complete. A great resource for monster pictures is the book *Go Away, Big Green Monster* by Ed Emberly.

Experienced Learner: Magnetic Monster Face Shapes

Cover three different sized coffee cans with various colors and kinds of patterns of contact paper. Place tissue paper inside the coffee can for "hair." Invite the children to cut out various geometric shapes from colored construction paper. Laminate the shapes and attach a piece of magnetic tape to the back of each shape. Encourage the children to use the shapes to create silly monster faces on the coffee cans.

SCIENCE CENTER

Beginning Learner: Monster Muck

Pour cornstarch and water in the water table and add green food coloring. Have the children put on paint smocks before playing with the monster muck. Discuss how the cornstarch changes consistency as the children hold it in their hands.

■ ■ **Developing Learner:** Measuring Monster Muck

Make monster muck as described for the beginning learner. Provide wooden spoons and measuring spoons and cups. Discuss the different units of measurement as the children use the measuring devices in their play with the muck. Talk about the concepts of liquids and solids as the children hold the muck. The muck feels hard and solid as the children hold it in their hands, but when they release it, the muck changes to a liquid.

■ ■ **Experienced Learner:** Monster Mountain

Make "monster mountains" with the children. Give each child a small mound of wet sand on a tray to form into the shape of a volcano. Have them use a finger to make a small hole at the top of their "volcanoes." Each child puts one teaspoon of baking soda in the opening, and then adds one tablespoon of vinegar. A chemical reaction will cause the monster mountain to erupt like a volcano! Let the children repeat the experiment, adding food coloring for a colorful eruption.

LANGUAGE/DRAMATIC PLAY CENTER

■ **Beginning Learner:** Dancing Shadows

Remind the children that the monsters in the story had fun dancing and moving in interesting and strange ways. Tell them they are going to experiment with making shadows that move and dance like the monsters in the story. Hang a large white sheet from the ceiling or staple it to a wall. Invite the children to use flashlights to make shadows on the sheet.

■ ■ **Developing Learner:** Shadow Puppets

Prior to doing this activity, cut black construction paper into interesting shapes that resemble the outlines of monsters. Glue the monster shapes to craft sticks to make puppets. Hang a large white sheet from the ceiling or staple it to a wall as described for the beginning learner. Encourage the children to use the "puppets" behind the sheet to make a shadow puppet show.

■ ■ **Experienced Learner:** Monster Story

Encourage the children to bring their monster masks that they made in the Art Center to this center. Have them name their monster and dictate a story about it. Write down their words, and encourage them to illustrate their stories. Invite the children to put on their monster masks and act out their stories.

VOCABULARY

dark, frightening, furry, make-believe, monster, night, scary, teeth, wild

Reflect

Say to the children, "Yesterday, we learned about giants and giant beanstalks. Today, we learned about monsters, and we created monster masks. Tomorrow, we will learn about fairy godmothers and we will make our own magic wands."

Extend and Enrich

Use the following ideas to extend and enrich what children know about monsters.

◆ Read the story *Go Away, Big Green Monster!* by Ed Emberly.

◆ Provide monster stories in the reading center.

◆ Make green monster shakes by mixing lime sherbet and milk in a blender.

Fairy Godmothers

Morning Circle

Prior to the children's arrival, sprinkle glitter and foil confetti around the room. Just for fun, greet the children wearing a tiara or crown and carrying a wand. Tell them that you are pretending to be "someone who makes wishes come true," and encourage the children to guess what they will be learning about today.

Storytime

The Youngest Fairy Godmother Ever by
   Stephen Krensky

Daily Center Activity Ideas

ART CENTER

Prior to doing this activity, send a note home asking parents to donate empty toilet tissue or paper towel tubes. All levels of learners will use the tubes.

■ **Beginning Learner:** Magic Wands
Cover the empty toilet-tissue and paper-towel tubes with construction paper. Invite the children to decorate the "wands" using colored markers, crayons, and star stickers.

■■ **Developing Learner:** Magic Wands with Sound Effects
Give each child an empty paper towel tube, colored construction paper, star stickers, curly ribbon, and tape. Help the children cover their tubes with construction paper and tape it in place. Children decorate their wands using markers and star stickers, and attach curly ribbon at the end of the wands. Invite the children to seal one end of their magic wand with duct tape, add a few spoonfuls of aquarium gravel, and seal the other end shut with duct tape. The magic wands will now make noise as the children cast their magic spells.

Experienced Learner: Magic Wands with Stars

Provide empty toilet paper tubes, construction paper, star stencils, glue, scissors, glitter, markers, and ribbon. The children wrap their tubes with construction paper and glue it in place. Invite the children to trace stars on construction paper using a star stencil and cut them out. The

children spread glue on the stars and sprinkle with glitter. Set them aside to dry. Encourage the children to decorate their tubes using markers and ribbons. When the stars are dry, children may glue them to their magic wands.

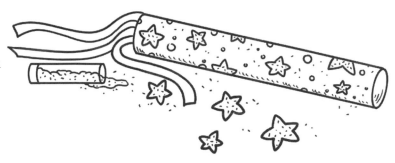

MATH CENTER

Beginning Learner: Star Counting

Cut out a five-pointed star from tagboard for each child. Discuss the shape of the star and encourage the children to help you count the number of sides and the number of points it has. Provide star stickers and invite the children to fill in their stars with the stickers. Help them count how many star stickers they placed on their stars.

Developing Learner: Star Graphs

Make a graph for each child with five vertical columns labeled from 1–5. Provide foil star stickers and invite the children to place the number of stars in each column to match the numeral at the top of the column. Encourage the children to write the correct numeral under each column.

Experienced Learner: Star Headband/Identifying Numerals

Give each child a tagboard sentence strip and foil star stickers. Encourage the children to write the numeral 1 and place one star sticker next to it, then write the numeral 2 and place two star stickers next to it, and so on until they get to 5. Staple the strips to make headbands.

SCIENCE CENTER

Beginning Learner: Confetti in the Water Table

Explain that fairy godmothers and fairies often use "fairy dust" or "magic dust" to perform their magical spells. Show the children foil confetti ("fairy dust") and ask them if they think the confetti will sink or float in water. Fill a water table with colored water (use food coloring) and confetti. Provide small fishing nets for the children to use to catch the confetti. Ask them to describe the colors and shapes that they catch in their nets.

■ ■ **Developing Learner:** Confetti Playdough

Show the children a star shape and ask them how many sides and points it has. Provide white playdough, star-shaped cookie cutters, rolling pins, mixing tools (egg beater and wooden spoon), and star-shaped foil confetti. Discuss what they think the different tools are used for and which they think would make mixing confetti into the playdough the easiest. Place playdough on the table or on a tray, and encourage the children to mix the confetti into the playdough using a rolling pin, egg beater, and wooden spoon. Encourage them to roll out the dough and use cookie cutters to make star shapes.

■
■ ■ **Experienced Learner:** Hidden Objects

Fill clear plastic jars or containers with play sand. Put small toy objects such as a marble, toy boat, key, toy turtle, and so on into each container of sand. Make picture cards of the different items that you have "hidden" in each jar. Explain that fairy godmothers sometimes place magic spells on people or things that are hard to see. Let each child choose a picture card and shake the mystery containers to try to locate the hidden objects.

LANGUAGE/DRAMATIC PLAY CENTER

■ **Beginning Learner:** Writing on Gel Bags

Prior to doing this activity, fill three large plastic storage bags with clear hair gel and silver or gold glitter. Secure the openings of the bag with duct tape. Explain that fairy godmothers often use "fairy dust" and "magic potions" to conduct their magic. Tell the children they are going to use fairy potion to practice writing their letters. Encourage the children to feel the bags and squish them between their fingers. After an initial exploration, encourage the children to use their fingers to practice drawing letters.

■ ■ **Developing Learner:** Sequined Names

Discuss that there are many interesting things associated with fairy godmothers, including magic, spells, fairy dust, wishes, and magic wands. Write some of these words as well as each child's name on tagboard cards. Each child chooses a fairy-related word or her own name and writes it on a sentence strip. Encourage the children to trace over their names or other words with glue and then add sequins. Discuss the letters in their names or the words.

■
■ ■ **Experienced Learner:** If I Had a Fairy Godmother…

Prior to this activity, write the following sentence on paper for each child. "If I had a fairy godmother, I would wish for _____." Encourage the children to complete the sentence and illustrate their wishes.

VOCABULARY

castle, fairy godmother, fun, happiness, magic, magic wand, make-believe, pixie dust, potion, wishes

Reflect

Say to the children, "Yesterday we learned about monsters, and we made shadow puppets. Today we learned about fairy godmothers and we made our own magic wands. Tomorrow we will learn about elves and we will read *The Elves and the Shoemaker*.

Extend and Enrich

Use the following ideas to extend and enrich what children know about fairy godmothers.

◆ Provide several different versions of the Cinderella story and talk about the special things that the fairy godmother did for Cinderella. Encourage the children to compare the different versions. Ask them what is alike and what is different in each story.

◆ Help the children make star mobiles and write wishes on each star.

◆ Encourage the children to help make a list of all of the things they would like to do if they were fairy godmothers or fairy godfathers. Ask them how they would get around, where they would live, and what they would wear.

Elves

Morning Circle

Have the children remove their shoes at the classroom door when they arrive and place them in neat rows by the door. Give each child a small piece of leather. (This can be found at a local craft store.) Encourage the children to touch, smell, and hold the leather while they wait for you to read the story. Explain that they are going to learn about some very special make-believe "helpers" who are often found in places where there is a lot of work to do and who help the workers get their jobs done. Ask the children what they know about elves. (**Note:** Be careful not to refer to Santa's elves as make-believe because most children this age believe in Santa and his elves.)

Storytime

The Elves and the Shoemaker by the Brothers Grimm

Daily Center Activity Ideas

ART CENTER

■ **Beginning Learner:** Shoe Tracing

Show the children different types of leather shoes (sandals, boots, tennis shoes, and loafers). Ask them to choose a shoe that they would like to make. Help them to trace their shoe on construction paper or draw a shoe. Cut out their shoes for them and punch holes in them. Help the children thread yarn (laces) through the holes. Have them crinkle the paper to make it look worn and wrinkled like leather.

■ ■ **Developing Learner:** Painted Paper Shoes

Give each child two shoe patterns cut out of a brown paper grocery bag. Encourage them to wad their shoe patterns up until they are wrinkled and then unfold them. Children paint their shoe cutouts with brown and black watercolors to make them look like leather. Help them punch holes in the shoe cutouts and tie yarn through the holes to make laces.

Experienced Learner: Wallpaper Shoe Cutouts

Provide a collection of different kinds of shoes so the children can see that shoes come in all types, sizes, and colors. Encourage them to look at their own shoes for ideas. Provide shoe patterns, an old wallpaper book, scissors, and markers. The children trace their shoe pattern on a piece of wallpaper and cut it out. (Make sure children cut out two shoes to make a pair.) Encourage them to use a hole punch to punch holes around the outside of the shoe pattern. Help them to lace yarn through the holes.

MATH CENTER

Beginning Learner: Pairs of Shoes

Ask the children to look at their shoes. Discuss that the shoes match, and they are called a "pair." Talk about the concept of pairs, and ask the children to name other things that come in pairs. Encourage the children to remove their shoes and place them in a pile. Have them match the pairs of shoes.

Developing Learner: Shoe Patterns

Have the children remove their shoes. Show them how to make a simple ABAB pattern using their shoes, for example, sneaker, sandal, sneaker, sandal. After some initial exploration, encourage the children to use the shoes to create their own patterns.

Experienced Learner: Shoe Patterns II

Have the children remove their shoes. Write the following pattern possibilities on a chart: ABAB, ABCABC, AABB, and AABBCC. Provide sentence strips and markers and invite the children to choose a pattern and write it on their sentence strip. Encourage the children to use their shoes and those of their classmates to complete their chosen pattern. Encourage the children to trade sentence strips and try to complete each other's patterns.

SCIENCE CENTER

■ **Beginning Learner:** Hammering Nails

Remind the children that the elves in the story used mallets and nails to make the shoes in the workshop. Show the children a real hammer and small nails and demonstrate how to hammer the nails into a block of wood (adult only). Put the hammer and nails away, and tell the children that they are going to practice hammering using rubber mallets and golf tees as pretend nails. Provide large Styrofoam blocks, golf tees, and small rubber mallets or plastic toy hammers. Encourage the children to hammer the golf tees into the Styrofoam just as the shoemaker hammered the nails into the leather in the story.

■ ■ **Developing Learner:** Screwdrivers

Show the children different tools that are often used in a workshop, such as a hammer, screwdriver, wrench, and nails. Explain that elves are make-believe characters that often use many kinds of tools to help people get their work done. Provide child-sized screwdrivers and small screws and start the screws into boards for the children. Demonstrate how to use a screwdriver to get the screws into the board. (**Note:** This activity requires one-on-one supervision between each child and an adult.)

■
■ ■ **Experienced Learner:** Sandpaper Shoes

Trace several children's shoes on sandpaper and cut them out. Show the children a piece of sandpaper and pass it around for them to feel its texture. Encourage them to describe how the sandpaper feels. Ask the children to look at the bottom of their shoes and use their hands to feel the textures on the soles of their shoes. Give the children sandpaper shoe patterns and peeled crayons to make sandpaper shoe rubbings. Then provide sandpaper for the children to trace their own shoes and cut them out to make rubbings.

LANGUAGE/DRAMATIC PLAY CENTER

■ **Beginning Learner:** Describing Shoes

Encourage the children to trace their shoes on a piece of paper and use markers and crayons to decorate their shoe pictures. Encourage language development by asking the children to take turns describing what their shoes look like. What color are they? Do they have lights on them? Do they have shoelaces, Velcro, or buckles? Write some of the words on the children's pictures that they use to describe their shoes

■ ■ **Developing Learner:** Spoon Puppets

Draw pictures of the shoemaker, his wife, and the elves from the story. Make enough pictures for each child to have a set of story characters. Let the children color their pictures and cut them out. Give each child four plastic spoons and help them to tape their characters to the spoons to make puppets. Encourage the children to use the spoon puppets to retell the story *The Elves and the Shoemaker*.

■ ■ **Experienced Learner:** Storytelling

Provide the following items for the children to use in their storytelling: a green sweat suit (or something similar) to represent the elves, an apron to wear to represent the shoemaker, a dress to represent the shoemaker's wife, a rubber mallet, and several pairs of shoes. Encourage the children to take turns using the props to retell the story.

VOCABULARY

cut, elves, hammer, money, nails, pounding, shoemaker, shoes, stitch, table, work

Reflect

Say to the children, "Yesterday, we learned about fairy godmothers, and we made magic wands. Today, we learned about elves and we had fun pretending to make shoes with hammers and golf tees."

Extend and Enrich

Use the following ideas to extend and enrich what children know about elves.

◆ Provide fake leather for the children to explore.

◆ Encourage the children to write a different ending to the story of *The Elves and the Shoemaker*.

Index

Index of Children's Books

Index

A

Acorns, 140, 144–147, 164
Acrylic paint, 113, 149, 323
Addition, 207, 225, 303–304, 324
Alarm clocks, 52, 405
Alike and different, 10, 17, 42, 134, 142, 183, 194, 198, 228, 274, 411
Alphabet beads, 32
Alphabet blocks, 194
American Sign Language, 29
Animal feeders, 212
Animal figures, 35, 122–123, 127–128, 135, 215, 220, 230, 256, 274, 284, 286–287, 292, 303, 307–309, 381, 409, 428
Animal fur, 19, 155, 158, 224, 236, 239, 422
Animals, 23, 29, 35, 73, 399, 409–412
  bats, 192–195
  bears, 236–239
  elephants, 302–305
  farm, 119, 122–125
  hibernating, 224–227
  in the classroom, 125
  kangaroos, 371
  nocturnal, 405
  octopuses, 272–275
  owls, 180–183
  parrots, 415–416
  penguins, 232–235
  pets, 42–45
  polar bears, 236–239
  safety, 157
  squirrels, 144–147
  starfish, 284
  stuffed, 42–45, 48, 66, 224–228, 230–231, 234, 239, 274, 292, 359, 382, 385, 403–404, 412, 416
  whales, 284–287
Ant farms, 296
Antlers, 155, 158
Ants, 294–297
  plastic, 295–296, 385
Apple pies, 173
  making, 174
Apples, 35, 161, 171–175, 297, 337–338, 384
  butter, 173
  cider, 173
  jelly, 173
  juice, 173
Applesauce, 173
  making, 173–174
Appliance boxes, 28, 49, 126, 126, 417
Aprons, 86, 319, 336, 369, 432
Aquariums, 276, 286
  gravel, 44, 196–197, 248, 286, 324–325, 426
  nets, 44, 277, 286, 321, 324, 427
  plants, 284

Art center, 10, 14, 18–19, 22, 26–27, 30, 34, 38, 42, 46, 49–50, 54, 58–59, 62, 66–67, 70–71, 76, 80–81, 84, 88–89, 92–93, 102–103, 106, 109, 113–114, 118–119, 122–123, 126–127, 130–131, 134–136, 140, 144, 148, 151, 155–156, 160, 164, 167–172, 175, 180, 184, 188–189, 192, 196–197, 202–203, 206, 210–211, 214, 219, 224–225, 228–229, 232–233, 236–237, 236–237, 240–241, 246, 250, 254, 258, 262–263, 268–269, 272–273, 276–277, 280–281, 284–285, 290–291, 294–295, 298–299, 302–303, 306, 312, 316, 320, 323, 326, 332, 336–337, 340, 344, 348–349, 354–355, 358, 362–363, 365–366, 369, 374, 378, 382–383, 386–387, 390–391, 396–397, 400, 403, 406–407, 409–410, 415, 418–419, 422, 426–427, 430–431
Autoharps, 25

B

Baby bath thermometers, 327
Baby food jars, 64, 67–68, 103, 124–125, 162, 165, 207, 220, 338
  lids, 106
Bags, 387, 412
  flour, 104–105
  gift, 375
  grocery, 40, 44, 133, 136, 180, 209, 240, 262, 301–303, 337, 417, 422, 430
  laundry, 228, 230
  lunch, 64, 77, 81–82, 128, 180, 212, 233, 273, 323, 362, 422
  paper, 89, 128, 135, 140, 167, 182, 186, 290
  plastic, 82–83, 85, 93, 132, 174, 194, 316, 318, 340, 345, 348, 350, 367, 398
  popcorn, 81
  sandwich, 158, 164, 219, 344
  storage, 342
  sugar, 104–105
  trash, 142, 272
  zippered plastic, 29, 55, 102, 142, 204, 279, 350, 356, 365, 380, 402, 420, 428
Baking soda, 388, 424
Balance scales, 168, 407
Balancing activities, 45, 60, 67–68, 255, 407
Balloons, 54, 109, 167, 254, 374, 406
  helium, 272
Balls, 60, 110, 137, 235, 292, 359, 361, 389
  baseballs, 110
  basketballs, 110
  beach, 210, 400, 402
  golf, 46, 110, 219, 356
  ping-pong, 46, 81, 110, 208, 356, 363–364

  plastic, 202
  rubber, 356
  soft, 207
  Styrofoam, 81, 171–172, 184, 208, 219, 291
  tennis, 110
Bananas, 35, 130–131, 161, 175, 378–380, 384
Bandanas, 134, 358
Bar soap, 62, 110, 264
Barns, 135
Baseballs, 110
Basketballs, 110
Baskets, 128, 133, 146, 160, 172, 175, 190, 219, 225, 230–231, 252, 295, 407, 415
  berry, 105, 160, 163, 340
  laundry, 37, 81
  picnic, 297, 382, 385
  shopping, 133
Bath time, 262–265
Bathroom scales, 19, 168, 238
Bats, 192–195
Beach balls, 210, 400, 402
Beaches, 400–402
Beads, 38, 44, 89, 135, 154, 196–197, 246, 261, 277, 415
  alphabet, 32
  wooden, 420
Beanbags, 127, 255, 397
Beans, 99, 132, 419
Bears, 236–239
Bees, 298–301
Beeswax, 300
Beetles, 290–293
  plastic, 290–291
Beginning learners, 10
Bells, 93, 196–197
  jingle, 67, 99
Berries, 104, 121, 157, 160–163, 175, 204, 340–342
Berry baskets, 105, 160, 163, 340
Bingo markers, 354
Binoculars, 60
Bird's nests, 128, 182
Birdfeeders, 165–166, 212
Birthdays, 374–377
  banners, 376
  candles, 375
Blackberries, 340–342
Black-eyed peas, 132, 419
Blankets, 28, 39, 213, 236, 382, 384–385, 402
Blenders, 124–125, 173, 341, 350–351, 425
Blindfolds, 58, 64, 67, 69, 358
Blocks, 19, 46–47, 51, 189, 297, 314, 360, 405
  alphabet, 194
  Duplos, 404
  Legos, 46
  milk carton, 207
  stacking, 47
  Styrofoam, 342
  Unifix cubes, 286